Lecture Notes in Computer Science 7440

Commenced Publication in 1973
Founding and Former Series Editors:
Gerhard Goos, Juris Hartmanis, and Jan van Leeuwen

Yang Xiang   Ivan Stojmenovic
Bernady O. Apduhan   Guojun Wang
Koji Nakano   Albert Zomaya (Eds.)

Algorithms and Architectures for Parallel Processing

12th International Conference, ICA3PP 2012
Fukuoka, Japan, September 4-7, 2012
Proceedings, Part II

 Springer

Volume Editors

Yang Xiang
Deakin University, Burwood, VIC, Australia
E-mail: yang@deakin.edu.au

Ivan Stojmenovic
University of Ottawa, SEECS, Ottawa, ON, Canada
E-mail: stojmenovic@gmail.com

Bernady O. Apduhan
Kyushu Sangyo University, Fukuoka, Japan
E-mail: bob@is.kyusan-u.ac.jp

Guojun Wang
Central South University, Changsha, Hunan Province, P.R. China
E-mail: csgjwang@csu.edu.cn

Koji Nakano
Hiroshima University, Higashi-Hiroshima, Japan
E-mail: nakano@cs.hiroshima-u.ac.jp

Albert Zomaya
University of Sydney, NSW, Australia
E-mail: albert.zomaya@sydney.edu.au

ISSN 0302-9743   e-ISSN 1611-3349
ISBN 978-3-642-33064-3   e-ISBN 978-3-642-33065-0
DOI 10.1007/978-3-642-33065-0
Springer Heidelberg Dordrecht London New York

Library of Congress Control Number: 2012945393

CR Subject Classification (1998): F.2, H.4, D.2, I.2, F.1, G.2, H.3, C.2

LNCS Sublibrary: SL 1 – Theoretical Computer Science and General Issues

Typesetting: Camera-ready by author, data conversion by Scientific Publishing Services, Chennai, India

Printed on acid-free paper

Springer is part of Springer Science+Business Media (www.springer.com)

Message from the ICA3PP 2012 General Chairs

We are privileged and delighted to welcome you to the proceedings of the 12th International Conference on Algorithms and Architectures for Parallel Processing (ICA3PP 2012).

Following the traditions of the previous successful ICA3PP conferences held in Hangzhou, Brisbane, Singapore, Melbourne, Hong Kong, Beijing, Cyprus, Taipei, Busan, and Melbourne, this year ICA3PP 2012 was held in Fukuoka, Japan. The objective of ICA3PP 2012 was to bring together researchers and practitioners from academia, industry, and government to advance the theories and technologies in parallel and distributed computing. ICA3PP 2012 focused on two broad areas of parallel and distributed computing, i.e., architectures, algorithms and networks, and systems and applications. The ICA3PP 2012 conference was organized by Kyushu Sangyo University, Japan, and Deakin University, Australia.

We sincerely thank the many people who helped organize ICA3PP 2012. We would like to thank the Program Chairs, Ivan Stojmenovic, University of Ottawa, Canada, Bernady O. Apduhan, Kyushu Sangyo University, Japan, and Guojun Wang, Central South University, China, for their leadership in providing the excellent technical program. We are also grateful to the members of our Program Committee and other reviewers who helped us in producing this year's exciting program.

September 2012

Koji Nakano
Albert Zomaya
Yang Xiang

Message from the ICA3PP 2012 Program Chairs

A warm welcome to the proceedings of the 12th International Conference on Algorithms and Architectures for Parallel Processing (ICA3PP 2012) held in Fukuoka, Japan.

ICA3PP 2012 was the 12th in this series of conferences started in 1995 that are devoted to algorithms and architectures for parallel processing. ICA3PP is now recognized as the main regular event in the world covering the many dimensions of parallel algorithms and architectures, encompassing fundamental theoretical approaches, practical experimental results, and commercial components and systems. As applications of computing systems have permeated in every aspect of daily life, the power of computing systems has become increasingly critical. ICA3PP 2012 provided a widely known forum for researchers and practitioners from countries around the world to exchange ideas on improving the computation power of computing systems.

In response to the ICA3PP 2012 call for papers, we received 156 submissions from 27 countries. These papers were evaluated on the basis of their originality, significance, correctness, relevance, and technical quality. Each paper was reviewed by at least three members of the Program Committee. Based on these evaluations, of the papers submitted, 39 regular papers and 26 short papers were selected for presentation at the conference, representing 25% of acceptance for regular papers and 16.7% of acceptance for short papers.

We would like to thank the Program Committee members and additional reviewers from all around the world for their efforts in reviewing the large number of papers. We appreciate all the associated Workshop Chairs for their dedication and professionalism. We would like to extend our sincere thanks to the ICA3PP Steering Committee Chairs, Wanlei Zhou, Yi Pan, and Andrzej Goscinski, and the General Chairs, Koji Nakano, Hiroshima University, Japan, Albert Zomaya, The University of Sydney, Australia, and Yang Xiang, Deakin University, Australia. They provided us with invaluable guidance throughout the process of paper selection and program organization. We also thank Yu Wang for his help in completing the final proceedings.

Last but not least, we would also like to take this opportunity to thank all the authors for their submissions to ICA3PP 2012.

September 2012

Ivan Stojmenovic
Bernady O. Apduhan
Guojun Wang

Organization

ICA3PP 2012 Committees

Honorary General Chair

Iwao Yamamoto   Kyushu Sangyo University, Japan

General Chairs

Koji Nakano   Hiroshima University, Japan
Albert Zomaya   The University of Sydney, Australia
Yang Xiang   Deakin University, Australia

Program Chairs

Ivan Stojmenovic   University of Ottawa, Canada
Bernady O. Apduhan   Kyushu Sangyo University, Japan
Guojun Wang   Central South University, China

International Advisory Committee

Tadashi Dohi   Hiroshima University, Japan (Chair)
Takashi Naka   Kyushu Sangyo University, Japan
Toshinori Sueyoshi   Kumamoto University, Japan

Steering Committee

Wanlei Zhou   Deakin University, Australia
Yi Pan   Georgia State University, USA
Andrzej Goscinski   Deakin University, Australia

Workshop Chairs

Xu Huang   University of Canberra, Australia
Bin Xiao   Hong Kong Polytechnic University, Hong Kong

Publicity Chairs

Kejie Lu   University of Puerto Rico at Mayaguez,
                                    Puerto Rico
Wen Tao Zhu   Chinese Academy of Sciences, China
Muhammad Khurram Khan   King Saud University, Saudi Arabia
Toshinori Sato   Fukuoka University, Japan

Demo/Exhibition Chair

Jun Zhang   Deakin University, Australia

Local Arrangements Committee

Kai Cheng   Kyushu Sangyo University, Japan
Kazuaki Goshi   Kyushu Sangyo University, Japan
Masaki Hayashi   Kyushu Sangyo University, Japan
Toshihiro Shimokawa   Kyushu Sangyo University, Japan
Toshihiro Uchibayashi   Kyushu Sangyo University, Japan
Yoshihiro Yasutake   Kyushu Sangyo University, Japan

Program Committee

Bechini Alessio   University of Pisa, Italy
Giuseppe Amato   ISTI-CNR, Italy
Srinivas Aluru   Iowa State University, USA
Hideharu Amano   Keio University, Japan
Henrique Andrade   Goldman Sachs, USA
Cosimo Anglano   Università del Piemonte Orientale, Italy
Dorian Arnold   University of New Mexico, USA
Purushotham Bangalore   University of Alabama, USA
Novella Bartolini   University of Rome La Sapienza, Italy
Ladjel Bellatreche   ENSMA, France
Jorge Bernal Bernabe   University of Murcia, Spain
Ateet Bhalla   NRI Institute of Information Science and
                                    Technology, India
Arndt Bode   Technische Universität München, Germany
George Bosilca   University of Tennessee, USA
Luc Bougé   ENS Cachan, France
Rajkumar Buyya   The University of Melbourne, Australia
Surendra Byna   Lawrence Berkeley National Lab, USA
Massimo Cafaro   University of Salento, Italy
Andre Carvalho   Universidade de Sao Paulo, Brazil
Tania Cerquitelli   Politecnico di Torino, Italy
Ruay-Shiung Chang   National Dong Hwa University, Taiwan

CDCN 2012 Preface

It is our great pleasure to welcome you to the proceedings of the First International Workshop on Cognitive Distributed Computing and Networking (CDCN 2012) held in conjunction with the 12th International Conference on Algorithms and Architecture for Parallel Processing (ICA3PP-12) in Fukuoka, Japan, September 4–7, 2012.

The CDCN Workshop focuses on major research streams in algorithms and architectures for various types of processing. This workshop offers researchers a good opportunity to present their work in a more focused way than the main conference itself and to obtain feedback from the community interested in the focused theme areas.

The CDCN Workshop invited new and original submissions addressing theoretical and practical topics in algorithms and architectures relevant to cognitive distributed computing and networking. The proceedings of the CDCN Workshop, published by Springer in their *Lecture Notes in Computer Science* (LNCS) series in the same proceedings as ICA3PP-12 (EI indexed), were available to all conference registrants on site.

The CDCN 2012 Workshop attracted a total of 19 original submissions. The peer-review process was carried out by international reviewers who are experts in relevant cognitive distributed computing and networking areas. Each paper was reviewed by at least two reviewers and checked by the workshop committee. After the peer-review process, eight papers were accepted giving an acceptance rate of 42%. We would like to thank all the reviewers and the workshop committee members for their careful evaluation, feedback provided to the authors, and personal contribution to the peer-review process that resulted in the high-quality papers included in these proceedings.

We express our gratitude to the ICA3PP 2012 Conference Committee for their great support of the CDCN Workshop.

Xu Huang
Dat Tran

Table of Contents – Part II

ICA3PP 2012 Short Papers

CDCN 2012 Workshop Papers

Table of Contents – Part I

ICA3PP 2012 Regular Papers

Analytical Modeling for Multi-transaction Bus on Distributed Systems

Jih-Ching Chiu, Kai-Ming Yang, and Chen-Ang Wong

Department of Electrical Engineering, National Sun Yat-Sen University,
Kaohsiung, 804, Taiwan, R.O.C.
d953010024@gmail.com

Abstract. Network-on-Chip (NoC) has been proposed to perform high performance and scalability in System-on-Chip (SoC) design. Interconnection modeling was widely used to evaluate performance, especially for large-scale NoCs. In this paper, the router modeling for multi-transaction bus architecture on distributed system with bufferless microarchitectures was presented to analyze and evaluate the performance and model the success rate of each node respectively. It will facilitate the analysis of impact for different priorities. The accuracy of our approach and its practical use is illustrated through extensive simulation results.

Keywords: On-Chip Interconnect, Analytical Performance evaluation.

1   Introduction

On-chip network architectures constitutes the infrastructure of Systems-on-Chip (SoC) and multiprocessor systems. As the increasing number of transistors in progress technology, the number of components on a single chip continues to achieve the high performance. Much research adopted off-chip networks methods in on-chip network for modeling the performance of on-chip networks [1][2]. Because of design complexity, the on-chip network architecture will not scale properly. Therefore, many researches present the router modeling by M/G/1/N queuing models [19][20][21][22]. However, current products and applications usually use the bufferless microachitecture. These approaches based on queuing models will not be suitable for current applications. Regarding high performance, the novel bus architecture, multi-transaction bus architecture, is proposed and used widely for current products. Modeling the multi-transaction bus with bufferless microarchitecture to evaluate performance is practical and up-to-date. Considering trade-off between performance and hardware complexity in interconnections, there are three considered factors as follows:

1). Single and multi transaction bus architecture. Traditional single bus architecture consumes all bus resources to one component. While a component is communicating with another, others cannot access bus at any time. The connecting ability of single transaction bus limits the performance of SoC and communication of multi-processors. These growing requirements also push the attention of

Y. Xiang et al. (Eds.): ICA3PP 2012, Part II, LNCS 7440, pp. 1–9, 2012.

multi-transaction communication architectures to abandon traditional bus architectures. The multi-transaction communication can perform multiple accesses in one bus cycle by multiple transactions [7]. This concept of multi-transaction bus can improve efficiently the bandwidth and has been widely used in the current products, such as IBM Cell BE [8][9]. However, the multi-transaction bus architecture increases significantly the complexity of arbitrations to maintain the fairness for communications. Therefore, applying this multi-transaction bus technique simultaneously with a low complexity design is another crucial issue while providing the high performance.

2). Centralized and distributed arbitration. Centralized architectures concentrate all requests in the single arbitration unit as the Fig. 1(a). The main problem is that the latency and complexity of hardware increases significantly as the number of routers increases. The centralized architectures cannot be performed efficiently for large numbers of routers due to the complex arbiter from centralized management. For better scalability, distributed communication managements are proposed in as shown Fig. 1 (b). In [7], they verified also that centralized arbitrations are much more complex, leading to higher arbitration delay. As a result, the distributed arbitration becomes consequential choice.

3). Buffering and bufferless router microarchitecture. For on-chip network router, many researches proposing the buffer NoC router or buffering switch will be not properly used for on-chip network [1][3][8][9][10][11][12][13]. The bufferless router microarchitectures are proposed without queuing buffers and has been used many products, such as the Intel Larrabee and IBM Cell BE ring network [4] [15]. At each port, there are no separate queuing buffers to place packets. For the low design complexity, on-chip network router prefers the bufferless router microarchitecture. Therefore, in bufferless router microarchitecture, the packets with bus contention cannot be retained by the input and output queuing buffer. Considering trade-off between performance and hardware complexity, the current products and applications prefer to the bufferless router microarchitecture.

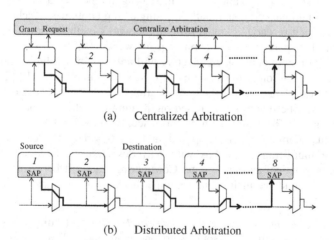

(a)   Centralized Arbitration

(b)   Distributed Arbitration

Fig. 1. Structure of Multi-transaction bus Architecture

Topology: The network topologies are another significant factor which dominates the performance. On distributed systems, the complexity of routers depends on the router degree for network topologies rather than the number of routers. As a viable interconnects for future CMPs(Chip MultiProcessor). Rings may offer a preferred compromise between speed, scalability, complexity, and resource usage. Rings are also used by the IBM Cell [8][9][14][15][16][17] and are under consideration by Intel for future CMPs [16] [17] [18]. As this result, the proposed scheduler will focus on the ring bus network in this paper.

According to previous discussions, using multi-transaction bus architecture on distributed system becomes the consequential selection. Therefore, our research will focus on the multi-transaction bus architecture, distributed arbitration and bufferless router environment for ring network as Fig. 1 (b). The multi-transaction bus architecture on distributed system with bufferless router microarchitecture was abbreviated as *MDBL* in this paper. Although current approaches proposed analytical modeling by M/G/1/N queuing theory for buffer router microarchitecture [19][20][21][22], *MDBL* has been applied by current many products and researches considering performance and scalability [8][16]. In this paper, we will propose a simple analytical model for the impact of weights. By useful feedbacks of *MDBL* network model, NoC designers can evaluate throughput about the arbitration strategy in advance.

2   Previous Works and Background

In this section, we introduce the multi-transaction communication architecture. The centralized and distributed arbitrations on the multi-transaction bus are shown as the Fig. 1. For examples in the Fig. 1(a), there are two communication requests from source router (router *1* and *3*). The destinations of bus transaction are router *3* and router *n* respectively. In the multi-transaction bus, two bus transactions using two different partial networks, can communicate at the same time. Therefore, these bus transactions can be performed *1~3* and *3~n* transactions simultaneously. The multi-transaction architecture has the better utilize bus for resource and the bus bandwidth. Therefore, it is used in general system and performed for multi-processor system such as IBM Cell BE [17]. However, the centralized arbitrations need to obtain the destination addresses of all pending transactions in addition to their source module addresses. Suppose the number of routers is N, the centralized arbitrations must determine at least $N/2$ of bus transactions.   In [7], they have verified that multiwinner centralized arbitrations are much more complex, leading to higher arbitration delay. Considering the latency and scalability, the distributed architectures at each local router are proposed, called the distributed arbitration, as the Fig. 1(b). The distributed arbitration at the location only determines one of the pending paths among conflicting paths. The complexity of arbitration can be reduced significantly. As this result, the distributed system can be more suitably performed than the traditional system.

3   Analysis Mechanism

This section mainly focuses on the model of the above-statement network architecture for performance analysis. The system environment and definition of connection rule will be described in subsection A. In subsection B, we present the basic assumptions and notations for router modeling on *MDBL*.

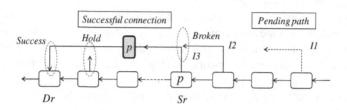

Fig. 2. Definitions for *MDBL* Architecture

3.1   System Environment

The system environment and definition of connection rule with only pipeline registers are shown as Fig. 2. We assume that each router has one unique priority, called *P*. When contention occurs (as broken and hold marks in Fig. 2), the arbiter must determine a winner based on priority *P*. The *P* numbers from large to small indicate priorities from high to low. In the example of Fig. 2, the direction of connections is towards the west. When a connection does not arrive at the destination router yet, this connection, called *pending path*, will forward along the topology continuously. A head flit injected into the network will attach a priority of source router. This flit makes progress towards its destination. While communications has been connected successfully and transferring body flits, this path, called successful connection, is non-interruptible. It means that new requests cannot interrupt a successful connection. Therefore, before transferring body flits, a connection must be built in advance. For this mechanism, these body flits cannot closely follow after the head flit for the pipelining operation. The interval between head and body flits, called bubbles, may decrease the throughput. Considering tradeoff between the performance and hardware complexity, this mechanism can simplify the router microarchitecture to reduce the amount of buffers needed with minimal loss in performance. In fact, bubbles occupy only the faction of overall transmission. Beside, because communicating frequently processors usually are arranged near each other as possible, the length of bubbles usually is short. According to Amdahl's law, the loss throughput caused by bubbles will be minimal [6]. As a result, this work prefers this communication mechanism.

3.2   Router Modeling for MDBL

In this subsection, the router modeling methodology for *MDBL* is presented. Fig. 2 shows *MDBL* for on-chip interconnect to illustrate the methodology. This proposed modeling for performance analysis consists of pass, hold, and broken rate. The pass rate represents the probability of pending paths which can pass a router with lower priority. The broken rate as shown Fig. 2 represents the probability of pending paths which are broken by another pending path with higher priority from east. The hold rate represents the probability of pending paths which must be stall at a router with higher priority. Beside, all parameters are defined as table 1. We will analysis the performance via these factors and discuss as follows:

Table 1. List of Parameter Notation in analytical model

Param.	Description
N	The number of routers
Sr	Source router
Dr	Destination router
P	The current router priority.
λ	Injection rate (Flits/routers/cycle)
λ_t	The mean traffic rate through t unit interval
d	The distance of communication from Sr to Dr
bl	The length of body flits.

Assume a communication pattern shown in Fig. 2 with three injections I1, I2 and I3, each with a corresponding weight p1, p2 and p3. The total number of routers is N. Therefore, weights are between 1 and N. The probability of p1 grants P (I1) being asserted with probabilistic arbitration is equal to the following.

$$P(I1) = \frac{p1}{N\text{-}1} \tag{1}$$

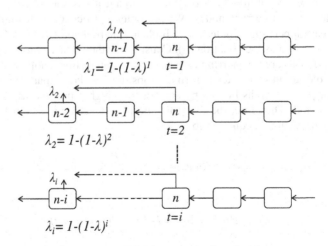

Fig. 3. Structure of Multi-transaction bus Architecture

In the practical condition, the injection rate (λ), the average number of flit at each router per cycle, must be considered. As table 1, the λ_t indicates the probability of a node to incur network, through t unit interval time. In other words, the λ_t means that the probability of a pending path encountering another pending path at t unit interval time. As shown Fig. 3 when a pending path travels at the first interval time, it will travel at the node n-1. In this time, the probability of this node n-1 to incur networks is 1-$(1$-$\lambda)^1$ and exhibited as λ_1. It means that a pending path encounter contention λ_t is estimated as:

$$
\begin{aligned}
T=1: & \quad \lambda_1 = \lambda \\
T=2: & \quad \lambda_2 = 1-(1-\lambda)^2 \\
T=3: & \quad \lambda_3 = 1-(1-\lambda)^3 \\
& \cdots\cdots \\
T=d: & \quad \lambda_d = 1-(1-\lambda)^d
\end{aligned}
\tag{2}
$$

Pass rate (t): The definition of pass rate is the probability of a pending path which passes a router after t unit interval. Therefore, when the current position router does not incur network (as $(1$-$\lambda_t)$ term in equation (3)) or it with lower priority incur network at t unit interval (as $(\lambda_t * P$-$1/N$-$1)$ term), the pass rate is donated as equation (3). Based on the equation (3), the probability of a pending path from Sr to Dr can be donated as equation (3).

$$
Pass\,Rate(t):\ (1-\lambda_t)+\lambda_t*\ \frac{P\text{-}1}{N\text{-}1}
\tag{3}
$$

$$
Total\,Pass\,Rate:\ \prod_{t=1}^{d} Pass\,rate(t)
\tag{4}
$$

Broken rate: The probability of breaking communications indicates that a higher priority router crosses current nodes. When contention occurs with higher priority comes from east, a pending path has to be broken. The probability of broken paths at t unit interval is shown as the equation (5). Considering the impact of transferring body flits, when body flits are transferring on a successful connection, another pending path has to be hold at this transferring router position as hold mark in Fig.2. The probability of pending paths broken by another with higher priority also increases as the holding period. Therefore, the interval time for connections becomes $d+bl$. The broken rate is presented as equation (6).

$$
Broken\,Rate(t):\ \lambda_{d\text{-}t}*\frac{N\text{-}P}{N\text{-}1}
\tag{5}
$$

$$
Final\,Broken\,Rate = 1-\prod_{t=1}^{d+bl}[1\text{-}Broken\,rate(t)]
\tag{6}
$$

Holds rate: the probability of holding connection indicates that forward communications should be held due to the head packet meets the higher priority node which incurs bus as shown in the equation (7).

$$Hold\ rate:\ \lambda * \frac{N\text{-}P}{N\text{-}1} \qquad (7)$$

Finally, the success rate can be modeled by equations (4) and (6) as equation (8).

$$Success\ rate = Pass\ rate * (1\text{-}Broken\ rate)$$
$$= \prod_{t=1}^{d+bl} Pass\ rate(t) * \prod_{t=1}^{d+bl} [1\text{-}Broken\ rate(t)] \qquad (8)$$

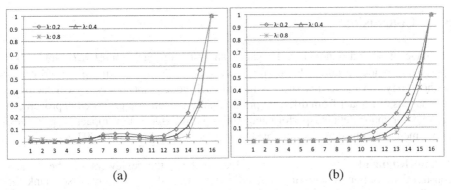

(a)   (b)

Fig. 4. Results of simulations and router modeling for 16 components under the different mean traffic ratio

4   Experiment Results

By the model in the section 3, the simulation and router modeling for 16 components under the different mean traffic ratio are shown Fig. 4(a) and Fig. 4(b). The experiment environment is based on *MDBL* on 16-node ring network. The length of body flits is ten packets for every communication. The X-axis denotes successful rate of all routers with priorities itself respectively. These numbers from large to small indicate priorities from high to low. The y-axis denotes the ratio of successful connection. As the results of models, routers with lower priorities cannot incur bus because other routers with higher priorities will occupy the network. Therefore, the lower priority has seriously starvation problem as the mean traffic ratio increases. The simulation and router modeling have similar curves about O (n^2). The difference between simulation and modeling are shown as Fig. 5. The proposed modeling have higher error for λ =0.8   condition. As the simulation, the highest error is not over 3%.

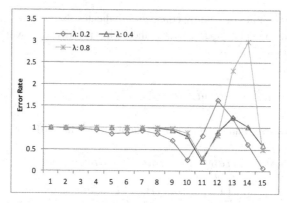

Fig. 5. Difference of successful rate between simulation and modeling

5   Conclusion

We have presented a novel performance analysis approach for *MDBL* NoCs. Our approach provides accurate for performance metrics. Moreover, the proposed router methodology can model the success rate of each node respectively. It will facilitate the analysis of impact from different priorities. As a result, the proposed approach can be used for more detailed performance analysis to explore the impact of priorities. Experimental results demonstrate that the accuracy can achieve about 97%.

Acknowledgment. The authors would like to thank the reviewers for their many constructive comments and suggestions in improving this paper. We also thank the contributions of National Sun Yat-Sen University and aim for the top university project under grant 01C030710.

References

1. Kim, J.: Low-cost router microarchitecture for on-chip networks. In: Proceedings of the 42nd Annual IEEE/ACM International Symposium on Microarchitecture, New York, December 12-16 (2009)
2. Owens, J.D., Dally, W.J., Ho, R., Jayasimha, D.N., Keckler, S.W., Peh, L.-S.: Research challenges for on-chip interconnection networks. IEEE Micro, 96–108 (September/October 2007)
3. Ramanujam, R.S., et al.: Design of a high-throughput distributed shared-buffer NoC router. In: Proc. of NoCs, pp. 69–78 (2010)
4. Seiler, L., Carmean, D., Sprangle, E., Forsyth, T., Dubey, P., Junkins, S., Lake, A., Cavin, R., Espasa, R., Grochowski, E., Juan, T., Abrash, M., Sugerman, J., Hanrahan, P.: Larrabee: A many-core x86 architecture for visual computing. IEEE Micro 29(1), 10–21 (2009)
5. Fossum, T.: Keynote: On-die interconnect and other challenges for chip-level multi-processing. In: Proc. of Hot Interconnects, Stanford, CA (August 2007)

6. Hennessy, J.L., Patterson, D.A.: Computer Architecture A Quantitative Approach, 3rd edn. Morgan Kaufmann Publichsers (2003)
7. Lu, R., Cao, A., Koh, C.: SAMBA-Bus: A High Performance Bus Architecture for System-on-Chips. IEEE Transactions on VLSI Systems 15(1), 69–79 (2007)
8. Handbook, Cell Broadband Engine Programming Handbook, Version 1.1, IBM (published on April 24, 2007)
9. Gschwind, M., Peter Hofstee, H., Flachs, B., Hopkins, M.: IBM,Yukio Wata-nabe, Toshiba,Takeshi Yamazaki, Sony Computer Entertainment. In: Synergistic Processing in Cell's Multicore Architecture. Published by the IEEE Computer Society
10. Lee, K., Lee, S.J., Yoo, H.J.: A distributed on-chip crossbar switch scheduler for on-chip networks. In: Proc. Custom Integrated Circuits Conf., pp. 671–674 (May 2003)
11. Rodrigo, S., Flich, J., Roca, A., Medardoni, S., Bertozzi, D., Camacho, J., Silla, F., Duato, J.: Cost-Efficient On-Chip Routing Implementations for CMP and MPSoC Systems. IEEE Trans. Computer-Aided Design of Integrated Circuits and Systems 30, 534–547 (2000)
12. Peh: A High-Throughput Distributed Shared-Buffer NoC Router. Li Computer Architecture Letters 8(1), 21–24 (2009)
13. Lee, K., Lee, S.-J., Yoo, H.-J.: A Distributed Crossbar Switch Scheduler for On-Chip Networks. In: IEEE Proceedings of Custom Integrated Circuits Conference, pp. 671–674 (2003)
14. Kahl, J., Day, M., Hofstee, H., Johns, C., Maeurer, T., Shippy, D.: Introduction to the Cell Multiprocessor. IBM Journal of Research and Development 49(4) (2005)
15. IBM. Unleashing the Cell Broadband Engine Processor (November 2005), http://www-128.ibm.com/developerworks/power/library/pa-fpfeib/
16. Borkar, S.Y., Dubey, P., Kahn, K.C., Kuck, D.J., Mulder, H., Pawlowski, S.S., Rattner, J.R.: Platform 2015: Intel processor and platform evolution for the next decade. Technical report, Intel White Paper (March 2005)
17. Kahl, J.A., et al.: Introduction to the Cell Multiprocessor. IBM J. Research and Development 49(4), 589–604 (2005)
18. Marty, M.R., Hill, M.D.: Cache coherence techniques for multicore processors. University of Wisconsin at Madison, USA (2008)
19. Bakhouya, M., Suboh, S., Gaber, J., El-Ghazawi, T.: Analytical modeling and evaluation of on-chip interconnects using network calculus. In: NoCS Proc., pp. 74–79 (2009)
20. Suboh, S., Bakhouya, M., Gaber, J., El-Ghazawi, T.: Analytical Modeling and Evaluation of Network-on-Chip Architectures. In: Proc. High Performance Computing and Simulation (HPCS), pp. 615–622 (2010)
21. Lai, M., Gao, L., Xiao, N., Wang, Z.: An accurate and efficient performance analysis approach based on queuing model for Network on Chip. In: ACM/IEEE Int. Conference on Computer-Aided Design, ICCAD (2009)
22. Ogras, U.Y., Marculescu, R.: Analytical router modeling for networks-on-chip performance analysis. In: Proc. Des., Autom. Test Eur. Conf., p. 1096 (2007)

Leveraging the Strengths of Transactional Memory While Maintaining System Performance for a Multiplayer Gaming Application

LihChyun Shu[1,2], Ying-Cheng Su[1], Chang-Ming Tasi[2], and Huey-Min Sun[2,*]

[1] Dept. of Accounting, National Cheng Kung University, Taiwan 701, ROC
[2] Dept. of Information Management, Chang Jung Christian University, Taiwan 711, ROC
prince@mail.cjcu.edu.tw

Abstract. With the technology of multi-core on the rise, many applications have started to support concurrency control on shared resources for raising performance and accuracy such as locks, semaphores, and monitors. A new mechanism called transactional memory (TM) can provide serilizability for using shared resources and ease for programming. However, the TM performance of most studies has been relatively poorer than traditional methods. This is the reason why these applications still use the locks to handle the problem of concurrency control. We propose two mechanisms named Barrier Transactional Memory and Aggregate Physics Update to detect and release signals without conflict and to update all calculation results using parallel multi-threading in a multi-player gaming system. Experimental results show the improvement and the comparison of the proposed mechanisms to traditional locking and single thread update, especially in the area of physics calculations and updating.

Keywords: transactional memory, aggregate update, concurrency control.

1 Introduction

In a multi-core computing environment, providing a safe and efficient access mechanism for the concurrent control of shared resources and speeding up overall performance through the scalability of CPU core numbers has become an important issue. Transactional Memory (TM)provides atomicity, consistency, isolation, and serializability to ensure that shared resources can be used safely. In contrast to traditional block-based mechanisms such as semaphores, which allow programmers to handle the conflict and may cause deadlock or starvation. Although TM mechanisms can guarantee data and resources with atomicity, consistency, and isolation, a number of studies concerning TM mechanisms [4–9] have shown lower performance than traditional semaphore, locks, and monitors methods.

---

* Corresponding author.

Y. Xiang et al. (Eds.): ICA3PP 2012, Part II, LNCS 7440, pp. 10–20, 2012.

TL2[4] was a well known TM mechanism that used a time stamp, a memory lock, and validation to ensure serializability. Autolocker[5] was a lock-based transactional memory system that had a read/write lock and table/entry lock data structures. Swiss TM[6] was a lock-based STM that used invisible reads and counter based heuristics. It featured eager write/write and lazy read/write conflict detection. SNZI STM[7] used a node data structure for more memory space to exchange the performance of the transactional memory system, and SkySTM[8] combined with a new SNZI-R mechanism using scalable-read sharing and solved the privatization problems of the TL2. The SigTM[9] was a hybrid TM system with software transactional memory and hardware transactional memory. It provided a difficult strong isolation guarantee.

Even though some problems in this new mechanism with a parallel computing environment need to be solved[10–12], TM still provides a safe and convenient mechanism for programmers to operate with shared resources. The nested problem in a TM system is a popular issue on discussing how to solve the nested transactions but still maintain the serializability and performance[10]. In privatization problems, Spear et al.[11] introduced several examples in a delayed commit situation with redo and undo logs and also presented an I/O problem entering an atomic block and a method for the use of a barrier validation to solve it. In communication problems, Dash and Demsky[12] discussed the communication problems in a distributed system with a transactional mechanism. It is important to determine which mechanism is adaptive in the design of a transactional memory system, such as whether it should have a strong isolation guarantee or not[13] or should use a lock or non-block mechanism[14].

Therefore, more and more studies have started to move TM mechanisms from simple benchmark/algorithms to real applications. One of the areas in which this has taken place is in a multi-player gaming application.

In[1–3], the researchers showed real-shooting game server performed with TM mechanisms, but unfortunately the performance was not satisfactory. We try to find a new solution using the characteristics of TM mechanisms combined with aggregate update mechanisms to acquire better performance in overall game systems. We do a number of simulations compared with lock and TM mechanisms in the multi-player gaming system model.

For the problem of parallel computing physics steps in a multi-player gaming system [2, 3, 18], especially in handling the conflict of threads that access shared resources, we design a Barrier TM using the concept of transactional memory to detect the conflict of thread accesses and combine with an aggregate physics update scheme that makes the physics steps in a game system parallel through multi-threading for speeding up overall performance. These parallelling tasks need extra conflict detections and conflict management mechanisms to roll-back or block the threads in the physics steps. The responsibility will be on programmers who need to design appropriate algorithms for conflict management, and due to complex program structure, it is difficult for programmers to handle the conflict problem.That is, to reduce the difficulty of programming a concurrent physics steps and to achieve better performance, the physics steps often run in single threads[2, 3, 18]. We employ the Barrier TM to detect the conflict by prevalidaiton for each thread and block the conflict threads in a buffer. Each of the threads passing the Barrier TM in a cycle has no conflict and can be concurrently executed in physics steps. Even though the Barrier TM takes time in server when processing the signals (threads), but with the higher resources the physics calculations need, the higher performance we gain because we can run physics calculation in multi-thread and without any complex conflict control. Because of the benefit from the Barrier TM, we can do aggregate updating for the results that are derived from physics calculating and return concurrently the results to the game world, which is called Aggregate Physics Update. We replace the traditional single-thread physics updating with it.

Baldassin and Burckhardt[1] performed a real game application on Spacewar 3D using transactions to handle shared resource conflicts. The authors extended the TM application area into the game world. The TM system named Quake TM[2] and Atomic Quake[3] were both real game applications on a physics multiple-player gaming server using transactional memory mechanisms. The results showed the performance for Quake TM and Atomic Quake was relatively lower than lock mechanisms, but Lupei et al.[19] studied the load balancing of the thread in a game application, tried to separate the conflict area, and allocated the area to a single thread combined with the TM to avoid the frequency of conflict and gain the performance.

Aggregate update is a well-known database approach that still has a great deal of application research focusing on it, such as using an aggregate update for online transaction processing (OLTP) and online analytical processing (OLAP)[15], sensor data of a web portal[16], and an online virtual environment[17]. In the aggregate update mechanism, the updating can concurrently control shared resources without conflict for each cycle, but in order to keep the fairness of multiplayer games, we need to return the correct sequence sent by players.

In the aggregate physics update mechanism, even we do the updating concurrently without conflict for each cycle, but in order to keep the fairness of multi-player games, we still need to return the correct sequence sent by players, thus we use a conception of virtual time constructed in aggregate physics steps to make sure the return sequence will be correct. Experimental results show that the overall performance of the game system using the Barrier TM and aggregate physics update is higher than traditional lock mechanism with single-thread updating in general cases. Our contributions provide a possibility for the use of TM in a specific application area and promote performance if keeping the characteristics from TM and combining with the aggregate physics update mechanism.

2   Methodology

Our research model is based on a multiple-player gaming system. The model collects the players' signals after receiving the request. Then, it processes signals and sends them to physics step for calculating. The computed results update and reply to the game world and display on monitors. After processing the signals, these data send to physics step with physics engines doing the physics calculation to calculate how fast the ball should move or where it should move to, and then update the results to the game world for the players.

The first phase based on the model is to update the physics game world to the players. Thus, we can see the progress of the interaction between the players and the game world. In this virtual world, we present three kinds of shared objects, and using these shared data structures is the reason why we need to use TM to handle the conflicts caused by the players.

The second phase is to receive signals that are sent from the players. The content of the signals may be someone shooting something or kicking some object, for example. These signals will be sent to the server and will go through a lock or TM mechanism to make sure the signal will execute following the correct sequence in multi-core or even cloud computing hardware. Then the signal can be calculated such as health point decrees or which object should be broken and if necessary physics calculations will be done. In this phase, we need to do physics calculations in order to calculate the physics statuses for each object, including speed, rolling, and where it should move following the physics formulas. In the replying phase, we send the result to the players and the server for game world updating and then call it a frame.

We combine a TM mechanism with a parallel update to speed up the total efficiency for the game system. For comparability, we perform a simulation of the game system with a barrier TM processing and aggregate physics updating to see if the total efficiency will be better than a traditional lock mechanism.

2.1   Aggregate Physics Update

The physics calculations include the Verlet algorithm, rolling, and moving actions. In the case of the lock mechanism, we do the physics calculations in a single thread and update the whole world once a frame. There is a slight variation when we do the Aggregate Physics update parallel since a conflict may happen in each 1/60sec cycle. Therefore, we may do the physics steps many times in order to see if a conflict occurs. For example, in the worst case as seen in Fig. 1 and Fig. 2, we assume that player 1, player 2, and player 3 are sending signals to modify the same object in a cycle. If we use a lock mechanism, the lock will force the players' signals to execute one after another on the shared object, then the physics calculations are done one by one, and the result is updated one by one to a frame. If we use an aggregate update, at first, the barrier TM will detect the shared object conflict, then release the signals one at a time; the conflicting signals will be blocked by the barrier TM until the conflict situation is gone; the signals without conflicts will do the processing on the shared object in the barrier TM, send them to the physics steps to do the physics calculating and then update to the frame buffer. After all signals in this cycle are calculated, a frame updating is done. Still we may face a rare case in the real game system that is if the signals send to players' PCs have been delayed in the Internet communication and lost their sequence, we may need a return signal to make sure one physics calculation

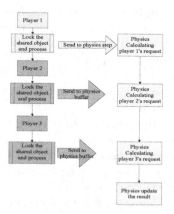

Fig. 1. Worst case scenario for the lock mechanism

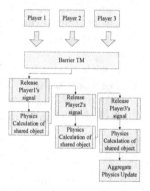

Fig. 2. Worst case scenario for the barrier TM mechanism

task is done. Since we run a simulation on only one computer with single thread, this communication problem will happen and be ignored. In order to perform an aggregate update, we design two mechanisms to avoid the incorrect result. One is based on more memory space to give a time stamp for each signal in a cycle. The other mechanism in aggregate updating is update-sorting. Because we do the physics step as a parallel operation, we cannot ensure which player's signal will be finished first if there is no conflict between them. Therefore, before these signals are updated, we need to do update-sorting according to their receiving time stamp in order to ensure each physics calculation on the shared object is an atomic operation and to make sure the results follow the correct sequence.

2.2   Barrier Transactional Memory

The concept of a barrier TM is a software transactional memory system that will help the server detect the signal conflicts in order to release the computed signals without conflict and to make sure the conflict signals will execute following the serializability principle. In our simulation of a barrier TM, the granularity of the detecting conflict is signals, and we assume each signal is sent in order to modify the status and physics of one object. In a real case, one player's signal may cause two or more objects to be modified, and it will be regarded as two or more signals being executed in a 1/60sec cycle.

The following steps are the rules for Barrier TM work:

Record the time stamp to each of the signals (threads). When the signals are sent to the server, before the prevalidation starts, each signal will be assigned a time stamp. Here, we use the receiving time, but not the sending time, because there might be delayed by the Internet communication since we are running a multi-player gaming server. Following the principle of serilizability, we cannot afford one signal to be sent first and even though it is delayed by the Internet, still needing to be executed first. In some cases, these delayed signals will be ignored or cancelled; therefore, it will be more fair and convenient if we use the receiving time to record the signals.

Count the number of signals in a 1/60sec cycle. The server will collect the signals for each 1/60sec and use these signals to update a frame. Here, we need to record the number of the signals in a frame. In other words, we can determine how many signals will be executed in parallel and then use this number to request extra memory space in order to perform our Barrier TM mechanism.

Request memory space for two data structures. With the counting number of the signals in one frame, we will ask for memory space to store the needed information. The reason why a counting number is necessary is because we don't want to see a conflict in these data structures, and each signal will be assigned a memory space and can be validated by any other signal with the prevalidation mechanism. The first data structure is a waiting buffer. It will store the signal numbers. This signal is willing to modify along with the time stamp. The second data structure is a processing buffer, used to store the signals and the object number that passes the prevalidation but still under execution.

Prevalidation(an atomic validation) and executing signals. After the request for extra memory space, before the signals are executed, we will conduct a prevalidation first as an atomic operation. In the case of each signal, the prevalidation will check the waiting buffer first to see if there are conflicts in the waiting buffer (modifying the same object). If not, then the process moves to check the processing buffer to see if there are any signals executing the same object at that time. If the second check passes, the signal is added to the processing buffer and the signal is executed to the physics steps. If there is a signal modifying the same object but waiting in the waiting buffer, we will compare the time marks. When time stamp is earlier (smaller) or equal to the signals in the waiting buffer with the same object number, the signal will pass to the processing buffer check or else the signal will be put back to the waiting buffer and will sleep for a very short time. In the case of a signal waking up from the waiting buffer and requiring the right to pass to the processing check, we will remove it from the waiting buffer when this signal passes to the next checking step. In the case of processing buffer checking, if there are signals with the same object number executing, the Barrier TM will add the signal back to the waiting buffer and force the thread to sleep for a very short time waiting for the next prevalidation. If there are no signal conflicts in the processing buffer, we can pass it to the physics steps and finish the prevalidation. This mechanism is designed to avoid the abort that happened when we detect a conflict after the physics calculation is finished or being updated and ensures that all signals will follow the correct sequence (time stamp) to be executed. After the computing of the signal (process step), the Barrier TM will release this signal to the physics step and remove the record from the processing buffer.

Check the count number, release extra memories. For each frame, we check the signals passing the prevalidation and compare the number with the counting number. If all signals in a frame have been executed and the physics calculations and physics updating are completed, we can release the memory space of this 1/60 cycle, finish a frame, and can execute the next one.

3   Experimental Results

In the experiment, we simulated that a number of players sent their signals to the server using the barrier TM or the lock mechanism. After processing the signals, these signals were released to the physics steps and updated back to the clients. The programming language we used was visual basic .net with .net framework 4.0 which provided a complete mechanism for multi-threading and supported for concurrency control in parallel computing.

To record the information for each player, we designed a simple data structure and sub-program to send out a signal recording the player's identifying number, the object number this player wanted to modify, and the value it could be modified with. Our simulation randomly created the signals for each player, but in order to control the experimental condition, we still could force players to send out the signals of experimental requirements.

For each physics calculation of the game objects in our simulation, we ran three kinds of algorithms for experiment. One was the Verlet algorithm, with a given vector, used to calculate the transformation of a mass point in a specific period of time. Another used a matrix to perform a rolling algorithm. The other calculated where each mesh point should move.

As we indicated earlier, because of running the physics in a single thread without the conflict problem, it was relatively easy to construct an aggregate physics update. We used multithreading to run the physics steps and to control the number of CPUs by a function provided from the windows operating system. The problem was that because we wanted to avoid the situation in which a same-signal conflict happened in parallel physics calculations, we needed a lock to make sure the physics calculation to be an atomic operation.

For the Barrier TM mechanism, each player's signal was sent into the server and became one of the threads. The Barrier TM started prevalidation and memory space control until it released. For the lock mechanism, using synchronously locking accessed the shared objects and the shared variables between processes.

Our simulation ran on an Inteli7 950, a 4 core machine with a windows.net framework 4.0 environment.

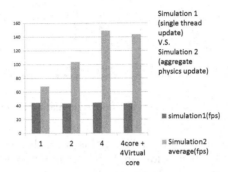

Fig. 3. Frame per second of single thread update vs. aggregate physics update

First, we ran an aggregate physics update in order to compare with a traditional single thread update without adding a conflict control, i.e., assuming no conflict, mechanism to make sure the aggregate physics update can actually level up the performance. We set the same condition to 30 objects, and each of them had 800 mesh points. These 30 objects were calculated in a frame time. The performance of frames with increasing CPU numbers shown in Fig. 3 is rasing. However, we were interested in determining why an aggregate update was faster in only one core. In this situation, it should be the same efficiency since when we did the parallel computing, there was only one CPU computing the task. The reason was that each physics step was outputted once for each 30 objects in the single thread updating, but a final aggregate updating was done (if there was no conflict) and only input and output once, and the passing of the I/O showing the results on monitor only took a short time to execute in the parallel physics steps.

Furthermore, with the Intel hyper threading technology, the performance was not scalable because the physics cores were all filled with threads, and this made no difference in the case of virtual cores.

Second, we tested the overall processes in our system simulation, from players' sending signals, passing through the Barrier TM, to the end of the physics calculations and updating steps.

The lock mechanism is compared with 1, 2, and 4 cores shown in Fig. 4 and Fig. 5 where TM1, TM8, and TM16 stand for 1, 8, and 16 players signal in a frame using Barrier TM and Lock1, Lock8, and Lock16 for 1, 8, and 16 players signal in a frame using lock mechanism, respectively.

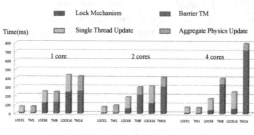

Fig. 4. The worst case of Barrier TM and Aggregate Physics Update vs. locks

The worst case is shown in Fig. 4. In this case, the conflicts were forced to occur. The effect of efficiency for single core computing was the same as that for single thread computing. However, when we added to 2 cores and 4 cores, the effect of conflicts on performance was decreasing. Especially in the 4 cores environment with 16 players, the conflicts took place when each of the threads was going through prevalidation. The conflicts occurred with 16 players and 8 players, and the number of conflicts was 120 times and 33 times in a cycle, respectively. Even with the number of conflicts causing the performance of the Barrier TM to be unacceptable, the aggregate physics updating was still fast, and the total execution time was around 2 to 3 times faster than the lock mechanism.

If we used random signals, the performance was better. As shown in Fig. 5, with a growth in the number of CPUs, the conflicts occur and raise the calculation time for the Barrier TM, but the number of conflicts is less than that of the worst case. With the safe-aggregate physics updating mechanism, the overall performance on average is faster than that of the lock mechanism.

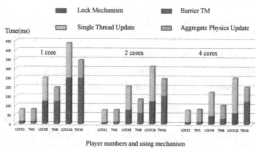

Fig. 5. The average case of Barrier TM and Aggregate Physics Update vs. locks

4   Conclusions

We have introduced two mechanisms to perform a simulation of multiple players gaming system. The results show a possibility of extending the efficiency of the system using a TM concept and aggregate updating. Even though in some rare cases, a TM may cause low performance, it can still provide the safety characteristic of serializability, and we use this characteristic combined with an aggregate updating mechanism to develop a new method for the game application. The reason for the use of the general TM as a standard mechanism to handle the parallel computing conflict is that the performance of TM is still worse than that of a traditional lock. Even though the lock mechanism needs programmers to respond to conflicts and deadlocks, starvation, or any other concurrency control problems, the simple mechanism still provides a high performance speed, and that is what we are always seeking in the world of computers. However, in our research, as can be observed in the experimental results, it is possible that the performance is improved with a Barrier TM combined with aggregate physics updating for the game application. The experimental results show the possibility that if we can use the safety characteristic of serializability combined with other mechanisms, there may be a chance of acquiring higher performance instead of using a lock and still keep the existing safety characteristic.

Furthermore, the mechanism of the Barrier TM could still be improved, especially with regard to conflicts. One of the possibilities is that if we can lower the number of conflicts, there may still be a chance to speed up the performance of overall systems. With a better TM mechanism, we may get a chance to extend our mechanism to more computer application areas, since the trend of multi-core environment is not going to reverse. Determining a method for the provision of a mechanism with safety characteristic and good performance for computer applications will be an important issue in the future.

Acknowledgments. This research is partially supported by NSC grant NSC 100-2221-E-006-159.

References

1. Baldassin, A., Burckhardt, S.: Lightweight Software Transactions for Games. In: First USENIX Workshop on Hot Topics in Parallelism, CA, USA, p. 13 (2009)
2. Gajinov, Zyulkyarov, F., Unsal, O.S., Cristal, A., Ayguade, E., Harris, T., Valero, M.: QuakeTM: Parallelizing a Complex Sequential Application Using Transactional Memory. In: Proceedings of the 23rd International Conference on Supercomputting, New York, USA, pp. 126–135 (2009)
3. Zyulkyarov, F., Gajinov, V., Unsal, O.S., Cristal, A., Ayguade, E., Harris, T., Valero, M.: Atomic Quake: Using Transactional Memory in an Interactive Multiplayer Game Server. In: Proceedings of the 14th ACM SIGPLAN Symposium on Principles and Practice of Parallel Programming, Raleigh, North Carolina, USA, pp. 14–18 (2009)
4. Dice, D., Shalev, O., Shavit, N.N.: Transactional Locking II. In: Dolev, S. (ed.) DISC 2006. LNCS, vol. 4167, pp. 194–208. Springer, Heidelberg (2006)

5. McCloskey, B., Zhou, F., Gay, D., Brewer, E.: Autolocker: Synchronization Inference for Atomic Sections. In: The 33rd ACM SIGPLAN-SIGACT Symposium on Principles of Programming Languages, Charleston, South Carolina, USA, pp. 346–358 (2006)

6. Dragojevic, A., Guerraoui, R., Kapalka, M.: Stretching Transactional Memory. In: Proceedings of the 2009 ACM SIGPLAN Conference on Programming Language Design and Implementation, PLDI 2009, Dublin, Ireland, pp. 155–165 (2009)

7. Ellen, F., Lev, Y., Luchangco, V., Moir, M.: SNZI: Scalable NonZero Indicators. In: Proceedings of the 26th Annual ACM Symposium on Principles of Distributed Computing, PODC 2007, Portland, Oregon, USA (2007)

8. Lev, Y., Luchangco, V., Marathe, V.J., Moir, M., Nussbaum, D., Olszewski, M.: Anatomy of a Scalable Software Transactional Memory. In: 4th ACM SIGPLAN Workshop on Transactional Computing (2009)

9. Minh, C.C., Trautmann, M., Chung, J., McDonald, A., Grasso Bronson, N.G., Casper, J., Kozyrakis, C., Olukotun, K.: An Effective Hybrid Transactional Memory System with Strong Isolation Guarantees. In: ISCA 2007, San Diego, California, USA, June 9-13, pp. 69–80 (2007)

10. Agrawal, K., Lee, I.-T.A., Sukha, J.: Safe Open-Nested Transactions Through Ownership. In: Proceedings of the 14th ACM SIGPLAN Symposium on Principles and Practice of Parallel Programming, PPOPP 2009, Raleigh, North Carolina, USA, pp. 151–162 (2009)

11. Spear, M.F., Virendra, J.M., Dalessandro, L., Scott, M.L.: Privatization Techniques for Software Transactional Memory. In: Proceedings of the 26th Annual ACM Symposium on Principles of Distributed Computing, PODC 2007, pp. 338–339 (2007)

12. Dash, A., Demsky, B.: Integrating Caching and Prefetching Mechanisms in a Distributed Transactional Memory. IEEE Transactions on Parallel and Distributed Systems-PrePrints 22(10) (October 2011)

13. Dalessandro, L., Scott, M.: Strong Isolation is a Weak Idea. In: TRANS-ACT (2009)

14. Dice, D., Shavit, N.: TLRW: Return of the Read-Write Lock. In: SPAA 2010 Conference Program, Thira, Santorini, Greece, pp. 284–293 (2010)

15. Plattner, H.: A common Database Approach for OLTP and OLAP Using an In-Memory Column Database. In: Proceedings of the 35th SIGMOD International Conference on Management of Data, pp. 1–2 (2009)

16. Ahmad, Y., Nath, S.: COLR-Tree: Communication-Efficient Spatio-Temporal Indexing for a Sensor Data Web Portal. In: IEEE 24th International Conference on Data Engineering, Cancun, Mexico, pp. 784–793 (2008)

17. Esch, M., Botev, J.: Distance-Aware Avatar Interaction in Online Virtual Environments. In: International Conference on Advances in Future Internet, Venice, Italy, pp. 56–62 (2010)

18. Dawson, B.: Coding For Multiple Cores on Xbox 360 and Microsoft Windows (June 2010)

19. Lupei, D., Simion, B., Pinto, D., Misler, M., Burcea, M., Krick, W., Amza, C.: Towards Scalable and Transparent Parallelization of Multiplayer Games Using Transactional Memory Support. In: Proceedings of PPOPP, pp. 325–326 (2010)

Enhancing the Performance of a Distributed Mobile Computing Environment by Topology Construction

Il-Young Kim[1] and Jong-Kook Kim[2]

[1] LG Electronics, Seoul, South Korea,
[2] School of Electrical Engineering, Korea University, Seoul, South Korea
{humbo,jongkook}@korea.ac.kr

Abstract. Topology construction methods for a distributed mobile computing environment where the devices are heterogeneous, mobile, and use dynamic voltage scaling and variable transmission power control methods to efficiently use the overall system energy are developed in this research. The final goal of the research is to complete as many tasks as possible using the distributed mobile computing system. The tasks in this system are heterogeneous and must be completed by their deadline to have value. The tasks must be intelligently distributed among the devices to efficiently use the system resources. The reason for the new topology methods was that as the number of devices increase for the example environment the number of communications dropped because of communication collision increased. We propose two major ideas for topology algorithms to enhance the performance and compared it with the all-connected environment and the one that uses the MSMR method which showed improved performance over previous ones. Different methods proved to be better than MSMR in different scenarios for the distributed mobile computing environment.

Keywords: distributed mobile computing, scheduling, topology.

1 Introduction

As more and more mobile devices are operational, it would be beneficial to use those devices for computing resources when they become idle. A mobile ad hoc network (MANET) is a peer-to-peer network where each device is mobile, has limited battery capacity, and uses wireless communication for data transfers. A distributed mobile computing (DMC) environment (e.g., [1], [2]) may be based on the MANET where users can share their computational load and the system-level energy is efficiently used to complete as many tasks as possible. The DMC environment is usually heterogeneous in the sense that various devices have different characteristics such as computing capabilities, different battery duration, and architecture. The tasks or applications may have affinity to certain devices, thus they are heterogeneous. All aspects of a heterogeneous DMC system must be exploited to maximize the performance or the cost-effectiveness of the system.

Y. Xiang et al. (Eds.): ICA3PP 2012, Part II, LNCS 7440, pp. 21–30, 2012.

In the mobile distributed computing environment, the power/energy management is accomplished by using dynamic voltage scaling (DVS) [3] and variable-range transmission power control (VTPC) [4]. DVS is based on the relationship between the CPU supply voltage of a device and the power usage (e.g. Crusoe [5] and ARM7D [6]). The relationship between power and energy is that energy consumed is equaled to power multiplied by the amount of time that the power is used. The relationship between power and voltage is a strictly increasing convex function, represented by a polynomial of at least second degree [7]. Most processors that support DVS use discrete levels. The DVS technique allows the reduction of a CPU's energy usage (through CPU voltage (clock frequency) reduction) at the expense of increasing the task execution time. The VTPC technique can improve the overall network energy usage because different transmission power levels can be used to send data according to the distance between the source and the destination devices. The DVS and VTPC mechanism in this research may be managed by the system administrator or the resource manager and can be transparent to the user.

A good protocol to send data to devices while considering the overall performance is needed for the DMC environment. The destination sequenced distance vector (DSDV) routing protocol (e.g., [8]) is used in this research because, the DSDV routing protocol periodically updates the routing information regardless of the system state and therefore always have the routing information ready for use. In the DMC environment described, it would be best if the routing information is known before the decision to execute task on a device is made because, when a decision is being made, the energy consumption of the device (i.e., processing energy and communication energy) may be taken into consideration. And the estimated communication energy consumption will be determined by the route that will be taken between nodes.

The contribution of this paper is that it enhanced the overall performance of the DMC system by constructing the appropriate topology for the system. The problem is that if a lot of the devices are connected to each other when they are in range there can be a lot of communication collisions resulting in loss of data communication thus increasing the delay in which to send data. Some of the topology construction methods presented in this research uses and enhances the multi-sector multi range control (MSMR) [9] idea which is to decrease the out-degree of devices and tries to save energy. The main idea of MSMR is to select one device from a θ degrees sector considering the transmission power of the devices inside the sector. There are other topology construction methods designed for the DMC environment and all of the designed methods are compared to the original MSMR method. Preliminary tests using the cone-based distributed topology-control (CBTC) method [10] (a well known topology construction scheme) showed that the results were not comparable to the results of other methods so they are not presented. In some cases, the methods designed in this research were better than the MSMR method by increasing the performance of the DMC environment.

The next section describes the DMC environment considered in this research. In Section 3, topology construction methods are proposed. The simple heuristic methods to test and analyze the overall system are depicted in Section 4. In Section 5, the simulation setup is presented. Section 6 presents the results and the last section summarizes the paper.

2   Distributed Mobile Computing Environment

The system model assumed in this research is a distributed mobile computing (DMC) environment. This environment is an ad hoc environment where, devices have mobility and can communicate with other devices that are in range or that have routes to them. All of the mobile devices have a constraint on the energy each can use and their battery capacities can be different. In addition, the devices use dynamic voltage and frequency scaling (DVFS) [3] to control the energy usage of the processor and variable-range transmission power control (VTPC) [4] to adjust transmission power depending on the range between two communicating devices to increase energy efficiency. All devices' direction, duration, and the speed of mobility are determined using a random distribution. It is assumed that there is a central entity called the resource management system (RMS) that controls the whole system. The RMS decides where the requested tasks will be sent for execution, it is located at the center and does not move, and assumed to have unlimited energy.

It is assumed that the RMS knows all of the devices' information and the tasks' execution times on those devices. The estimated execution times of each task on each device is assumed to be known based on user supplied information, experiential data, task profiling, and analytical benchmarking, or other techniques. Other information such as the arrival times of the tasks, the requested task, where the task will be requested is not known a priori. The tasks have a hard deadline and if the deadline is not met, the task has no value.

Fig. 1 shows an example of a multi-hop DMC environment. The task scheduling and operation procedure of the DMC is as follows:

1. Task executions are requested from various users (i.e. source) to the RMS (e.g., ①).
2. The RMS decides on a destination device that can complete the task while considering the energy consumption, task deadline, and expected task completion time.
3. The RMS sends the decision to the source device. If the task needs input data from another device (i.e. input-device), RMS will send a request(s) to that device(s) (②).
4. When the source receives the decision information, it sends the task execution command plus relevant data to the destination device. If inputs are required, inputs are sent to the destination device and the task starts when all inputs arrives (③).
5. After the task execution is completed ($t_n \rightarrow t_{n+1}$), the destination device sends back the information to the RMS (task completed) and the results to the source device (④).

3   Topology Construction Methods

The **802.11 topology construction method** in the NS-2 simulator ([11]) connects all the devices that are in communication range of each other. Therefore, if there are a lot of devices that are in close proximity, there will be a lot of communication collisions. This would mean that communications will be delayed and need to be retried. Thus, the completion of requested tasks by their deadline becomes increasingly difficult. If the overall system is loosely populated, this method may be preferred but as more and more devices are introduced, there will be more communication collisions as the system need to send execution commands, data to start executing tasks, and results to send back to the task requester. Moreover, as there are multiple attempts to communicate, the more energy is wasted as attempts increased.

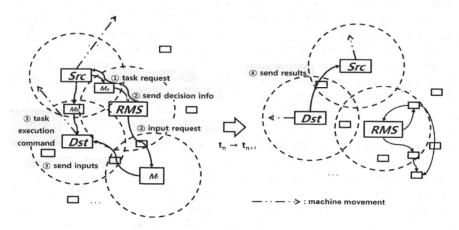

Fig. 1. The centralized RMS for the distributed ad hoc mobile computing environment

The **Multi-Sector Multi-Range Control (MSMR)** [9] is a topology construction method that limits the communication range (shorter than the maximum communication range) and divides the communication range into equal sectors. For each of the sectors, the devices in the sectors are connected to form a minimum spanning tree using the distance. Using the suggestion in [9] and some of our own preliminary results, the transmission range is limited to 250 meters and the number of sectors is three for the results in this research.

The **range constrained (RC)** method is basically a simple method where, the communication range is shortened from the maximum range and all devices in the range is connected to each other. In this research, RC-250, RC-300, and RC-354 methods are designed and compared with other methods. The numbers after "RC" is the maximum distance that each of the device is allowed to communicate. After some preliminary experiments, above three are chosen for this research.

The **Per-Sector Remaining Energy (PSRE)** is similar to the MSMR that was previously described. The PSRE method chooses one device that has the largest remaining energy from each of the sectors. In this research number of sectors is four. The PSRE-250 and PSRE-500 methods are shown for this environment, where the numbers after PSRE are the maximum communication range considered for the topology construction.

4   Heuristic Methods for Resource Management

The **selectively random (SR)** heuristic maps the new task on a randomly selected device from the list of devices that are currently within the communication area of the task requester device (selectable devices). If the selected device cannot complete the task by its deadline, the task will have no value. Even if the task fails, it will use the battery while it is being executed and the energy consumption is updated whenever there is a new task request. All tasks are executed using the highest DVFS level which means using the fastest speed level and thus, the highest energy consuming level.

The **Estimated Minimum Total Energy (EMTE)** heuristic uses the estimated coordinates of the source and destination device to calculate the estimated total energy consumption for all selectable devices. The DVFS is applied such that the device can complete the task by its deadline while trying to minimize the energy being used. The device that cannot complete the task by its deadline is not considered. The detailed procedure of EMTE is in [15].

The first part of the **K-Percent-Energy (KPE)** heuristics is a variation of the k-percent best heuristic found in [12]. Let M be the total number of devices within the DMC environment. The idea behind KPE is to assign a task to one of the m < M machines which can complete within the task's deadline while choosing m number of devices using a metric and then determining a single device to execute a task using another metric. That is, while limiting the number of machines (m) using the energy consumption information, assign a task to the fastest execution time device. From preliminary experiments, the k was best when it is 70. That is, 70% of from the selectable devices is chosen for the final determination of the "best" device. The detailed procedure of KPE is in [15].

The **Minimum Execution Time (MET)** heuristic executes the task on the device that has the minimum estimated computation time. The advantage of this method is that a task is sent to the fastest execution device for the task chosen from the selectable devices. The device that cannot complete the task by its deadline is not selected. The DVS level used to execute a task on a device is the highest level. The detailed procedure of MET is in [15].

5   Simulation Setup

Simulations are performed using a NS-2 based simulator for distributed computing environments called EArDruM [2].For the environment in this research, six types of wireless devices are assumed (based on information in [13]) and each device has three different number (i.e.., two, four, and eight) of voltage levels. So, there can be eighteen different types of devices for the simulation. The maximum battery capacity (energy) of each device is set to the maximum CPU energy consumption level plus the maximum transmission energy consumption, multiplied by the maximum operation time of the device. The maximum operation time is determined using a Gamma distribution with a mean of two hours using the method in [14]. This means that if the CPU and wireless module use the maximum (highest) level, then the battery capacity is only enough to operate the device for two hours on average.

To simplify DVFS, this research assumes that each voltage level of a processor corresponds to a clock speed level for the processor. Each device can have two, four, or eight discrete speed levels with equal probability. After the number of levels for each device is decided, the relative speed of each level is determined. The lowest speed level of a device is assumed to be one third of the maximum speed level. The rest of the levels are determined dividing the gap between the maximum and lowest speed level equally according to the number of levels in each device (linearly). In order to determine the power usage at each of the levels, using the simplifying relationship of power being proportional to voltage squared, a constant is calculated using the voltage and the active power in [13]. This constant and the fractions calculated using the above method are used to determine the power consumption. We make the simplifying assumption that task execution time varies linearly with the discrete speed level. It is assumed that the voltage switching is done dynamically and that the overhead associated with the switching is negligible (20 μs ~ 150 μs).

In each simulation of a system, 20, 50, and 100 devices among the eighteen types are picked with equal probability. The arrival (request) of tasks is simulated using a Poisson distribution with the mean inter-task arrival time of 6 seconds. For each of the eight scenarios (one mean inter-task arrival time × two mean execution times × four types of device number), 30 trials are run for 28800 seconds (i.e., 8 hours) for each heuristic.

For all tasks, the estimated time to complete (ETC) values on 18 types of devices taking heterogeneity into consideration is randomly generated using the Gamma distribution method described in [14]. The mean execution time of 200 seconds is used for the ETC matrix. The mean execution time is chosen to represent applications such as processing data (such as maps or weather reports), generating strategies, etc. The size of the task and output (result to the source) data was calculated using a Gamma distribution and a mean of 100 Kbytes. The size of the input and the other communication data was calculated using a Gamma distribution with 1 Kbytes as the mean.

This research assumes that when the task arrives, the deadline of the task is given. For our simulation studies the deadline calculation is done as follows, the deadline of task i is equal to its arrived time plus the overall mean execution time of all tasks plus the median execution time of task i on all devices plus the expected communication time of task and result. This is a simple attempt that tries to give a task a fair chance of being completed within its deadline. The calculation method is not used for any other purpose than to present a number for a task's deadline.

IEEE 802.11b standard is applied for wireless communication and communication power consumption value is based on specification in [13]. Based on the two-ray ground reflection model [5] in NS-2, whenever communication is occurred, the transmission power and the discrete transmission power level are determined according to the transmission range (for 10, 50, 100, 150, 200, 250 and 500 meters) by using VTPC. Because the two-ray ground model does not consider the interference influence, our simulation model also does not consider the interference influence. It is also assumed that only one way communication is available (i.e., only the communication of one source/destination device pair is possible at a moment).

6   Results

Figure 2 shows the percentage of completed tasks using the SR, EMTE, KPE, and MET heuristics for different topology construction methods. A task is successful or completed when the final result is received by the task requester by the deadline. A task is failed when it did not start execution or when the task's overall time taken to complete passes the stated deadline. The number of devices in the system is increased from 20 to 50 to 100. The average of 30 trials for each scenario is shown in the graphs.

The selectively random method did pretty well considering that the method is mainly random as shown in Figure 2(a). The small amount of intelligence put in to the randomness (i.e., random determination of device among the selectable devices) proved to be quite important for the overall performance as just random performed very poorly.

The RC methods typically produced lower number of connections than the 802.11 method and some of the devices could not connect to any device because the transmission range is reduced. Thus, as shown in all of the figures the 802.11 method was better than the RC methods in 20 devices where the system density is low. However, when100 devices are introduced to the system, RC methods perform better than the 802.11 method because the lower number of connections means lower number of communication collisions. As the maximum transmission range for the RC methods increased, the performance for the 20 device case increased, but it is the opposite for the 100 devices case. In figure 2(c), the RC-300's performance is the best among the RC methods.

The MSMR method proved to be comparable to the newly designed and enhanced methods. In the 20 devices case, the performance is slightly lower than that of 802.11 method. This may be because the devices are mobile and some of the connections can disconnect and if there are a lot of paths to transmit, as with the 802.11 method, it can be an advantage. As the number of devices increase, the MSMR performs better than the 802.11 method in figures 2(a) and 2(b) as the lower number of connections allow for lower number of communication collisions.

The PSRE methods use the energy information of the devices around the target device to build the topology. Thus, rather than using the distance information, using the device that has a lot more energy left may be the reason why the PSRE performs pretty well. For the 20 devices case, the 802.11 is a little better as the device density is low but as the number of devices increases PSRE methods perform better in figures 2(a), 2(b), and 2(c). The performance of the PSRE methods is comparable to the MSMR method when using the EMTE heuristic for the resource management of the system as shown in Figure 2(b).For the KPE and the MET methods (in Figure 2(c) and 2(d)), PSRE-250 does better than the MSMR method. This may be due to the fact that the KPE and MET methods use the time information, while the EMTE only uses the energy information to decide on the device to execute a given task. The PSRE-250 and PSRE-500 methods are presented in this paper and the numbers after the PSRE represent the maximum transmission range when building the topology for the system.

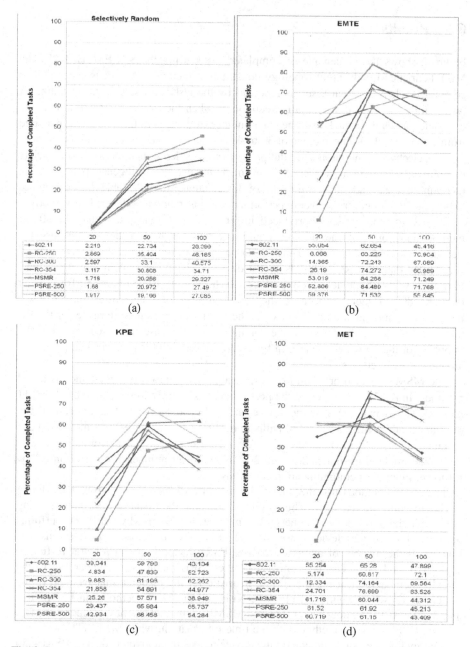

Fig. 2. Percentage of completed tasks for the selectively random, EMTE, KPE, and MET method using various topology construction methods

Overall, the PSRE-250 performs well. Although for different cases, different combination of topology construction and resource management heuristic was the best. In the 20 devices case, the MSMR method and the MET combination was the best (shown in Figure 2(d)). While in the 50 devices case, PSRE-250 using the EMTE proved to be the best (shown in Figure 2(b)). When there are 100 devices in the system, RC-250 using the MET method was the best (shown in Figure 2(d)). This indicates that as the number of devices increase or as the device density increases, limiting the transmission range and limiting the number of connection between the devices is better for system performance.

7 Summary

In this paper, we propose two major topology construction ideas (the range constrained and the per sector remaining energy methods) to increase the performance of the distributed mobile computing environment. Where, the goal is to complete as many tasks as possible by their deadline, while efficiently utilizing the system energy (the aggregate energy of the devices). We tested the topology construction methods using simple resource management methods and compared it to the most recent method in the literature which was the multi sector multi range (MSMR) method.

Topology construction methods such as the per sector remaining energy with transmission range 250 meters (PSRE-250) performed well as well as the range constrained 250 meters (RC-250). Although limiting the transmission range and the number of connections between the devices in the system was the general method to increase the performance of the system, we found out that different resource management methods prefer different topology construction method. And different number of devices also affected the performances of the topology construction methods. Thus, for the best performance of the environment, different resource management method and topology construction method pair should be used for the different number of devices scenarios. For this research, in the 20 devices case, the MSMR method and the MET combination; in the 50 devices case, PSRE-250 using the EMTE; and in the 100 devices case, RC-250 using the MET method was the best.

Acknowledgement. This research is funded in part by the National Research Foundation of Korea grant no. 2009-00763.

References

1. Kim, J.-K., Siegel, H.J., Maciejewski, A.A., Eigenmann, R.: Dynamic Resource Management in Energy Constrained Heterogeneous Computing Systems Using Voltage Scaling. IEEE Trans. Parallel and Distributed Systems 19(11), 1445–1457 (2008)
2. Kim, J.S.: Energy-Aware Distributed Mobile Computing for Real-time Single-hop Ad hoc Mobile Environments. Master's thesis, Korea University, p. 60 (February 2010)
3. Weiser, M., Welch, B., Demers, A., Shenker, S.: Scheduling for Reduced CPU Energy. In: Proc. Usenix Symp. Operating Systems Design and Implementation, OSDI 1994, pp. 13–23 (1994)

4. Gomez, J., Campbell, A.T.: A Case for Variable-Range Transmission Power Control in Wireless Multihop Networks. In: IEEE INFOCOM 2004, pp. 1425–1436 (2004)
5. Crusoe/Efficeon Processor, http://www.transmeta.com
6. ARM Processor, http://www.arm.com
7. Altman, E., Avrachenkov, K., Miller, G., Prabhu, B.: Discrete Power Control: Cooperative and Non-Cooperative Optimization. In: IEEE INFOCOM 2007, pp. 37–45 (2007)
8. Perkins, C.E., Bhagwat, P.: Highly dynamic destination-sequenced distance-vector routing (DSDV) for mobile computers. In: Proc. of the SIGCOMM 1994 Conference on Communications Architectures, Protocols and Applications, pp. 234–244 (1994)
9. Ryoo, J.H., Kim, H.: Multi-sector multi range control for self-organizing wireless networks. J. of Network and Computer Applications 34, 1848–1860 (2011)
10. Li, L., Halpern, J.Y., Bahl, P., Wang, Y.M., Wattenhofer, R.: A Cone-Based Distributed Topology-Control Algorithm for Wireless Multi-hop Networks. IEEE/ACM Trans. on Networking 13, 147–159 (2005)
11. Fall, K., Varadhan, K.: The ns manual, http://www.isi.edu/nsnam/ns/
12. Maheswaran, M., Ali, S., Siegel, H.J., Hensgen, D., Freund, R.F.: Dynamic mapping of a Cass of Independent Tasks onto Heterogeneous Computing Systems. J. Parallel and Distributed Computing 59, 107–121 (1999)
13. Intel PXA270 Processor Datasheet, http://www.phytec.com/pdf/datasheets/PXA270_DS.pdf
14. Ali, S., Siegel, H.J., Maheswaran, M., Hensgen, D., Ali, S.: Representing Task and Machine Heterogeneities for Heterogeneous Computing Systems. Tamkang Journal of Science and Engineering, Special 50th Anniversary Issue 3(3), 195–207 (2000)
15. Kim, I.-Y.: Energy-Aware Ad Hoc Routing Protocol for a Distributed Mobile Computing Environment.: Master's Thesis, Korea University, p. 81 (2011)

Frame Error Rate Testing
for High Speed Optical Interconnect

Yi Dai, Ke-fei Wang, Wei-xia Xu, He-ying Zhang, and Shao-gang Wang

School of Computer Science, National University of Defense Technology
Changsha, Hunan, 410073, P.R. China
y_dai@163.com, {kfwang,wxxu,hyzhang,sgwang}@nudt.edu.cn

Abstract. Fault tolerance network demands the router provide graceful degradation in the presence of faults such as a noisy high-speed serial lane that causes excessive retransmissions. Auto-degrade network links dynamically map out a faulty lane and keep operating, albeit at a lower bandwidth. In this paper we design a Frame Error Rate Testing (FERT) circuit at link-level in order to prevent the use of a faulty link. We show the design and implementation of frame error rate testing circuit operating at line speed. Furthermore we describe the fault tolerance mechanism at link layer using frame error rate testing. We also present and evaluate the power and logic cost of the ASIC based as well as FPGA based FERT implementation.

1   Introduction

Due to the growing scale and complexity of HPC, today's supercomputers run for only a few days before rebooting. The major challenge in fault tolerance is that faults in extreme scale systems will be continuous rather than an exceptional event [1]. This requires the router must be designed to detect and adapt to frequent failure such as a failed network cable or connector, a noisy high-speed serial lane that causes excessive retransmissions, even a faulty router chip. Link-level reliability is very critical to guarantee the integrity of end-to-end communication. First CRC protection through the router data path to detect soft errors in the buffering as the packet traverses the router switch. The errors detected by CRC will trigger retransmission from source to destination. However end-to-end packet retry is too expensive for large-scale $O(N^2)$. To resolve this problem flexible routing table to specify the set of allowable output ports prevents the use of a faulty link. This paper design a frame error rate testing at link level to detect faulty link or lane, thus the router can avoid offending link by adaptive routing.

As shown in Fig. 1 FERT module is directly connected with Physical Coding Sublayer (PCS). FERT can be considered a bypass of link layer coexisting with normal data path. Before FERT the link layer must complete handshake while enabling FERT in the process of handshake. As a result the data path is switched to FERT. Generally FERT is performed between two ports, single-port loopback mode also being supported in our design. The minimum data unit of link-level flow control is called flit. Packet consists of several flits, the first flit is tagged with head sign and the

Y. Xiang et al. (Eds.): ICA3PP 2012, Part II, LNCS 7440, pp. 31–39, 2012.

last flit is tagged with tail sign. Each flit is attached with sideband information of link-level such as the configure parameter of FERT. When FERT is enabled via link handshake the number of flits being sent during FERT is configured. Therefore FERT always sending fixed number of flits, in particular FERT flits is not real flit of normal data path but PRBS codes with the same width of flit. During FERT test flits will be sent directly to the physical coding sublayer. PCS transmits test data via 8x lanes in parallel, each lane operating at 10Gbps. So the line speed of each port is 80Gbps. The main task of Physical Media Attachment (PMA) is to serialize/deserialize data by 8x SERDES units.

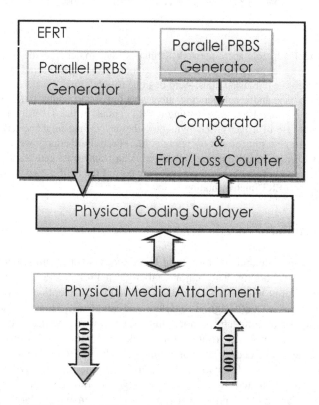

Fig. 1. Link layer FERT. Parallel PRBS generators can be integrated on the same chip as the device under test for built-in self-test (BIST) purposes.

As we have briefly mentioned, implementing an FERT circuit based 80Gbps poses two main design challenges: Firstly, the test data must be validated and generated at the required line speed while keeping the resource utilization down in terms of power demands and logic consumption; and secondly, FERT can be initiated whenever needed this requires the test data must coexist with normal data path. Pseudo-random bit sequence (PRBS) generators and checkers are widely used for testing the correct functionality of broadband integrated circuits, such as re-timers, SERDES blocks, and transceivers [2]. Previously, the design of PRBS generators has been limited to full-rate [3], half-rate [4], or quarter-rate [5], series architectures. For the frame error rate testing at link level of router chips, the test flits must be validated at the required line speed and the PRBS generator should produce as long a sequence as possible. In this paper we design 80-Gb/s PRBS generator with a $x^{31}-1$ sequence length [6] and 96-bit parallel outputs. As the synthesis results demonstrate our scheme generating parallel PRBS sequence can be easily scale to wider parallel outputs such as 512 bits with minimal circuitry, thus the maximum clock frequency of PRBS generator maintaining high and stable with the increased parallel wide of PRBS. In the following sections, we describe in detail the design of parallel PRBS-31 implementation and fault tolerance mechanism at link layer using frame error rate testing. We also evaluate the power and logic cost of the ASIC based as well as FPGA based FERT implementation.

2   Parallel PRBS Implementation

Generally the implementation of PRBS generator is based on the linear feedback shift register (LFSR). The PRBS generator produces a predefined sequence of 1's and 0's, with 1 and 0 occurring with the same probability. A sequence of consecutive n*(2^n - 1) bits comprise one data pattern, and this pattern will repeat itself over time. Serial PRBS generator produces only one bit per clock cycle by means of a LFSR would require an internal clock frequency of 80GHz, which is not feasible in current technology. A well-known approach for implementing parallel PRBS generators is to utilize multiple serial PRBS generators in parallel. These are initialized in such a way that the resulting multiplexed output corresponds to the serial sequence [7]. In investigating this approach, even the serial generator at a very high frequency of 1GHz a minimum of 80 PRBS generators must be running in parallel to produce 80Gb/s. In order to avoid the large resource consumption and high clock speed of such a system, we use the parallel PRBS circuit design depicted in Fig. 3. This system is based on a serial Fibonacci LFSR [7], but parallelized to generate 96 bits of the PRBS sequence in a single clock cycle keeping the system complexity to minimum.

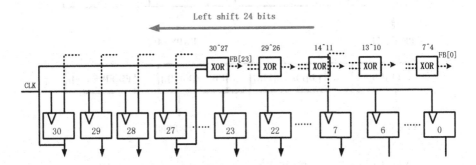

Fig. 2. 24-bit parallel PRBS generator for the polynomial x31+x28+1

Since the data width of link-level flit is 96bits we implement a 96bit width PRBS generator by using four LFSRs each generating 24-bit PRBS in parallel. The schematic of 24-bit parallel PRBS-31 generator defined by the polynomial equation $x^{31}+x^{28}+1$ is shown in Fig. 2. A common clock source drives all 31 flip-flops'clock inputs. Each exclusive-OR gate generates the register's feedback signals. The successive 24-bit PRBS-31 of next clock cycle is generated by these feedback signals. LFSR outputs 24bits PRBS-31 per clock cycle while prepared to output next 24-bit PRBS-31 by left shifting 24bits. The calculation of each output bit and each new register value can then be performed in parallel.

As shown in Fig. 2 the XOR equations to computer feedback values as follows:

```
FB[23]=LFSR[30]^ LFSR[27];

FB[22]=LFSR[29]^ LFSR[26];
FB[21]=LFSR[28]^ LFSR[25];
FB[20]=LFSR[27]^ LFSR[24];
              ...
FB[0] =LFSR[7] ^ LFSR[4];
```

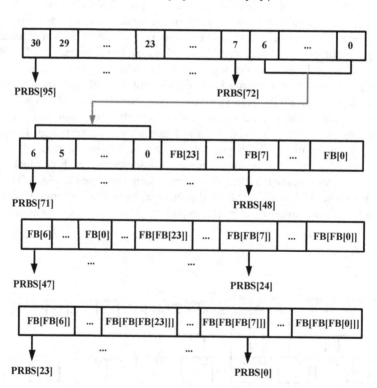

Fig. 3. 96-bit parallel PRBS-31 generator consisting of   four LFSRs

For the above equations FB[a] denotes the feedback value (input value) of ath flip-flop in LFSR. To generate 96-bit parallel PRBS per clock cycle four LFSRs generate PRBS-31 in parallel. As shown in Fig. 3. The first LFSR computers PRBS[95:72] of 96-bit PRBS. In order to computer the next 24-bit PRBS the initial value of the second LFSR should equal to the successive 31bits PRBS of PRBS[95:72]. Therefore the value of $LFSR_1[6:0]$ along with the new 23-bit PRBS being denoted as [FB[23]:FB[0]] will be the initial value of the second LFSR. Then the second LFSR generates PRBS[71:48] the following   PRBS can be computed in the same way. Especially the last $LFSR_4[6:0]$ along with its corresponding 23-bit feedback values should be the inputs of the first LFSR thus proceeding the calculation of next 96-bit PRBS.

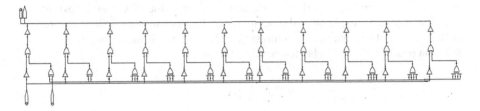

Fig. 4. The flattened gates view of 96-bit parallel PRBS-31 generator and the maximum inputs of XOR gates is four

The flattened gates view of 96-bit parallel PRBS-31 generator (see Figure3) is shown in Fig.4. The low-power performance of the circuit is facilitated by topology choice and transistor-level circuit optimization. At the system level, power is optimized by employing a parallel, as opposed to series, PRBS generator topology, which avoids additional phase shifting circuitry and is suitable for generating signals that can be multiplexed directly. After the transistor-level circuit optimization the implementation circuits of 96-bit parallel PRBS generator shown in Fig. 3 is converted into a combinatorial circuit for calculating the 96 bits PRBS-31 in a single clock cycle. Precisely speaking there is a 31-bit register not shown in Fig. 4, which holds current state of the PRBS generator for calculating the next 96 output bits and the next state of the register based on the current register state. Actually this register can be considered as the first LFSR shown in Fig.3 while other LFSRs in Fig.3 are removed and substituted by combinational logic. The next state of the register equal to $LFSR_4[6:0]$ along with its corresponding 23-bit feedback values should be loaded in the 31-bit registers at rising edge of clock to trigger the combinational logic to calculate next 96-bit PRBS-31 as well as the next state of the registers corresponding to 96 serial shifts.

The resulting parallel generator circuit is able to produce the desired PRBS-31 sequence at 80Gb/s while keeping both the resource and the power consumption to a minimum. As shown in Fig.4, the maximum inputs of XOR gates is only four after synthesis, thus the combinatorial circuit can achive very high clock frequency. In section 4 we evaluate the resource consumpion of parallel PRBS generator with diifferent parallel output width varying from 96 bits to 512 bits. The synthesis results show that the total combinational Look-Up Tables (LUTs) taken up by parallel PRBS calculation circuit increase smoothly as the width of parallel outputs increases, which suggests better scalability of generating algorithm of parallel PRBS-31generator.

3   Frame Error Rate Testing

3.1   Process of Frame Error Rate Testing

The heart of the 80G FERT is the test pattern generation and validation mechanisms, which are located on the transmit (TX) side and receive (RX) side respectively (see Fig. 1).The test traffic is generated in the transmitter using a 96-bit parallel PRBS generator. Once the data path is switched to FERT the TX starts best effort transmission of test flits. In brief the main task of TX is to send prescribed number of test flits in best effort manner. In contrast the RX of FERT is more complicated. The validation process of RX can be described as follows.

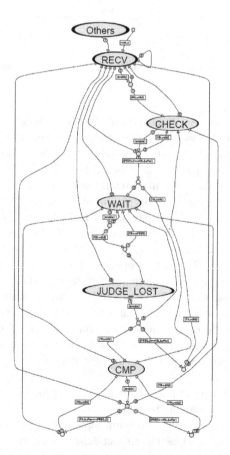

Fig. 5. RX FSM transition

The RX module starts computing the PRBS-31 sequence when receiving the first flit. By using the same initial value of the first LFSR RX module will obtain the same PRBS sequence as the source port sending. As shown in Fig. 3 the RX module extract the high 31-bit of the first received flit as the initial value of the first LFSR thus getting the right 96-bit PRBS. In fact the RX module performs two kind of calculation in parallel. After receiving the first right flit the RX module will compute the next 96-bit PRBS of PRBS-31 sequence. On the other hand the RX module computers the received flit itself to identify whether the test flit is a right PRBS-31 code.   If the receiving flit equal to the next 96-bit PRBS-31 computed by the generator the right-flit counter is increased.   If the test flit is not equal to the next 96-bit flit but it is a right PRBS-31 code the right-flit counter as well as the lost-flit counter are increased and the PRBS-31 sequence is recalculated from this right test flit. The third circumstance is that the test flit itself is not a right PRBS-31 code and the error-flit counter should be increased.

The schematic of RX FSM transition with junctions is shown in Fig. 5. When the RX is to computer a new PRBS-31 sequence the FSM transfer to the RECV state to receive the first test flit of this sequence. After the arrival of first flit FSM transfers to CHECK state to verify whether the arriving flit itself is a right PRBS-31 code. If it is right add the right-flit counter by one while computing the value of next flit. Otherwise recompute the PRBS-31 sequence with the next right flit. The WAIT state is to verify whether the arriving flit is equal to the next 96-bit PRBS of previous right flit. If the received flit is not equal to the precomputed next flit the FSM will transfer to JUDGE_LOST state from WAIT state to verify whether this arriving flit itself is a right PRBS-31code. If it is a right 96-bit PRBS code, flit loss must have taken place then return to RECV state to recompute the PRBS-31 sequence using this received flit. As we have briefly discussed above if the received flit itself is an error PRBS-31 code the RX will recompute the PRBS-31 sequence with next arriving flit. Due to the complexity of the RX FSM transition only typical state transitions are presented. Other FSM transitions under complicated conditions can be inferred from Fig. 5.

3.2   Link-Level Fault Tolerance Based on FERT

As an independent data path coexisting with normal data path of link layer, FERT have no CRC protection through the test data as well as flit retry for error flits. So FER testing can objectively reflect the link quality. As we have briefly mentioned, FER testing is actived in the process of link handshake. The number of test flits sent during FERT and the bandwidth of link should also be configured during link handshake.

Once the handshake process is completed and FER testing between two ports is enabled the link data path is switched to FERT. If the TX of FERT has sent prescribed number of test flits the link layer will send control flit indicating the completion of test data transmission while starting the local timeout timer.   If the two participants of FERT complete the transmission of test flits and also receive the complementation flit sent from the other port the FERT process is finished successfully. Read the error-flit counter, if its value is equal to zero the corresponding link is available for packet transmission otherwise there may exist a noisy serial lane that causes excessive retransmissions. When the value of error-flit counter is beyond the preset value the flexible routing table should remove this faulty link from the set of allowable paths thus avoiding excessive retransmissions and frequent reboots of applications. If the local TX have failed to send test flits or failed to receive complementation flit from another testing port the same operations presented above should be executed.

4   Synthesis Results

For the ASIC based FERT implementation the synthesis results as follows: the number of nets is 4186, the number of combinational cells is 3538, the number of sequential cells is 483, and the total cell area of FERT is 8352um^2 under 40ns technology. In our design 8x10Gbps lanes are used at physical layer, flits being transmitted over multiple lanes in parallel. For 96-bit frame error rate testing the require clock frequency for 80Gbps is 833MHz. In fact 1GMHz can be achieved for FERT ASIC implementation.

To verify our design with FPGA prototype we also synthesize FERT design to a Xilinx Virtex6 FPGA (XC6VHX565T) [8]. The entire FERT circuit implementing both the transmitter and the receiver takes up 1029 combinational LUTs and 490 registers with a maximum frequency of 295.8MHz. The 96-bit parallel PRBS generator only takes up 127 combinational LUTs and zero registers. The maximum frequency of Tx side including 96-bit parallel PRBS-31 generator is 374.9MHz (see Table.1). As anticipated, the statistic function for error or lost flits on the transmission side is by far the most critical component in terms of critical path delay and logic utilization. Even so, the proposed design offers a very compact solution, which can be easily pipelined to support even greater throughput or implementation in more modest FPGAs.

Table 1. Parallel PRBS-31 generator synthesis results

	96-bit parallel PRBS-31 generator	158-bit parallel PRBS-31 generator	256-bit parallel PRBS-31 generator	512-bit parallel PRBS-31 generator
Total Luts	127	195	326	424
Register bits	31	31	31	31
Maximum clock frequency	374.9MHZ	359.9MHZ	374.9MHZ	378.1MHZ

The resulting resource usage for the PRBS generators alone, without any counting and control logic, is depicted in Table 1. In order to avoid the large resource consumption and high clock speed of such a system, we use the method depicted in Fig. 3 generating the parallel XOR equations for calculating parallel PRBS-31 sequence. We evaluate the resource consumption and maximum clock frequency of parallel PRBS-31 generator with parallel outputs varying from 96 to 512. As shown in Table1 with the width of parallel PRBS-31generator increasing the number of combinational LUTs used by parallel PRBS-31 generator increases smoothly and the maximum clock frequency remains high and stable, which reflect the better scalability of generating algorithm for combinatorial circuit of parallel PRBS-31 generator. Take the 512-bit parallel generator for example, the required clock speed is reduced to 195.3125MHz to generate 100Gb/s.

5 Conclusions

In this paper, we have presented an overview of a novel design for a Frame Error Rate Testing which statists frame error rate at link layer and assists the link-level fault tolerance. In particular, FERT can be performed over appointed lanes thus preventing the use of noisy high-speed serial lane that causes excessive retransmissions. By means of parallelization of the PRBS the FERT has been efficiently synthesized to current ASIC technology with minimal resource and energy requirements. The synthesis results demonstrate our method calculating the parallel XOR equations for PRBS-31 sequence can be easily scale to wider parallel outputs such as 512 bits with minimal circuitry, thus the combinatorial circuit generating parallel PRBS-31 can achieve very high clock frequency even doubling the width of parallel outputs. In a word, running frame-error-rate tests at link layer provide an effective tool for testing both internal PCS/PMA functions as well as providing quality measurements of network links for link-level fault tolerance of high speed optical interconnect.

Acknowledgements. This work was supported by the National Natural Science Foundation of China under Grant No.61003301 and by the National High-Tech Research and Development Plan of China under Grant No.2012AA01A301.

References

1. Geist, A., Lucas, R.: Whitepaper: Major Computer Science Challenges at Exascale (2009)
2. Laskin, E., Voinigescu, S.P.: A 60 mw per lane, 4x23-gb/s 2(7)-1 prbs generator. IEEE Journal of Solid-State Circuits 41(10), 2198–2208 (2006)
3. Malasani, R., Bourde, C., Gutierrez, G.: A SiGe 10-Gb/s multipattern bit error rate tester. In: Proc. IEEE Radio Frequency Integrated Circuits (RFIC) Symp., pp. 321–324 (2003)
4. Veenstra, H.: 1–58 Gb/s PRBS generator with <1.1 ps RMS jitter in InP technology. In: Proc. ESSCIRC, pp. 359–362 (2004)
5. Dickson, T.O., Laskin, E., Khalid, I., Beerkens, R., Xie, J., Karajica, B., Voinigescu, S.P.: A 72 Gb/s 2^{32} -1 PRBS generator in SiGe BiCMOS technology. In IEEE ISSCC Dig. Tech. Papers, San Francisco, CA, pp. 342–345 (2005)
6. LAN/MAN Standards Committee of the IEEE Computer Society. IEEE p802.3ba d2.1 - amendment: Media access control parameters, physical layers and management parameters for 40 gb/s and 100 gb/s operation, pp. 144–156 (2009)
7. Veenstra, H., Long, J.R.: Circuit and interconnect design for rf and high bit-rate applications (2008)
8. Xilinx Corporation: Virtex-6 FPGA Data Sheet: DC and Switching Characteristics (2009)

Maintaining Consistency in Software Transactional Memory through Dynamic Versioning Tuning

Ehsan Atoofian and Amir Ghanbari Bavarsad

Electrical Engineering Department, Lakehead University, Thunder Bay, Canada
{atoofian,aghanbar}@lakeheadu.ca

Abstract. A popular method to maintain consistency in software transactional memory (STM) is global version clock whose values are used to tag memory locations. This method is not efficient when transactional commit occurs frequently since contention over the global clock generates costly cache coherence invalidations and degrades performance. The alternative method is thread local clock (TLC) which exploits decentralized local variables to maintain consistent states in transactions. However, TLC may lead to false aborts and increase run-time of programs. In this work, we introduce Adaptive Versioning (AV) which dynamically selects one of the two validation techniques based on probability of conflicts. We show that AV is effective and improves performance of transactional applications significantly.

Keywords: Transactional Memory, Validation, Performance.

1 Introduction

Chip multiprocessors (CMPs) are prevalent in server and desktop systems, making parallel programming a necessity to harness computational power of underlying hardware. The traditional method for parallel programming is lock which is too difficult and error prone for most of programmers and is the domain of experts. Deadlock, race, and other synchronization bugs are some of the challenges of lock-based programming. Transactional Memory (TM) [1] is a programming model which makes parallel programming easier by allowing a programmer to mark sections of a program that should be executed atomically. Instead of having to carefully compose the correct sequence and set of locks to protect an atomic section, a programmer simply has to provide where to begin and end the atomic section. This suggests TM can be an important model for creating parallel programs for multi-core processors.

In the last few years, many software toolkits for implementation of transactional memory have been proposed [5, 8, 9]. Recent software transactional memory (STM) systems exploit a centralized synchronization mechanism to maintain consistency of transactional data. For example, the TL2 STM [9] uses a timestamp mechanism to allow the system to verify in constant time that a transaction has consistent view of transactional reads. TL2 associates a lock with each memory location and uses a global shared clock to generate unique timestamps for transactions. When a

Y. Xiang et al. (Eds.): ICA3PP 2012, Part II, LNCS 7440, pp. 40–49, 2012.

transaction commits it increments the clock and uses the new value of the clock as its timestamp to tag all memory locations that it writes into. Thus, a transaction can quickly check the consistency of a new transactional read by recording the global clock when it begins, and comparing that value to the timestamp of the lock corresponding to the transactional read.

While global clock in TL2 reduces cost of validation in those STMs that iterate over the entire transactional reads on every validation, its centralized synchronization mechanism may increase cache coherence traffic. In its default mode, called GV4 [9], TL2 increments the clock every time a transaction commits. This makes transactions experience ping-pong effect across caches and induces costly coherence misses, even when transactions do not conflict with each other. An alternate scheme is thread local clock (TLC) [3] which exploits local clocks to maintain coherency of transactions. In TLC, each transaction has a local array to record timestamp of other transactions in the system. By using a combination of local clock and local array, TLC is able to support coherent states without the need for a global notion of time. However, this advantage comes with a cost and that is false abort. Transaction A may write to a memory location and commit before transaction B reads the memory location, yet transaction B may fail because its local array recorded an old timestamp of transaction A.

In this work, we propose Adaptive Versioning (AV) which dynamically selects GV4 or TLC based on probability of conflicts among transactions. AV exploits a history-based predictor to speculate chance of conflicts in future. AV dynamically selects one of the two validation schemes based on feedback received from the predictor. If it is likely a transaction conflicts then AV selects GV4 to reduce false aborts. On the other side, if the predictor speculates successful commit then TLC is selected to reduce overhead of the global clock.

The remainder of the paper is organized as follows. In section 2, we discuss time-based STMs and explain details of GV4 and TLC. In section 3, we explain AV and discuss how the predictor is implemented in software. In section 4, we present experimental results that illustrate the effect of AV on overall system performance. We review related work in section 5. Finally, in section 6 we offer concluding remarks.

2   Background

In this work, we use TL2 [9] which is a time-based validation STM. It is important to note that although we use TL2 for evaluation of AV, our method is general and can be used in any other time-based STMs [5, 12]. TL2 associates locks to the shared memory locations to handle concurrent accesses to the memory. The locks are organized as a large table and memory is striped using a hash function to map memory locations to the table entries.

In its default mode, called GV4, TL2 uses a global clock to synchronize transactional read and write operations. The global clock is implemented as a shared variable and is incremented using atomic compare-and-swap [2]. When a transaction commits, it increments the global clock and writes the new value of the clock in the lock entries corresponding to its write-set. At the start of a transactional section, global clock is read and copied into a thread local variable called read version (*rv*). When a transaction reads a memory location, it compares its *rv* with the lock corresponding to the read memory location. If *rv* is less than the version number of the lock, then the transaction aborts since the memory location is modified after the transaction has started; otherwise, the most recent write to the read memory location has happened before the start of the transaction and the transactional read passes validation.

One of the problems associated with the global clock in GV4 is cache coherence traffic. Since each writing transaction updates the clock at least once, it results in frequent cache coherence invalidations. An alternative method is thread local clock (TLC) [3] which supports coherent states without the need for a global clock. In TLC, each thread has a local clock and a local array. The local clock is initially zero and is incremented when a transaction commits. The local array has an entry per thread and records timestamps of threads. It is important to note that this array is local to each thread and is never read by other threads.

In TLC, before a transaction commits, it acquires locks for all entries in the write-set. Then, it checks entries in the read-set to ensure that they are not locked by other threads. In the next step, the transaction validates entries in the read-set to guarantee that other threads have not modified read memory locations. If thread j writes into a memory location after the transaction has started, its timestamp extracted from the lock entry is more than timestamp in entry j of the local array and so validation fails. In this case, entry j of the local array is updated with the new timestamp and the transaction aborts. When the transaction successfully validates all entries of its read-set, it increments its own local clock and writes the new value of the clock and its ID into the lock entries corresponding to its write-set. At this point, the locks are released and the commit process is over.

Although TLC eliminates the need for a global timestamp, it introduces false aborts. Assume that thread A has completed its transaction before current transaction in thread B, but local array in thread B holds an old timestamp of thread A. When current transaction in thread B reads a memory location written by thread A, it aborts since the timestamp recorded in entry A of local array in B is not current enough. These false aborts in TLC waste processor resources and degrade performance of STM systems.

3   Adaptive Versioning (AV)

In this section, first we discuss motivation behind our work. Then, we explain AV.

3.1   Motivation

Table 1 compares the performance of Gv4 and TLC in Stamp v.0.9.10 benchmark suite [4] (For detail of experimental framework, please refer to section 4). For each benchmark, the number of threads changes between two and 16. Positive numbers represent speedup under TLC.

Table 1 proves that neither GV4 nor TLC is optimal across all benchmarks. Except *Vacation*, the rest of the benchmarks are sensitive to the validation technique. While in *Ssca2*, TLC works better than GV4, in *Kmeans*, GV4 is the preferred validation method. In *Bayes*, when the number of threads is equal to two or four, GV4 is faster than TLC. However, when the number of threads is equal to eight or 16, TLC works better than GV4. In *Labyrinth*, when the number of threads is eight, TLC is slightly better than Gv4. For other cases, GV4 is the preferred validation policy. *Vacation* is not sensitive to the validation methods. The performance of *Vacation* changes less than 2.5% when the number of threads changes from two to 16.

Table 1. Performance of Stamp v.0.9.10 benchmarks in TLC relative to GV4. The number of threads changes from two to 16 in each benchmark. Positive numbers represent speedup in TLC.

Benchmarks	2	4	8	16
Bayes	-8.6%	-9.9%	7.8%	24%
Kmeans	-6.9%	-37%	-34.8%	-58%
Labyrinth	-2.9%	-7.8%	1.3%	-43.1%
Ssca2	14.9%	21.6%	38.1%	58.3%
Vacation	-1.7%	-1.8%	-1.4%	2.3%

The two validation methods, GV4 and TLC, have conflicting effects. While GV4 reduces false abort it unnecessarily serializes transactions and increases cost of central global clock even if transactions do not conflict. On the other side, TLC reduces cost of global clock but results in false aborts. We conclude that the optimum validation method depends on access pattern of shared data and changes within and across applications. In the next section, we discuss AV which is an adaptive technique and changes validation method dynamically and in run-time.

3.2   Adaptive Versioning (AV)

GV4 and TLC validation schemes have different advantages. A natural question is whether the different advantages can be combined in a new validation scheme. One such method is selecting one of the two techniques based on probability of conflicts. If conflict rate is high, then GV4 is the preferred validation scheme since TLC may result in false abort. If conflict rate is low, then the preferred validation scheme is TLC since GV4 unnecessarily serializes the committing transactions. However, in order to bring about all of these benefits, a mechanism is required to accurately predict whether a transaction succeeds or aborts.

To speculate the outcome of a transaction, we use a history-based contention predictor (CP). The predictor relies on outcome of transactions in the past to predict the outcome of transactions in the future. Each thread has its own predictor. We avoid using a central predictor since the central predictor moves back and forth among the caches and results in coherence traffic. Figure 1 shows structure of the CP in a program with four threads. Each thread has a local CP and the local CP is composed of N link-lists. Each node of the link-list records starting address of a transaction and a saturating counter (SC). We use inline assembly to read Program Counter (PC). The PC is written into the starting address fields of the link-list nodes.

The saturating counter (SC) has one or more bits and is similar to the saturating counters used in branch predictors [10]. When a transaction finishes it updates its corresponding SC. If the transaction commits successfully it increments the SC; otherwise, the SC is reset to zero.

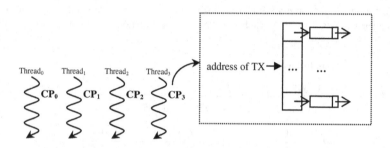

Fig. 1. A program with four threads. Each thread has its own local contention predictor. Each contention predictor is implemented using a table of link-lists.

When a transaction starts, the starting address of the transaction is hashed into the table of link-lists. Then, a node with matching starting address in the link-list is selected (if there is no matching node, then we assume that the transaction commits successfully). Based on the value of SC, the transaction is predicted to commit or abort. If SC is more than a pre-determined threshold, then the transaction is predicted to commit; otherwise, it is predicted to abort. The value of an n-bit saturating counter changes from 0 to 2^{n-1}. The number of the bits and the threshold are configured once and are used for all applications. Repeatedly successful transactions will be predicted to commit, and repeatedly aborted transactions will be predicted to fail. By using an n-bit SC, the predictor can tolerate a transaction that has unusual outcome one time and keep predicting the usual behavior. Details of AV are explained in Figure 2.

Proof of Correctness in AV Algorithm

In this section, we prove that AV always operates on consistent state. We assume the correctness of underlying TL2 [9] and TLC [3] algorithms. To prove correctness of AV, we show that every writing transaction can be serialized at the point in which it acquires all locks corresponding to its write-set.

For a location X in memory read by a transaction in thread A, assume that the last transaction that wrote to X before A reads X belongs to thread B. If the transaction in B commits after the transaction in A starts, then we claim that the transaction in A will abort. Transaction in thread B may write into X using either GV4 or TLC versioning. If B updates X with GV4 policy, then it increments global clock. So, transaction A finds that version number of X is more than rv and aborts. If B updates X with

TLC policy, then the transaction in A aborts. The reason is that the last value stored in entry B of local array in A was read in a transaction which was completed before current transaction in A. Since B increments its local clock before it commits, the value it wrote was at least one greater than the one recorded for entry B in the local array of A. Thus, A will detect an inconsistent state and abort its current transaction.

TxStart()
```
{
  If (CP_predicted_abort)
    Set version policy to GV4;//if CP predicts conflict, then
                              //version policy is set to GV4
  else
    Set version policy to TLC;//if CP predicts no conflict,
                              //then version policy is set to TLC
  ...
}
```

TxCommit()
```
{
  if(!acquire_lock())//if lock acquisition fails, then TX
                     //aborts
    return 0;
  if(!read_set_consistency())//if read-set
                             //consistency check fails, then TX aborts
    return 0;

  if(GV4)//if version policy is GV4
  {
    global_clock++;//increment global clock
    update_locks(global_clock);//write the new
                 //global clock into locks corresponding to write-set
  }
  else//if version policy is TLC
  {
    local_clock++;//increment local clock
    update_locks(local_clock);//write the new
                 //local clock into locks corresponding to write-set
  }
}
```

Fig. 2. A thread calls *TxStart()* when it starts a transactional section and calls *TxCommit()* when the transactional section finishes successfully. In *TxStart()*, if CP speculates contention, then the version policy is set to GV4; otherwise, the version policy is set to TLC. When the transaction commits (*TxCommit()*), it acquires locks and checks consistency of its read-set. If the version policy is GV4, it increments global clock and update locks with the new value of the global clock; otherwise, it increments its own local clock and updates locks with the new value of the local clock. Each lock entry has a dedicated bit which shows whether the lock entry is in GV4 format or TLC format.

4   Evaluation

We use the Stamp v0.9.10 benchmark suite [4] to evaluate AV and quantify its performance impact. Table 2 presents input arguments of the Stamp benchmarks used in our experiments. The set of benchmarks includes a Bayesian learning network (*Bayes*), a k-means clustering algorithm (*Kmeans*), a maze routing algorithm (*Labyrinth*), a set of graph kernels (*Ssca2*), a client-server reservation system simulator (*Vacation*). We run benchmarks up to completion and measure statistics over a set of ten test runs to reduce variations in collected data.

We use Sun T6340 server module for our simulation. The server has two Ultra SPARC T2 Plus processors and each processor is an 8-way CMP running at 1.2 GHz. Each core is capable of running up to 8 threads and totally the server can run up to

Table 2. Stamp v0.9.10 benchmarks and input parameters

Benchmarks	Input Parameters
Bayes	-v32 -r4096 -n10 -p40 -i2 -e8 -s1
Kmeans	-m15 -n15 -t0.00001 -i inputs/random-n65536-d32-c16.txt
Labyrinth	-i inputs/random-x512-y512-z7-n512.txt
Ssca2	-s20 -i1.0 -u1.0 -l3 -p3
Vacation	-n4 -q60 -u90 -r1048576 -t4194304

128 threads simultaneously. The processor has a 4MB, 16-way set associative L2 cache which is organized in 8 banks with 64B cache lines. Each core has a 16KB instruction cache and an 8KB data cache.

4.1   Performance

Figure 3 reports number of committed transactions per second in AV, GV4, and TLC for Stamp v0.9.10 benchmarks [4]. The number of threads varies from two to 16 for each benchmark. The contention predictor uses 5-bit saturating counters with threshold equal to 15.

AV improves performance of *Ssca2* relative to GV4 drastically. This aligns with performance of benchmarks under GV4 and TLC reported in Table 1. In *Ssca2*, TLC is faster than GV4 and AV quite often selects TLC for validation. On the flip side, in *Kmeans*, GV4 is faster than TLC and so, AV selects GV4 for validation most of the time. In *Bayes* and *Vacation*, performance of all the three schemes is similar. In *Labyrinth*, AV is slightly better than GV4 and TLC.

5   Related Work

Transactional memory was originally proposed as a hardware technique by Herlihy and Moss [1] and later by Stone et al. [6]. Shavit and Touitou [13] introduced the first transactional memory relying on software. There are two types of STMs: word-based [9] and object-based [8]. Word-based STMs access memory at granularity of memory words or larger blocks. Object-based STMs access memory at the granularity of objects. While object-based STMs need compiler or manual insertion of lock fields, word-based STMs do not require modification of data structures [9].

Spear et al. [7] proposed global commit counter to reduce overhead of incremental validation. In invisible read policy, a reader detects read-write conflicts by incrementally validating open objects at the cost of quadratic number of objects. To reduce cost of validation, a global counter records the number of transactions that attempt to commit. When a transaction opens an object, the transaction skips incremental validation if the counter has not changed since the last time the reader checked its objects.

As such, costly exhaustive validations can be avoided if transactional write operations happen rarely. However, this method does not distinguish access to different fields of an object and results in unnecessary serialization, if transactions access disjoint memory locations. On the other side, AV serializes transactions only when it is likely transactions conflict over the same memory location.

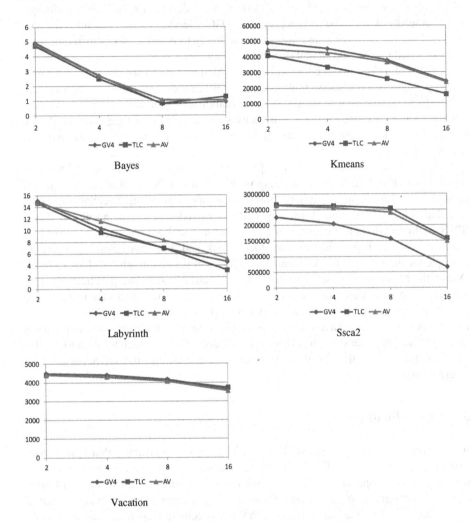

Fig. 3. Number of committed transactions per second in AV, GV4, and TLC. For each benchmark, the number of threads changes from two to 16. AV uses predictors with 5-bit saturating counters and thresholds equal to 15.

Avni and Shavit [3] introduced thread-local clock (TLC) technique to allow transactions to operate on consistent states without the global clock. While TLC eliminates central global clock, it increases abort rate. We have exploited TLC and proposed AV which dynamically selects GV4 or TLC based on feedback received from CP. Our results reveal that AV improves performance of Stamp benchmarks over both TLC and GV4. In addition, Avni and Shavit evaluated TLC with micro benchmarks which are not representative of real applications. In contrast, we have evaluated AV with the comprehensive Stamp benchmark suite.

Atoofian and Bavarsad [11] proposed adaptive global clock (AGC) which dynamically selects GV4 or GV5 [15]for validation. AGC decides on validation technique based on feedback received from a program. AGC selects GV4 for contended transactions and selects GV5 for transactions that are likely to commit. AV is different since it works based on centralized and decentralized clocks.

Riegel et al. [12] introduced a mechanism which uses real-time clocks to optimistically synchronize concurrent transactions. They also exploited externally synchronized clocks as the time base for better scalability. In contrast to our work, their scheme requires external support and focuses on scalability of time base itself. AV focuses on reducing the cost of the global clock and does not require any external hardware support.

Mannaeswamy and Govindarajan [14] studied cache behavior of STMs and showed that global clock misses are responsible for up to 38% of transactional misses in Stamp benchmark suite. They proposed a compiler optimization technique, which is called selective partition timestamp (SPTS), to reduce cost of the global clock. SPTS partitions disjoint instances of data structures and assigns each partition to a separate pool. Each pool has its own local clock and data structures within a pool compete for the local clock. As such, contention over the central global clock reduces. One of the restrictions of SPTS is that it decides on data structure partitions in compile-time and so it needs to use a conservative approach to select candidate shared data structures for partitioning. As an example, if a data structure is passed to an external function, whose source code is not visible to the compiler, the compiler can not apply SPTS to the data structure. However, AV does not have such a limitation and is able to reduce cost of the global clock for those data structures that are accessed in an external function.

6   Conclusion

In this paper, we have evaluated GV4 and TLC and demonstrated that applications react differently to these validation methods. The ideal validation method may change not only across applications, but also within an application and through different phases of a program. We described AV as an optimization technique which dynamically selects GV4 or TLC for validation. AV is a speculative approach and decides on validation method based on a contention predictor. The predictor exploits saturating counters and speculates whether a transaction will commit or fail. AV selects GV4 for contended transactions and selects TLC for transactions that are likely to commit. AV which has been implemented in TL2 and evaluated using Stamp v0.9.10 shows significant performance gain in Stamp benchmarks.

References

1. Herlihy, M., Moss, J.E.B.: Transactional memory: Architectural support for lock-free data structures. In: Proceedings of the Twentieth Annual International Symposium on Computer Architecture (1993)
2. Culler, D.E., Singh, J.P., Gupta, A.: Parallel Computer Architecture: a Hardware/Software Approach. Morgan Kaufmann Publishers (1998)
3. Avni, H., Shavit, N.N.: Maintaining Consistent Transactional States without a Global Clock. In: Shvartsman, A.A., Felber, P. (eds.) SIROCCO 2008. LNCS, vol. 5058, pp. 131–140. Springer, Heidelberg (2008)
4. Minh, C.C., Trautmann, M., Chung, J., McDonald, A., Bronson, N., Casper, J., Kozyrakis, C., Olukotun, K.: An Effective Hybrid Transactional Memory System with Strong Isolation Guarantees. In: The Proceeding of International Symposium on Computer Architecture (June 2007)
5. Dragojevic, A., Guerraoui, R., Kapalka, M.: Stretching transactional memory. In: The Proceedings of the 2009 ACM SIGPLAN Conference on Programming Language Design and Implementation (2009)
6. Stone, J.M., Stone, H.S., Heidelberger, P., Turek, J.: Multiple reservations and the Oklahoma update. IEEE Parallel & Distributed Technology: Systems & Technology, 58–71 (November 1993)
7. Spear, M.F., Marathe, V.J., Scherer III, W.N., Scott, M.L.: Conflict Detection and Validation Strategies for Software Transactional Memory. In: Dolev, S. (ed.) DISC 2006. LNCS, vol. 4167, pp. 179–193. Springer, Heidelberg (2006)
8. Herlihy, M., Luchangco, V., Moir, M., Scherer III, W.: Software transactional memory for dynamic-sized data structures. In: Proceedings of PODC, pp. 92–101 (July 2003)
9. Dice, D., Shalev, O., Shavit, N.N.: Transactional Locking II. In: Dolev, S. (ed.) DISC 2006. LNCS, vol. 4167, pp. 194–208. Springer, Heidelberg (2006)
10. Yeh, T.-Y., Patt, Y.: Alternative implementations of two-level adaptive branch prediction. In: Proceedings of the 19th Annual International Symposium on Computer Architecture (May 1992)
11. Atoofian, E., Bavarsad, A.G.: AGC: adaptive global clock in software transactional memory. In: The Proceedings of the International Workshop on Programming Models and Applications for Multicores and Manycores (2012)
12. Riegel, T., Fetzer, C., Felber, P.: Time-based transactional memory with scalable time bases. In: SPAA 2007: Proceedings of the Nineteenth Annual ACM Symposium on Parallel Algorithms and Architectures, pp. 221–228. ACM, New York (2007)
13. Shavit, N., Touitou, D.: Software transactional memory. In: The Proceedings of ACM Symposium on Principles of Distributed Computing (August 1995)
14. Mannarswamy, S., Govindarajan, R.: Making STMs Cache Friendly with Compiler Transformations. In: Proc. of the 20th International Parallel Architectures and Compilation Techniques, PACT 2011, Galveston Island, TX (October 2011)
15. Lev, Y., Luchangco, V., Marathe, V., Moir, M., Nussbaum, D., Olszewski, M.: Anatomy of a scalable software transactional memory. In: TRANSACT 2009: 4th Workshop on Transactional Computing (February 2009)

Solving a 2-Covered Path Problem
with Variable Radii for Wireless Sensor Networks

Da-Ren Chen[2], Chiun-Chieh Hsu[1], You-Shyang Chen, and Jun-Fu Guo[1]

[1] Department of Information Management,
National Taiwan University of Science and Technology, Taipei, Taiwan, R.O.C.
[2] Department of Information Management,
National Taichung University of Science and Technology, Taichung, Taiwan, R.O.C.
[3] Department of Information Management,
Hwa Hsia Institute of Technology, Taipei, Taiwan, R.O.C.
{cchus@mail.ntust.edu.tw}

Abstract. In this paper, we propose two techniques to solve a 2-covered path problem. Given a set of n antennas with m available radii and two points A and B on the plane, our goal is to find a suitable radius $p \in m$ (as well as transmission power) for each antenna so that the active antennas in a 2-covered path with endpoints A and B consumes minimum transmission power. The proposed techniques called 2-covered area stretching planning (TASP) and radii shrinking planning (RSP) that apply different strategies to reduce power consumption. Experimental results show that RSP derives less power consumption than TASP, and RSP and TASP take $O(n^2)$ and $O(n^3)$ time complexity, respectively.

Keywords: wireless sensor networks, 2-covered path, power consumption.

1   Introduction

Problems related to wireless sensor networks (WSN) has emerged in the last few years as a result of the fast development of the associated technology. These networks has great economic potential and used to solve a great diversity of problems that range from battlefield monitoring to weather detection, security services and even wildlife protection [4]. WSN applications to detection and monitoring problems usually have limited battery power [6]. The transmission range of each antenna depends directly on its transmission power which, in turn, is responsible for the costs associated to the service it provides. The problem solved in this paper is related to 2-covered path planning in which the antennas may have different transmission ranges defined in m radii. The goal is to find a 2-covered path between points A and B in the plane and reduce or minimize power consumption of the antennas.

Disks covering problems [9, 10, 11] try to find the minimum number of disks of pre-described radius r, which cover a given set of n points in the plans. These problems have many interesting applications [1, 6, 7, 12]. The most popular application is the problem of locating the least number of energy facilities such that

Y. Xiang et al. (Eds.): ICA3PP 2012, Part II, LNCS 7440, pp. 50–61, 2012.

all potential users are located within a reasonable small distance from one of the facilities. It is known that optimal covering in the plane is strongly NP-complete [8] and is usually applied in the applications with fixed-location antennas.

In this paper, let M denote a set of discrete transmission strength (voltage) of microwave where $m=|M|$. The main purpose is to develop the methods for finding the 2-covered paths with m variable radii. The remainder of the paper is organized as follows. In Section 2 and Section 3, we introduce two methods for solving 2-path covering problem with m radii. We report the experimental results and their time complexities in Section 4. Conclusions and the future work are provided in Section 5.

2   TASP Method

The first step of TASP is creating intersection relations array for all antennas. It is used to reduce the execution time required in upcoming procedures. First of all, we have to compute the distances between any two antennas and use the double value of the largest radius R_m as a threshold to examine if they could intersect or not. For example, if the distance between antenna P_1 and P_2 is smaller than or equals to $2 * R_m$, then P_1 and P_2 intersects when R_m is utilized.

As shown in Fig. 1, the first position of array is used to save the intersection points of P_1, namely P_2, P_3, and P_5. The second position is used to save the intersection points of P_2, namely P_1 and P_4. After creating the intersection relations array, we can use it as a searching tool to find out all intersected antennas immediately.

$$\{(P_2, P_3, P_5), (P_1, P_4), (P_1, P_5), (P_2, P_5, P_6), (P_1, P_3, P_4, P_6), (P_4, P_5)\}$$

Fig. 1. Intersection relations array

2.1   The Nearest Intersected Antenna

In order to stretch 2-covered areas, the chosen antenna P_i must be intersected with the antennas forming 2-covered area. In Fig. 2(a), P_3 intersects with P_1, and P_5 intersects with P_2. The unique antenna stretching a 2-covered area is P_4 because it is intersected with both antennas P_1 and P_2.

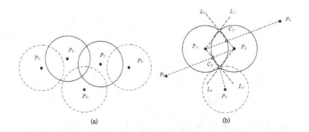

(a)   (b)

Fig. 2. (a)Intersection status and (b)Type I intersection relation

2.2   Calculate the Distance

While P_i has been selected, we need to calculate the distance D between 2-covered area and P_i and then choose a radius greater than or equals to D. There are three kinds of intersection relations between two antennas:

1. Two antennas intersect at two points.
2. Two antennas intersect at only one point outside the circles.
3. One antenna is the internal circle of another one.

As shown in Fig. 2(b), if two antennas intersect at two points, there are three cases discussing the locations of P_i:

1. P_i is located in the area intersected by L_3 and L_4:
In Fig. 2(b), the distance between P_3 and 2-covered area is the value subtracted radius of P_2 from $d(P_2, P_3)$. In Eq. 1, the distance between P_i and P_j is represented by $d(P_i, P_j)$. Note that the situation of antenna located in the area intersected by L_1 and L_2 is similar to P_3.

$$D = d(P_i, P_j) - r_i \tag{1}$$

2. P_i is located in the areas intersected by L_1 and L_3 or L_2 and L_4:
In Fig. 2(b), the distance between P_5 and 2-covered area cannot be calculated by Eq.1. The transmission range of P_5 formed with radius $d(P_5, C_2)$ only intersects at one point with 2-covered area. It means the distance between P_5 and 2-covered area is $d(P_5, C_2)$, either. As a result, we can utilize Eq.2 to calculate the distance. Note that C_1 and C_2 are intersection points of 2-covered area.

$$D = Min\{d(P_i, C_1), d(P_i, C_2)\} \tag{2}$$

We also define two types of intersection relations type II and type III to denote respectively that one antenna is the internal circle of another one, and two antennas intersect at one point outside the circles. For instance, in Fig. 3(a), we can use Eq.1 to compute $d(P_2, P_3)$ and subtract the radius of P_2 from the distance. It is the distance between P_3 and 2-covered area. While two antennas intersect at only one point outside the circles (see Fig. 3 (b)), the distance between P_3 and the intersection point is the distance required.

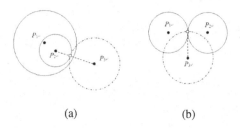

(a)   (b)

Fig. 3. The (a)type II and (2)type III intersection relations

2.3 Covering State of B

The main idea of TASP is stretching 2-covered areas from point A to point B. It uses potential 2-covered areas to look for all intersected antennas and choose the one closest to B, then plan the selected antenna P_i by the radius greater than or equals to the distance between 2-covered areas and P_i until B is covered by at least two antennas. The required steps of TASP are as follows:

1. Create intersection relations array for all antennas $P_1 \sim P_n$.
2. Find out two antennas Na_1 and Na_2 nearest to A and plan each of them using the radius as small as possible such that A is in 2-covered area.
3. Use potential 2-covered area to look for all intersected antennas and choose the one closest to B.
4. Calculate the distance between selected antenna P_i and 2-covered area, then plan P_i by the radius greater than or equals to the distance.
5. Amplify the radii of planned antennas if they are too small to stretch 2-covered areas.
6. Repeat steps 3, 4 and 5 until B is covered by two antennas.

2-Covered Area Stretching Planning Algorithm
1. //n is the number of antennas, r_m is the biggest radius.
2. //*PlannedRadius[ ]* records the planned antennas and radii.
3. *IntersectionArray[ ]* = CreateIntersectionArray(n, r_m); //intersection relations
4. Find two nearest antennas Na_1, Na_2 of point A.
5. Record the radii number used into array *PlannedRadius[ ]*.
6. **do**
7.   PlanNextPoint(*PlannedRadius[ ]*, *IntersectionArray[ ]*);
8. **until** (B is in 2-covered area)

Fig. 4. TASP algorithm-1

CreateIntersectionArray(n, r_m)
1. **for** (i = 1 to n)
2.   **for** (j = 1 to n)
3.   **if** (i != j && distance between antenna i and j <= 2 * r_m)
4.   *IntersectionArray[i]* += j + ',';
5.   **End for**
6. **End for**
7. **return** *IntersectionArray[ ]*;

Fig. 5. TASP algorithm-2

To create the intersection relations array with n antennas and m radii, we need to check each of the remaining $(n - 1)$ points for every antenna. The time complexity is $O(n^2)$. The second step is finding out the nearest two antennas of A and plans their radii. It takes $O(n + 2m)$ time. Besides, TASP needs to search for the common-intersected antennas and plan the radius until B is in 2-covered area. Finding the nearest common-intersected antenna of B takes $(n - 1)^2$ time computations. Planning

```
PlanNextPoint(PlannedRadius[], IntersectionArray[])
1.   if (B is in new antenna's covering range)
2.           count++;
3.       if (count > 1)
4.           return PlannedRadius[];
5.   else
6.       P_i = NextPoint(PlannedRadius[], IntersectionArray[]);
7.       if (P_i exists)
8.           Count the distance from 2-covered area to the next point P_i.
9.           Find the radius greater than or equal to the distance.
10.          Enlarge the radii if it's necessary.
11.          Record the radii number used into PlannedRadius[].
12.          PlanNextPoint(PlannedRadius[]);
13.      else
14.          return false;
```

Fig. 6. TASP algorithm-3.

```
NextPoint(PlannedRadius[], IntersectionArray[])
1.   //P_i, P_j are the antennas forming 2-covered area.
2.   //k is the number of intersection points in IntersectionArray[P_i].
3.   //l is the number of intersection points in IntersectionArray[P_j].
4.   for (i = 1 to k)
5.       for (j = 1 to l)
6.           if(antenna i and j are the same and it is not used in PlannedRadius[])
7.               P_k = antenna i if the distance between antenna i and point B is
8.                   nearer than previous antennas.
9.       End for
10.  End for
11.  return P_k;
```

Fig. 7. TASP algorithm-4.

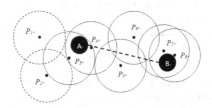

Fig. 8. An example of antennas elimination

radius takes m time computations. Enlarge 2-covered area takes $2m$ time computations. Step 3, 4, and 5 takes at most $n - 2$ time computations. In conclusion, TASP takes $O(((n - 1)^2 + 3m) * (n - 2)) = O(n^3)$ time.

3   RSP Algorithm

To eliminate all antennas that do not intersect $\overline{AB}$ is the main idea of RSP. As shown in Fig. 8, it simply utilizes the antennas covering $\overline{AB}$. Consequently, eliminating P_1 and P_2 is necessary.

While eliminating procedures are in progress, we can utilize Eq.3 to compute the distance between each antenna and $\overleftrightarrow{AB}$. If the distance is greater than the largest radius, then antenna is abandoned. The distance D between point (x_0, y_0) and $ax + by + c = 0$ could be calculated using Eq.3.

$$D = \frac{ax_0 + by_0 + c = 0}{\sqrt{a^2 + b^2}} \tag{3}$$

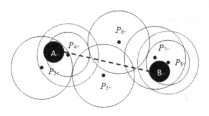

Fig. 9. An example of radii shrinking

In Fig. 9, we calculate the distances between P_4 and circle P_3, P_5, P_6, and point A, and find out the largest value D_m above. The smallest radius greater than or equals to D_m is the most suitable radius of P_4. In Fig. 9, the area covered by P_4 and P_6 is abandoned with connecting 2-covered areas. The followings are steps of RSP:

1. Plan antennas $P_1 \sim P_n$ by the largest radius.
2. Link the point A and point B to form a line segment $\overline{AB}$.
3. Eliminate all antennas that do not intersect $\overline{AB}$.
4. For each remaining antenna P_i, finding out all antennas intersecting P_i and calculating the smallest distance required for P_i. Plan P_i using the smallest radius greater than or equals to the distance.

Radii Shrinking Planning Algorithm
1. Record the biggest radii number into *PlannedRadius[ ]*.
2. Link point A and point B to create a line segment $\overline{AB}$.
3. Eliminate the antennas not crossed.
4. **Foreach** Planned antenna P_i
5. D_{max} = IntersectionAntennasDistance(P_i, *PlannedRadius[ ]*);
6. Find the smallest radius greater than or equal to D_{max}.
7. Record the radius into *PlannedRadius[P_i]*.

Fig. 10. RSP algorithm-1

Planning all antennas by the largest radius and forming $\overline{AB}$ takes O(n) time. Eliminating all antennas not intersecting $\overline{AB}$ also takes O(n) time. In step 4, we have to examine the remaining ($n - 1$) antennas for each antenna while calculating the distance. It takes $n * (n - 1)$ time computations. Finding out the smallest radius greater than or equals to the distance required takes m time computations. As a result, the time complexity of RSP is O($n(n - 1 + m)$) = O(n^2).

```
IntersectionAntennasDistance(Pᵢ, PlannedRadius[])
1.    //k is the number of remaining antennas
2.    for (i = 1 to k)
3.        if (i != Pᵢ && PlannedRadius[i] + PlannedRadius[Pᵢ]
4.                ≥ distance between antenna i and Pᵢ)
5.            D = distance between Pᵢ and circle i;
6.            if (D > Dₘₐₓ)
7.                Dₘₐₓ = D;
8.    End for
9.    return Dₘₐₓ;
```

Fig. 11. RSP algorithm-2

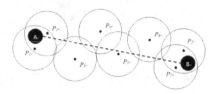

Fig. 12. Limitation of RSP

4   Experiment Results

The resource required of one antenna is estimated by EIRP (Equivalent Isotropically Radiated Power) [18]. It is assumed that the isotropic radiator radiates its wireless signals through all directions. Moreover, the power density of a point is D (W/m²) if the distance between antenna and this point is r. As shown in Eq.4, EIRP is in direct proportion to $4\pi r^2$ if D is given.

$$D = \frac{\text{EIRP}}{4\pi r^2} \tag{4}$$

While comparing the costs of solutions obtained from the algorithms proposed here, we use the percentages of r^2 to estimate the power consumption of antennas. As shown in Eq.5, S is the set of antennas planned and r_i is the radius used by the ith antenna.

$$PC = \sum_{i \in S} r_i^2 \tag{5}$$

4.1   Experiment Data

There are three different parameters including antennas number, radii number, and antennas density in our simulations. We have done 30 time experiments under each condition. The parameters are shown in Table 1.

We apply three antennas densities, four antennas numbers, and four radii numbers to estimate the performances and time elapsed by the algorithms. While density is 0.005, the randomization range is controlled in 0~100. The computer program will

Table 1. Parameters

Densities	Radii	Antennas #	Randomization Ranges
0.005	8,9,10,11	50	0~100
		100	0~142
		250	0~223
		500	0~316
0.01	5,6,8,8	50	0~80
		100	0~100
		250	0~158
		500	0~223
0.05	3,4,5,6	50	0~32
		100	0~45
		250	0~81
		500	0~100

generate 50 points to represent the locations of antennas. If the antennas number is extended to 100, the randomization range will be enlarged to 0~142 such that the density of antennas is guaranteed to be 0.005.

In addition to the densities described, we also use four different kinds of antennas numbers to observe the variations in the algorithms' performances. Moreover, the number of radii is significant while planning the transmission range of each antenna. It is absolutely more flexible if we can provide a large amount of options to choose from. Unfortunately, the costs of emitters will increase rapidly as one selection added. As a result, we only utilize 2 to 4 radii during simulations.

While setting the size of radii, we must be care of a significant factor called covering rate. It is used to indicate the covering number in one area with given antennas and radii. In order to simulate the environments practically, we have to restrain the value such that the number of antennas covered by one emitter is small enough. The formulation utilized to calculate CR (covering rate) is shown in Eq.6. Note that n is the number of antennas, r is the size of radius, and x is the randomization range. The numerator represents the size of area covered by n antennas and the denominator indicates the size of simulation environment.

$$CR = \frac{n\pi r^2}{x^2} \tag{6}$$

For example, if we have 50 antennas generated in a 100 * 100 square and the radius of each antenna is 8, the covering rate under this circumstance is $50 * 3.14 * 8^2/100^2 \approx 1$. While radius is 11, the covering rate is then increased to $50 * 3.14 * 11^2/100^2 \approx 2$. In this paper, we substitute n, x, and $CR = 1$ into Eq.6 and obtain the radius required in different densities, then increase the radius 1 by 1 three times to set four radii as our parameters.

4.2   Experimental Results

In the experiments, a graph transformation planning (GTP) is a brute-force algorithm which always produces the optimal solution (i.e., the minimum energy consumption).

Table 2. The experimental results of 250 antennas

Densities	Radii #	Algorithms	Time	Time Percentages	PC Percentages
0.005	2	TASP	0.080	30.82%	105.65%
		RSP	0.011	9.10%	110.39%
		GTP	0.558	100.00%	100.00%
	3	TASP	0.085	12.28%	106.04%
		RSP	0.011	2.48%	112.12%
		GTP	1.911	100.00%	100.00%
	4	TASP	0.092	9.84%	105.49%
		RSP	0.011	2.35%	111.92%
		GTP	5.130	100.00%	100.00%
0.01	2	TASP	0.120	41.12%	105.02%
		RSP	0.009	5.34%	111.50%
		GTP	5.858	100.00%	100.00%
	3	TASP	0.081	15.32%	106.15%
		RSP	0.009	3.09%	115.01%
		GTP	3.622	100.00%	100.00%
	4	TASP	0.103	8.40%	108.59%
		RSP	0.011	1.85%	119.82%
		GTP	19.122	100.00%	100.00%
0.05	2	TASP	0.028	41.89%	106.03%
		RSP	0.012	19.28%	121.04%
		GTP	0.068	100.00%	100.00%
	3	TASP	0.034	22.95%	108.83%
		RSP	0.012	8.89%	123.08%
		GTP	0.151	100.00%	100.00%
	4	TASP	0.034	14.26%	111.25%
		RSP	0.012	5.10%	128.88%
		GTP	0.309	100.00%	100.00%

We analyzed TASP, RSP, and GTP under 2, 3, 4 radii numbers, respectively. The experimental results are shown in Table 3.

Table 3. Percentages of PC and execution time under different radii numbers

Radii #	Algorithms	Average Time Percentages	Average PC Percentages
2	TASP	45.38%	106.02%
	RSP	16.58%	115.86%
	GTP	100.00%	100.00%
3	TASP	20.00%	106.83%
	RSP	8.25%	118.14%
	GTP	100.00%	100.00%
4	TASP	12.31%	108.68%
	RSP	4.58%	118.80%
	GTP	100.00%	100.00%

In Fig. 13(a), the differences of average percentages of PC between TASP, GTP and RSP, GTP are 6%~8% and 15%~18%, separately. As the number of radii increased, the differences of PC between TASP, GTP and RSP, GTP also raised. Nevertheless, the costs of emitters increase rapidly as new radius added in real life. We always provide 2 to 4 kinds of radii while planning transmission ranges. As a result, the influence of variations in radii numbers is negligible.

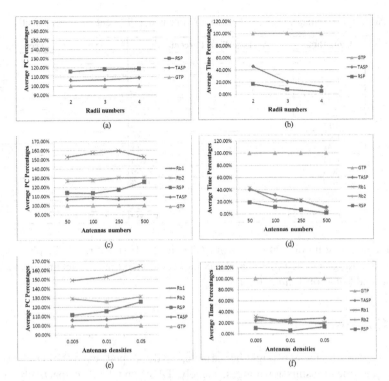

Fig. 13. Percentages of (a) PC under different radii numbers, (b) execution time under different radii numbers, (c) PC under different antennas numbers, (d) execution time under different antennas numbers, (e) PC under different antennas densities, (f) execution time under different antennas densities

Fig. 13(b) shows the differences of execution time elapsed between TASP, RSP and GTP. In contrast to GTP, TASP and RSP only need a bit of time to finish their algorithms. While 4 radii are used, TASP and RSP require less than 20% of the execution time GTP spent. The tradeoff between power consumption and execution time is thus a considerable issue for users.

4.3   Different Antennas Density

This section presents the performances between TASP, RSP, and GTP as the density of antennas increases. The average percentages under different densities (e.g. 0.005, 0.01, and 0.05) are shown in Table 4.

While antennas density is 0.005, TASP and RSP are ideal algorithms since the differences of average percentages of PC between TASP, GTP and RSP, GTP are 5% and 11%, respectively. Unfortunately, as antennas density increases, especially on 0.05, the difference of power consumption between RSP and GTP is higher than 20%. Therefore, RSP is not suitable under high density environments (see Fig. 13(3)).

Table 4. Percentages of PC and execution time under different antennas densities

Densities	Algorithms	Average Time Percentages	Average PC Percentages
0.005	Rb1	31.12%	149.11%
	Rb2	26.88%	129.12%
	TASP	23.98%	105.85%
	RSP	10.18%	111.52%
	GTP	100.00%	100.00%
0.01	Rb1	21.95%	152.86%
	Rb2	20.65%	125.69%
	TASP	25.55%	106.51%
	RSP	5.54%	115.42%
	GTP	100.00%	100.00%
0.05	Rb1	18.03%	164.49%
	Rb2	19.83%	131.14%
	TASP	28.18%	109.28%
	RSP	12.68%	125.66%
	GTP	100.00%	100.00%

Although the solution obtained from GTP is the best approach in planning the transmission range of each antenna, the complicated backtracking technique makes it a tedious and time-consuming algorithm.

5   Conclusion

Due to the radii of antennas might be variable, we developed two different algorithms used to plan the transmission ranges, namely TASP and RSP, respectively. TASP stretches 2-covered areas from source point to destination point. RSP plans the largest radius initially and shrinks the antennas intersecting the line segment described in section 3.

Although the fastest algorithm in this paper is RSP, the power consumption of the solution obtained is not always satisfactory for wireless communication system providers. How to economize the use of power is still an important issue for us to study in the future. Besides, the execution time elapsed by GTP is determined by the connection relations of the nodes in the graph. It could be reduced if the characteristics of unnecessary nodes can be generalized.

References

1. Aardal, K., van Hoesel, C.P.M., Koster, A.M.C.A., Mannino, C., Sassano, A.: Models and solution techniques for the frequency assignment problem. 4OR 1, 261–318 (2006)
2. Abellanas, M., Bajuelos, A.L., Matos, I.: Optimal 2-coverage of a polygonal region in a sensor network. Algorithms 2, 1138–1154 (2009)
3. Abellanas, M., Bajuelos, A.L., Matos, I.: 2-Covered paths by a set of antennas with minimum power transmission range. Information Processing Letters 109(14), 868–883 (2009)
4. Boukerche, A., Fei, X., Araujo, R.B.: An energy aware coverage-preserving scheme for wireless sensor networks. In: Proocedings of the 2nd ACM International Workshop on Performance Evaluation of Wireless Ad Hoc, Sensor and Ubiquitous Networks, Montreal, Canada, October 13, pp. 205–213 (2005)

5. Chen, L., Yuan, D.: Solving a minimum-power covering problem with overlap constraint for cellular network design. European Journal of Operational Research 203, 814–823 (2010)
6. Eisenblatter, A., Geerdes, H.F., Grotschel, M.: Planning UMTS radio networks. OR/MS Today 35, 41–46 (2008)
7. Eisenblatter, A., Koch, T., Martin, A., Achterberg, T., Fugenschuh, A., Koster, A., Wegel, O., Wessaly, R.: Modelling feasible network configurations for UMTS. In: Anandalingam, G., Raghavan, S. (eds.) Telecommunications Network Design and Management. Kluwer Academic Publishers (2002)
8. Fowler, R.J., Paterson, M., Tanimoto, S.L.: Optimal Packing and Covering in the Plane are NP-Complete. Information Processing Letter, 133–138 (1981)
9. Franceschetti, M., Cook, M., Bruck, J.: A geometric theorem for approximate disk covering algorithms. Technical report, California Institute of Technology (2001)
10. Gonzalez, T.F.: Covering a set of points in multidimensional space. Information Processing Letters 40(4), 181–188 (1991)
11. Hochbaum, D.S., Maass, W.: Approximation Schemes for Covering and Packing Problems in Image Processing and VLSI. Journal of ACM 32(1), 130–136 (1985)
12. Nawrocki, M., Aghvami, H., Dohler, M. (eds.): Understanding UMTS RadioNetwork Modelling, Planning and Automated Optimisation: Theory and Practice. Wiley (2006)
13. Xiao, B., Zhuge, Q., Zhang, Y., Sha, E.H.M.: Algorithms for disk covering problems with the most points. In: Proceedings of the IASTED International Conference on

Design of an Application-Dependent Static-Based Shared Memory Network

Yoshimasa Ohnishi and Takaichi Yoshida

Kyushu Institute of Technology,
680-4 Kawazu, Iizuka, Fukuoka 820-8502, Japan
ohnishi@el, takaichi@ci.kyutech.ac.jp
http://www.kyutech.ac.jp/english/

Abstract. The latency of network switching is of particular importance for fine-grained communication processes such as memory access. We propose a specialized network switch that reduces communication latency because many scientific computing applications have specific access patterns. In this paper, we describe the basic concept and design of our reconfigurable shared memory network. Our evaluation results show that there is no significant difference between the port-to-port latency of our network switch and that of an 8-port InfiniBand network switch. Furthermore, the hardware size of the routing stack in the network switch does not increase with the number of nodes.

Keywords: cluster computer, network switch, reconfigurable, shared memory, static route.

1 Introduction

In large-scale cluster configurations, the performance of scientific applications is affected by many factors, including, routing, network topology, resource assignment, and application characteristics. Many high-performance network switches have been developed to maintain performance and prevent any possible degradation in performance by configuring custom network topologies. Hoefler et al. showed [4] that static routing is superior in high-performance networks and it avoids network congestion. In scientific computation, it is important to ensure that the static routing and the memory allocation are programmed correctly. A network analysis and monitoring tool proposed by Dandapanthula [2] provides some useful characteristics for effective static routing.

Previously, we proposed a shared memory network architecture that can configure a minimum necessary communication route, and we designed an application-dependent specialized network switch. We also described a simple scientific application example for a shared memory network and explained the implementability of the network switch using reconfigurable devices [10]. Reconfigurable devices are slower than ASIC devices, but when using reconfigurable devices for network switching, we expect that scientific application users will be able to configure an efficient topology more easily in a shared memory network.

Y. Xiang et al. (Eds.): ICA3PP 2012, Part II, LNCS 7440, pp. 62–71, 2012.

In this paper, we describe a specific network interface and a reconfiguration model of a network switch in a shared memory network. We present a static route example using scientific computation matrix data and we evaluated the capacity of our proposed network switch compared with a small-scale InfiniBand switch. We also consider a shared memory network that provides a beneficial combination of a static route and reconfigurable devices.

2   Overview of the Basic Concept

Our reconfigurable network architecture can construct personal networks using application data. For example, if an HPC user wants to address certain problem using the same application program, our network switch reconfigures some of the routes according to the characteristics of the user's application data [10]. The objective of this study is to select the optimal network using the specific application data and application program for a user's scientific computations.

2.1   Shared Memory Access Model

Figure 1 shows the access model of a shared memory network. In our access model, each node has a private memory (PM) component and a shared memory (SM) component. Each SM component is connected via a cluster network and the cluster system shares only the requisite memory space. To reduce the network switch latency, we introduce a model where the CPU accesses a shared memory via a requisite static route for each application.

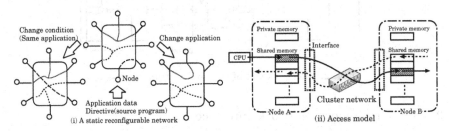

Fig. 1. Proposed shared memory network

When write memory access is performed, the CPU can access another node's SM via a network switch, if necessary. For example (see Fig. 1 (ii)), the CPU at node A accesses the SM of node A, and the interface at node A transmits data to the network switch simultaneously. If required, the network switch distributes the data, in which case it delivers the data to the interface at node B. The data are then written to the SM of node B. Thus, the same data exist in the SM components (shaded regions of Fig. 1 (ii)) of both nodes A and B. If the CPU writes data to the SM, the CPU sends the data to another SM via the network. Thus, we assume that there is a specific memory interface (for example, a memory channel-like [3] interface, a DIMMnet [11] interface, or our interface model(see Fig. 3)) between the CPU and the physical memory.

3   Design of the Shared Memory Network

3.1   Model of the Shared Memory Space

Memory access is divided into PM space access and SM space access. Local data and local variables are assigned to the PM space, and shared data and shared variables are assigned to the SM space. As shown in Fig. 2, the global virtual space is composed of the SM space at each node so we introduced a single address space method into the global virtual space management method, which reduces the complexity of the address mapping mechanism.

When the CPU writes to the SM in a global virtual address space, the specific memory interface simultaneously transmits the data to be written to the same global virtual address space. In contrast, the CPU only accesses its own node's SM when a read memory access is performed because the requisite data are received by the specific memory interface via the network switch beforehand. Naturally, an address mapping mechanism is required between a global virtual address and a physical address for each node.

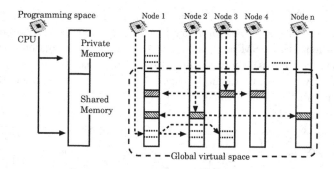

Fig. 2. Access model of a global virtual address

3.2   Shared Memory Network Interface

As shown in Fig. 3, we designed a node computer model. The shared memory network interface (SMNI) consists of a physical memory component and a network component. The SMNI transmits the data to the network switch when it detects a write memory access signal from the memory controller. An address translator between the virtual addresses on the shared memory network and the physical addresses on the memory bus must be implemented in the SMNI before a global virtual space can be realized.

We now describe the flow of the address data in the shared memory network. After memory access, the virtual addresses are transferred to the physical addresses by a memory controller in the CPU. As shown in Fig. 3, the physical addresses flow to the physical memory before the shared memory, according to the memory access sequence, and they are transmitted simultaneously to the reverse address translator on the SMNI. The reverse address translator converts

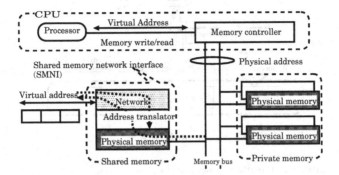

Fig. 3. Shared memory network interface model

the physical addresses to virtual addresses (global virtual addresses). The information in the address mapping table of the SM is obtained from the CPU beforehand. The global virtual address used on the shared memory network is again converted to the physical addresses on the SMNI of the destination node.

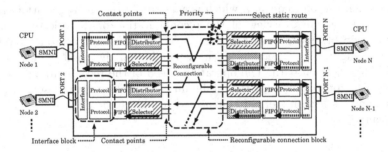

Fig. 4. Shared memory reconfigurable network switch model

3.3 Shared Memory Network Switch

Figure 4 shows an overview of the network switch, where the arrows indicate the direction of data flow. The network switch consists of a selector component, a distributor component, an interface block, and a reconfigurable connection block. We can configure a static route via the reconfigurable connection blocks and we can create a shared memory network using a selector component and a distributor component, according to the problem's characteristics. Thus, the distributor component on the source side transmits the communication data to the selector component on the destination side via the reconfigurable connection block. The interface block receives and sends the communication data between the nodes and the network switch via the port.

The distributor component of each port delivers the data to the selector component via the reconfigurable connection block. Contact points exist around the reconfigurable connection block because the network switch needs to connect

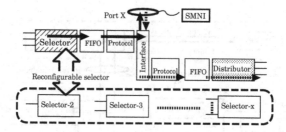

Fig. 5. Choosing the optimal selector component

certain communication routes. The number of contact points differs according to the number of connection nodes. The contact points must be regenerated for the application, according to the characteristics of the problem and the data, because the number of communication routes changes after each execution.

The selector component of each port receives data from the source nodes. The contact points only connect the requisite communication routes, as does the distributor component. The selector component of each port selects the optimal static route according to the communication priority when a conflict occurs in the selector component. The communication priority is calculated on the basis of the communication frequency, which is generated from the application data.

Figure 5 shows an overview of the reconfiguration of the selector component. The network switch can prepare a selector with suitable contact points on the reconfigurable connection block, depending on the number of decisions in the communication path. The operation speed of the reconfigurable connection block is improved by using the minimum necessary hardware resources. The use of a simple selection method is expected to reduce the delay of the selector component.

4   Configuration Results for the Shared Memory Network

We simulated several functions to demonstrate a static route for the shared memory network. We used simple calculations, i.e., multiplying matrix A by vector p, and we described examples of a static route (shared memory network) using several sparse matrices taken from the Matrix Market [7].

To calculate $q = Ap$ on the shared memory network, the system used an evaluation composed of several node computers and one network switch. In this case, our tools distributed all of the shared variables over 10 nodes and the requisite number of nonzero elements for the matrix data.

4.1   Examples of Static Routes

We simulated a small-scale cluster system (i.e., 10 nodes and one network switch) using six matrices. These sparse matrices contained 1.5% to 2.1% nonzero entries. Table 1 shows the set and the number of selector components used by the network switch. The optimal communication pattern was different for each problem in these results. Because of the neighbor effect, a few static routes and a small selection of selector types were sufficient to configure the shared memory network. For example, the network switch configured using only M1 matrix data required selector-2 and selector-3, while a reconfigurable connection block that was configured with only two static routes and 16 static routes had priority.

Table 1. Matrix summary and configuration results

Sparse matrix summary		M1	M2	M3	M4	M5	M6
Matrix size in terms of the number of rows ($n \times n$)		1086	1473	2003	1086	1473	2003
Nonzero entries		22070	34241	83883	22092	19659	21181
Submatrix size ($n \times n$)		109	148	201	109	148	201
	Component name	Number of selector components					
	Selector-2	2	1	-	2	1	1
	Selector-3	8	5	-	8	5	6
Configuration of 10 ports network SW	Selector-4	-	1	3	-	1	3
	Selector-5	-	3	1	-	3	-
	Selector-6	-	-	2	-	-	-
	Selector-7	-	-	3	-	-	-
	Selector-8	-	-	1	-	-	-

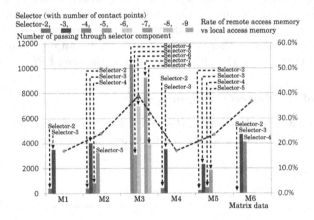

Fig. 6. Communication frequency of remote access memory

4.2 Remote Access Communication

Figure 6 shows the communication frequency for each type of selector (within the network switch) with six matrices (as shown in Table 1). The communication frequency indicates the number of remote communications when accessing a shared variable at another node. Each selector had a different communication frequency. For example, the number using the selector-3 component (two remote access + one local access) was maximized, with the exception of the M3 matrix data. When there is a large difference in the number using the selector components, we need a design that reduces the latency for the critical static route and the critical selector components.

5   Evaluation of the Network Switch

5.1   Latency

We analyzed the latency of our prototype network switch, which was implemented using a small-scale FPGA device. To make these measurements, we used an experimental SMNI that could generate transmission communications using 4-byte data instead of 2-byte practical memory access timing (32-bit address and 32-bit data). The latency of an 8-port InfiniBand switch was also measured using two node PCs (CentOS 5.7 32-bit Core i7-860 2.8 GHz, 40 Gb/s InfiniBand HCA). We analyzed the latency of the small-scale InfiniBand switch using ibv_rc_pingpong.

As a result, the port-to-port latency of our prototype network switch was 0.36μs (56 clock, 156.25 MHz). Figure 7 shows the latency of the InfiniBand switch. We found the production latency of the InfiniBand switch on the Mellanox website [9].

During fine-grained remote communication, such as memory access, the transmission data during a single memory access must not exceed 16 bytes. The realistic grain size for remote communication may be a few bytes; hence, the latency of our proposed network switch was not degraded. Our proposed method is likely to play an important role in a shared memory network because we could configure a system to further reduce the latency by using high-speed FPGA devices.

5.2   Delay of the Selector Components

Table 2 and Fig. 8 show the delay of the selectors on a prototype network switch design. The delays of both types of selector components were derived from FPGA

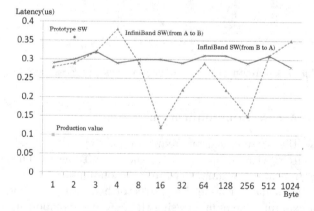

Fig. 7. Port-to-port latency

design tools, whereas the other values were estimated from the prototype design of our network switch. We analyzed the delay of the selector component using large sparse matrices (as shown in Table 3) to evaluate the performance of our shared memory environment (memory network). The application we evaluated was a simple calculation, i.e., multiplying matrix A by vector p.

The total communication delay was calculated as both the delay and the communication frequency when our shared memory network topology was configured using an L1 matrix and an L2 matrix. The network topology was a single cluster structure that was connected directly to one network switch and several nodes.

Table 2. Delay of the selector components with the prototype design

	Selector component	
Number of contact points	3	6
Maximum delay (ns)	1.8	1.9

Table 3. Sparse matrix summary used for the evaluation

	L1	L2
Matrix size $(n \times n)$	10974	11948
Nonzero entries	428650	149090

Figure 8 shows that the communication frequency with remote access increased with the number of nodes. The results for these sparse matrix data show that the total communication delay of the reconfigurable connection block could be reduced using all topologies of the cluster systems. For instance, the total communication delay was reduced by 30% in a network switch with 549 ports (L1 matrix).

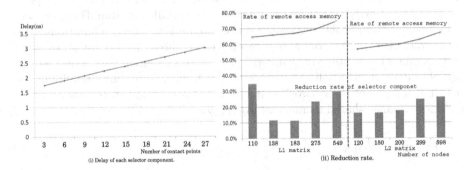

Fig. 8. Reduction rate for the requisite static route (contact points) vs a fully connected route

6 Related Work

Hoefler et al. showed [4] that static routing is better for avoiding network congestion in high-performance networks with multistage switches. They analyzed some real-world applications and described how an effective static route could affect the application performance. We used a similar concept and focused on static routing in reconfigurable high-performance networks. We studied the reduction in the latency of remote memory access using reconfigurable devices and we developed an effective large-scale shared memory network.

DIMMnet [11] is a network interface that can be installed in a memory slot, and it is an efficient network interface for a PC cluster offering SM. A key feature of this architecture is that a memory access transaction can be detected with a low communication overhead. We proposed a network switch for a distributed shared memory that operates cooperatively with a shared memory network interface. By considering the processing of communication data in a network switch, we selected the requisite static route using a low latency switching method.

Many studies have reported topology changes in cluster computers. Kamil proposed HFAST[8], which is a hybrid switch architecture that uses circuit switches to dynamically reconfigure lower degree interconnects, depending on the topological requirements. Our network switch cannot reconfigure a communication route dynamically. However, the advantage of our method is that we can easily reduce the overall hardware utilization by using only the requisite communication information for remote memory access. In addition, the configuration of a dynamic reconfigurable switch needs to use complex hardware.

7   Conclusion

In this paper, we described a static route example for a reconfigurable network switch using several matrix datasets. We demonstrated that our network can configure the requisite communication paths and that a static route based on circuit-like communication can reduce the latency. The performance of our prototype network switch is not inferior to that of the small-scale InfiniBand switch.

Our reconfigurable network switch is effective for scientific computations that are characterized by memory access based on a neighbor effect. Only static connection minimum routes are required in the network switch when using reconfigurable devices, which limits the necessary hardware resource requirements [10]. The latency of the network switch is reduced by using static routes; thus, high-performance shared memory can be provided.

8   Future Work

We need to consider restrictive conditions while extending the present implementation to a large-scale shared memory network. In addition, we will implement an address management system for a shared memory to facilitate memory allocation in the operating system.

A description of the shared memory is required because the proposed network switch needs to collect information about shared variables and application data (matrix data). Some programming languages have been reported for shared variables. Wei-Yu Chen demonstrated the effectiveness of analysis and optimization using several benchmarks [1]. We are also interested in global address space languages such as UPC [6] and XcalableMP [5].

References

1. Chen, W.Y., Iancu, C., Yelick, K.: Communication optimizations for fine-grained upc applications. In: Proceedings of the 14th International Conference on Parallel Architectures and Compilation Techniques, PACT 2005, pp. 267–278. IEEE Computer Society (2005)
2. Dandapanthula, N., Subramoni, H., Vienne, J., Kandalla, K., Sur, S., Panda, D.K., Brightwell, R.: INAM - A Scalable InfiniBand Network Analysis and Monitoring Tool. In: Alexander, M., D'Ambra, P., Belloum, A., Bosilca, G., Cannataro, M., Danelutto, M., Di Martino, B., Gerndt, M., Jeannot, E., Namyst, R., Roman, J., Scott, S.L., Traff, J.L., Vallée, G., Weidendorfer, J. (eds.) Euro-Par 2011, Part II. LNCS, vol. 7156, pp. 166–177. Springer, Heidelberg (2012)
3. Fillo, M., Gillett, R.B.: Architecture and implementation of memory channel 2. Digital Tech. J. 9, 27–41 (1997)
4. Hoefler, T., Schneider, T., Lumsdaine, A.: Multistage switches are not crossbars: Effects of static routing in high-performance networks. In: 2008 IEEE International Conference on Cluster Computing, October 1-29, pp. 116–125 (2008)
5. The Xcalable MP: Directive-based language extension for scalable and performance-aware parallel programming, http://www.xcalablemp.org/
6. The Berkeley UPC Compiler (2002), http://upc.lbl.gov/
7. Matrix Market (2007), http://math.nist.gov/MatrixMarket/
8. Kamil, S., Pinar, A., Gunter, D., Lijewski, M., Oliker, L., Shalf, J.: Reconfigurable hybrid interconnection for static and dynamic scientific applications. In: Proceedings of the 4th International Conference on Computing Frontiers, CF 2007, pp. 183–194. ACM (2007)
9. Mellanox InfiniBand switches (2012), http://www.mellanox.com/
10. Ohnishi, Y., Yoshida, T.: Design and evaluation of a distributed shared memory network for application-specific pc cluster systems. In: Proceedings of the 2011 IEEE Workshops of International Conference on Advanced Information Networking and Applications, WAINA 2011, pp. 63–70. IEEE Computer Society (2011)
11. Tanabe, N., Yamamoto, J., Nishi, H., Kudoh, T., Hamada, Y., Nakajo, H., Amano, H.: Low latency high bandwidth message transfer mechanisms for a network interface plugged into a memory slot. Cluster Computing 5(1), 7–17 (2002)

Determining Quality of S-Boxes Using Pseudo Random Sequences Generated from Stream Ciphers

Anh P. Nguyen and Thuc D. Nguyen

Faculty of Information Technology, University of Science
227 Nguyen Van Cu st, Dist 5, Hochiminh city, Vietnam
{npanh,ndthuc}@fit.hcmus.edu.vn

Abstract. In this paper, two stream ciphers, SOBER-t32 and SNOW 2.0 are used to generate sequences of pseudo random numbers. The original S-Boxes of these ciphers are replaced by Skipjack, IRSC, AES-Rijndael S-Box, and variants of AES-Rijndael S-Boxes. Pseudo-random sequences generated by SOBER-t32 and SNOW 2.0 using these S-Boxes are then tested by statistical test suite and analyzed by linear distinguishing cryptanalysis for randomness properties. The results show that these S-Boxes do not have much contribution to the statistical randomness of the pseudo-sequences but play significant roles on the nonlinearity of the ciphers. Hence, affect the randomness of sequences in cryptanalysis aspect.

Keywords: stream cipher, S-Box, pseudo-random generator, linear cryptanalysis.

1   Introduction

Random number and Pseudo-random number are used in simulation, gambling as well as in cryptography such as key generation and authentication protocols. Pseudo-random numbers usually produced by a deterministic algorithm called pseudo random generator, which takes a short truly random sequence and output long, deterministic sequences of number. Synchronous stream cipher is an algorithm that produces keystreams which are XORed with plain/cipher text in the encryption/decryption process. In this context, keystreams may be considered as a sequence of pseudo random numbers generated from corresponding pair of one secret key and one vector of initialization.

To determine the randomness of output generated from synchronous stream cipher, these keystreams can be passed in to statistical test like NIST [11]. However, in cryptographic application, a cipher must pass all known cryptanalysis attack. One type of attack that concerns the randomness quality of number sequences generated from stream cipher is linear distinguishing attack. This attack is a variant of linear cryptanalysis, which determines whether a sequence of numbers is generated from a truly random source or from a given deterministic algorithm. We concentrate on linear distinguishing attack on stream ciphers using linear feedback register. A general method for this type of stream cipher is analyzing the non-linear parts of stream cipher algorithm, combining these non-linear parts based on linear feedback shift register to calculate the complexity of the attack [2].

Y. Xiang et al. (Eds.): ICA3PP 2012, Part II, LNCS 7440, pp. 72–79, 2012.

In symmetric encryption, S-Boxes are important parts of many encryption algorithms which provide non-linearity. In this paper, S-Boxes which are studied under the randomness properties are two original S-Boxes in two stream cipher algorithms, SOBER-t32 and SNOW 2.0, AES-Rijndael S-Box, two variants of AES-Rijndael S-Boxes [4, 5], and Skipjack S-Box.

SOBER-t32 is an encryption algorithm in NESSIE project. There is no public attack that could practically break the cipher completely. SOBER-t32 has passed the NESSIE statistical tests [7]. Patrik used linear cryptanalysis method on SOBER-t32 with the complexity of 2^{87} [8]. Detail of SOBER-t32 is described in [12]. The other cipher, SNOW 2.0 [6], is an improvement of SNOW. This cipher was used along with RC4 and AES as benchmark ciphers for candidates in eStream project. The best linear cryptanalysis on SNOW 2.0 up to now has the complexity 2^{174} [10].

2 Method

2.1 Statistical Tests

Keystream sequences generated from SNOW 2.0, corresponding to five S-Boxes: AES-Rijndael, LCUI, an instance of [4], Skipjack, and IRSC are passed into NIST test suite [11]. NIST provides fifteen independent tests. Each examines a randomness aspect of a given sequence. All the results are in P-values. Based on the set of P-value, NIST give conclusions about the randomness of the sequence.

We generate 7 sets of 200 independent sequences, each sequences has 2.10^6 bit long. Each set of sequences corresponds to a given S-Boxes. In addition, we generate a set of sequences from SHA-1 random generator, and a set of sequences corresponds to SNOW 2.0 without S-Boxes (Figure 5).

2.2 Linear Distinguishing

Linear distinguishing is a type of attack on stream cipher originates from linear cryptanalysis. Copper Smith generalized this attack by a framework for stream cipher algorithms [2]. A stream cipher (figure 1) in this framework has two parts, non-linear function F and linear states y_{i1}, y_{i2}. Linear states are often considered as random while non-linear function F has a bias ε. This bias is covered by the linear states before and after the function F. The attacker is assumed to observer keystream z_i. There always exist J steps on combination of keystreams, in which the linear states are vanished.

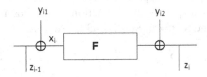

Fig. 1. A simple stream cipher

$$\sum_J l\,(z_{i-1},\,z_i) = \sum_J l\,(x_i,\,F(x_i)) + \sum_J l\,(y_{i1},\,y_{i2}) = \sum_J l\,(x_i,\,F(x_i)) \qquad (1)$$

When l is a linear function, $l\colon \{0,\,1\}^{2n} \to \{0,\,1\}$. A cipher may have more than one non-linear part. In this case, the bias of these non-linear parts may accumulate using pilling-up lemma [13].

$$\varepsilon = \tfrac{1}{2}\,(\Pi\varepsilon_i^6) \qquad (2)$$

SOBER-t32

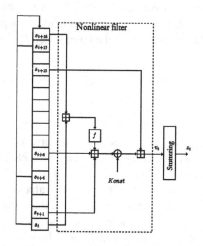

Fig. 2. The stream cipher SOBER-t32, source [9]

SOBER-t32 [12] uses a linear feedback shift register and a nonlinear filter. The filter has three additions with carry, one XOR operator, a nonlinear function f containing S-Boxes. The stuttering can be ignored since this is only the enhancement part in the cipher. We use directly the attack on SOBER-128[1] on SOBER-t32. The attack utilizes the first bit of states in nonlinear filter since the first bit in addition with carry is always linear. The nonlinear filter in the figure 1 can be expressed as

$$z_t = ((f_{32}\,(S_{n+1}\,\mathrm{S}_{n+1}\,\boxplus\,S_{n+17}) \,\boxplus\, S_{n+2} \,\boxplus\, S_{n+7}) + Konst\,) \,\boxplus\, S_{n+14} \qquad (3)$$

S_i represents a state in linear feedback register, Konst is the constant. The symbol $\boxplus$ is modulo addition with carry. Since the first bits in the additions with carry are always linear, when using linear approximation on the first bit of operands on (3), the solely remaining non-linear part is the f function which has first output bit of the f function involves with one S-Box in SOBER-t32. We have (4)

$$z_t = S_{n+1(k_1)} + S_{n+17(k_2)} + S_{n+2(0)} + S_{n+7(0)} + Konst_{(0)} + S_{n+14(0)} \qquad (4)$$

The k_1 and k_2 in S_{n+1} and S_{n+17} states are the input masks of the linear-approximation. Since SOBER-t32 using linear feedback shift register, we can dismiss the linear states base on the expression of linear states on the register. The authors in [2] and [3] have found a way to make α coefficient in the LNSR of SOBER-t32 to vanish (6).

$$S_{t+17.2^{32}-4} + S_{t+15.2^{32}-4} + S_{t+4.2^{32}-4} + S_{t+13} + S_{t+11} + S_t = 0 \tag{5}$$

Using pilling-lemma (2), the total bias of (5) is six time the bias in the linear approximation in (4).

SNOW 2.0

SNOW 2.0 has one linear feedback shift register with two coefficients α and α-1. The non-linear filter has two additions with carry, two register caching the result of previous calculation step, a non-linear transformation S' using S-Boxes.

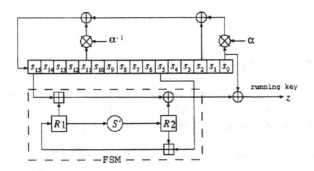

Fig. 3. The SNOW 2.0 cipher, source [9]

Two linear distinguishing attacks have been launched on SNOW 2.0. Wantanabe [9] used the masking method directly on linear feedback shift register with the assumption of four independent non-linear parts, three additions with carry and a non-linear transformation S'. These non-linear parts appear when combining two adjacent keystreams in order to diminish the register R1, R2 (figure 3). In [10], this attack was improved with the assumption of two non-linear parts, two consecutive additions with carry and the other is S' with an addition with carry.

Our attack is the combination of the two heuristics in [9] and [10] with the assumption of three independent non-linear parts, one non-linear transformation S', one addition with carry, and two consecutive additions with carry.

To use the method in [2], the non-linear part S' and additions with carry need to be approximated. With 32 bit input and output, it is infeasible to calculate the bias of all input output cases. We use the assumption in [9] that with sparse mask no more than six bit, the result bias of addition with carry is large in most case. We also reuse the heuristic in [10] that bias of two consecutive additions with carry is better than two independent additions. The approximation expressions have the forms [10]:

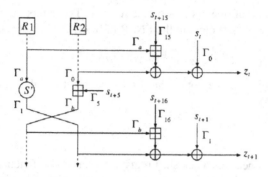

Fig. 4. The non-linear filter of SNOW 2.0 when combine two adjacent keystreams, source [9]

$$\Gamma x = \Gamma S'(x) \tag{7}$$

$$\Gamma x \boxplus \Gamma y = \Gamma x + \Gamma y \tag{8}$$

$$\Gamma x \boxplus \Gamma y \boxplus z = \Gamma x + \Gamma y + \Gamma z \tag{9}$$

According to [9], when directly apply approximations with masks on linear feedback shift register with coefficients α and α-1 on SNOW 2.0, linear states in the combination of two consecutive keystreams (figure 4) vanish.

$$\Gamma(z_{t+2} + z_{t+3} + z_{t+16} + z_{t+17}) + (\Gamma\alpha^{-1})(z_{t+11} + z_{t+12}) + (\Gamma\alpha)(z_t + z_{t+1}) \tag{10}$$

3   Results

3.1   Statistical Tests

We use the P-values proportion criteria given in NIST test suite. The proportions imply the number of independent sequences passes the NIST tests, which must follow uniform distribution in case of truly random sequences.

The result shows that in statistical test criteria, all S-Boxes, including NULL S-Box, passed the NIST statistical test. Moreover, no S-Box has clearly good or bad results over the others (figure 5).

3.2   Linear Distinguishing Attack

SOBER-t32

Based on the method on SOBER-t32, we implement the attack using C language in a Pentium D 2.8 GHz, 2Gb Ram computer. S-Box with best results is the original S-Box of SOBER-t32, the ISRC, and the S-Box in [4].

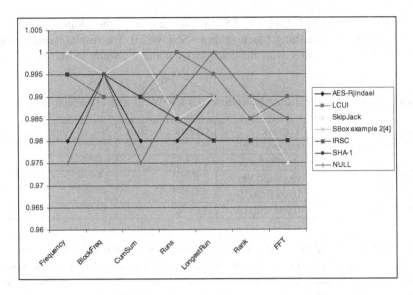

Fig. 5. Result on statistical test of given S-Boxes

Table 1. Result on linear distinguishing attack on SOBER-t32

Mask \ S-Box	Mask S_{n+1}	Mask S_{n+17}	Bias ($\frac{1}{2}(1 + \varepsilon)$)	Cumulative bias	Complexity of attack
CUI [5]	0xfc	0xfc	$2^{-3.3561}$	$2^{-20.1366}$	2^{40}
AES-Rjindael	0xd0	0xe0	$-2^{-3.2721}$	$-2^{-19.6326}$	2^{39}
SKIPJACK	0xee	0xee	$-2^{-3.2056}$	$-2^{-19.2336}$	$2^{38.5}$
S-Box [4]	0xfe	0xff	$-2^{-3.7473}$	$-2^{-22.4838}$	2^{45}
ISRC	0xf7	0xf7	$2^{-3.7146}$	$-2^{-22.5126}$	2^{45}

SNOW 2.0

The linear distinguishing attack on SNOW 2.0 was implemented using Matlab on a 2.8 Gb Pentium D, 2 Gb RAM computer, with the 6 bit sparse mask. In this attack, S-Box AES-Rijndael show best results over others. ISRC has much larger bias compared with AES-Rijndael.

Table 2. Result of linear distinguishing on SNOW 2.0

S-Box	ε_{total}	Mask Γ	No. of steps required
AES-Rijndael	$2^{-106.20}$	0x60018006	2^{212}
LCUI	$2^{-105.5}$	0x18018180	2^{210}
SkipJack	$2^{-104.51}$	0x60018001	2^{208}
S-Box [4]	$2^{-103.21}$	0x18018004	2^{206}
ISRC	$2^{-91.54}$	0x03000031	2^{182}

To clarify the roles of S-Boxes in SNOW 2.0, we remove the additions with carry and using linear distinguishing attack again on SNOW 2.0. The results (table 3) show that LCUI has best quality with the complexity about 2^{94} while ISRC are still the worst.

Table 3. Result on linear distinguishing attack on SNOW 2.0 without addition with carry

S-Box	Γ mask	Cumulative Bias	No. of steps required
AES-Rjindael	0x004382e0	$2^{-45.7978}$	$2^{91.5956}$
LCUI	0x9f8c5c00	$2^{-46.928}$	$2^{93.856}$
SkipJack	0xe0a8539a	$2^{-45.0014}$	$2^{90.0028}$
S-Box[4]	0xe97c0019	$2^{-45.3724}$	$2^{90.7448}$
ISRC	0xe97c0019	$2^{-44.0847}$	$2^{88.1694}$

The total biases on the modified SNOW 2.0 depend only on S-Boxes and the combination of masks (Γ, $\Gamma\alpha$-1, $\Gamma\alpha$). In this case, all masks must be examined instead of the sparse mask since there is no addition with carries. However, the heuristic in which, input and output mask are the same, is maintained. The results on two attacks show that except ISRC, which having bad qualities, the others have similar result on linear distinguishing attack.

4   Conclusion and Discussion

Results on the statistical tests show no differences between S-Boxes when used to generate pseudo-random sequences. However, results of linear distinguishing attack on SNOW 2.0 show that in the total bias, the S-Boxes does have important roles in the cipher, and hence the randomness of the sequences generated. The AES-Rijndael, AES-Rijndael extensions, Skipjack have good results and can be used interchangeable under the viewpoint of randomness of sequences. Thus, S-Boxes with good qualities may have good randomness properties and bad S-Boxes may affect the randomness generated from the cipher. To have more confident results, more statistical test suites may be used such as DIEHARD or Knuth test. In the linear distinguishing attack, other ciphers should be inspected to clarity the roles of S-Boxes.

Acknowledgement. This research was supported by a grant from Nafosted.

References

1. Cho, J.Y., Pieprzyk, J.: Distinguishing Attack on SOBER-128 with Linear Masking. In: Batten, L.M., Safavi-Naini, R. (eds.) ACISP 2006. LNCS, vol. 4058, pp. 29–39. Springer, Heidelberg (2006)
2. Coppersmith, D., Halevi, S., Jutla, C.S.: Cryptanalysis of Stream Ciphers with Linear Masking. In: Yung, M. (ed.) CRYPTO 2002. LNCS, vol. 2442, pp. 515–532. Springer, Heidelberg (2002)

3. Ekdahl, P., Johansson, T.: Distinguishing Attacks on SOBER-t16 and t32. In: Daemen, J., Rijmen, V. (eds.) FSE 2002. LNCS, vol. 2365, pp. 210–224. Springer, Heidelberg (2002)
4. Tran, B.N., Nguyen, T.D., Tran, T.D.: A New S-Box Structure to Increase Complexity of Algebraic Expression for Block Cipher Cryptosystems. In: 2009 International Conference on Computer Technology and Development (2009)
5. Cui, L., Cao, Y.: A new S-box structure named Affine-Power-Affine. International Journal of Innovative Computing, Information and Control, 751–759 (June 2007)
6. Ekdahl, P., Johansson, T.: A New Version of the Stream Cipher SNOW. In: Nyberg, K., Heys, H.M. (eds.) SAC 2002. LNCS, vol. 2595, pp. 47–61. Springer, Heidelberg (2003)
7. Dichtl, M.: Statistical Test Results for the NESSIE Submission SOBER-t32. NESSIE Document NES/DOC/SAG/WP3/016/2
8. Ekdahl, P., Johansson, T.: Distinguishing Attacks on SOBER-t16 and t32. In: Daemen, J., Rijmen, V. (eds.) FSE 2002. LNCS, vol. 2365, pp. 210–224. Springer, Heidelberg (2002)
9. Watanabe, D., et al.: A Distinguishing Attack of SNOW 2.0 with Linear Masking Method. In: Matsui, M., Zuccherato, R.J. (eds.) SAC 2003. LNCS, vol. 3006, pp. 222–233. Springer, Heidelberg (2004)
10. Nyberg, K., Wallén, J.: Improved Linear Distinguishers for SNOW 2.0. In: Robshaw, M. (ed.) FSE 2006. LNCS, vol. 4047, pp. 144–162. Springer, Heidelberg (2006)
11. Rukhin, A., et al.: A Statistical Test Suite for Random and Pseudorandom Number Generators for Cryptographic Applications. NIST, Special Publication 800-22
12. Hawkes, P., Rose, G.G.: Primitive specification and supporting documentation for SOBER-t32 submission to NESSIE. In: Procedding of First Open NESSIE Workshop (2000)
13. Matsui, M.: Linear Cryptanalysis Method for DES Cipher. In: Helleseth, T. (ed.) EUROCRYPT 1993. LNCS, vol. 765, pp. 386–397. Springer, Heidelberg (1994)

Exploring Object-Level Parallelism
on Chip Multi-processors

Weixing Ji, Yizhuo Wang, Zhi Huang, Junqing Zhao, and Xi Li

Beijing Institute of Technology, Beijing 100081, China
jwx@bit.edu.cn

Abstract. Object-oriented programming languages are prevalent at present and the inherent parallelism of a wide range of applications can be expressed as groups of concurrent objects. This paper proposes a new object-level parallel programming model to meet the challenge of parallel programming on chip multi-processors. This object-based computation model maps multiple software objects onto different physical processor cores at runtime. Independent objects can run concurrently and communicate with each other by synchronous, asynchronous, future and broadcast messages. In order to verify the efficiency of this model, a library implementation CPPLib of this model based on C++ is presented. The library implementation of this model requires no extension to existing object-oriented programming languages and provides good salability and portability. The performance of CPPLib is evaluated on both a dual-core desktop computer and an 8-core server using standard benchmarks. Experimental results show that CPPLib achieves average speedup levels of 1.5 and 3.6 on the dual-core desktop computer and the 8-core server, respectively, compared with their serial version.

Keywords: Parallel computing, Object-orientated programming, Multi-core processor, Message passing, Multi-thread programming.

1 Introduction

There is an ongoing multi-core revolution in computer systems, and the number of cores on a single chip is expected to double every two or three years. 2-core and 4-core processor chips are widely used in the common desktop computers these days, and it is nearly impossible to buy a desktop or laptop that has just a single core in it. As multi-core processor based systems evolve and take over the mainstream, software providers need to threadlize their applications to take advantage of these new platforms. Multi-threaded programming models are relatively well-known despite the fact that threading sequential applications tends to be complex. Software developers face the challenge of obtaining optimal results while overcoming the difficulties of synchronization, scheduling and debugging. In recent years, researchers have proposed a variety of parallel programming languages and associated development tools[1]. Most of these are either completely newly designed concurrent object-oriented programming(OOP) languages or extensions to existing sequential ones. In general, programmers need time to learn

Y. Xiang et al. (Eds.): ICA3PP 2012, Part II, LNCS 7440, pp. 80–89, 2012.

and master these new languages and supporting tools. At present, the existing mature parallel programming language and tools are mainly used to boost the performance of high performance computers, while issues involving the development of parallel software applied to desktop computers remain as active research topics in the field.

Object-based computing model can better describe inherent parallelism in a number of application, because the execution of one object-oriented program performs as a group of active software objects at runtime. The parallel object computing model is not only a combination of OOP and parallel computing, but also a combination of different parallel computing models, such as task parallelism and data parallelism. Multi-core processors can achieve genuine parallel execution of multiple software objects, because they have more than one processing units in a single chip. When a program is running, activated objects can be mapped simultaneously to different physical cores. This paper combines the present object-oriented programming model and the multi-core processor architecture to explore object level parallelism on multi-core processors. A message-based object-level parallel computing model is proposed, and a library-based implementation CPPLib of this model, which uses existing programming language, is presented. The proposed model maps the software objects onto physical cores and schedules active objects to run concurrently. It is flexible in the expression of task parallelism, data parallelism and other parallel patterns through various messages. Moreover, programmers can be trained in mere hours for a quick start on parallel programming, with the help of the library CPPLib. Since the programming language has not changed, programmers can take advantage of the existing integrated development environment for parallel program design and verification.

The rest of this paper is organized as follows: Section 2 introduces the proposed execution model of objects. In Section 3, we show the programming framework of library-based implementation. The evaluation methods and experimental results are given in Section 4. Section 5 discusses the related work, and Section 6 concludes this paper.

2 Object-Based Parallel Programming Model

The main components of object-level parallel computing model include: parallel objects, object aggregations, messages, message manager and worker threads, as shown in Fig. 1.

2.1 Parallel Objects

First, we partition the objects instantiated in the user application into two groups: parallel objects and serial objects. There is no difference between the serial object in our model and the object defined in traditional serial object-oriented programs, which is a compilation of attributes combined with a set of methods for accessing and managing the data. Parallel objects are enhanced serial objects and they indeed have attributes and methods; however, they are mainly entities of parallel tasks and communicate with others via messages. From a programmer's point of view, execution of parallel objects are expected to take up most of program's time, and as such, they are scheduled to run concurrently by the runtime system. In order to define the behaviors clearly, parallel objects are separated into two classes, in accordance with the way that messages are processed. A parallel object with lock(POWL) processes messages one by one and it dose not process a new message until the previous one is totally served. In contrast, a parallel object without lock(PONL) can process multiple messages simultaneously.

2.2   Object Aggregations

Philippsen pointed out in [1] that it is inefficient to spawn activities sequentially; concurrent OOP languages must offer spawning constructs with high fan-out, so that programmers can create more than one new activity at a time. Otherwise, on a machine with p processors it may take p steps to keep all processors busy; such codes are often hard to read and maintain. Object aggregation is provided so that operations can be performed on a collection of parallel objects, thus increasing the fan-out of parallel activities in our model. An aggregation can be initialized either using an object array or adding objects into it one by one. Sending a message to an aggregation is the same as sending this message simultaneously to all the objects in the aggregation. There is no need for all the objects gathered in the same aggregation to be the same type. However, all objects in the same aggregation should have interfaces to process the same message that sent to the aggregation.

2.3   Messages

Parallel objects communicate with one another only through messages. This model supports the following one-to-one messages:

- Asynchronous message: a parallel object can continue to execute and does not need a response;
- Synchronous message: a parallel object is blocked and waits for a response from the receiver;
- Future message: a parallel object dose not need a response from the receiver immediately and can continue to execute forward. When it reaches the point at which the response is needed and the message has not been processed, the sender is blocked and has to wait.

Broadcast messages can be sent to object aggregations. Parallel objects that send broadcast messages must wait for responses from all the objects in the aggregation. Broadcast message and object aggregation facilitate the creation of more than one new activities at a time compared with traditional models.

2.4   Message Manager and Worker Threads

The message manager and worker thread reside in the runtime system and these are transparent to programmers. The message manager is responsible for message construction, delivery, dispatch, and destruction. Once a new message is created, it is delivered to the message manager and stored in a queue. All the messages in the queue can be rescheduled and reordered according to schedule policies. The worker thread retrieves a message from the queue for the idle state, and transfers it to the busy state to process the message. Worker threads run on different physical cores, at this point, processing a specific message is the same as scheduling an object to run on the hosted physical core. Multiple worker threads running in parallel resembles a number of parallel objects running on different processor cores concurrently. Programmers need only to focus on problem analysis and program design, while the runtime system takes care of message management and worker threads.

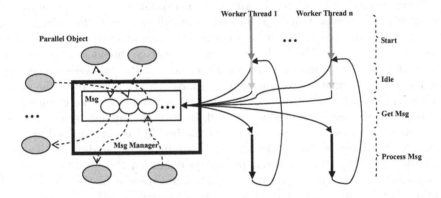

Fig. 1. The execution model of object-level parallelism based on message passing

3   Library-Based Implementation

In this Section, we present a library implementation based on C++ to verify the correctness and efficiency of the proposed model.

3.1   Library Programming Interfaces

We have defined a base class CCObject with various of interfaces for message encapsulation and sending. Only objects of classes derived from CCObject can send messages to other parallel objects. Most of the parallel objects' classes are user declared and contain a number of public interfaces to receive and process messages. The runtime system requires a way to build relationship between the message ID and class interface, so that the runtime system can properly process a message. Therefore, all the child classes derived from CCObject have to implement a message dispatch interface defined in CCObject. Programmers use message-sending interfaces to build one-to-one mapping from the interfaces to the message IDs; meanwhile, they use the message dispatching interface to build one-to-one mapping from message to the interface methods. Although messages plays an important role in this model, most operations on messages are performed in the library to ease the burden on programmers. The message interface provided by CCObject is presented below.

- SendAsyMsg(CCObject* pObj, ulong iMsgID, uint iParaNum, ...)
- SendSyncMsg(CCObject* pObj, ulong iMsgID, uint iParaNum, ...)
- SendFutureMsg(CCObject* pObj, ulong iMsgID, uint iParaNum, ...)
- SendBdctMsg(CAggregation pAgg, ulong iMsgID, uint iParaNum, ...)
- Dispatch(CMsgHandle* pHandle)

We have replaced traditional method calls in object-oriented programs with message passing. The first three interfaces are used to send one-to-one messages, in which the receiver is explicitly designated as pObj. Given that object invoking this interface is implicitly denoted and automatically passed by the compiler to the callee as "this" parameter, it dose not need to appear in the parameter list. The second parameter iMsgID denotes how the message should be processed; it can be the function pointer or any other identifier of the receiver's processing interface. The parameters contained in the message are listed from the third parameter. The number of message parameters is not limited. we cannot predict the type of message processing method, because the number of parameters, parameter types and the return type of the method in the class defined by programmers are different. So the SendAsyMsg, SendSynMsg, SendFutureMsg and SendBdctMsg methods use variable parameter definitions.

A class CAggregation is also declared and implemented in the library as a container of CCObject and CCObject subtypes instances. CAggregations provide interfaces, in which one or multiple instances can be inserted at a time. A barrier synchronization mechanism is realized based on object aggregation to achieve synchronization between multiple objects. Broadcast messages can be sent to multiple objects in the same aggregation and achieve concurrent operation of multiple objects. At the same time, synchronization between concurrent objects can be achieved through barrier synchronization of objects on the specific location of implementation path. Only when all the objects have run to a synchronization point, they can continue to run forward.

3.2   An Example Using the Library Interfaces

Fig. 2 (a) shows the common style to declare two classes *CA* and *CB* in the current object-oriented C++ programs, where an instance object *oa* of class *CA* is declared as a local variable in *CB*'s method *fun2*. The method *fun1* is invoked with parameter *10* passing in and its code segment is executed sequentially. The parallel version of this code segment is shown in Fig. 2 (b), in which all parallel transformations are labeled in bold style. *CA* and *CB* are both declared as the child classes of CCObject, and the instances of these two classes can send messages to each other. Meanwhile, the dispatch interface defined in class CCObject must be implemented in order to map message IDs to method invocations. In this context, the instance object *oa* of class *CA* is a parallel object that can receive messages from other parallel objects. Hence, the method invocation in function *fun2* in the traditional style is changed to send an asynchronous message. As a result, the sender object can run concurrently with the receiver object *oa*.

```
class CA {                      class CA :public CCObject{
public:                         public:
        void fun1(int i){...}            void fun1(int i){...}
...};                                   virtual void Dispatch(CMsgHandle MsgHandle)      {
class CB {                                      if(MsgHandle->GetMsgID() == MSGID(CA::fun1) )
public:                                                 this->fun1(MsgHandle->GetPara(1));
        void fun1(int i){}              ...
...};                                   ...}
CB::fun2()
{       ...                     };
        CA oa;                  class CB :public CCObject{
        oa.fun1(10);            public:
        ...                             void fun1(int i) {... }
}                                       ...
                                };
                                CB::fun2(){  ...
                                        CA oa;
                                        This->SendAsyMsg(&oa,MSGID(CA::fun1), 1, PARA(10))
                                        ...
                                }
        (a)                                     (b)
```

Fig. 2. Comparison of two programming styles

3.3   Object Mapping and Scheduling

In this model, the worker thread attaches to a target parallel object when it receives a message from the queue and detaches from it once the message is completely processed. However, a deadlock may appear if the objects are not well scheduled and some specific messages sequences are generated. We use an active backoff algorithm instead of the typical preemptive ones to reduce context switches in our implementation. The objects detach from the worker thread actively to break the holding and waiting state as it waits for a response from another object.

4   Experiments and Evaluations

4.1   Experiments Setup

Microsoft Windows has dominated the world's personal computer market for several decades occupying approximately 80% of the desktop operating systems market share according to usage share of operating systems [3]. The experiments of this paper are conducted in such an environment where general object-objected design and developing are performed. We tested the scalability of our implementation in 8-core server systems and our detailed system configurations are shown in Table 1.

Table 1. System configuration setup for the experiment

Platform	Processor			Memory(GB)	OS	Compiler	
	Type	Freq.(GHz)	Cores			Compiler	Compiler Para.
Desktop	Core2	2.4	2	2	XP	VS 2008	/O2
Server	Opteron 852	2.6	8	32	Server 2003	VS 2008	/O2

In the current paper, we selected four benchmarks from the PARSEC benchmarks suite [4], which also provides the Intel TBB implementation for these four benchmarks. These TBB implementations were used in our experiment as a comparison.

4.2   Experimental Results

First, we measured the speedup of these benchmarks using CPPLib to show the effectiveness of the CPPLib. Fig. 3 shows the speedup obtained by different parallelization approaches in a desktop dual-core system. As can be seen, the CPPLib and Intel TBB achieved almost the same speedup as the input size increasing. Even in the case of Streamcluster and Blackscholes, CPPLib performed a little better for large inputs; however, for Swaptions and Fluidanimate, CPPLib performed worse than TBB when the input size was small. It gradually matched TBB as inputs size increased. This is mainly due to the current implementation of this library on working threads creation and messages management; it is not well optimized and generates a large overhead in creating threads and messages even when the input set is small.

Fig. 4 shows the speedup comparison when different methods and different number of processor in an 8-core server system are used. 3 different sets of input were used in this test. For Blacksholes, experimental results with input sizes of 16KB, 64KB and 10MB were given. The execution time of benchmarks in this figure was normalized to the serial version. Similar to dual-core desktop system results, the speedups of Streamcluster and Blackscholes using CPPLib were significantly higher than that of TBB. It is noteworthy that in the case of Blackscholes, data size and speedup were inversely proportional, such that the smaller the input data, the bigger speedup. This is mainly due to the manner by which the input data is read. In the beginning of this test procedure, input data were read from file and initialized. When the procedure ended, the data were written back to the file. All these operations were serial, thus taking up a great deal of time. So when the input data was 10M, the speedup we obtained was even lower than what we obtained for 64KB and 16KB. For Swaptions and Fluidanimate, CPPLib and TBB obtained almost the same speedup.

These results shows the good scalability of CPPLib. Given that OOP language has become the mainstream of programming, object-oriented analysis and design methods have a broad and solid industrial base. Compared with the task parallel model used in TBB, the message-based object-oriented parallel computing model is easier to understand and learn. Its expression is also more flexible, thus guaranteeing a wide range of applications.

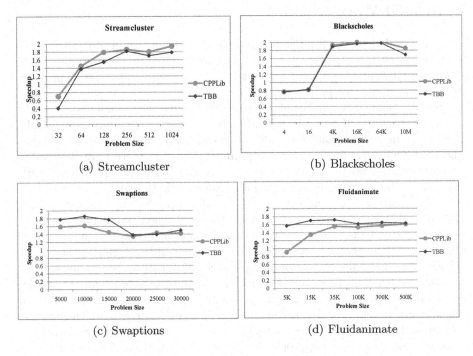

(a) Streamcluster

(b) Blackscholes

(c) Swaptions

(d) Fluidanimate

Fig. 3. Performance of CPPLib on a dual-core processor

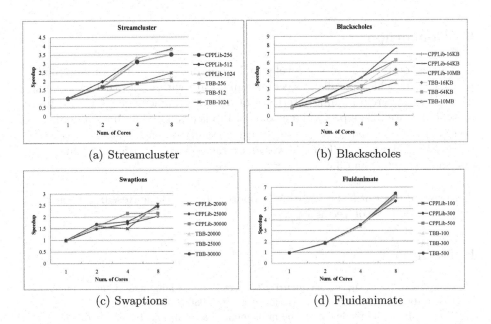

(a) Streamcluster

(b) Blackscholes

(c) Swaptions

(d) Fluidanimate

Fig. 4. Performance of CPPLib on an 8-core sever

5   Related Work

Many proposals have been made to combine the advantages of object-oriented design with increased power of parallel machines. Most of these studies have proposed either new concurrent OOP languages or parallel libraries to provide explicitly constructs for programmers.

Currently, some new parallel object-oriented languages are under study, such as Sun's Fortress [5], IBM's X10 [6] and Cray's Chapel [7]. In addition, PROOF [8] and Erlang [9] are solid examples of parallel languages that combine the concept of OOP and functional programming. Although there have been various parallel language proposed in the past decades [1,10], no concurrent OOP language has been generally accepted and widely used. Mentat [11], pC++ [12], CC++ [13], HPC++ [14] and ICC++ [15] are all concurrent object-oriented language derived from C++. Compared with designing a new parallel language, it is easier to extend a new language than design a new one. However, the compiler must be revised so that it can support the expansion of the parallel part.

Javar [16] can realize the automatic parallelization in Java programs. Giacaman and Sinnen have proposed the task-based object-oriented semi-automatic parallel programming tool [17], which is a source to source compiler and a run-time support system. Liu has provided a basic framework to achieve the object-level parallelism in a cluster system build by multi-core processors [18]; however, no implementation of this approach has been reported so far. Yu have studied and designed a Java source code refracturing compiler JAPS-II [19], which has been used to realize the object-level parallelism in Java programs.

6   Conclusion

This paper proposes an object-level parallel programming model for chip multi-processors, in which parallel objects communicate with each other by sending messages. The programming interfaces of a library implementation have been presented as well. The performance of CPPLib is evaluated on both a dual-core desktop computer and an 8-core server using standard benchmarks. Experimental results show that CPPLib achieves an average speedup of 1.5 on the dual-core desktop computer, and 3.6 on the 8-core server.

Acknowledgements. This work is supported by the Basic Research Programs of Beijing Institute of Technology.

References

1. Philippsen, M.: A survey of concurrent object-oriented languages. Concurrency and Computation: Practice and Experience 12, 917–980 (2000)
2. Boehm, H.-J.: Threads cannot be implemented as a library. In: Proceedings of the 2005 ACM SIGPLAN Conference on Programming Language Design and Implementation, Chicago, IL, USA, pp. 261–268 (June 2005)

3. Wikipedia, Usage share of operating systems (2011),
   http://en.wikipedia.org/wiki/Usage_share_of_operating_systems
4. Bienia, C., Kumar, S., Singh, J.P., Li, K.: The PARSEC Benchmark Suite: Characterization and Architectural Implications. In: Proceedings of the 17th International Conference on Parallel Architectures and Compilation Techniques (October 2008)
5. Sun Microsystems Inc., The Fortress Language Specification, Version 1.0 (2008),
   http://research.sun.com/projects/plrg/fortress.pdf
6. IBM Inc., The X10 Programming Language, http://domino.research.ibm.com/comm/research_projects.nsf/pages/x10.index.html
7. Chamberlain, B.L., Callahan, D., Zima, H.P.: Parallel Programmability and the Chapel Language. International Journal of High Performance Computing Applications 21(3), 291–312 (2007)
8. Stephen, S.: PROOF: a parallel object-oriented functional computation model. Journal of Parallel and Distributed Computing 12(3), 202–212 (1991)
9. http://www.erlang.org
10. Yu, M., Zang, W.Y., Xie, L., Guo, Y.M.: A Survey of Parallel Object-Oriented Language. Journal of Software 12(6), 822–829 (2001)
11. Grimshaw, A.S.: Easy-to-Use object-oriented parallel processing with Mentat. IEEE Computer 26(5), 39–51 (1993)
12. Gannon, D., Yang, S.X., Beckman, P.: User guide for a portable parallel C++ programming system: pC++. Technical Report, Indiann University (1994)
13. Carlin, P., Chundy, M., Kesselman, C.: The CC++ language definition,
    http://globus.isi.edu/ccpp/
14. Diwan, S., Johnson, E., Gannon, D.: HPC++ and the Europa call reification model. ACM Applied Computing Review 4(1), 251–269 (1996)
15. Chien, A., Dolby, J., Ganguly, B., et al.: Supporting high level programming with high performance: the Illinois concert system. In: Proceedings of the 2nd International Workshop on High-Level Parallel Programming Models and Supportive Environments, pp. 147–162 (1997)
16. Bik, A.J.C., Gannon, D.B.: Automatic exploiting implicit parallelism in java. Concurrency, Practice and Experience 9(6), 576–619 (1997)
17. Giacaman, N., Sinnen, O.: Task Parallelism for Object Oriented Programs. In: Proceeding of the International Symposium on Parallel Architectures, Algorithms and Networks, pp. 13–18 (2008)
18. Liu, X.: Exploiting Object-Based Parallelism on Multi-Core Multi-Processor Clusters. In: Eighth International Conference on Parallel and Distributed Computing (2007)
19. Yu, M., Chen, G.H., Yang, X.L., Xie, L., Guo, Y.M.: JAPS-II: a Parallelizing Compiler for Java. Journal of Software 13(4), 739–746 (2002)

The Hamiltonicity of WK-Recursive Pyramid

Yi-Chun Wang and Justie Su-Tzu Juan*

Department of Computer Science and Information Engineering
National Chi Nan University, Nantou, R.O.C.
{s96321901,jsjuan}@ncnu.edu.tw

Abstract. Fernandes and Kanevsky proposed an important structure in interconnection network, WKR Pyramid Networks ($\text{WKP}_{(d,t,L)}$, for short), in 1993. They are constructed by taking difference size WK-recursive network as difference layers. That paper discussed about the orders sizes and connectivity. $\text{WKP}_{(d,L)}$ is a simple version of $\text{WKP}_{(d,t,L)}$. In $\text{WKP}_{(d,L)}$, each vertex has exactly d children and the nth layer is isomorphic to a $\text{WK}_{(d,n)}$. In this paper, we show that $\text{WKP}_{(d,L)}$ is Hamiltonian-connected, for $d \geq 3$.

Keywords: WK-recursive, $\text{WKP}_{(d,L)}$, Hamiltonian-connected, Pyramid, topology.

1 Introduction

The interconnection network plays a central role in determining the overall performance of a multiprocessor/multicomputer system. If the networks cannot provide adequate performance for a particular application, nodes will frequently be forced to wait for data to arrive. Therefore, it is important to design an interconnection network with better performance for those properties. Let processes or cores be considered as vertices, and communication channels be considered as edges, thus all problems on interconnection networks can be discussed on graphs.

Suppose that G is a graph. A path (cycle) in G is called a *Hamiltonian path* (*Hamiltonian cycle*) if it contains every node of G exactly once. G is called *Hamiltonian* if there is a Hamiltonian cycle in G, and it is called *Hamiltonian-connected* if there is a Hamiltonian path between every two distinct nodes of G [2]. Some topologies, such as the hierarchical cubic network [6], are Hamiltonian-connected.

A parallel algorithm is an algorithm which can be executed a piece at a time on many different processing devices, after that, put the results back together to get the correct result. It is usful because it has a great improvement on efficiency of the multiprocessing systems. If a network can embed the longest linear array between any two distinct nodes with dilation, congestion and load all equal to one, all parallel algorithms designed for linear arrays can be executed on this network as well. Hence, we discuss the Hamiltonian properties of graphs.

---

* Corresponding author.

Y. Xiang et al. (Eds.): ICA3PP 2012, Part II, LNCS 7440, pp. 90–99, 2012.
© Springer-Verlag Berlin Heidelberg 2012

In 1986, Lu [8] proposed Hanoi graphs. It is corresponding to the allowed moves in the tower of Hanoi problem. Compare Hanoi graphs with triangular meshs, meshs and toroidal meshs. They are all Hamiltonian. For the same dimensions, although Hanoi graphs have more vertices than triangular meshs, but it have less vertices than meshs and toroidal meshs. At the same time, Hanoi graphs have lower degree for any internal vertex than each internal vertex in triangular meshs, toroidal meshs or meshs. [1] and [10] are also two research on Hanoi graphs. So we can say Hanoi graphs have good performance in some way that triangular meshs, toroidal meshs and meshs.

The d dimension n amplitude WK-recursive network (WK$_{(d,n)}$, for short), proposed in 1992 by Fernandes [4], is a network that is recursively defined and is expandable to any level. This is also well-known networks in network computing, there are several researches on WK-recursive network ([3], [7], [9]). In fact, The WK$_{(d,n)}$ is a general version of Hanoi graphs, i.e. the Hanoi graphs is isomorphic to WK$_{(3,n)}$.

In 1993, Fernandes and Kanevsky proposed two hierarchical WK-recursive topologies, Hierarchical WK-Recursive networks and WKR Pyramid Networks (HWK$_{(d,t,L)}$ and WKP$_{(d,t,L)}$, for short, respectively) [5]. They are constructed by taking difference size WK-recursive network as difference layers. [5] discussed about the orders sizes and connectivy of HWK$_{(d,t,L)}$ and WKP$_{(d,t,L)}$.

In 2008, Razavi and Sarbazi-Azad claimed that a special graph, called WKP, is Hamiltonian and pancyclic, and also prove those properties [9]. In fact, this paper only discusses a special case of WKP$_{(d,t,L)}$. In topology WKP, each vertex has exactly 4 children, and those children form a complete K_4.

In this paper, we discuss another special version of WKP$_{(d,t,L)}$, denoted by WKP$_{(d,L)}$. In WKP$_{(d,L)}$, each vertex has exactly d children and the nth layer is isomorphic to a WK$_{(d,n)}$. Therefore, the topology that proposed by Razavi and Sarbazi-Azad in 2008 [9] is WKP$_{(4,L)}$ by our definition.

We will give some definitions and show some preliminaries in Section 2. Section 3 prove the main result that WKP$_{(d,L)}$ is Hamiltonian-connected for any positive integer $d \geq 3$, $L \geq 1$. Some conclusion are given in Section 4.

2   Definitions and Perlimilaries

In this section, we give the definition of WKP$_{(d,L)}$ and show some preliminaries of WK$_{(d,t)}$ and WKP$_{(d,L)}$. At first, we review the definition of WK-recursive network. Fig. 1 is an illustration of WK$_{(3,3)}$.

Definition 1. [4] *A radix-t WK-recursive network, denoted as WK$_{(d,t)}$, consists of a set of nodes $V(WK_{(d,t)}) = \{a_{t-1}a_{t-2}...a_1a_0 | 0 \leq a_i \leq d, 0 \leq i \leq t-1\}$. Each node $a_{t-1}a_{t-2}...a_1a_0$ is adjacent to 1) $a_{t-1}a_{t-2}...a_1b$, where $b \neq a_0$; and adjacent to 2) $a_{t-1}a_{t-2}...a_{j+1}b_1(b_0)^j$, if $a_j \neq a_{j-1}$ and $a_{j-1} = a_{j-2} = ... = a_0$, where $b_1 = a_{j-1}, b_0 = a_j$, where $(b_0)^j$ denotes j consecutive b_0s.*

For convenience, $a_{t-1}a_{t-2}...a_1a_0$ is called the *labelling* of a node in $V(WK_{(d,t)})$.

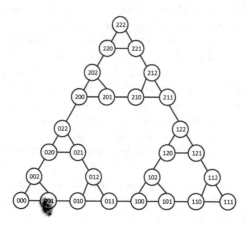

Fig. 1. The structure of $WK_{(3,3)}$

Definition 2. [5] *A WK-recursive pyramid network of height* $L, WKP_{(d,t,L)}$, *consists of a set of nodes* $V(WKP_{(d,t,L)}) = \{(k, a_{tk-1}a_{tk-2} \ldots a_1 a_0)|\ 1 \le k \le L, 0 \le a_i < d, 0 \le i \le tk - 1\}$ *arranged in* L *levels of WK-recursive network. A node is addressed as* $(k, a_{tk-1}a_{tk-2} \ldots a_1 a_0)$ *and is said to be a node at level* k. *The part* $a_{tk-1}a_{tk-2} \ldots a_1 a_0$ *of the address determines the address of a node within the layer* k *of the WK-recursive network. The nodes at level* k *form a network of* $WK_{(d,tk)}$, *i.e., a node with the address* $(k, a_{tk-1}a_{tk-2} \ldots a_1 a_0)$ *placed at level* k *of the* $WK_{(d,tk)}$ *network, is connected to adjacent nodes as defined in Definition 1. This node is also connected to nodes* $(k+1, a_{tk-1}a_{tk-2} \ldots a_1 a_0 (0)^t), (k+1, a_{tk-1}a_{tk-2} \ldots a_1 a_0 (1)^t), \ldots, (k+1, a_{tk-1}a_{tk-2} \ldots a_1 a_0 (d-1)^t)$ *in level* $k + 1$, *as childnodes, and to node* $(k-1, a_{tk-1}a_{tk-2} \ldots a_{t+1}a_t)$ *as the parent, if* $a_{t-1} = a_{t-2} = \ldots = a_0$.

Fig. 2 shows $WKP_{(4,2,2)}$. In this paper, we consider the variable $t = 1$ in $WKP_{(d,t,L)}$, i.e., this is a simple version $WKP_{(d,t,L)}$. Because the Lth leval of this topology is a $WK_{(d,L)}$, we denote the simpler structure by $WKP_{(d,L)}$, and we give the definition as follows.

Definition 3. *A WK-recursive pyramid network,* $WKP_{(d,L)}$, *consists of a set of nodes* $V(WKP_{(d,L)}) = \{(k, a_{k-1}a_{k-2} \ldots a_1 a_0)|\ 1 \le k \le L, 0 \le a_i < d, 0 \le i \le k-1\}$ *arranged in* L *levels of WK-recursive network. A node is addressed as* $(k, a_{k-1}a_{k-2} \ldots a_1 a_0)$ *and is said to be a node at level* k. *The part* $a_{k-1}a_{k-2} \ldots a_1 a_0$ *of the address determines the address of a node within the layer* k *of the WK-recursive network. The nodes at level* k *form a network of* $WK_{(d,k)}$, *i.e., a node* v *with the address* $(k, a_{k-1}a_{k-2} \ldots a_1 a_0)$ *placed at level* k *of the* $WK_{(d,k)}$ *network, is connected to adjacent nodes as defined in Definition 1. This node is also connected to nodes* $(k + 1, a_{k-1}a_{k-2} \ldots a_1 a_0 0), (k + 1, a_{k-1}a_{k-2} \ldots a_1 a_0 1) \ldots (k+1, a_{k-1}a_{k-2}, \ldots, a_1 a_0 (d - 1)$ *in level* $k + 1$, *as childnodes, and to node* $(k-1, a_{k-1}a_{k-2}, \ldots, a_1)$ *as the parent,* $p(v)$. *Conversely,* v *is a child of* $p(v)$. *In the other words, the node* $p(v)$ *has* d *children, and* v *is one of them.*

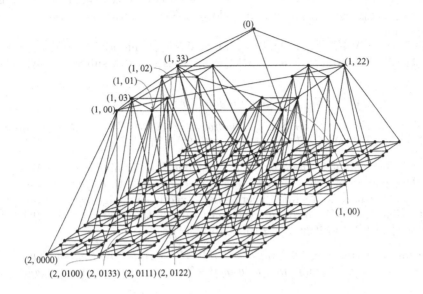

Fig. 2. The structure of $WKP_{(4,2,2)}$

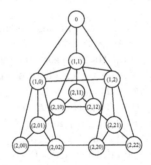

Fig. 3. The structure of $WKP_{(3,2)}$

Fig. 3 shows $WKP_{(3,2)}$. For convenient, a level k of $WKP_{(d,L)}$ is denoted by $WK^*_{(d,k)}$ in this paper. For $1 \leq k \leq L$, $V(WK^*_{(d,k)}) = \{(k, x_{k-1}x_{k-2} \ldots x_1x_0)|1 \leq k \leq n, 0 \leq x_i \leq d - 1 \text{ and } 0 \leq i \leq k - 1\}$, and $E(WK^*_{(d,k)}) = \{(k, x_{k-1}x_{k-2} \ldots x_1x_0) (k, x_{k-1}x_{k-2} \ldots x_1\alpha)|\alpha \neq x_0\} \bigcup \{(k, x_{k-1}x_{k-2} \ldots x_i\beta_1(\beta_2)^{i-1})(k, x_{k-1}x_{k-2} \ldots x_i \beta_2(\beta_1)^{i-1})|\beta_1 \neq \beta_2 \text{ and } 2 \leq i \leq k\}$.

In addition, we define another subgraph of $WKP_{(d,L)}$. Let $c_{t-1}c_{t-2} \ldots c_m$ be a specific $(t - m)$-digit radix d number. Define $c_{t-1}c_{t-2} \ldots c_m \cdot WKP_{(d,m)}$ as the subgraph of $WKP_{(d,t)}$ induced by $\{(m-t+k, c_{t-1}c_{t-2} \ldots c_m a_{k-1}a_{k-2} \ldots a_1a_0)|$

$0 \leq k \leq m - 1$ and $a_{k-1}a_{k-2}\ldots a_1a_0$ is a k-digit radix d number}; that is, $c_{t-1}c_{t-2}\ldots c_m \cdot \text{WKP}_{(d,m)}$is an embedded $\text{WKP}_{(d,m)}$ with the identifier c_{t-1} $c_{t-2}\ldots c_m$.

In Fig. 3, $0 \cdot \text{WKP}_{(3,1)}$ is the subgraph of $\text{WKP}_{(3,2)}$ induced by $\{(1,0),(2,00),$ $(2,01),(2,02)\}$. Note that each $c \cdot \text{WKP}_{(d,L-1)}$ is called a subgraph with level $L-1$.

Lemma 1. [11] $WK_{(3,t)}$ *is Hamiltonian, for* $t \geq 1$.

Lemma 2. *For* $t \geq 1$, *for any a Hamiltonian cycle of* $WK_{(3,t)}$, *it must contain* $\{(0(1)^{t-1})(1(0)^{t-1}),(1(2)^{t-1})(2(1)^{t-1}),(2(0)^{t-1})\,(0(2)^{t-1})\}$.

Proof. By Lemma 1, there exists at least one Hamiltonian cycle in $\text{WK}_{(3,t)}$. By the defintion of $\text{WK}_{(d,t)}$, $\text{WK}_{(3,t)}$ can be divide into three parts by the first digit of each node's labeling. There exists exactly one edge between any two parts. Hence, each Hamiltonian cycle must contain those three edges $\{(0(1)^{t-1})$ $(1(0)^{t-1}),(1(2)^{t-1})\,(2(1)^{t-1}),(2(0)^{t-1})(0(2)^{t-1})\}$. □

Lemma 3. *In* $WKP_{(3,L)}$, *for any* $L \geq 2$, *if* $WKP_{(3,L-1)}$ *is Hamiltonian-connected, there exists an* x-y *Hamiltonian path in* $WKP_{(3,L)}$ *for any* $y \in WK^*_{(3,L)}$ *and* $x = p(y)$.

Proof. Because $x = p(y)$, we assume $x = (L-1,a_{L-1}a_{L-2}\ldots a_1)$ and $y = (L,a_{L-1}a_{L-2}\ldots a_1a_0)$. Without loss of generality, let $a_{L-1} = 0$. Hence, $x,y \in V(0 \cdot \text{WKP}_{(3,L-1)})$. We divide the proof into two cases.

Case 1: $L = 2$. There exist three conditions in this case. we show the x-y Hamiltonian path in Fig. 4.

Case 2: $L \geq 3$. By assumption, there exists an x-y Hamiltonian path P in $0 \cdot \text{WKP}_{(3,L-1)}$. Hence, the vertex $(1,0)$ and one of edges $\{(1,0)(2,01),$ $(1,0)(2,02)\}$ must be in P, say $e = (1,0)(2,01) \in E(P)$. We break the edge e, and obtain two subpaths of P, x-z path P_1 and z'-y path P_2, where z is one of $\{(1,0),(2,01)\}$ and z' is the other. Without loss of generality, let $z = (2,01)$ and $z' = (1,0)$. By assumption, $\text{WKP}_{(3,L-1)}$ is Hamiltonian-connected, there exist $(2,10)$-$(L,1(2)^{L-1})$ Hamiltonian path Q_1 and $(L,2(1)^{L-1})$-$(1,2)$ Hamiltonian path Q_2 in $1 \cdot \text{WKP}_{(3,L-1)}$ and $2 \cdot \text{WKP}_{(3,L-1)}$, respectively. Then, we construct a x-y Hamiltonian path $\langle x, P_1, z = (2,01),(2,10), Q_1,(L,1(2)^{L-1}),(L,2(1)^{L-1}), Q_2,(1,2),$ $(0), z' = (1,0), P_2, y\rangle$ in $\text{WKP}_{(3,L)}$. (See Fig.5) □

Lemma 4. [7] *For* $d \geq 4$, *any two verties* $A = a_{t-1}a_{t-2}\ldots a_1a_0$ *and* $B = b_{t-1}b_{t-2}\ldots b_1b_0$ *in* $WK_{d,t}$, *there exist an* A-B *Hamiltonian path.*

3   Hamiltonian-Connectedness of $\text{WKP}_{(d,L)}$

In this section, we divide the main result of this paper into two theorems. First is the Hamiltonian-connectedness of $\text{WKP}_{(3,L)}$. Another is the Hamiltonian-connectedness of $\text{WKP}_{(d,L)}$, for $d \geq 3$. For conveniens, we say $P^{-1} = \langle u_{m-1},$

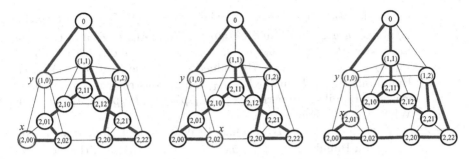

Fig. 4. The constrution of Case 1 of Lemma 3

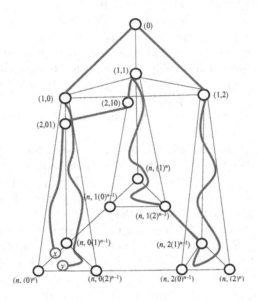

Fig. 5. The constrution of Case 2 of Lemma 3

$u_{m-2}, \cdots, u_1, u_0\rangle$ is a u_{m-1}-u_0, where $P = \langle u_0, u_1, \cdots, u_{m-2}, u_{m-1}\rangle$ is a u_0-u_{m-1} path.

Theorem 1. *For $L \geq 1$ is a positive interger, any two vertices $x = (k_1, x_{k_1-1}$ $x_{k_1-2} \cdots x_1 x_0)$ and $y = (k_2, y_{k_2-1} y_{k_2-2} \cdots y_1 y_0) \in V(WKP_{(3,L)})$.*

1) there exists a x-y Hamiltonian path P,

2) P contains at least one of $\{(L, 0(1)^{L-1})(L, 1(0)^{L-1}), (L, 1(2)^{L-1}) (L, 2(1)^{L-1}), (L, 2(0)^{L-1})(L, 0(2)^{L-1})\}$.

Proof. We prove the theorem by induction on L. It is clear for $L = 1$. Assume it holds for $L = n - 1$. Now we consider $L = n$, without loss of generality, we assume $k_1 \leq k_2$. The proof can be divided into three cases.

Case 1: $k_1 = k_2 = n$. By Lemma 1, $WK^*_{(3,n)}$ is a Hamiltonian. There exists a Hamiltonian cycle $C = \langle u_0, u_1, \ldots, u_{m-1}, u_0\rangle$ such that $x = u_0$,

$y = u_1$ for some $0 \leq i \leq m-1$, where $m = |V(\mathrm{WK}^*_{(d,k)})|$. We delete $u_0 u_1$ and $u_i u_{i+1}$ in C, and obtain two subpaths of C and C^{-1}: x-u_{i+1} path $P_1 = \langle x = u_0, u_{m-1}, \ldots, u_{i+2}, u_{i+1} \rangle$ and u_1-y path $P_2 = \langle u_1, u_2, \ldots, u_{i-1}, u_i = y \rangle$. By induction hypothesis, a $p(u_{i+1})$-$p(u_1)$ Hamiltonian path P_3 in $\mathrm{WKP}_{(3,n-1)}$ can be constructed. Hence, There exists an Hamiltonian path $\langle x, P_1, u_{i+1}, p(u_{i+1}), P_3, p(u_1), u_1, P_2, y \rangle$ in $\mathrm{WKP}_{(3,n)}$. (See Fig.6(a))

Case 2: $k_1 \neq n$ and $k_2 = n$. By Lemma 1, $\mathrm{WK}^*_{(3,n)}$ is a Hamiltonian. We can find a Hamiltonian cycle $\langle u_0, u_1, \ldots, u_{m-1}, u_1 \rangle$ such that $y = u_0$, where $m = |V(\mathrm{WK}^*_{(3,n)})|$. We consider the positions of u_{m-1}, u_0, u_1 and x, then have two subcases.

  Case 2.1: $\{p(u_m), p(u_1)\} - \{x\} \neq \emptyset$. Let $z \in u_{m-1}, u_1$ such that $p(z) \neq x$. Without loss of generality, we assume that $z = u_{(m-1)}$. Hence, $Q_1 = \langle u_0, u_1, \ldots, u_{m-1} = z \rangle$. And, there exists an x-$p(z)$ Hamiltonian path Q_2 on $\mathrm{WKP}_{(3,n-1)}$. by induction hypothesis. Hence, the Hamiltonian path $\langle x, Q_2, p(z), z, Q_1, y \rangle$ in $\mathrm{WKP}_{(3,n)}$ is constructed. (See Fig.6(b))

  Case 2.2: $p(u_{m-1}) = p(u_1) = x$. In this situation, $p(u_0) = x$, too. By Lemma 3, there exists an x-y Hamiltonian path in $\mathrm{WKP}_{(3,n)}$.

Case 3: $k_1, k_2 < n$. By induction hypothesis, we construct an x-y Hamiltonian path R in $\mathrm{WKP}_{3,n-1}$ such that this Hamiltonian path contains at least one of $\{(n-1,0(1)^{n-2})(n-1,1(0)^{n-2}), (n-1,1(2)^{n-2})$ $(n-1,2(1)^{n-2}), (n-1,2(0)^{n-2})(n-1,0(2)^{n-2})\}$. Without loss of generality, we assume that R contains $(n-1,0(1)^{n-2})(n-1,1(0)^{n-2})$. If we deleted the edge $(n-1,0(1)^{n-2})(n-1,1(0)^{n-2})$, we obtain two sunpaths of R and R^{-1}, R_1 and R_2, respectively. Without loss of generality, we assume that R_1 is x-$(n-1,0(1)^{n-2})$ path, and R_2 is y-$(n-1,1(0)^{n-2})$ path. When we consider $\mathrm{WK}^*_{(3,n)}$, there exists a Hamiltonian cycle C that contains $(n,0(1)^{n-1})(n,1(0)^{n-1}), (n,1(2)^{n-1})$ $(n,2(1)^{n-1})$ and $(n,2(0)^{n-1})(n,0(2)^{n-1})$ by Lemma 2. We delete the edge $(n,0(1)^{n-1})($ $n,1(0)^{n-1})$ and let R_3 be the $(n,0(1)^{n-1})$-$(n,1(0)^{n-1})$ Hamiltonian path in $\mathrm{WK}^*_{(3,n)}$ such that $R_3 = C - (n,0(1)^{n-1})(n,1(0)^{n-1})$. Hence, the Hamiltonian path $\langle x, R_1, (n-1,0(1)^{n-2}), (n,0(1)^{n-1}), R_3, (n,1(0)$ $^{n-1}), (n-1,1(0)^{n-2}) R_2, y \rangle$ in $\mathrm{WKP}_{(3,n)}$ is constructed. (See Fig.6(c))

Because of Lemma 2 and only one or two edges of Hamiltonian cycle in $\mathrm{WK}^*_{(3,n)}$ at Case 1, Case 2.1 and Case3 are deleted; and because of Lemma 3 will made one of these three edges be included in the constructed x-y Hamiltonian path of Case 2.2, the Hamiltonian path in $\mathrm{WKP}_{(3,n)}$ still contains at least one of $\{(n,0(1)^{n-1})(n,1(0)^{n-1}), (n,1(2)^{n-1})$ $(n,2(1)^{n-1}), (n,2(0)^{n-1})(n,0(2)^{n-1})\}$. $\square$

Theorem 2. *For $d \geq 4$, $L \geq 1$, $WKP_{(d,L)}$ is Hamiltonian-connected.*

Proof. We proved this theorem by induction on L. Clearly, the theorem holds for $L = 1$, because $\mathrm{WKP}_{(d,1)}$ isomorphic to K_{d+1}, the complete graph. Assume it holds

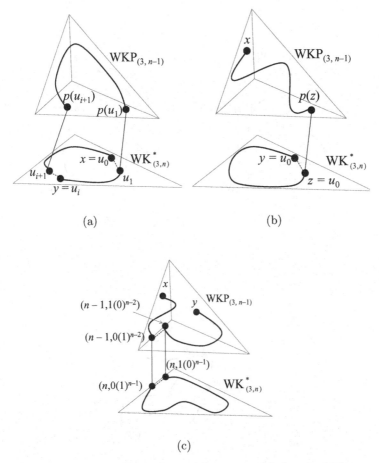

Fig. 6. The constrution of (a) Case 1 (b) Case 2.1 (c) Case 3 of Theorem 1

for $L = n - 1$. The condiction in the case of $L = n$ is discussed below. We consinder any two vertices $x = (k_1, x_{k_1-1}x_{k_1-2} \cdots x_1 x_0)$ and $y = (k_2, y_{k_2-1}y_{k_2-2} \cdots y_1 y_0) \in V(\mathrm{WKP}_{(d,n)})$. Without loss of generality, we assume $k_1 \leq k_2$. Three cases will be considered:

Case 1: By Lemma 4, we find an x-y Hamiltonian path $P = \langle x = u_0, u_1, \ldots, u_{m-1} = y \rangle$ of $\mathrm{WK}^*_{(d,t)}$, where $m = |V(\mathrm{WK}^*_{(d,n)})|$. We choose an integer $1 \leq z \leq m - 2$ and delete the edge (u_z, u_{z+1}) such that $p(u_z)p(u_{z+1})$, then we obtain two subpaths, x-u_z path P_1 and u_{z+1}-y path P_2, of P. By induction hypothesis, there exists a $p(u_z)$-$p(u_{z+1})$ Hamiltonian path P_3 in $\mathrm{WKP}_{(3,n-1)}$. Hence, a Hamiltonian path $\langle x, P_1, u_z, p(u_z), P_3, p(u_{z+1}), P_2, y \rangle$ of $\mathrm{WKP}_{(d,n)}$ is constructed. (See Fig.7(a))

Case 2: $k_1 \neq n$ and $k_2 = n$. There exists a vertex $y' \in V(\mathrm{WK}^*_{(d,n)})$ such that $y' \neq y$ and $p(y') \neq x$. By Lemma 4, we find a y'-y Hamiltonian path $Q_1 = \langle y' = u_0, u_1, \ldots, u_{m-1} = y \rangle$ of $\mathrm{WK}^*_{(d,t)}$, where

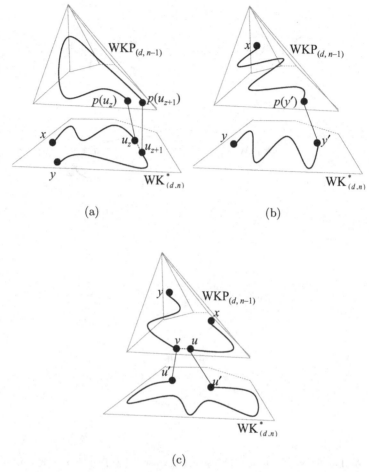

(a)

(b)

(c)

Fig. 7. The constrution of (a) Case 1 (b) Case 2.1 (c) Case 3 of Theorem 2

$m = |V(\mathrm{WK}^*_{(d,n)})|$. In $\mathrm{WKP}_{(d,n-1)}$, there exists an x-$p(y')$ Hamiltonian path Q_2 by induction hypothesis. Hence, a Hamiltonian path $\langle x, Q_2, p(y'), y', Q_1, y \rangle$ of $\mathrm{WKP}_{(d,n)}$ is constructed. (See Fig.7(b))

Case 3: $k_1, k_2 < n$. That is, x and y are in $\mathrm{WKP}_{(d,n-1)}$. There exists an x-y Hamiltonian path R in $\mathrm{WKP}_{d,n-1}$ by induction hypothesis. For any vertex $u \in V(\mathrm{WK}^*_{(d,n-1)})$, there exists exactly one neighbor in $\mathrm{WK}^*_{(d,n-2)}$, i.e., there exists a edge $uv \in E(\mathrm{WK}^*_{(d,n-1)}) \bigcap E(R)$ (it is possible that $u = x$ or $v = y$). If we deleted the edge uv, we obtain two subpaths R_1 and R_2 of R. Without loss of generality, we assume that R_1 is x-u path, and R_2 is v-y path. Let u' and v' be one child of u and

v, respecively. By Lemma 4, there exists an u'-v' Hamiltonian path R_3 in $\mathrm{WK}^*_{(d,n)}$. Hence, A Hamiltonian path $\langle x, R_1, u, u', R_3, v', v, R_2, y \rangle$ of $\mathrm{WKP}_{(d,n)}$ is constructed. (See Fig.7(c))   □

By above two theorems, we have the following corollary.

Corollary 1. *For $d \geq 3$, $L \geq 1$, $WKP_{(d,L)}$ is Hamiltonian-connected.*

4 Conclusion

In this paper, showed that $\mathrm{WKP}_{(d,L)}$ is Hamiltonian-connected, for any $d \geq 3$ and $L \geq 1$. That is, there exists a Hamiltonian path between any two distinct nodes of $\mathrm{WKP}_{(d,L)}$.

In the near future, we will try to find the diameter, radius and average distance of $\mathrm{WKP}_{(d,L)}$. At the same time, we also try to find the Hamiltonian-connectedness with node or edge faults in $\mathrm{WKP}_{(d,L)}$. After that, we will also develop the routing and broadcast algorithm of $\mathrm{WKP}_{(d,L)}$. Because $\mathrm{WKP}_{(d,L)}$ is a variant of Pyramid, all properities of $\mathrm{WKP}_{(d,L)}$, Pyramid, Enhance Pyramid and Trangular Pyramid will be compared.

References

1. Berend, D., Sapir, A.: The diameter of hanoi graphs. Information Processing Letter 98, 79–85 (2006)
2. Buckley, F., Harary, F.: Distance in Graphs. Addisson-Wesley, Reading (1990)
3. Chen, G.H., Duh, D.R.: Topological properties, communication, and computation on wk-recursive network. Networks 24(6), 303–317 (1994)
4. Fernandes, R.: Recursive interconnection networks for multicomputer networks. In: Proceedings of the 1992 International Conference on Parallel Processing, vol. I, pp. 76–79 (1992)
5. Fernandes, R., Kanevsky, A.: Hierarchical wk-recursive topologies for multicomputer systems. In: Proceedings of the 1993 International Conference on Parallel Processing, vol. I, pp. 315–318 (1993)
6. Fu, J.S., Chen, G.H.: Hamiltonicity of the hierarchical cubic network. Theory of Computing Systems 35(1), 59–79 (2002)
7. Fu, J.-S.: Hamiltonicity of the wk-recursive network with and without faulty nodes. IEEE Transactions on Parallel and Distribured Systems 16(9), 853–865 (2005)
8. Lu, X.M.: Towers of hanoi graphs. International Journal Computer Mathematics 19, 23–28 (1986)
9. Razavi, S., Sarbazi-Azad, H.: The triangular pyramid: Routing and topological properties. Information Sciences 180, 2328–2339 (2010)
10. Romik, D.: Shortest paths in the tower of hanoi graph and finite automata. SIAM Journal on Discrete Mathematic 20, 610–622 (2003)
11. Zivkovic, D.: Hamiltonianicity of the tower of hanoi problem. Univ. Beograd. Publ. Elektrotehn. Fak. Ser. Mat. 17, 31–37 (2006)

Towards Multi-level Adaptation
for Distributed Operating Systems
and Applications

Djawida Dib[1,*], Nikos Parlavantzas[1,2], and Christine Morin[1]

[1] INRIA, Campus de Beaulieu, 35042 Rennes Cedex, France
[2] INSA de Rennes, Campus de Beaulieu, 35708 Rennes Cedex, France
{Djawida.Dib,Nikos.Parlavantzas,Christine.Morin}@inria.fr

Abstract. Distributed operating systems simplify building and executing applications on large-scale infrastructures, such as clusters, grids and
clouds. These systems operate in a constantly changing environment
characterized by varying application needs and varying physical infrastructure capabilities. To handle the diversity and dynamism of both the
applications and the underlying infrastructures, the distributed Operating System (OS) should continually adapt to its changing environment.
Two challenges arise in this context: how to design the distributed OS in
order to facilitate dynamic adaptation, and how to ensure that OS-level
adaptation does not conflict with application-level adaptation. This paper proposes to address these challenges by: (1) building the distributed
OS as an assembly of adaptable services following the service-oriented
architecture; and (2) using a common multi-level adaptation framework
to adapt both the OS and the application layers in a coordinated way.
Moreover, the paper presents experimental evidence of the usefulness of
this approach in adapting the distributed shared memory service of a
specific distributed OS.

Keywords: distributed operating system, service-oriented architecture,
multi-level adaptation, distributed shared memory.

1 Introduction

Distributed Operating Systems (OSs) provide common services and abstractions
for building applications on large-scale infrastructures such as clusters [14][3],
grids [13][8] and clouds [1][2]. These systems operate in a constantly changing
environment characterized by varying application needs and physical infrastructure capabilities. To deal with this dynamicity, it is essential for the distributed
OS to support dynamic adaptation. For example, it should support dynamically
modifying communication protocols depending on application usage patterns or
network conditions.

Service-Oriented Architectures (SOAs) have recently emerged as a popular
approach for building flexible software systems [15]. A service-oriented system

---

* The research leading to these results is co-funded by the Brittany Region.

Y. Xiang et al. (Eds.): ICA3PP 2012, Part II, LNCS 7440, pp. 100–109, 2012.

is an assembly of services, where each service represents a well-defined function. The flexibility of SOA results from the dynamic capability to publish, discover and use services as well as modify their implementations without impacting their consumers. While SOA has been widely applied to build distributed applications [20], it is less explored in building the supporting system software. In this paper, we propose to apply the SOA at the OS level in order to facilitate the OS dynamic adaptation.

Supporting dynamic adaptation of the distributed OS is introducing further challenges, such as detecting when adaptation is needed and deciding what and how to adapt in order to achieve specific objectives. One important challenge, which is not addressed by related research work, is ensuring that OS-level adaptation does not conflict with application-level adaptation. For example, a particular performance problem could be addressed by replacing a service at the application layer or by allocating more resources at the OS layer; performing both adaptations could be inefficient or damaging. To address this challenge, we propose to use a multi-level adaptation framework that coordinates the adaptation of both the application and the OS layers based on configurable policies. Experimental results are provided to demonstrate the usefulness of this approach.

This paper is organized as follows. Section 2 introduces the service-oriented OS. Section 3 discusses the need for a multi-level adaptation framework. Section 4 presents the multi-level adaptation architecture. Section 5 shows the usefulness of the proposed approach with the distributed shared memory example. Section 6 presents some related work. Finally, Section 7 concludes this paper and discusses future work.

2   Distributed Service-Oriented Operating Systems

Current distributed operating systems provide for distributed infrastructure users what a traditional OS provides for single computer users [3][14][13]. Specifically, a distributed OS extends in a transparent way traditional OS functionalities. For example, the memory management functionality in a traditional OS is extended to form the Distributed Shared Memory (DSM) functionality in a distributed OS. Previous research works have proposed, compared and classified several algorithms to implement each OS functionality (e.g., DSM [18] and resource management [11]). Depending on the system environment, usually only one algorithm provides optimal performance. For example, a resource management algorithm can be very efficient to manage a small number of resources but it could be less efficient than other algorithms to manage a lot of resources.

Furthermore, distributed OSs operate in a constantly-changing environment, characterized by two levels of dynamicity: the dynamicity of the underlying infrastructure (resources may connect and disconnect at any time leading to variable resource availability), and the dynamicity of the application requirements (such as resource requirements). To accommodate this dynamicity while providing the best quality of service to applications, we believe that the distributed OS

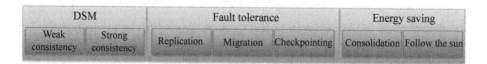

DSM		Fault tolerance			Energy saving	
Weak consistency	Strong consistency	Replication	Migration	Checkpointing	Consolidation	Follow the sun

Fig. 1. Service-oriented operating system overview

should be dynamically adaptable. Specifically, we believe that the OS should support selecting the best algorithm for each functionality at runtime. The selection could be done either according to the state of the whole system or in a more customized way, for each kind of application. In the latter case, two or more algorithms for the same functionality should be able to operate simultaneously, each one supporting the applications for which it was selected. For example, the fault tolerance functionality may use checkpointing for some applications while using replication for others.

To build such a dynamically-adaptable OS we propose to use SOA, thus enabling its well-known benefits in terms of interoperability and dynamic recomposition to be extended to the OS layer. Then, the OS is built as a composition of services, each service representing a distributed OS functionality. Figure 1 illustrates this idea with examples of some existing algorithms for three distributed OS services. The DSM service may use the weak or the strong consistency models, the fault tolerance service may use replication, migration or checkpointing, and the energy saving service may use a consolidation protocol [6] to minimize the number of used resources or use the "follow the sun" protocol [21] to utilize mostly sun energy.

The main challenge in building such a dynamically-adaptable OS is to determine when and how to change algorithms while taking into account the overhead of the change. Indeed, selecting the appropriate algorithm for each service is a complex task and involves thoroughly evaluating the algorithms as well as the parameters influencing their behaviors. To demonstrate this point, we investigate in Sect.5 two algorithms for the DSM service as well as the parameters influencing their behaviors.

3   Multi-level Adaptation Framework

Apart from the distributed OS, it is frequently necessary to dynamically adapt the distributed applications themselves. This may be motivated by changes in user requirements, such as demands for higher precision in calculation results; or in the available computing resources, such as node failures or new nodes joining the system. The application adaptation is required in such cases to enable applications to work correctly despite all possible environment degradations, and to take advantage of new opportunities that can occur. Indeed, modern distributed applications are increasingly built according to SOA in which applications are composed of multiple services and are prepared to handle services appearing and disappearing at any time.

Traditionally, the adaptation of each layer of a distributed system is managed separately based on layer-specific knowledge and objectives. For example, there are research works focusing exclusively on OS layer adaptation [17][19] and other works focusing exclusively on application layer adaptation [20]. However, the adaptation of one layer clearly impacts the others. As a result, adapting each layer separately can create conflicts, unpredictable results, or redundancies. For example, adapting the OS to accommodate reduced network bandwidth may be unnecessary if the application reacts to the same situation by replacing the remote service with a locally available one. To avoid such interference between adaptation actions, we propose to use a multi-level adaptation framework (such as SAFDIS [7]), capable of interacting and dynamically adapting both layers in a coordinated way. The framework must maintain knowledge about the whole system and perform adaptation actions according to application-specific and system-wide goals.

4   Architecture

This section presents a generic architecture to apply the concept of multi-level adaptation. This architecture is composed of two service-oriented layers, application and OS layers, which are on top of a physical infrastructure layer (see Fig.2). The considered physical infrastructure layer is composed of the hardware and a traditional OS installed on each node. All layers expose rich monitoring mechanisms and are controlled by the multi-level adaptation framework. Service-oriented layers expose also actuation mechanisms enabling the framework to trigger adaptation actions. The adaptation process of the framework follows the four main phases of the MAPE model [10]: Monitoring, Analysis, Planning and Execution. A description of the phases is given below.

1. **Monitoring:** the framework collaborates with the sensors of each layer in order to provide a dynamic view of the whole system. At the physical infrastructure layer, the sensors inform the framework about the availability and the workload of resources. At the OS layer, the sensors inform the framework about all available algorithms for each OS service, either statically at the start-up of the system or dynamically when a new algorithm component is added to the system. At the application layer, the sensors inform the framework about all available services in the repository as well as applications requirements. The mechanism used to monitor data may be either push or pull, depending on the nature of data and its frequency changes. The gathered information is stored in a knowledge base to be used later in the other phases.

2. **Analysis:** the framework analyzes the monitored data and uses policies to decide whether an adaptation is required or not. For instance, when the monitored data shows a deterioration of the system performance, the analysis policy determines if the OS, the application, or both should be adapted. The analysis policy triggers next phases only if the estimated overhead of the adaptation is less important than its benefit.

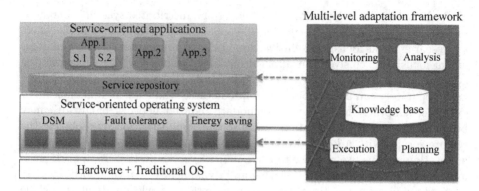

Fig. 2. Multi-level dynamic adaptation architecture – solid arrows represent the communication between sensors of each layer (sensors are not shown in the figure) and the Monitoring component of the framework; dashed arrows represent the communication between actuators of service-oriented layers (actuators are not shown in the figure) and the Execution component of the framework; dotted arrows represent the sequence of phases in an adaptation cycle.

3. **Planning:** the framework defines a plan to apply the decided adaptation at the analysis phase. The plan consists of set of actions which are scheduled properly. For example, if both application and OS layers should be adapted then the planning strategy will specify which layer will be adapted first.
4. **Execution:** the framework collaborates with actuators of the service-oriented layers to perform the plan defined at the planning phase. At the OS layer, actuators enable either to switch between algorithms or to ensure that two (or more) algorithms coexist. At the application layer, actuators may modify application parameters or modify the application structure, such as replacing services or changing service interconnections.

5 Illustrative Examples

In this section we investigate two algorithms of the DSM functionality to illustrate the usefulness of the proposed architecture. The objective of this section is not to improve or to optimize existing DSM algorithms, but to demonstrate that each algorithm can be better than others in particular cases.

The DSM service makes the main memory of a cluster of computers look like a single memory, using replicated data consistency models. We have evaluated two algorithms of the sequential consistency model: Broadcast-on-write and Invalidate-on-write. Both algorithms guarantee that any read of a data copy returns the last value assigned to this data. This is done by invalidating all remote data copies when a process access in write mode its local copy. The main difference takes place once the write operation finishes. In the broadcast-on-write algorithm, the owner of the modified copy updates automatically all the other copies. Whereas in the invalidate-on-write algorithm, the invalidated copies will be updated on demand when a page fault exception occurs. If the OS uses the broadcast algorithm, no fault page exception will occur. Nevertheless, some invalidated copies may be unnecessary updated if these copies are never subsequently used by their owners. Therefore, it is difficult to predict which algorithm will perform better. In this perspective we measure, in the next subsection, the execution time of a synthetic application with each algorithm while varying some parameters likely to impact the system performance.

5.1 Experiment Environment

To carry out these experiments, we have used and extended the Kerrighed OS [14]. The existing implementation of Kerrighed uses the invalidation algorithm for the DSM functionality. We have implemented the boadcast algorithm and an actuator to switch between the two algorithms at runtime. In addition to the Kerrighed modification, we have developed a synthetic distributed application that uses shared memory objects for its inter-process communications. This application consists of a configurable *number of processes* that share data objects, each process run on a different node. One process creates a configurable *number of shared data objects* with different *sizes* and all other processes can access them either in read or in write mode. The application *access pattern* follows the notion of *Write-Run* defined in [5]. A write-run is a sequence of write accesses to a shared object by a single process uninterrupted by any access of the other processes. The number of the sequential writes, called the write-run length, represents in these experiments the access pattern parameter. Attention has been paid to these parameters because of their dynamicity during the execution of a distributed shared memory application. The experiments were performed on the paradent cluster of the Grid'5000 site of Rennes that consists of Carri System CS-5393B nodes supplied with 2 Intel Xeon L5420 processors (each with 4 cores at 2.5 GHz), 32 GB of memory, and Gigabit Ethernet network interfaces. The results are discussed in the next subsection.

5.2 Results

Figure 4(a) shows the impact of the number of data object copies on the application execution time. The application parameters were set at one data object of 10 bytes size with a write-run length equal to one, only the number of data object copies was adjusted. We notice that the performance with both algorithms is equal when there are two data object copies. The invalidation algorithm performs better when there is only one copy, but the broadcast algorithm performs increasingly better when there are at least three copies.

Figure 4(b) shows the impact of the write-run length on the application execution time. The application parameters were set at one data object of 10 bytes size with 4 data object copies, only the write-run length was adjusted. The application execution times with both algorithms converge when the write-run length is set at 13. If the write-run length is smaller then the convergence point, the broadcast algorithm performs better and conversely if it is greater.

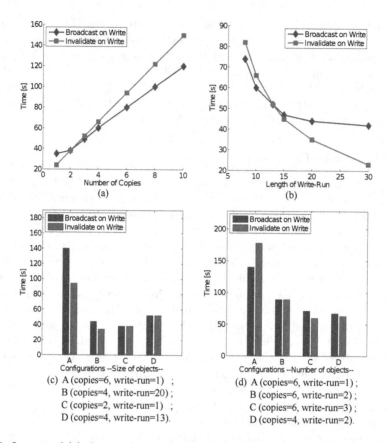

Fig. 3. Impact of (a) the number of data object copies, (b) the write-run length, (c) the data object size, and (d) the number of data objects on the execution time of the application

Figure 4(c), compared to Fig.4(a) and Fig.4(b) shows the impact of the data object size on the application execution time. The application parameters were set at one data object of 10^3 bytes size. The number of data object copies and the write-run length were adjusted to define four configurations (A,B,C,D). Each configuration was previously tested with an object size set at 10 bytes (see Fig.4(a) and Fig.4(b)). This comparison shows that the object size does not impact the application execution time in our experimental environment.

Figure 4(d) shows the impact of the number of data objects on the application execution time. The application parameters were set at two data objects of 10 bytes size. The number of data object copies and the write-run length was adjusted to define four configurations. The first configuration (A), compared to its analogous one with one shared object in Fig.4(a), shows an increase of the application execution time with both algorithms. In configurations (B) and (C), we have increased the write-run length and there we notice that the invalidation algorithm, respectively, catches up and overtakes the broadcast algorithm in terms of performance. In the configuration (D), we have decreased the number of data object copies and set the write-run length at 2. In this case the invalidation algorithm outperforms the broadcast algorithm. As a result, we conclude that the increase of the data objects number has an impact on the performance.

The results shown in Fig.3 demonstrate that the appropriate algorithm depends on application-layer parameters, thus showing the benefit of dynamically adapting the OS based on application-layer knowledge. Based on the data obtained from these experiments and machine learning techniques, we plan to generate a function that predicts from these parameters which algorithm will be better to use. When there is a change in parameters, the adaptation framework will use this function to decide whether to switch algorithms.

5.3   Possible Extensions

As a following step, we plan to validate our approach by providing support for adaptation involving multiple layers. We will first take into account the different network requirements of the algorithms. We then plan to extend the analysis phase to take into account not only the application-layer parameters but also the current state of the network.

Another planned extension is investigating coordinated adaptation across both OS and application layers through an application that transfers audio over the network and processes it in a parallel way using distributed shared memory. The audio compression rate of this application can be adapted based on network conditions. The multi-level framework enables this adaptation to be implemented in coordination with OS-level algorithm changes, thus avoiding unpredictable results. Indeed, performing this adaptation in an isolated way, without taking into account OS bandwidth needs, may cause instabilities. For example, if there is no coordinated adaptation and the bandwidth is low, the application increases its compression rate, freeing up available bandwidth. This causes the operating system to use a more bandwidth-demanding algorithm, which reduces the available bandwidth and the cycle continues. A coordinated adaptation, as enabled by our approach, avoids this problem.

6   Related Work

The dynamic adaptation of operating systems has been investigated under different angles. Seltzer and Small proposed a design for self monitoring and self adapting an extensible kernel [17]. They have defined a mechanism that uses online and offline analysis of the system behavior to adapt its policies. Teller and Seelam investigated the dynamic adaptation of OS policies in order to improve the application and the system performance. They have proposed a multi policy system that aims to satisfy different constraints by dynamically switching between policies. They have demonstrated their concept in the context of I/O scheduling [19].

The above works do not apply the service-oriented approach for structuring their OS. In this context Milanovic and Malek [12] investigated possible architectures to integrate the OS and the service-oriented computing. Among the investigated architectures, the closest one to our approach is to consider the OS as a set of collaborating services. The main difference with our model is the way of building the kernel. They propose to build it according to available kernel services while we propose to build it by selecting the most appropriate algorithm for each service according to its environment. Another interesting project in this context is SoOS, which tries to extend the limited capabilities of local devices with remote ones [16]. In this project local and remote resources are virtualized on top of the networking and Input/Output interfaces and are then made transparent to the running applications. Thus, the OS is considered as a collection of independent computational entities that appears to its users as a single coherent system. Unlike our proposal, this work focus on the physical infrastructure layer.

Recently, multi-level adaptation frameworks have also been investigated. The authors of [4] and [9] aim to provide a coherent solution to monitor and adapt service-based applications. The considered service layers are : business service, composition and coordination service, and the infrastructure service. The main difference with our proposal is the considered layers. They focus exclusively on service-oriented application layers while we also include the OS layer.

7   Conclusion

Modern distributed operating systems must operate reliably in constantly-changing environments. As a result, dynamic adaptability is an essential requirement for such systems. This paper made two contributions in this context. First, it proposed a service-oriented approach for building distributed OSs, which enables adapting the OS algorithms in a dynamic, on-demand fashion. Second, it proposed using a common framework to adapt both the OS and application layer in a coordinated way, thus avoiding any possible conflict or redundancy.

To demonstrate the usefulness of the proposed architecture, the paper investigated the DSM functionality and provided examples and experimental results using the Kerrighed distributed OS. As future work, we plan to implement further adaptation examples involving real applications on Kerrighed and extending the SAFDIS adaptation framework to control and adapt both layers.

Acknowledgment. We cordially thank the late professor Françoise André for her precious ideas and comments which helped to define the objectives of this work. We thank Dr. Louis Rilling for providing documentation support concerning Kerrighed. Experiments presented in this paper were carried out using the Grid'5000 experimental testbed, being developed under the INRIA ALADDIN development action with support from CNRS, RENATER and several Universities as well as other funding bodies (see https://www.grid5000.fr).

References

1. Openstack, http://www.openstack.org
2. Opennebula, http://opennebula.org
3. Barak, A., Guday, S., Wheeler, R.G.: The MOSIX Distributed Operating System: Load Balancing for UNIX. Springer, New York (1993)
4. Bratanis, K., Dranidis, D., Simons, A.J.H.: Slas for cross-layer adaptation and monitoring of service-based applications: a case study. In: Proceedings of the International Workshop on Quality Assurance for Service-Based Applications (2011)
5. Eggers, S.J., Katz, R.H.: A characterization of sharing in parallel programs and its application to coherency protocol evaluation. SIGARCH Comput. Archit. News (1988)
6. Ferreto, T.C., Netto, M.A.S., Calheiros, R.N., De Rose, C.A.F.: Server consolidation with migration control for virtualized data centers. Future Gener. Comput. Syst. (2011)
7. Gauvrit, G., Daubert, E., André, F.: SAFDIS: A Framework to Bring Self-Adaptability to Service-Based Distributed Applications. In: Proceedings of the 36th EUROMICRO Conference (2010)
8. Grimshaw, A.S., Wulf, W.A.: The Legion Team, C.: The legion vision of a worldwide virtual computer. Commun. ACM (1997)
9. Kazhamiakin, R., Pistore, M., Zengin, A.: Cross-Layer Adaptation and Monitoring of Service-Based Applications. In: Dan, A., Gittler, F., Toumani, F. (eds.) ICSOC/ServiceWave 2009. LNCS, vol. 6275, pp. 325–334. Springer, Heidelberg (2010)
10. Kephart, J.O., Chess, D.M.: The vision of autonomic computing. Computer (2003)
11. Krauter, K., Rajkumar Buyya, M.M.: A taxonomy and survey of grid resource management systems for distributed computing. Softw. Pract. Exper. (2002)
12. Milanovic, N., Malek, M.: Service-Oriented Operating System: A Key Element in Improving Service Availability. In: Malek, M., Reitenspieß, M., van Moorsel, A. (eds.) ISAS 2007. LNCS, vol. 4526, pp. 31–42. Springer, Heidelberg (2007)
13. Morin, C.: Xtreemos: A grid operating system making your computer ready for participating in virtual organizations. In: IEEE International Symposium on Object-Oriented Real-Time Distributed Computing (2007)
14. Morin, C., Gallard, P., Lottiaux, R., Vallée, G.: Towards an efficient single system image cluster operating system. Future Gener. Comput. Syst. (2004)
15. Papazoglou, M.P., Heuvel, W.J.: Service oriented architectures: approaches, technologies and research issues. The VLDB Journal (2007)
16. Schubert, L., Kipp, A., Koller, B., Wesner, S.: Service oriented operating systems: Future workspaces. IEEE Wireless Communications (2009)
17. Seltzer, M., Small, C.: Self-monitoring and self-adapting operating systems. In: Proceedings of the Sixth Workshop on Hot Topics in Operating Systems (1997)
18. Tam, M.C., Smith, J.M., Farber, D.J.: A taxonomy-based comparison of several distributed shared memory systems. SIGOPS Oper. Syst. Rev. (1990)
19. Teller, P.J., Seelam, S.R.: Insights into providing dynamic adaptation of operating system policies. SIGOPS Oper. Syst. Rev. (2006)
20. Tosi, D., Denaro, G., Pezze, M.: Towards autonomic service-oriented applications. Int. J. Autonomic Comput. (2009)
21. Treinen, J.J., Miller-Frost, S.L.: Following the sun: case studies in global software development. IBM Syst. J. (2006)

FIDs Classifier for Artificial Intelligence and Its Application

Chih-Chiang Wei

Department of Information Management, Toko University
No. 51, Sec. 2, University Rd., Pu-Tzu City, Chia-Yi County 61363, Taiwan
d89521007@ntu.edu.tw

Abstract. Fuzzy ID3 (FIDs) is popular and efficient method of making fuzzy decision trees in recent years. This paper presents FIDs algorithm for the precipitations during typhoon periods for a reservoir watershed. The FIDs was constructed as the quantitative precipitation forecast (QPF) model. This study also constructed the traditional C4.5 and the average statistical model (AVS) to compare with the performance by FIDs model. The steps involve collecting typhoon data, preprocessing the typhoon patterns, building QPF models, and training and testing the models. The experiment was in Shihmen Reservoir watershed. The results include the analysis of the 1-, 3-, and 6-hr accumulated rainfalls. The results showed that the superior RMSE and the categorical statistics of BIAS and ETS scores by using FIDs in contrast to those by using traditional C4.5 and AVS. Consequently, the FIDs model demonstrated its feasibility for predict rainfalls.

Keywords: FIDs, Artificial intelligence, Rainfall, Prediction.

1 Introduction

Forecasting the behavior of complex systems has been a broad application domain for artificial intelligence [1,2]. A technology called decision tree algorithms has been in widespread use. Decision trees such as ID3 and C4.5 [3], based on information theory are designed for efficient dataset classification. Fuzzy ID3 (FIDs) is popular and efficient method of making fuzzy decision trees in recent years. FIDs and its variations can be seen in [4-6].

In meteorology and atmospheric sciences, rainfall predictions in typhoon periods are an important research topic that attracted the interest of scientists for a long time. In the past years, Lee et al. [7] proposed a climatology model (so-called the average statistical model (AVS) in this paper) for forecasting typhoon rainfall in Taiwan. Fan and Lee [8] employed Bayesian approach to analyze the data in which the distribution of the response variable is considered to be a mixture of a continuous distribution and a point mass at zero. Then, their proposed model predicted the rainfalls during typhoon periods. Wei [9] developed the principal component analysis combining with radial basis function network to establish the quantitative precipitation forecast model.

Y. Xiang et al. (Eds.): ICA3PP 2012, Part II, LNCS 7440, pp. 110–119, 2012.

Wei [10] presented traditional Gaussian support vector machine (SVM) and the advanced wavelet SVM models for forecasting hourly precipitations.

In this paper, the FIDs algorithm was constructed as the quantitative precipitation forecast (QPF) model to predict precipitations. This study also constructed the traditional C4.5 and the average statistical model (AVS) to compare with the performance of the FIDs model. The experiment was in Shihmen Reservoir watershed in northern Taiwan. The analyzed cases included the 1-, 3- and 6-hr accumulated rainfalls during typhoon periods.

2   Algorithm

2.1   C4.5 Model

C4.5 uses a divide-and-conquer approach to growing decision trees that was pioneered by Hunt and his co-workers [11]. The detailed description of the method can be seen in Quinlan [3] for a more complete treatment.

2.2   FIDs Model

The design of an optimal FIDs proposed by Umano et al. [4] is presented in the following.

Fuzzy Sets. In classical set theory, an element either belongs to a certain set or does not. In this case, a two-valued characteristic function can be used. Systems developed with this assumption are called crisp. However, in real world, this is often unrealistic because of imprecise measurements and noise. To deal with this problem, symbolic systems have often attempted to include additional numerical components [6]. Fuzzy sets provide another alternative.

The cognitive uncertainties can be well represented by Zadeh's fuzzy set theory [12]. Let U be a collection of objects denoted generically by $\{x\}$. U is called the universe of discourse and x represents the generic element of U. In fuzzy set theory, a fuzzy subset A of the universe of discourse U is characterized by a membership function μ_A that takes values in the interval [0, 1].

For $x \in U$, $\mu_A(x) = 1$ means that x is definitely a member of A, $\mu_A(x) = 0$ is definitely not a member of A, and $0 < \mu_A(x) < 1$ means that x is partially a member of A. If either $\mu_A(x) = 0$ or $\mu_A(x) = 1$ for all $x \in U$, A is a crisp set. The detailed concepts on fuzzy set theory can also be found in various textbooks such as [13,14].

Fuzzy Decision-Tree Construction. The fuzzy decision-tree construction procedure is also similar to that for conventional decision trees, except the entropy measurement. In the fuzzy ID3, the information gain G is calculated by incorporating membership functions of fuzzy sets. In this method, the intersection of fuzzy sets with arithmetic product operator is defined as [4]

$$p_k^b = \left|D_k^b\right|/\left|D^b\right| \tag{1}$$

$$\left|D^b\right| = \sum_{x \in D}\left(\prod_{(i,j) \in Q} \mu_{ij}(x)\right) \tag{2}$$

$$\left|D_k^b\right| = \sum_{x \in D_k}\left(\prod_{(i,j) \in Q} \mu_{ij}(x)\right) \tag{3}$$

where μ_{ij} is a membership function of the attribute value, (i,j) means the jth attribute value (fuzzy set) of the ith attribute and Q is a set of the pair (i,j) along the branches from the root to node b. H, H_v, E and G are calculated in the same manner as the original ID3 method. Let L represent the set of leaf nodes and l represent an element of the set. A sample data x then belongs to class k with the probability

$$Prob^k(x) = \sum_{l \in L} p_k^l \cdot \left(\prod_{(i,j) \in Q_l} \mu_{ij}(x_i)\right) = \sum_{l \in L} p_k^l \cdot \mu_l(x) \tag{4}$$

where p_k^l is the relative frequency of a class k at the lth leaf node, Q_l is the set of (i,j) branches from the root to lth leaf node, and $\mu_l(x)$ is a multidimensional membership function corresponding to the lth leaf node.

AVS Model. In the past, one of the most popular methods is the average statistical method developed by Wang et al. [15]. The AVS method is based upon the simple assumptions; that is, the hourly rainfall prediction at a given location is a function of typhoon position, moving direction, and terrain effects. When a typhoon track is predicted, the hourly rainfall can be predicted readily from the rainfall statistical diagram, which is derived from AVS model [16].

The steps of generating the statistical diagram are as follows.

Step 1: Choose a rain gauge station to represent the predicted region;

Step 2: Investigate the observed typhoon tracks and precipitation over the past years;

Step 3: Delimit geographical boundaries which typhoon activities may affect that predicted region;

Step 4: Divide the space domain selected from Step 3 into many small nest grids;

Step 5: Analyze the various statistics at a certain grid, including the average, maximum, minimum, standard deviation of rainfalls and the number of times, as all the observed typhoon eyes passed that grid; and

Step 6: Repeat Step 5 to analyze all the grids.

Through Steps 1–6, the statistical diagram for predicting rainfall can be obtained.

3   Experiment

3.1   Study Site

The Shihmen Reservoir completed in 1964 is located on the upstream reaches of the Tahan River, and is one of the largest water reservoirs in Taiwan. The watershed covers an area of 763.4 km². The Shihmen Reservoir is currently managed by the Water Resources Agency [17]. There are 13 rainfall gauges in the watershed.

3.2   Data

The collected data involved the precipitations at rainfall stations and the typhoon characteristics including pressure in the typhoon center, position of typhoon center, the radius of typhoon, the predicted moving speed and direction, the center maximum wind speed, and the predicted typhoon path. In Shihmen Reservoir watershed, 45 years (1964–2008) of fully hourly historical data are available. During these years, 122 typhoon events have occurred. This study collected the hourly typhoon precipitations and then averages the 13-gauge hourly dataset in each time period. Then let the average rainfall amounts represented as the precipitations of reservoir watershed. For all the input-output patterns of the reservoir watershed, 3,679 hourly records (cases) are available. Years from 1964 to 2004 were for training set (2,521 records) and years from 2005 to 2008 for testing set (1,158 records).

3.3   Attributes Selected

Table 1 demonstrates attributes and targets during typhoon periods. For the complicated forecasting system, this study selected 10 attributes as inputs to predict precipitations. That is to say the hourly rainfall prediction at a given location is a function of these attributes (i.e. $\alpha_1, \alpha_2, \ldots, \alpha_{10}$). These attributes include typhoon level (α_1), pressure of typhoon center (10^2 Pa) (α_2), relative direction angle of typhoon to watershed (rad.) (α_3), relative distance of typhoon to watershed (km) (α_4), radius of typhoon (km) (α_5), predicted moving speed (km/hr) (α_6), center maximum wind speed (km/hr) (α_7), relative direction angle after 24 hours (rad.) (α_8), relative distance after 24 hours (km) (α_9), and hourly watershed precipitation at the current time (mm) (α_{10}). The target is the hourly watershed precipitation at the adjacent time (mm) (β).

In the above attributes, the relative direction angle of typhoon to watershed (α_3) can be defined as

$$\alpha_3 = \tan^{-1}\left(\frac{y - y_0}{x - x_0}\right) \times \frac{360}{2\pi} \tag{5}$$

where x and y are the longitude (°E) and latitude (°N) of typhoon center at the current moment during typhoon periods, respectively; and x_0 and y_0 are the longitude (°E) and latitude (°N) of reservoir dam, respectively.

The relative distance of typhoon to watershed (α_4) is defined as

$$\alpha_4 = 111.1\sqrt{\left((x - x_0)\cdot\cos\left(\frac{y + y_0}{2}\right)\right)^2 + (y - y_0)^2} \tag{6}$$

Table 1. Examples of the input-output patterns

Date	Hour	Attribute											
		Typhoon level (a_1)	Pressure of typhoon center ($a_2 .10^2$Pa)	Relative direction angle of typhoon to watershed (a_3, rad.)	Relative distance of typhoon to watershed (a_4, km)	Radius of typhoon (a_5, km)	Predicted moving speed (a_6, km/hr)	Center maximum wind speed (a_7, km/hr)	Predicted relative direction angle after 24 hours (a_8, rad.)	Predicted relative distance after 24 hours (a_9, km)	Hourly watershed precipitation at current time (a_{10}, mm)	The 1-hour ahead hourly watershed precipitation time (β_1, mm) (for continuous)	The 1-hour ahead hourly watershed precipitation (β_1') (for categorical)
2001/9/15	18	1	975	20.41	298.7	150	12	110.0	-51.74	98.2	0.00	0.13	Class_0
2001/9/15	19	1	975	18.50	294.8	150	12	110.0	-51.74	98.2	0.13	1.78	Class_2
2001/9/15	20	2	970	18.50	294.8	150	12	120.0	-55.34	107.3	1.78	4.78	Class_5
2001/9/15	21	2	970	19.17	285.0	150	12	120.0	-55.34	107.3	4.78	14.88	Class_15
2001/9/15	22	2	970	17.80	271.4	150	12	120.0	-55.34	107.3	14.88	8.59	Class_9
2001/9/15	23	2	970	17.80	271.4	150	8	120.0	-16.30	115.9	8.59	5.03	Class_5
2001/9/15	24	2	970	18.51	261.5	150	8	120.0	-16.30	115.9	5.03	5.63	Class_6
2001/9/16	1	2	970	18.51	261.5	150	8	120.0	-16.30	115.9	5.63	8.69	Class_9
2001/9/16	2	2	970	16.98	248.1	150	8	120.0	-19.82	96.2	8.69	4.78	Class_5
2001/9/16	3	2	970	16.98	248.1	150	8	120.0	-19.82	96.2	4.78	2.50	Class_3
2001/9/16	4	2	970	17.72	238.2	150	8	120.0	-19.82	96.2	2.50	3.38	Class_3

The Shihmen Reservoir hourly watershed precipitation serves as the target for extracting typhoon rainfall rules.

3.4   FIDs Construction

In FIDs algorithm, each attribute has an associated fuzzy membership function. Each fuzzy membership function contains several fuzzy sets. Design of a powerful fuzzy classifier requires more flexible membership functions. Therefore, the flexible trapezoid fuzzy sets are used. A trapezoid fuzzy set here is represented by four parameters $\{L_b, L_t, R_t, R_b\}$, as illustrated in Fig. 1. The membership grade of attribute x for a fuzzy set can be determined by

$$\mu(x) = \begin{cases} 0 & x \le L_b \ \text{and} \ x \ge R_b \\ 1 & L_t \le x \le R_t \\ \dfrac{x - L_b}{L_t - L_b} & L_b < x < L_t \\ \dfrac{R_b - x}{R_b - R_t} & R_t < x < R_b \end{cases} \tag{7}$$

For the 10 attributes, each trapezoid membership function assumed consists of three fuzzy sets. These three fuzzy sets can be given names {Low, Medium, High}. An intelligent genetic algorithm is employed to optimize the large number of parameters in fuzzy decision-tree design.

Genetic algorithm (GA) [18] is a technology for search, optimization or machine learning according to the mechanics of natural selection and natural genetics. In general, GA involves six steps [19,20]: (1) select an initial population of chromosomes, (2) evaluate the fitness of each chromosome, (3) select chromosomes from current populations to mate, (4) perform crossover (mating) for the selected chromosome, (5) perform mutation for the selected chromosome, and (6) repeat Steps (2) to (5) for the required number of generations.

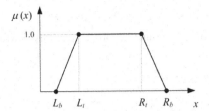

Fig. 1. Schematic of trapezoid fuzzy set

The combination of genetic algorithm and FIDs algorithm can be shown in Fig. 2. In this computing process, chromosomes are employed to encode the fuzzy membership functions. A chromosome contains variables of fuzzy membership function. The fitness function used for designing an optimal fuzzy decision tree in GA algorithm is maximizing the number of correctly classified training patterns (or maximizing the accurate percentage).

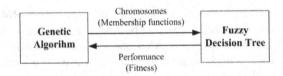

Fig. 2. Combination of genetic algorithm and FIDs

3.5   Results and Discussion

Three cases were designed for predicting future rainfalls. The targets of Cases 1, 2 and 3 are 1-, 3-, and 6-hr ahead hourly accumulated precipitations, respectively. The continuous-type target (denoted as β) was employed in AVS, while categorical-type target (β') was for C4.5 and FIDs. The inputs of AVS model are attributes α_3, α_4, α_6, α_8, and α_9. As well as, the inputs of C4.5 and FIDs model are attributes α_1 to α_{10}.

In GA processing of FIDs model, the parameters are population size = 100, crossover rate = 0.9, and mutation rate = 0.1. The maximal generation is equal to 300. All variables of fuzzy sets are encoded as a real number string in GA. The optimal fitness value was obtained at generation = 218, 144, 191 for 1-, 3-, and 6-hr ahead hourly accumulated prediction, respectively.

Fig. 3 depicted the scattered plots of observation versus simulation of testing sets in 1-hr ahead hourly predictions by AVS, C4.5 and FIDs. These figures showed that FIDs forecasted approximate the general behavior of the observed data.

The performance of root mean square error (RMSE) is used to assess the forecasted results. The formula is

$$\text{RMSE} = \sqrt{\sum_{i=1}^{n} \left(\hat{P}_i - P_i \right)^2 \Big/ n} \qquad (8)$$

where $\hat{P}_i$ is the estimated precipitation at record i, P_i is the observed precipitation at record i, and n is the number of hourly records. Generally, RMSE having lower values mean better performance.

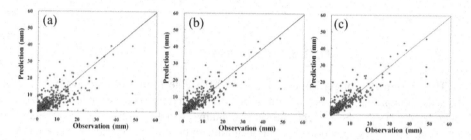

Fig. 3. Observation versus prediction 1-hr ahead hourly precipitation by (a) AVS, (b) C4.5, and (c) FIDs

The AVS, C4.5 and FIDs models were compared in respect of RMSE statistics in Table 2. The performance of the 1-, 3-, and 6-hr accumulated rainfalls by using FIDs performed better than those by using AVS and C4.5 models. Moreover, it can be obviously seen that the 1-hr ahead predicted rainfall was more accurate than those of 3- and 6-hr ahead for the two models.

Table 2. RMSE measures of predicted precipitation

Model	target β_1	target β_3	target β_6
AVS	3.523	10.751	22.674
C4.5	2.962	9.040	18.508
FIDs	2.661	7.901	16.217

3.6   Evaluation by Skill Scores

In this section, two categorical statistics measures, including bias score (BIAS), and equitable threat score (ETS), are used, computed from the elements of this rain/no-rain contingency table. As seen in Table 3, the term categorical refers to the yes/no nature of the forecast verification. Then at each retrieval, each verification time is scored as falling under one of the four categories of correct non-rain forecasts, false alarms, misses, or hits (denoted as Z, F, M, and H, respectively). In the ideal situation of perfect forecast, both M and F equal to 0. By considering retrievals of the rainfall rate greater than a certain threshold, the problem can be broken down into a series of 2×2 contingency tables, each for a different threshold value [21].

Definitions of Skill Scores. BIAS measures the ratio of the predicted rain frequency to the observed frequency, regardless of forecast accuracy. That is, bias can be employed to assess the tendency of the model to under- or over-predict rain occurrence. It is defined as

$$\text{BIAS} = \frac{F + H}{M + H} \tag{9}$$

If BIAS > 1.0, the model over-predicts rain occurrence; otherwise, the model under-predicts rain occurrence.

Table 3. Rain contingency table

Observed	Predicted	
	No rain	Rain
No rain	Z	F
Rain	M	H

The equitable threat score (ETS) allows the scores to be compared "equitably" cross different regimes and is insensitive to being influenced by systematic over- or under-forecasting [22].

$$\text{ETS} = \frac{H - G}{(H + M + F) - G} \tag{10}$$

where

$$G = \frac{(H + M)(H + F)}{H + M + F + Z} \tag{11}$$

ETS ranges from -1/3 to 1, with a value of 1 indicating perfect correspondence between predicted and observed rain occurrence.

Evaluation. Because prediction of the 1-hr ahead rainfall is relatively important in meteorology and atmospheric sciences, this section will focus on discussing the skill scores in 1-hr ahead rainfall forecasts. Fig. 4a shows the bias score as a function of the threshold value, which ranges from 0.1 to 40 mm/hr, chosen to separate the rain/no-rain events. As mentioned above, if the BIAS > 1.0, the model over-predicts the rain occurrence; otherwise, the model under-predicts the rain occurrence. In the figure, the straight line "BIAS = 1" divided the figure into two regions. For C4.5 and FIDs, the threshold is less than about 9 mm/hr (BIAS > 1.0). Meanwhile, AVS, C4.5 and FIDs have a relatively higher bias at the threshold of 0-2 mm/hr. This means that the three models overestimate the light rains. For FIDs, it has approximately horizontal lines with a BIAS between 10 and 18 mm/hr. In the region of BIAS < 1.0, biases in C4.5 and FIDs demonstrate close to the bias value of 1.0. On the contrary, bias in AVS is relatively far from the horizontal line. This means that AVS strongly underestimates the peak values than C4.5 and FIDs.

ETS measures the number of retrieval fields that match the observed threshold amount. Fig. 4a illustrates the ETS as a measure of the relative skill for a distribution of rainfall amounts. For the three models, the ETS scores equal to about zero at the threshold of 0.1 mm/hr. Then ETS values increase until maximal ETS value of about

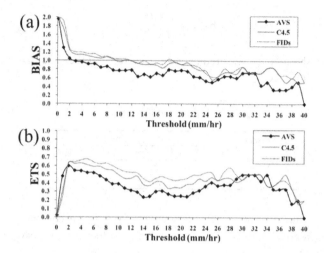

Fig. 4. BIAS and ETS scores of 1-hr rainfall forecasts for three models

0.6-0.7 at the threshold = 2, 2, 5 mm/hr for AVS, C4.5 and FIDs, respectively. At thresholds between 2 and 30 mm/hr, the ETS values in FIDs are better than those made by C4.5 and AVS. This means FIDs has good prediction ability at higher rainfalls.

4   Conclusions

This paper presented Fuzzy ID3 decision trees (FIDs) for the precipitations during typhoon periods for a specific reservoir watershed. The quantitative precipitation forecast (QPF) models have been developed to forecast hourly rainfalls during typhoon periods. The three classification technologies, namely AVS, C4.5 and FIDs models were employed and compared. The developed methodology is applied to the Shihmen Reservoir in the Tahan River Basin. The results showed that the FIDs model provide good RMSE performance in contrast to those by using traditional AVS and C4.5 models. Moreover, the categorical statistics of BIAS and ETS based on the rain contingency table is applied at each analysis model over the verification period. It also indicated that FIDs yields superior performance than C4.5 and AVS. Consequently, the proposed FIDs model can be used to predict precipitation during typhoon periods.

Acknowledgements. The support under Grant No. NSC101-2622-B-464-001-CC3 by the National Science Council, Taiwan is greatly appreciated. The authors would like to acknowledge data provided by the CWB and WRA.

References

1. Atiya, A.F., El-Shoura, S.M., Shaheen, S.I., El-Sherif, M.S.: A Comparison between Neural-network Forecasting Techniques-Case Study: River Flow Forecasting. IEEE Transactions on Neural Networks 10(2), 402–409 (1999)

2. Chau, K.W.: Particle Swarm Optimization Training Algorithm for ANNs in Stage Prediction of Shing Mun River. Journal of Hydrology 329, 363–367 (2006)
3. Quinlan, J.R.: C4.5: Programs for Machine Learning. Morgan Kaufmann, San Mateo (1993)
4. Umano, M., Okamoto, H., Hatono, I., Tamura, H., Kawachi, F., Umedzu, S., Kinoshita, J.: Fuzzy Decision Trees by Fuzzy ID3 Algorithm and its Application to Diagnosis Systems. In: Proc. 3rd IEEE Int. Conf. on Fuzzy Systems, Orlando, pp. 2113–2118 (1994)
5. Yuan, Y., Shaw, M.J.: Induction of Fuzzy Decision Trees. Fuzzy Sets and Systems 69, 125–139 (1995)
6. Janikow, C.Z.: A Genetic Algorithm Method for Optimizing Fuzzy Decision Trees. Information Science 89, 275–296 (1996)
7. Lee, C.S., Huang, L.R., Shen, H.S., Wang, S.T.: A Climatology Model for Forecasting Typhoon Rainfall in Taiwan. Natural Hazards 37, 87–105 (2006)
8. Fan, T.H., Lee, Y.H.: A Bayesian Mixture Model with Application to Typhoon Rainfall Predictions in Taipei. International Journal of Contemporary Mathematical Sciences 2(13), 639–648 (2007)
9. Wei, C.C.: Radial Basis Function Networks Combined with Principal Component Analysis to Typhoon Precipitation Forecast in a Reservoir Watershed. Journal of Hydrometeorology 13(2), 722–734 (2012)
10. Wei, C.C.: Wavelet Support Vector Machines for Forecasting Precipitations in Tropical Cyclones: Comparisons with GSVM, Regressions, and Numerical MM5 Model. Weather and Forecasting 27(2), 438–450 (2012)
11. Hunt, E.B., Marin, J., Stone, P.J.: Experiments in Induction. Academic Press, New York (1966)
12. Zadeh, L.A.: Fuzzy sets. Information and Control 8, 338–353 (1965)
13. Kosko, B.: Neural Networks and Fuzzy Systems. Prentice Hall, Englewood Cliffs (1992)
14. Pedrycz, W.: Fuzzy Control and Fuzzy Systems, 2nd edn. John Wiley, New York (1993)
15. Wang, S.D., Chen, T.J., Shieh, S.L.: Characteristics of Typhoon Rainfall and Forecasting in Taiwan (I). NSC Technique Report, Taipei (1983) (in Chinese)
16. Hsu, N.S., Wei, C.C.: A Multipurpose Reservoir Real-time Operation Model for Flood Control during Typhoon Invasion. Journal of Hydrology 336, 282–293 (2007)
17. Water Resources Agency: Guidelines of Shihmen Reservoir Operations. Water Resources Agency, Taipei (2002) (in Chinese)
18. Goldberg, D.E.: Genetic Algorithms in Search. Optimization and Machine Learning. Addison Wesley Publishing, Reading (1989)
19. Yuan, Y., Zhuang, H.: A genetic Algorithm for Generating Fuzzy Classification Rules. Fuzzy Sets and Systems 84, 1–19 (1996)
20. Wei, C.C., Hsu, N.S.: Derived Operating Rules for a Reservoir Operation System: Comparison of Decision Trees, Neural Decision Trees and Fuzzy Decision Trees. Water Resources Research 44, W02428 (2008)
21. Hall, T., Brooks, H.E., Doswell, C.A.: Precipitation Forecasting using a Neural Network. Weather and Forecasting 14, 338–345 (1999)
22. Schaefer, J.T.: The Critical Success Index as an Indicator of Warning Skill. Weather and Forecasting 5, 570–575 (1990)

On Affirmative Adaptive Failure Detection

Ahmad Shukri Mohd Noor[1], Mustafa Mat Deris[2], Tutut Herawan[3],
and Mohamad Nor Hassan[1]

[1] Department of Computer Science, Faculty of Science and Technology
Universiti Malaysia Terengganu,
21030 Kuala Terengganu, Malaysia
[2] Faculty of Computer Science and Information Technology
Universiti Tun Hussein Onn Malaysia
86400 Parit Raja, Batu Pahat, Johor Darul Takzim, Malaysia
[3] Faculty of Computer System and Software Engineering
Universiti Malaysia Pahang
Lebuh Raya Tun Razak, 26300 Gambang, Kuantan, Pahang, Malaysia
{ashukri,mohamadnor}@umt.edu.my, mmustafa@uthm.edu.my,
tutut@ump.edu.my

Abstract. Fault detection methodology is a crucial part in providing a scalable, dependable and high availability of grid computing environment. The most popular technique that used in detecting fault is heartbeat mechanism where it monitors the grid resources in a very short interval. However, the heartbeat mechanism-based technique for fault detection suffers from weaknesses of either fast detection with low accuracy or completeness in detecting failures with a lengthy timeout. In this paper, we propose Affirmative Adaptive Failure Detection (AAFD). In this technique, the integration of newly proposed failure detection algorithm and the ping service is essential not only for dynamically improving certainty level of accuracy, but it is also very significant in verifying the aliveness of a site for strong completeness failure detection and reduces waiting time. The model outperforms the existing techniques by 18% to 39% in term of algorithm performance. On the average, AAFD detection is about 30% better than other detection algorithms.

Keywords: Fault Detection, Heartbeat Methodology, Distributed system environment, System failure.

1 Introduction

Since current distributed computing such as grid computing and CLOUD computing become larger, increasingly dynamic and heterogeneous. These distributed systems become more and more complicated. Failures or error are arise due to the inherently unreliable nature of the distributed environment include hardware failures, software errors and other sources of failures [1]. Fault detection is the first essential phase for developing any fault tolerance mechanism or failure recovery systems [2]. Hence Fault detection is very important part in proving high availabity in distributed systems and thus widely used. Fault detections provide information on faults of components of

Y. Xiang et al. (Eds.): ICA3PP 2012, Part II, LNCS 7440, pp. 120–129, 2012.

these systems. Failure detection involves isolation and identification of a fault so that the proper recovery actions can be initiated. Depending on system architecture and assumptions about fault characteristics of components, the study found fault-detection latencies covered from 55% to 80% of non-functional periods [3]. This non-functional period happened when a system is unaware of a failure (failure detection latency) and periods when a system attempts to recover from a failure (failure-recovery latency) [4]. Therefore many failure detection and recovery techniques have been developed to improve the distributed system availability. However, these failure detection techniques suffer from weaknesses of either fast detection with low accuracy or completeness in detecting failures with a lengthy timeout. For instance the failures can be detected quickly but the probabilities of false detections are high. At the other hand, the failures can be detected completely but with a lengthy timeout. To this, these trade-offs have to be improved.

In this paper, we propose Affirmative Adaptive Failure Detection (AAFD). In this technique, the integration of newly proposed failure detection algorithm and the ping service is essential not only for dynamically improving certainty level of accuracy, but it is also very significant in verifying the aliveness of a site for strong completeness failure detection and reduces waiting time. This research focuses on improving failure detection technique for current distributed system. This work aims at reducing detection time with high accuracy and completeness, subsequently providing the system with more accurate information for recovery and fault tolerant purposes.

The rest of the paper is organized as follows: Section 2 presents the related work. Section3 discusses the proposed failure detection methodology, illustrates the mathematical equation and the algorithm to detect the failure. Section 4 discusses the performance measurements of an existing model and proposed model. Finally, in Section 5 we conclude the paper

2   Related Works

Stelling *et al.* proposed Globus Heartbeat Monitor (GHM) for a failure detection service in grid computing [5]. GHM is one of the most popular failure detection services in grid environment . GHM provides a fault detection service for applications developed with the Globus toolkit. It was developed under the assumption that both the grid generic server and the heartbeat monitor run reliably [6]. Stelling *et al.* stated two of the main concerns that should be addressed in the design of a fault detector for grid environments which are

a. Accuracy and completeness. The fault detector must identify faults accurately, with both false positives and false negatives being rare.
b. Timeliness. Problems must be identified in a timely fashion, so that responses and corrective actions can be taken as soon as possible.

However, few bottlenecks of GHM have been identified; they scale badly in the number of members that are being monitored , require developers to implement fault tolerance at the application level , difficult to implement ,and have high-overhead [7]. Failure Detection and Recovery Services (FDS) improves the GHM with early detection of failures in applications, grid middleware and grid resources[8]. The FDS also introduce an efficient and low-overhead multi-layered distributed failure detection service that release grid users and developers from the burden of grid fault detection and fault recovery. However, this technique has a weakness as it requires a period of times before detecting faulty and delaying the recovery actions to be taken. Recently, International Business Machines (IBM) utilizing the heartbeat releases 2 in achieving high availability on Linux for IBM System Z [9]. This heartbeat is able to scale up to 16 nodes. However, the heartbeat release 2 still maintains the fixed interval time and timeout delay as Released 1. Adaptive failure algorithm are able to adjust to changing network conditions [10,6] The algorithms are based on periodically sent heartbeat messages. The behaviour of a network can be significantly different during high traffic times as during low traffic times regarding the probability of message loss, the expected delay for message arrivals, and the variance of this delay. Adaptive failure detectors arrange their parameters in order to meet the current conditions of the system. Thus adaptive failure detectors are highly desirable. In large scale networks, adaptive algorithms are proved to be more efficient than algorithms with constant timeout [5]. Elhadef & Boukerch [11] proposed a method to estimate the arrival time of the heartbeat messages where the arrival time of the next heartbeat of a node is computed by averaging the n last arrival times. They improved and utilised Bertier's algorithm[12] in their implementation.

Khilar *et al.* proposed an adaptive failure detection service for large scale ad hoc networks using an efficient cluster based communication architecture [13]. This failure detection service adapts the detection parameter to the current load of the wireless ad hoc network.

The lack of failure detection techniques that suitable for current distributed system environments has thus motivated writer to do a research for improving detection time with completeness and high accuracy.

3   Affirmative Adaptive Failure Detection

The Affirmative Adaptive Failure Detection (AAFD) is designed to provide timely detection with completeness and high accuracy. Suppose that process p is monitoring q using a heartbeat style failure detector, thus q sends heartbeat messages to p every interval S_i while p uses them to draw conclusions about q's status. Heartbeat Monitor (HBM) manages a sample base list S. This sample base list S consists of the information about the inter-arrival times of the last heartbeats S_i it received. Meanwhile, n is the size of sample base list, $n = |S|$. Furthermore HBM stores the time of the latest received heartbeat called freshness point f. Based on the sampled inter-arrival times and freshness point, the proposed algorithm predicts the probability of the arrival of further heartbeat messages. Since network bandwidth and CPU load is unpredictable, this list is the key for the HBM to dynamically tailor to the prediction for maximum waiting time H_{max} of HB inter-arrival. Thus it can reduce the false detection. Basically, the inter-arrival times S_i times are mainly influenced by the following environmental circumstances:

Network delay: Heartbeats sent over the network are affected by network bandwidth and load. Therefore, in this work, it is necessary to consider the network delay in determined the maximum allocation time HB_{max} a node to send a HB.

HB message generating delay: a site sends heartbeat messages not at the time it is supposed to, For instance, due to processing overload or CPU busy. Based on this data, HBM generate q's status.

The equation of AAFD prediction for estimating the maximum HB message arrival waiting time is given by:

$$H_{max} = \sum_{i=1}^{n} S_i + S_{n+1},$$

(1)

where,

i) H_{max} = Maximum HB message arrival waiting time,

ii) $\sum_{i=1}^{n} S_i$ = the total time elapsed (total heartbeats time) and

iii)

$$S_{n+1} = \frac{\frac{\sum_{i=1}^{n-1} S_i}{S_{n-1}} + S_n}{2}$$

(2)

where, $\sum_{i=1}^{n-1} S_i$ is the total heartbeats time in S_{n-1}, $|S_{n-1}|$ is the number of elements (cardinality) in S_{n-1}, and S_n inter-arrival time of the last heartbeat arrive.

This equation is established based the sample heartbeat data analysis. HB messages are delays when the service is initialised. The delays then gradually reduce with some minor irregularities. The data show that the changes of HB messages flow (whether increase or reduce) is gradually. There are only few sudden changes happened. Assuming again p is monitoring q and p is waiting for the $(n+1)^{th}$ heartbeat from q, the probability of the q's $n+1$ heartbeat is influenced by the past heartbeats. Based on the analysis of the inter-arrival time, the last heartbeat S_n in the sample base list S has a big influence on the S_{n+1} probability. Thus, the influential factor for S_n is weighted 50 percent and the rest in sample S is 50 percent.

Figure 1 illustrates the AAFD algorithm. A site q sends heartbeat messages to the HBM for every T_i. The p's failure detector has the variables f , S, and n. The freshness point, f is the time when failure detector received the last heartbeat message. S is the list of the heartbeat message inter-arrival times. Meanwhile, n is the size of S, so called sample list size. Whenever p receives a heartbeat, if T_r, heartbeat arrival time within predicted time, H_{max} the failure detector append $S_i = T_r - f$ to S and sets new freshness point equal to T_r $(f = T_r)$. Failure detector p removes the head of S if the list grows to a size of $n+1$ in consequence of appending the latest inter-arrival time. If the expected T_r exceeded the prediction time H_{max}. The algorithm activates ping command to ping the suspicious site q. Then if the site acknowledges that, the algorithm will wait for the next HB message from the site q. Else the site q is set as permanently failed. This will cause the index manager to be updated and failure recovery procedure to be invoked.

```
1.  # intialise  the freshness point
2.  f = -1
3.  #  S is initialised as empty list
4.  S = nil .
5.  n = 100  # max size of S (e.g. 100)
6.  Detect  new monitorable site Nx
7.  /*check if Nx register with index log*/
8.  if       site q  in  index  manager then
9.     update index manager  N++;
10. endif
11. # upon receive of message q at time tr
12. if       f = -1 then
13.    f = tr
14. else
15.    Hmax =  tr + ti  + average (average(S1..Sn-2) Sn-1)
16. If  tr  ≤   Hmax
17.       # HB message is normal.
18.       s = tr  -f
19.       f  = tr
20.       append s to S
21.       if size of S > n then
22.           remove head of S
23.       end if
24. endif
25. else
26.       if   tr  >  Hmax
27.           activate  ping protocol to  site q
28.       If the site q  acknowledge then
29.       # site or network ok, but  busy , wait next interval
30.           Wait for  next tr
31.       else
32.         ping timeout then
33.         site q failed; # set inverval to 2 second to  every
34.         outgoing message
35.         update index manager  ;
36.         invoke  failure recovery procedure  ;
37. endif ; endif
38. endif
```

Fig. 1. Affirmative Adaptive Failure Detection algorithm

3.1   Utilizing Ping Service with AAFD

The integration of the heartbeat mechanism and the ping service is essential not only for dynamically improving certainty level of accuracy, but it is also very significant in verifying the aliveness of a site for strong completeness failure detection and reduces waiting time. This is due to the fact that under certain circumstances, a node fails to send heartbeat and it is still alive, and there could be other possibilities that may cause its failure to send heartbeat such as HB message generator malfunctions or the CPU is very busy to generate the HB messages within the given timeframe. In that case, it is important for the node monitor to find alternative solution in determine the aliveness of a node. Since the relationship between HBM and a node n is notated as $HB \Rightarrow n$. Thus, a ping command is utilised to determine the status of a missing heartbeats node. Thus this proposed failure algorithm called failure detection Affirmative Adaptive Failure Detection (AAFD). The following equation 3 shows Ping utilisation in AAFD;

$$T_r = \begin{cases} T_{HM} + T_i, & \text{for } T_r \leq H_{max} \\ T_{HM} + T, & \text{for } T_r > H_{max} \text{ and Ping} = 1 \\ Null, & \text{for } T_r > H_{max} \text{ and Ping} = 0 \end{cases} \tag{3}$$

where ,

    i) T_{HM} = time taken for a message to arrived at heartbeat monitor

    i) T_i = The interval between each message sent to the heartbeat monitor.

    ii) H_{max} = The timeout when the heartbeat monitor realized that it have not received the message from the node, T_r.

The monitored node periodically send heartbeat message to HBM within predicted waiting time H_{max} . However, if HBM does not receive the message within the predicted time H_{max} or the receiving hb message time T_r exceed the H_{max} , the effected site is considered as having a problem and consider in a suspicious state. The HBM will activate ping protocol for the suspected site. If the site acknowledges the pinging process then it waits for next heartbeat. Else, if the site does not acknowledge the pinging process and exceeded ping timeout, the nodes is considered as failed state and the status of the node will be updated in the node manager and finally, proper recovery action will be undertaken.

4   The Performance Result

The comparisons of failure detection performance are carried out between AAFD and the well known failure detection algorithms as listed in Table 1.

Table 1. AAFD and other failure detection techniques

Techniques	Type of detection	Equation	Note
GHM [16]	Static	Keepalive = 2 s Deadtime = 4 s	Keepalive = Hmax Deadtime = Failed
Elhadef [14]	Adaptive	$S_{n+1} = \dfrac{\sum_{i=1}^{n} S_i}{\lvert S \rvert}$	
Khilar [15]	Adaptive	$S_{n+1} = S_n$	New time out = f(Freshness)
AAFD	Affirmative adaptive	$S_{n+1} = \dfrac{\dfrac{\sum_{i=1}^{n-1} S_i}{S_{n-1}} + S_n}{2}$	The proposed algorithm

The aims of performance comparisons are to show how the failure detection algorithms reacts when heartbeats inter arrival times are irregular which cause by unreliable network and different CPU load. The best detection algorithm must adapt to the margin in order to optimize the detection time with accuracy and completeness.

Figure 2 shows a representative example of the HB inter-arrival time on site2 for 100 heartbeat messages in sequence manner.

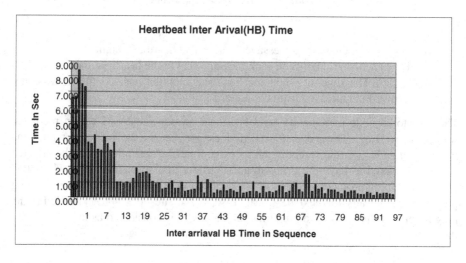

Fig. 2. An example of inter-arrival time on site2 for 100 HB in sequence manner

The graph in Figure 2 illustrates the heartbeats delay when the service is initialized. The delays gradually reduce with some minor irregularities. The graph also demonstrated the gradual changes of HB messages flow (whether increase or reduce). There are only few sudden changes inter-arrival time happened. The graph shows that the initial y axis is equal to 0 meaning interval or delay= 0. It means that, these simulations only consider the network delay and CPU load. But if the interval need to be considered then the y axis need to be initialised at required interval time. For instance, if interval is set to be two second then the time at y axis is started with two seconds. In order to compare and evaluate the failure detection performance results between algorithms in Table 1, the detection performance is plotted in Figure 3.

Figure 3 demonstrate the actual inter-arrival HB time with comparison to the listed algorithms predictions. The observation of Figures 3 show that AADF, Elhadef's and Khilar's algorithms have the ability to adapt to changing network conditions and this is the reason why they are called adaptive. The following situations are also observed:

a. In term of completeness and accuracy metric, Elhadef's algorithms perform better then the rest, however we can see an obvious gap between threshold and the actual HB arrival for this algorithm.

b. While for the prompt or timely detection, AADF and Khilar's algorithms show that they are better algorithms. However Khilar's algorithm generates a lot of false detections.

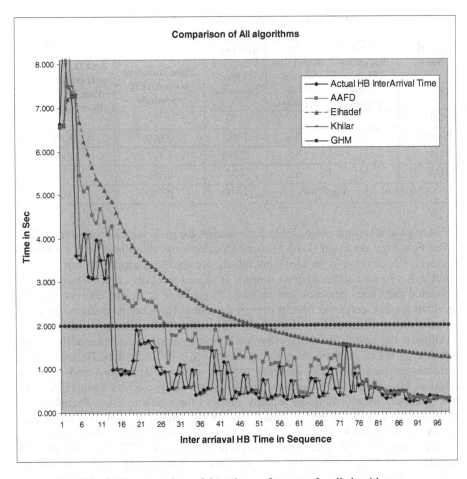

Fig. 3. The comparison of detection performance for all algorithms

c.   For Adaptive algorithms, AAFD points of line mostly located in between Elhadef's and Khilar's algorithm. This shows that AAFD prediction do not overestimate or underestimate the actual inter-arrival HB time
d.   A potential trade-off exists between the QoS metrics. Especially for Khilar's algorithm

From Figure 3, if the particular points of lines represented by the algorithms is the below the line of the actual HB point, this means that at that particular point, algorithm generated false detection. Otherwise if the points of lines predicted by the algorithms are above the actual HB point, the algorithms detected the inter arrival HB accurately. For instance, the Elhadef is triggered the false detection at point 72th. The Elhadef algorithm predicted that the HB data should arrive 1.55 second after the last heartbeat but that actual HB arrives after 1.56 second. The Figure 5 also shows that the Khilar algorithm produces false detection at points 18 to 20 and many other points. While for the AADF algorithm, one of the points that it sends false detection is at the 72th point.

Table 2. Summary of the performance results for site 2

Algorithm Name	False detections First-level-Detection	False detections Second-level-Detection	Average Detection Time (seconds)	Time Different with AAFD (Second)	AAFD outperform others (Percentage)
AAFD	14	0	1.83		
Elhadef	5	0	2.942	0.690	27.4%
Khilar	47	8	2.218	1.112	37.8%
GHM	14	4	2.52	0.388	17.5%
Average of other algorithms			2.560	0.730	30.0%

To complete this comparison, Table 2 summarises the performance results for site 2.

The First level detection is the prediction made by the algorithms before nested if statement. For example if an algorithm falsely predicted the actual HB arrival time, then it will wait for another interval (known as second level detection). After that it is considered third level detection and so forth. From Table 2, we can observe Khilar's algorithm maybe scores the best in prompt detection. However it produces the most false detections compared to the others. The table 2 also illustrates that AAFD algorithm is the best in archiving completeness and accuracy detection with prompt detection. AAFD algorithm embeds the ping service in the algorithm. The use of ping service is adapted in AAFD in order to archive the completeness and accuracy detection. Hence each time the actually HB exceed the prediction time, HBM ping back to the site for affirming the actually status of the monitored site. Therefore this algorithm can completely and accurately verify the site status with prompt timing. The average detection for AAFD is 1.83 which is the best compare to the others.

Table 2 also shows AAFD outperformed GHM's algorithm, Elhadef's and Khilar's algorithm by 27.4 %, 37.8% and 17.5 %, respectively. Subsequently Table 4 also shows AAFD detection is about 30% better than the average of other detection algorithms.

5   Conclusion

In the first part, we have described the design and implementation of a failure monitoring and detection service for high available distributed computing systems. A new failure detection framework and algorithm for reducing the latency of failures detection have been presented. This algorithm utilised heartbeat style interaction for distributed system. The mathematical formula for failure detection prediction in this algorithm is established based on the sample heartbeat data analysis. This algorithm has the ability to adapt to changing network conditions and that the reason why it is called adaptive. In case of the algorithm falsely predict that actually HB arrival time, it invokes ping service for affirming the aliveness status of the monitored site. Ping service is essential not only for reducing waiting time but also dynamically improving certainty level accuracy of completeness failure detection. Therefore this algorithm can completely and accurately verify the site status with prompt detection. Thus we call this failure detection Affirmative Adaptive Failure Detection (AAFD). The

AAFD is design for the purpose where the failure-detection thresholds are used for monitoring individual site and adjusted per-site basis. It is very important for autonomous recovery to achieve a complete and accurate detection with precise timing. A false detection will result in recovery malfunction, in other word the system will failover a functioning site to other functioning neighbour site. On the other hand, delaying in detecting a failure node will subsequently delay the recovery action. The results show that AAFD performs 18% to 39% better than other algorithms. In average AAFD detection is about 30% better than other detection algorithms.

References

1. Mohd. Noor, A.S., Mat Deris, M.: Extended Heartbeat Mechanism for Fault Detection Service Methodology. In: Ślęzak, D., Kim, T.-H., Yau, S.S., Gervasi, O., Kang, B.-H. (eds.) GDC 2009. CCIS, vol. 63, pp. 88–95. Springer, Heidelberg (2009)
2. Hwang, S., Kesselman, C.: Introduction, Requirement for Fault Tolerance in the Grid, Related Work. A Flexible Framework for Fault Tolerance in the Grid. Journal of Grid Computing 1, 251–272 (2003)
3. Mills, K., Rose, S., Quirolgico, S., Britton, M., Tan, C.: An autonomic failure detection algorithm. SIGSOFT Softw. Eng. Notes 29(1), 79–83 (2004)
4. Dabrowski, C., Mills, K., Rukhin, A.: A Performance of Service-Discovery Architectures in Response to Node Failures. In: Proceedings of the 2003 International Conference on Software Engineering Research and Practice, SERP 2003, pp. 95–101 (2003)
5. Stelling, P., Foster, I., Kesselman, C., Lee, C., Laszewski, G.: A Fault Detection Service for Wide Area Distributed Computations. In: Proceedings of HPDC, pp. 268–278 (1998)
6. Hayashibara, N., Defago, X., Yared, R., Katayama, T.: The φ accrual failure detector. In: Proceeding of 23rd IEEE International Symposium on Reliable Distributed Systems, SRDS 2004, pp. 66–78 (2004)
7. Abawajy, J.H., Dandamudi, S.P.: A Reconfigurable Multi-Layered Grid Scheduling Infrastructure. In: Proceedings of International Conference on Parallel and Distributed Processing Techniques and Applications, PDPTA 2003, pp. 138–144 (2003)
8. Abawajy, J.H.: Fault Detection Service Architecture for Grid Computing Systems. In: Laganá, A., Gavrilova, M.L., Kumar, V., Mun, Y., Tan, C.J.K., Gervasi, O. (eds.) ICCSA 2004. LNCS, vol. 3044, pp. 107–115. Springer, Heidelberg (2004)
9. Parziale, L., Dias, A., Filho, L.T., Smith, D., VanStee, J., Ver, M.: Achieving High Availability on Linux for System Z with Linux-HA Release 2. An International Business Machines (IBM) Corporation Redbooks Publication (2009)
10. Chen, W., Toueg, S., Aguilera, M.K.: On the quality of service failure detectors. IEEE Transactions on Computers 51(2), 13–32 (2002)
11. Elhadef, M., Boukerche, A.: A Gossip-Style Crash Faults Detection Protocol for Wireless Ad-Hoc and Mesh Networks. In: Proceeding of International Conference Performance Computing and Communications, IPCCC 2007, pp. 600–602 (2007)
12. Bertier, M., Marin, P.: Implementation and performance evaluation of an adaptable failure detector. In: Proceeding of International Conference on Dependable Systems and Networks, DSN 2002, pp. 354–363 (2002)
13. Khilar, P., Singh, J., Mahapatra, S.: Design and Evaluation of a Failure Detection Algorithm for Large Scale Ad Hoc Networks Using Cluster Based Approach. In: Proceeding of International Conference on Information Technology, ICIT 2008, pp. 153–158 (2008)

A New Low Latency Parallel Turbo Decoder Employing Parallel Phase Decoding Method

Wen-Ta Lee, Min-Sheng Chang, and Wei-Chieh Shen

Institute of Computer and Communication
National Taipei University of Technology
Taipei, Taiwan
wtlee@ntut.edu.tw

Abstract. In this paper, a new parallel phase algorithm for parallel turbo decoder is proposed. Traditional sliding window turbo algorithm exchanges extrinsic information phase by phase, it will induce long decoding latency. The proposed algorithm exchanges extrinsic information as soon as it had been calculated half the frame size, thus, it can not only eliminate (De-)Interleaver delay but also save the storage space. For verifying the proposed parallel phase turbo decoder, we have used FPGA to emulate the hardware architectures, and designed this turbo decoder chip with TSMC 0.18μm 1P6M CMOS process. The gate count of this decoder chip is 128284. The chip size including I/O pad is $1.91{\times}1.91\text{mm}^2$. The simulation result shows that, compared to traditional sliding window method, for different code size, parallel phase turbo decoding method has 51.23%~58.13% decoding time saved, with 8 iteration times at 100MHz working frequency.

Keywords: Parallel turbo decoder, Parallel phase algorithm, Low latency.

1 Introduction

In error correction codes, the turbo code is a famous error correction code, such as magnetic storage device, 3GPP [1] and digital video broadcasting (DVB-RCS) [2] adopt turbo code as channel coding scheme.

Turbo code was proposed in 1993 by Berrou, Glavieux and Thitimajashima [3]. It is a soft-in and soft-out (SISO) decoding scheme. Utilizing the nature of iterative decoding process, it can achieve very excellent decoding performance near Shannon's limit. Turbo code induced wildly research in recent years. However, the implementation of turbo code uses a lot of multipliers and exponent operations, and it is too complex to implement in hardware. To solve this problem, researchers proposed Log-MAP algorithm [4] that simple adders can replace complex multipliers. Besides, MAP algorithm needs a large of memory to store the state metrics. The memory and decoding latency increase along with the frame size. For this reason, the sliding window Log-MAP algorithm is proposed [5]. It can reduce the memory usage and make implementation of turbo decoder easier.

Recently, the era of multimedia is coming. We concern not only voice in wireless communication systems but also pictures, videos and multimedia etc. Consequently,

Y. Xiang et al. (Eds.): ICA3PP 2012, Part II, LNCS 7440, pp. 130–139, 2012.

high speed wireless communication is an important research topic. On the other hand, large frame size of turbo decoder, it will produce a long decoding latency in turbo decoding process. Therefore, low decoding latency is an essential issue for parallel turbo decoding algorithm [6], [7].

The section arrangement of this paper is shown as follows. In section 2, The encoder and decoder of turbo coding are described. In section 3, parallel phase decoding method for turbo decoder is presented. In section 4, the proposed method is simulated and compared with traditional sliding window algorithm. To verify our proposed method, we have designed a turbo decoder chip with this new method. The latency comparison result table is presented in Section 5 and conclusion in Section 6.

2   The Encoder and Decoder of Turbo code

2.1   Turbo Encoder and Decoder System

Fig. 1 shows a general turbo coding system. The turbo encoder consists of a parallel concatenation of two recursive systematic convolutional (RSC) encoders. An interleaver separates these two component codes, it permutes the ordering of symbol sequences at the input and produces identical symbols at the output but in a different temporal order. The general turbo decoder consists of two constituent SISO decoders, which one is working in sequential order (Phase1) and another is working in interleaved order (Phase2). An interleaver and a deinterleaver separate these two SISO decoders. In the SISO decoders, input data can be separated by three parts. The first input is the received systematic bits (y^s) multiplied by the reliability value of the channel. The second input of SISO decoder is the received parity-check bits (y^p) multiplied by the reliability value of the channel. The third input is the extrinsic information (L^e) output from the previous decoder. The error correcting performance can be improved by iterative decoding in the turbo decoder. Output data of turbo decoder are the extrinsic information and log-likelihood ratio (LLR). Hard decision is estimated from the LLR of the second SISO decoder output to reconstruct the original data sequence.

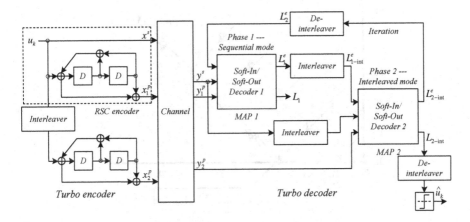

Fig. 1. Turbo encoder and decoder system

2.2   MAP Algorithm

MAP algorithm is mainly derived by Baye's rule and Markov model to measure the reliabilities of the decoded bits which is called LLR. The derivation of MAP algorithm is referred to [8] and the LLR can be described as the following equation (1) which u_k is estimated bit and y is received bit respectively.

$$L(u_k) = \log\left(\frac{p(u_k=+1|y)}{p(u_k=-1|y)}\right) \tag{1}$$

Because transmitted data is interfered in channel noise, the MAP algorithm uses the received bits to estimate as possible as original information bits. The MAP algorithm which consists of alpha (α), beta (β) and gamma (γ) calculations are tremendous due to many multiplication and exponentiation operations needed to calculate the LLR. For simplifying the MAP algorithm, [6] further applies logarithm operation to reduce the mathematics complexity. Then, we can get the equation (2).

$$L(u_k) = \max^*{}_{s^+}\left(\alpha_{k-1}(s') + \gamma_k(s',s) + \beta_k(s)\right) - \max^*{}_{s^+}\left(\alpha_{k-1}(s') + \gamma_k(s',s) + \beta_k(s)\right) \tag{2}$$

2.3   Sliding Window Algorithm

Sliding window algorithm [9] divides the coding block length into many sliding window which size is L, it can reduce the memory size and increase the decoding speed of SISO decoder. Fig. 2 shows the data process of traditional sliding window algorithm [10], [11] of SISO decoder. When the symbol at time t = 0L to 1L-1, the received block data D0 is available. From t = 1L to 2L-1, the reversed data D1 is received and decoded by βint unit at the same time. From t= 2L to 3L-1, D2 is received and decoded, D0 is decoded by β unit. Then, between t = 3L and 4L-1, the data D3 and D1 are decoded as above, D0 is decoded by α and compute the LLR and extrinsic information. The same process is then reiterated every L cycle. The decoding latency of this flow is 3L.

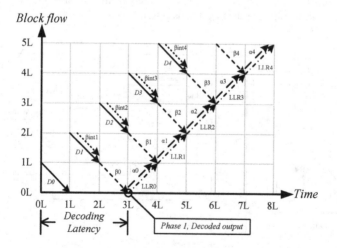

Fig. 2. Data process timing diagram of traditional sliding window algorithm

3   Parallel Phase Decoding Method for Turbo Decoder

Since traditional sliding algorithm exchanges L^e values phase by phase, it produces a long (De-)Interleaver delay, if the (De-)Interleaver delay can be eliminated , decoding speed can double. In concurrent decoding turbo decoding algorithm [12], although it eliminates the (De-)Interleaver delay, it decreases error correcting performance. Therefore, we propose a new parallel phase decoding algorithm. Parallel phase decoding algorithm is a combination of traditional sliding window algorithm and concurrent decoding turbo decoder algorithm. It eliminates not only decoding latency produced by loading data, but also (De-)Interleaver delay. By using this algorithm, it does not need to save all state metrics, and thus can reduce the chip size significantly.

3.1   The Sliding Window of Parallel Phase Decoding Algorithm

The sliding window of parallel phase decoding is shown in Fig. 3. It needs two SISO decoders like concurrent decoding turbo decoder algorithm. Each SISO decoder uses one forward recursive calculation units, two backward recursive calculation units, and one LLR calculation unit.

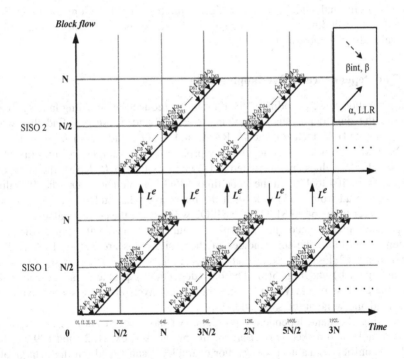

Fig. 3. Parallel phase decoding algorithm timing diagram

In parallel phase decoding algorithm, the SISO1 decoder only deals with phase1, and the SISO2 deals with phase2. We assume that N is 1024 bits, the window size (L) is 16 bits, so it is 64L in this algorithm. At time 1L, the SISO1 decoder starts to calculate βint1. At time 2L, the SISO1 decoder starts to calculate β0. At time 3L, the SISO1 decoder start to calculate α0 and LLR0, and we can get the first decoded output. The intrinsic values(L^i) will be calculated after the LLR calculation, and it will be stored in L^e RAM. At time 32L(N/2), L^i values have already been calculated from D0 to D30, and it can start the phase 2 calculation. The SISO1 decoder repeats the decoding process until 512L(8N). Once the SISO1 decoder calculates 512 bits L^i values, the L^i values will be feed into the SISO2 decoder as the L^e values.

At time 32L, The SISO2 decoder starts to do the decoding process like the SISO1 decoder. The SISO2 decoder is operated in phase2, so we need to interleave data first. We should avoid D29, D30 and D31 in the SISO1 are interleaved to D0, D1 and D2 in the SISO2. It will cause data dependence problem, and it will be discussed in the next section. At time 67L, the SISO2 has decoded 512 bits L^i values, and the L^i values will be stores in L^e RAM and feed back to the SISO1 decoder. At the same time, the SISO1 starts to do iteration 2 calculation until we terminate the iterative decoding process.

In parallel phase decoding algorithm, once the SISO decoder had been calculated 512 bits(N/2) L^i values, the L^i values will be sent to another SISO decoder. The SISO2 decoder will get the first decoded output at 35L, which is the first iteration output. In traditional sliding window algorithm, the first iteration output is 72L. Parallel phase decoding algorithm can reduce 37L decoding latency compared to traditional sliding window algorithm.

3.2   The Dependence of Overlapping Data

By using parallel phase decoding algorithm, it can reduce the decoding latency, but it will cause the data dependency problem. In Fig. 4 and 5, we can find that when SISO1 write(read) L^e to(from) the L^e RAM, and SISO2 read(write) L^e from(to) the L^e RAM, it will bring 3L data dependency problem. For example, in Fig. 4(a) when SISO1 at 32L, L^e values are calculated at D29 and written to L^e RAM, the addresses of D29 are from 464 to 479. At the same time, SISO2 is calculating D0, the L^e values addresses are read from π(15) to π(0). If the interleaved data π(15) to π(0) interleave addresses larger than 464 in SISO1, the SISO2 will not get the correct values.

In parallel phase decoding algorithm, four situations will cause the data dependency problem. The time indices of those situations are 32L~35L, 64L~67L, 96L~99L, and 128L~131L. Note that at time indices 64L~67L, two situations are shown at Fig. 4(b) and Fig. 5(a). The data dependency problem can be solved by limiting the address block. When we generate interleaver table, we should avoid the L^e RAM read and write at the same address.

For solving the data dependency problem, we have added address constraint to interleaver table, and make the overlapped sliding window ex. {0-2} and {29-31} has no address conflict, as Table 1 shows. For example, it can't read out the data greater than address 464 in interleaver index π(15); and the interleaver index π(14) can't read out greater than address 463 data, etc.

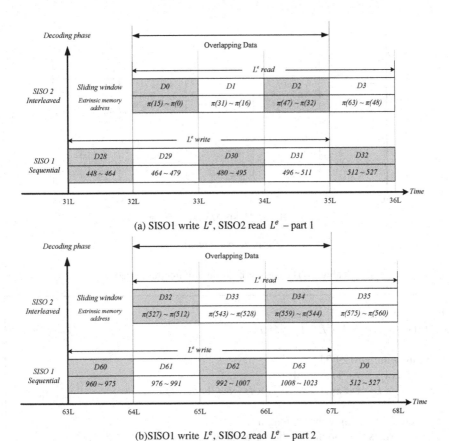

(a) SISO1 write L^e, SISO2 read L^e – part 1

(b) SISO1 write L^e, SISO2 read L^e – part 2

Fig. 4. The dependency of overlapping data-SISO1 write, SISO2 read

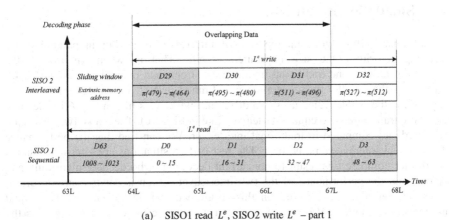

(a)   SISO1 read L^e, SISO2 write L^e – part 1

Fig. 5. The dependency of overlapping data-SISO1 read, SISO2 write

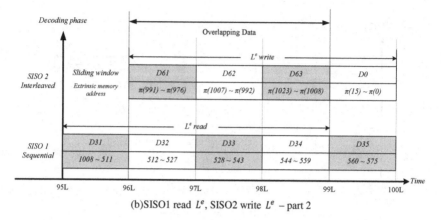

(b)SISO1 read L^e, SISO2 write L^e – part 2

Fig. 5. (*continued*)

Table 1. The address constraint of interleaver table

//sliding window {0-2}
$\pi(x) < sw_{phase\,2} \times L + L - 1 - x \% L$

//sliding window {29-31}
$\pi(x) > (sw_{phase\,1} + 1) \times L - 1$
$sw_{phase\,1} \times L - 1 < \pi(x) < sw_{phase\,1} \times L + L - 1 - x \% L$

   where L is sliding window length
         sw is the counter of sliding window

4   Simulation Result

In traditional turbo algorithm, the size of interleaver is N, but in parallel phase decoding algorithm, the size is limited to N/2. That is, when we arrange the interleaver address, the traditional interleaver is freer than parallel phase interleaver. Because of the parallel phase interleaver is limited to N/2, we can design it in two ways. First, the whole frame uses two different interleavers like in Fig. 6(b). Second, the whole frame uses two equal interleavers like in Fig. 6(c). The above two issues are simulated and compared to traditional interleaver. We can find that the performance of traditional interleaver is the best. The rest of two situations are almost the same. We further compare this result to concurrent decoding turbo decoder algorithm, and we can find the performance of the two interleaver design is better than concurrent turbo decoder algorithm. Based on this result, we choose the simpler two equal interleavers to implement our hardware, and it can save the chip size. Fig. 7 is the simulation result. The result shows the proposed algorithm losses only 0.4dB in compared with traditional algorithm.

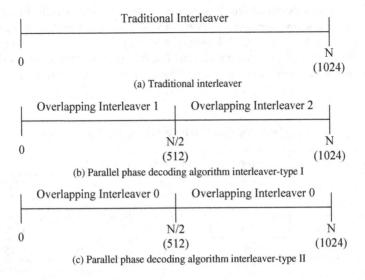

Fig. 6. Interleaver design

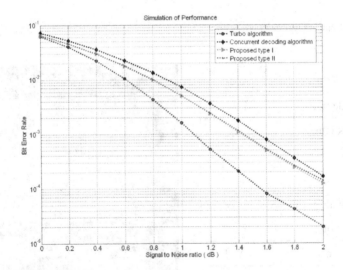

Fig. 7. Simulation result

5   Experimental Results

To emulate the proposed low latency turbo decoder, we use the Xilinx Virtex-5 FPGA to verify the parallel phase decoding method. Table 2 is the decoding time comparison of turbo decoders with different block length. Experimental results show this chip has 51.23%~58.13% decoding time saving with 8 iteration times.

Finally, we have designed this proposed turbo decoder with TSMC 0.18μm 1P6M process. Table 3 shows the specifications of our turbo decoder that using parallel phase decoding method. The block length of this decoder is 1024 and sliding window length is 16. This chip is 128284 gate count. The throughput of this chip is 11Mbps at 100MHz with 8 iterations. Chip size including I/O pad is 1.91×1.91mm^2 as shown in Fig. 8.

Table 2. Decoding time of different block length comparison

Block length	256-bit	512-bit	1024-bit	2048-bit
Traditional turbo decoding [11]	320L	576L	1088L	2112L
	-	-	-	-
Concurrent decoding [12]	144L	288L	576L	1152L
	55%↓	50%↓	47.06%↓	45.45%↓
Proposed parallel phase decoding	134L	262L	518L	1030L
	58.13%↓	54.51%↓	52.39%↓	51.23%↓

Table 3. Proposed turbo decoder chip specifications

Process	TSMC 0.18μm 1P6M
Code rate	1/3
Block length	1024
Constraint length	3
Window size	16
Decoding algorithm	SW-log-MAP
Gate counts	128284
Work frequency	100MHz
Throughput (8 iterations)	11Mbps
Power consumption	151.76mW
Chip area (include I/O pad)	1.91×1.91mm^2

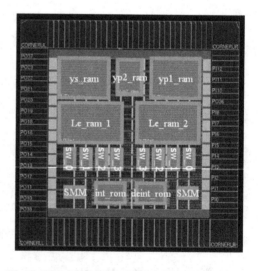

Fig. 8. IC layout of a low latency turbo decoder with parallel phase decoding method

6   Conclusions

This paper proposed a new parallel phase algorithm for turbo decoder. Different from traditional sliding window algorithm, the proposed algorithm can change extrinsic information as soon as it had been calculated half the frame size. Therefore, it can almost double the decoding speed. Simulation result shows that for different frame size, it can reduce the decoding latency 51.23%~58.13%.

Acknowledgment. The authors would like to thank the National Science Council and Chip Implementation Center of Taiwan, ROC, for financial and technical supporting. The work was sponsored by NSC-100-2221-E-027-064.

References

1. 3GPP specifications. 3rd generation partnership project (2000), http://www.3GPP.org/
2. DVB standards & bluebooks. Digital video broadcasting (2003), http://www.dvb.org/
3. Berrou, C., Glavieux, A., Thitimajshima, P.: Near Shannon limit error-correcting coding and decoding: Turbo codes. In: Proc. IEEE Int. Commun. Conf., pp. 1064–1070 (1993)
4. Robertson, P., Villebrun, E., Hoeher, P.: A comparison of optimal and suboptimal MAP decoding algorithms operating in the log domain. In: IEEE Int. Conf. on Commun., vol. 2, pp. 1009–1013 (1995)
5. Dawid, H., Meyr, H.: Real-time algorithms and VLSI architectures for soft output MAP convolutional decoding. In: IEEE Int. Symp. on Personal, Indoor and Mobile Radio Commun., vol. 1, pp. 193–197 (1995)
6. Sun, Y., Zhu, Y., Goel, M., Cavallaro, J.R.: Configurable and scalable high throughput turbo decoder architecture for multiple 4G wireless standards. In: Proc. IEEE Int. Conf. Application-Specific Systems, Architectures and Processors, pp. 209–214 (July 2008)
7. Wang, L., Yang, H., Yang, H.: A novel method for parallel decoding of turbo codes. In: IEEE Int. Conf. Circuits and Systems for Communications, pp. 768–772 (2008)
8. Bahl, L.R., Cocke, J., Jelinek, F., Raviv, J.: Optimal Decoding of Linear Codes for Minimizing Symbol Error Rate. IEEE Trans. Inform. Theory 20, 284–287 (1974)
9. Viterbi, A.J.: An intuitive justification and a simplified implementation of the MAP decoder for convolutional codes. IEEE J. Select. Areas Commun. 16, 260–264 (1998)
10. Lee, W.T., Chang, Y.C.: Turbo decoder design employing a new phase estimation hard decision stopping criterion method. In: Proc. IEEE Int. Conf. Computer Science and Information Technology, pp. 237–240 (June 2011)
11. Boutillon, E., Gross, W.J., Gulak, P.G.: VLSI architectures for the MAP algorithm. IEEE Trans. Commun. 51(2), 175–185 (2003)
12. Lu, Y.C., Chen, T.C., Lu, E.H.: Low-latency turbo decoder design by concurrent decoding of component codes. In: IEEE Int. Conf. Innovative Computing Information and Control, pp. 533–536 (2008)

A Regular Group Quorum System of Degree $\lceil \sqrt{n/2} \rceil$

Fouad B. Chedid[1,2]

[1] College of Arts and Applied Sciences
Dhofar University, Oman
[2] Department of Computer Science
Notre Dame University - Louaize, Lebanon
fchedid@du.edu.om, fchedid@ndu.edu.lb

Abstract. We consider the problem of constructing regular group quorum systems of large degree. In particular, we show that for every integer $p > 1$, there is a regular m-group quorum system over an $n = (\lfloor p(p+1)/2 \rfloor)$-element set of degree $\lfloor (p+1)/2 \rfloor = \lceil \sqrt{n/2} \rceil$ for every $m \le p$, where each quorum has size p.

1 Introduction

A fundamental problem in distributed systems is the problem of mutual exclusion [16]. In this problem, access to a critical section (shared resource) by concurrent processes must be synchronized so that only one process can enter the critical section (use the resource) at a time. The group mutual exclusion problem is a generalization of the original mutual exclusion problem, where each process may belong to different groups and members of the same group may be allowed simultaneous access to their critical sections. Members of different groups must access their critical sections in a mutually exclusive manner. Algorithms for group mutual exclusion appear in [1]-[8],[11]-[13],[15]-[17].

The idea of a quorum-based solution for mutual exclusion [12] is to rely on a set P of manager processes to control access to the critical section. An application process that wishes to enter the critical section has to collect enough votes from manager processes to form a quorum $Q \subseteq P$. Under the assumption that each manager process gives out its permission to at most one process at a time, if quorums are made such that $\forall Q_i, Q_j \subseteq P, Q_i \cap Q_j \ne \phi$, then mutual exclusion is automatically guaranteed. This is true because once an application process a_i enters the criticial section using the quorum Q_i, no other application process a_j can enter the criticial section using another quorum Q_j because of the requirement that $Q_i \cap Q_j \ne \phi$, which implies that there is at least one manager process in $Q_i \cap Q_j$ which has just given its vote to process a_i and now has to wait on a_i to exit the critical section before it can reassign its vote to process a_j.

In a m-group quorum system over a set of manager processes P, there will be m groups of application processes, where each group gets to use its own set of

Y. Xiang et al. (Eds.): ICA3PP 2012, Part II, LNCS 7440, pp. 140–147, 2012.

quorums, also called cartel, over P, such that every two quora of different cartels have a non-empty intersection. Quorum-based algorithms for mutual exclusion can be generalized to solve the group mutual exclusion problem [10] as follows. Following Joung [9], when attempting to enter the critical section, each process i of group j must acquire a quorum Q it has chosen from the cartel associated with the group j by obtaining permission from every member of Q. Upon exiting the critical section, process i returns the permission to the members of Q. By the intersection property between every two quora of different cartels, no two processes of different groups can enter the critical section simultaneously.

Define the degree of a cartel as the maximum number of pairwise disjoint quora in it (this tells us how many processes of the group associated with that cartel can be allowed into their critical sections simultaneously). The degree of a m-group quorum system is the smallest degree among its cartels (this tells us how many processes of any group can be allowed into their critical sections simultaneously). We say that a m-group quorum system is regular of degree k if all its cartels have the same degree k. Clearly, the high-degree of a group quorum system provides for a better protection against faults. On this last point, we have the following result from [9]:

Lemma 1. *Let P be an n-element set of manager processes. Then, for $m > 1$, the theoretical upper bound on the degree of a m-group quorum system over P is $OPT = \lfloor \sqrt{n} \rfloor$.*

In this paper, we show that for each integer $p > 1$, there is a regular m-group quorum system over an $n = \lfloor (p(p+1)/2) \rfloor$-element set of degree $\lfloor (p+1)/2 \rfloor = \lceil \sqrt{n/2} \rceil$ for every $m \leq p$, where each quorum has size p. Though our proposed group quorum system is not degree-optimal, it has a larger degree than the systems proposed in [9] and [5].

The rest of this paper is organized as follows. Section 2 reviews related work from the literature. Our contribution is included in Section 3. Section 4 is the conclusion.

2 Related Work

In 2003, Joung proposed a especially designed group quorum system for group mutual exclusion named the surficial system [9]. Given the number of manager processes n and the number of groups sought m, the surficial system has degree $k = \sqrt{\frac{2n}{m(m-1)}}$, for some integer k, and produces quorums of size $s = (m-1)k$.

In 2006, we described a regular group quorum system which has a larger degree and smaller quorum size than the surficial system of Joung. In particular, given n, m, k, and s as specified above, our system [5] has degree $k' = 1 + \sqrt{1 + \frac{n}{m}}$, for some integer $k' > 2$, which is much higher than k for $m > 3$. Moreover, the quorum size in our system is $s' = m(k' - 2)$, which is smaller than s for the same degree $k' = k$ and for $m > k/2$. These improvements are significant because the degree of a system is related to its fault-tolerance and the level of concurrency it allows. The quorum size is related to the lower bound on the cost of communication imposed on any solution based on the system. In this paper, we show how to construct a regular group quorum system of higher degree than k' above. In particular, we construct a system of degree $\lceil \sqrt{n/2} \rceil$, which is larger than k' $(= 1 + \sqrt{1 + \frac{n}{m}})$, for all $m > 2$.

With regard to group quorum systems of optimal degree $(= \sqrt{n})$, Joung observed [8] that the study of such systems is related to the study of finite projective geometries. The following is a rewrite of a theorem from [8] that is the result of such observation.

Theorem 1. *Let $n = p^{2k}$, where p is a prime, and k is a positive integer. Then there is a m-group regular quorum system of optimal degree $(= \sqrt{n})$ over an n-set for every $m \le \sqrt{n} + 1$, where each quorum has size $\sqrt{n}$.*

Proof. This theorem is an immediate result of the properties of an affine plane in projective geometry (see, e.g., [14]).

For the sake of clarity, we have defined below an affine plane and stated its properties.

Definition 1. *An affine plane is an ordered pair (P, L), where P is a non-empty set of elements called points, and L is a non-empty collection of subsets of P called lines satisfying the following properties:*

- *Every two points lie on exactly one line.*
- *Given a line L and a point $i \notin L$, there is exactly one line L' such that $i \in L'$, and L and L' are parallel.*
- *Each line has at least two points, and there are at least two lines.*

If each line of an affine plane contains exactly x points, the plane is said to have order x. We have the following theorem:

Theorem 2. *An affine plane (P, L) of order x has the following properties:*

- *P has x^2 points.*
- *L has $x^2 + x$ lines.*
- *Each point is on $x + 1$ lines.*
- *L can be partitioned into $x+1$ classes such that each class contains x parallel lines, and every two lines of different classes intersect.*

For example, for $n = 9$, we picture nine points $1, \ldots, 9$ arranged in the plane as follows:

$$
\begin{array}{ccc}
1 & 2 & 3 \\
4 & 5 & 6 \\
7 & 8 & 9
\end{array}
$$

Then, we construct an affine plane of order 3 consisting of 4 classes $C_1, \ldots, C_4$:

$$C_1 = \{\{1,4,7\}, \{2,5,8\}, \{3,6,9\}\}$$
$$C_2 = \{\{1,2,3\}, \{4,5,6\}, \{7,8,9\}\}$$
$$C_3 = \{\{3,5,7\}, \{1,6,8\}, \{2,4,9\}\}$$
$$C_4 = \{\{1,5,9\}, \{3,4,8\}, \{2,6,7\}\}$$

This construction implies a 4-group quorum system over the set of manager processes $\{1, \ldots, 9\}$ of optimal degree 3.

We reiterate that the main disadvantage of this construction method is that it is applicable only to those systems whose sizes are squares of powers of primes. This is true because it is known that an affine plane of order x exists if x is a power of a prime. Thus, while it is true that the properties of an affine plane provided Joung with an off-the-shelf method to construct a degree-optimal quorum system over a set of n processes, the requirement that n must be a square of a power of a prime limits the application of that method in practice.

3   This Work

We have the following theorem:

Theorem 3. *Let p be an integer greater than 1. Then, there is a regular m-group quorum system over an $n = \lfloor (p(p+1)/2) \rfloor$-element set of degree $\lfloor (p+1)/2 \rfloor = \lceil \sqrt{n/2} \rceil$ for every $m \le p$, where each quorum has size p.*

Proof. We propose the algorithm shown in Fig. 1 to construct the desired group quorum system. Let P be the set of integers $\{1, 2, \ldots, n\}$, where $n = \lfloor p(p+1)/2 \rfloor$. Algorithm Quorums divides the set P into $\lfloor (p+1)/2 \rfloor$ subsets $P_1, P_2, \ldots, P_{\lfloor (p+1)/2 \rfloor}$ of size p each. In particular, let P_1 contain the first p integers of P, P_2 the second p integers of P, etc. In general, let the subset P_j contain the integers in the range $[(j-1)p+1, j.p]$, $\forall j$ $(1 \le j \le \lfloor (p+1)/2 \rfloor)$. Notice that all P_j are mutually disjoint. Denote the ith element of P_j as $P_j[i]$, $\forall i, j$ $(1 \le i \le p, 1 \le j \le \lfloor (p+1)/2 \rfloor)$.

Algorithm Quorums uses the subsets P_j $(1 \le j \le \lfloor (p+1)/2 \rfloor))$ to construct p groups of $\lfloor (p+1)/2 \rfloor$ quorums each, where each quorum has size p. So, this is a regular p-group quorum system of degree $\lfloor (p+1)/2 \rfloor$. The algorithm assumes that the elements of each P_j are linked together with wraparound links so that $P_j[p+i]$ is equivalent to $P_j[i]$, $\forall i, j$, $1 \le i \le p, 1 \le j \le \lfloor (p+1)/2 \rfloor$. Also, denote the jth quorum of the ith group as Q_{ij}, $\forall i, j$ $(1 \le i \le p, 1 \le j \le \lfloor (p+1)/2 \rfloor)$.

Algorithm Quorums collects the elements of Q_{ij} as follows. First, starting with the element $P_j[i]$ $(=$ the ith element of the subset $P_j)$, the algorithm adds the next $p/2+1$ elements (with wraparound links) of P_j to Q_{ij} (These are steps 5-6 in Fig. 1). Then, depending on whether $j = 1$ or not, the algorithm follows two different sequences of steps to add $\lfloor (p+1)/2 \rfloor - 1$ additional elements to Q_{ij}. If $j = 1$; that is, if this is the first quorum of the group G_i, the algorithm adds the $(p+i-1)th$ element (with wraparound links) of each subset P_r $(2 \le r \le \lfloor (p+1)/2 \rfloor)$ to Q_{ij} (These are steps 7-9 in Fig. 1). If $j \ne 1$, the algorithm selects one element from each P_r $(1 \le r \ne j \le \lfloor (p+1)/2 \rfloor)$ and adds it to Q_{ij} (See steps 10-20 in Fig. 1).

Algorithm Quorums (p: an integer > 1)
1. Let P_j be the set of integers in the range $[(j-1)p+1, j.p]$, $\forall j$ $(1 \le j \le \lfloor (p+1)/2 \rfloor)$.
2. Let the elements of each P_j $(1 \le j \le \lfloor (p+1)/2 \rfloor)$ be linked together with a wraparound link.
3. for each group G_i $(1 \le i \le p)$ do
4.   for each quorum Q_j $(1 \le j \le \lfloor (p+1)/2 \rfloor)$ do
5.   for $r = i$ to $p/2 + i$ do
6.   Add $P_j[r]$ to Q_j.
7.   if $j = 1$ then
8.   for $s = 2$ to $\lfloor (p+1)/2 \rfloor$ do
9.   Add the element $P_s[p+i-1]$ to Q_j.
10.   else
11.   Let $t = p/2 + i$.
12.   for $r = j - 1$ down to 1 do
13. $t = t + 1$.
14.   Add the element $P_r[t]$ to Q_j.
15.   End for $r = j - 1$
16.   for $r = \lfloor (p+1)/2 \rfloor$ down to $j + 1$ do
17.   Add the element $P_r[t]$ to Q_j.
18. $t = t + 1$.
19.   End for $r = \lfloor (p+1)/2 \rfloor$
20.   End else
21.   End for each Q_j
22.End for each G_i

Fig. 1. Algorithm Quorums

Fig. 2 provides a pictorial view of the operations of Algorithm Quorums. In particular, Fig. 2 shows the steps made by Algorithm Quorums when collecting the elements of Q_{1j}; that is, the jth quorum of the $1st$ group G_1.

It is straighforward to compute the running time of Algorithm Quorums. Step 3 in Fig. 1 repeats p times. Step 4 repeats $\lfloor (p+1)/2 \rfloor$ times. Steps 5-6 repeat $\lfloor p/2 \rfloor + 1$ times. Steps 7-20 repeat $\lfloor (p-1)/2 \rfloor$ times. Thus, Algorithm Quorums runs in time $O(p.\lfloor (p+1)/2 \rfloor.(\lfloor p \rfloor/2 + 1 + \lfloor (p-1)/2 \rfloor)) = O(p^3)$, which is $O(\sqrt{n}^3) = O(n\sqrt{n})$.

We next show that Algorithm Quorums generates a group quorum system with the following property:

Lemma 2. *The generated system has p groups and is regular of degree $\lceil \sqrt{n/2} \rceil$.*

Proof. It follows by construction. This is true because Algorithm Quorums generates p groups of $\lfloor (p+1)/2 \rfloor$ quorums each. So, the generated system is regular of degree $\lfloor (p+1)/2 \rfloor$. In terms of n, we have $n = \lfloor p(p+1)/2 \rfloor$, or equivalently $\lfloor (p+1)/2 \rfloor = \lceil \sqrt{n/2} \rceil$.

We next have the following property:

Lemma 3. $\forall i, i', i \ne i', 1 \le i, i' \le p, \forall j, j', 1 \le j, j' \le \lfloor (p+1)/2 \rfloor,$

$$1 \le |Q_{ij} \cap Q_{i'j'}| \le \lfloor (p-1)/2 \rfloor.$$

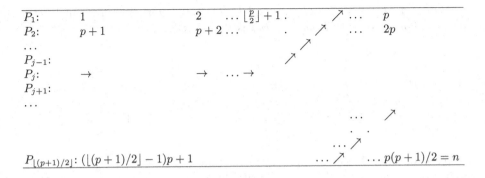

Fig. 2. A pictorial view of the operations of Algorithm Quorums

Proof. We distinguish between two cases depending on whether $j = j'$ or not. We use the notation $|A|$ to denote the size of the set A. We also use the notation $||a||$ to denote the absolute value of the number a.

Case $j = j'$. Steps 5-6 of Algorithm Quorums inserts $(\lfloor \frac{p}{2} \rfloor + 1)$ elements into the quorum Q_{ij}, for all i, j, $1 \le i \le p$; $1 \le j \le \lfloor (p+1)/2 \rfloor$. Observe that all elements inserted in these steps are drawn from the subset P_j of size p (See the straight line of arrows in Fig. 2). Hence, for $j = j'$, both Q_{ij} and $Q_{i'j'}$ contain more than half of the elements of P_j, which implies that these two quorums must have a nonempty intersection. In particular, since $1 \le i \ne i' \le p$, we have

$$1 \le ||i - i'|| \le p - 1$$

which implies that

$$1 \le |Q_{ij} \cap Q_{i'j'}| \le \lfloor p/2 \rfloor.$$

Case $j \ne j'$. Here, the first $(\lfloor \frac{p}{2} \rfloor + 1)$ elements of Q_{ij} and $Q_{i'j'}$ are drawn from two different sets P_j and $P_{j'}$. However, the elements inserted into each Q_{ij} in steps 7-20 of the algorithm are drawn from $\lfloor (p+1)/2 \rfloor - 1$ different subsets P_k, for $1 \le k \ne j \le \lfloor (p+1)/2 \rfloor$. By construction (See the diagonal lines of arrows in Fig. 2), we have

$$1 \le |Q_{ij} \cap Q_{i'j'}| \le \lfloor (p-1)/2 \rfloor.$$

Finally, since $\lfloor (p-1)/2 \rfloor \le \lfloor p/2 \rfloor$, we conclude that $\forall i, i', i \ne i', 1 \le i, i' \le p, \forall j, j', 1 \le j, j' \le \lfloor (p+1)/2 \rfloor$, we have

$$1 \le |Q_{ij} \cap Q_{i'j'}| \le \lfloor (p-1)/2 \rfloor.$$

This ends the proof of Lemma 3.   □

This and other properties of our proposed group quorum system are summarized in the following theorem:

Theorem 4. *Let $\mathcal{G} = \{G_1, G_2, \ldots, G_p\}$ be the group quorum system constructed by Algorithm Quorums. Then, $\mathcal{G}$ satisfies the following properties:*

1. *$\forall i, 1 \le i \le p, |G_i| = \lfloor (p+1)/2 \rfloor$.*
2. *$\forall i, i', i \ne i', 1 \le i, i' \le p, \forall j, j', 1 \le j, j' \le \lfloor (p+1)/2 \rfloor, |Q_{ij}| = |Q_{i'j'}| = p$.*
3. *$\forall p \in P$, let n_p be the size of the multiset $\{Q \mid \exists i, 1 \le i \le p : Q \in G_i$ and $p \in Q\}$. Then, $n_p = p$.*
4. *$\forall i, i', i \ne i', 1 \le i, i' \le p, \forall j, j', 1 \le j, j' \le \lfloor (p+1)/2 \rfloor, 1 \le |Q_{ij} \cap Q_{i'j'}| \le \lfloor (p-1)/2 \rfloor$.*

Proof. Properties 1 and 2 follow from Lemma 2. Property 3 is true because each group consists of $\lfloor (p+1)/2 \rfloor$ mutually disjoint quorums of size p each, where the members of each quorum are drawn from the set $\{1, \ldots, n\}$, where $n = p(p+1)/2$. Thus, each manager process appears exactly once in each group. Property 4 follows from Lemma 3.   □

This ends the proof of Theorem 3.   □

We have traced below Algorithm Quorums for $p = 5$. In this case, the number of manager processes $n = p(p+1)/2 = 15$ and the set of manager processes $P = \{1, \ldots, 15\}$. The algorithm uses the subsets $P_1 = \{1, 2, 3, 4, 5\}$, $P_2 = \{6, 7, 8, 9, 10\}$, and $P_3 = \{11, 12, 13, 14, 15\}$ to generate a regular 5-group quorum system over P of degree 3, where each quorum has size 5. Observe that this group quorum system is degree-optimal since for $n = 15$, we have $\lceil \sqrt{n/2} \rceil = \lfloor \sqrt{n} \rfloor$, which is optimal by Lemma 1 from Section 1. The resultant group quorum system is the following:

$$G_1 = \{Q_1 = \{1, 2, 3, 10, 15\}, Q_2 = \{6, 7, 8, 4, 14\}, Q_3 = \{11, 12, 13, 9, 5\}\}$$
$$G_2 = \{Q_1 = \{2, 3, 4, 6, 11\}, Q_2 = \{7, 8, 9, 5, 15\}, Q_3 = \{12, 13, 14, 10, 1\}\}$$
$$G_3 = \{Q_1 = \{3, 4, 5, 7, 12\}, Q_2 = \{8, 9, 10, 1, 11\}, Q_3 = \{13, 14, 15, 6, 2\}\}$$
$$G_4 = \{Q_1 = \{4, 5, 1, 8, 13\}, Q_2 = \{9, 10, 6, 2, 12\}, Q_3 = \{14, 15, 11, 7, 3\}\}$$
$$G_5 = \{Q_1 = \{5, 1, 2, 9, 14\}, Q_2 = \{10, 6, 7, 3, 13\}, Q_3 = \{15, 11, 12, 8, 4\}\}$$

It can be easily verified that quora belonging to the same group are mutually disjoint while quora belonging to different groups have a nonempty intersection.

4   Conclusion

In this paper, we presented a $O(n\sqrt{n})$-time algorithm that constructs a regular group quorum system over an $(n = p(p+1)/2)$-element set for some integer $p > 1$. The degree of the resultant system is $\lceil \sqrt{n/2} \rceil$. Moreover, our proposed group quorum system has some nice properties from which truly distributed quorum-based algorithms for group mutual exclusion can be easily constructed. Finally, taking a purely mathematical perspective, we find regular group quorum systems of large degree to be elegant mathematical objects whose study is an interesting theoretical problem in its own right.

References

1. Agrawal, D., El Abbadi, A.: An Efficient and Fault-Tolerant Solution for Distributed Mutual Exclusion. ACM Trans. Computer Systems 9(1), 1–20 (1991)
2. Alagarsamy, K., Vidyasankar, K.: Elegant Solutions for Group Mutual Exclusion Problem. Technical Report, Department of Computer Science, Memorial University of Newfoundland, Canada (1999)
3. Barbara, D., Garcia-Molina, H.: Mutual Exclusion in Partitioned Distributed Systems. Distributed Computing 1, 119–132 (1986)
4. Cantarell, S., Datta, A.K., Petit, F., Villain, V.: Token Based Group Mutual Exclusion for Asynchronous Rings. In: Proceedings of the 21th International Conference on Distributed Computing Systems, ICDCS 2001, pp. 691–694. IEEE Computer Society, Washington, DC (2001)
5. Chedid, F.B.: A Group Quorum System of Degree $1 + \sqrt{1 + \frac{n}{m}}$. In: Chaudhuri, S., Das, S.R., Paul, H.S., Tirthapura, S. (eds.) ICDCN 2006. LNCS, vol. 4308, pp. 70–81. Springer, Heidelberg (2006)
6. GarciarMolina, H., Barbara, D.: How to Assign Votes in a Distributed Systems. Journal of the ACM 32(4), 841–860 (1985)
7. Hadzilacos, V.: A Note on Group Mutual Exclusion. In: Proceedings of the Twentieth Annual ACM Symposium on Principles of Distributed Computing, PODC 2001, pp. 100–106. ACM, New York (2001)
8. Joung, Y.-J.: On Quorum Systems for Group Resources with Bounded Capacity. In: Guerraoui, R. (ed.) DISC 2004. LNCS, vol. 3274, pp. 86–101. Springer, Heidelberg (2004)
9. Joung, Y.-J.: Quorum-Based Algorithms for Group Mutual Exclusion. IEEE Transactions on Parallel and Distributed Systems 14(5), 205–215 (2003)
10. Joung, Y.-J.: Asynchronous Group Mutual Exclusion. Distributed Computing 13, 189–200 (2000)
11. Keane, P., Moir, M.: A Simple Local-Spin Group Mutual Exclusion Algorithm. In: Proceedings of the 18th Annual ACM Symposium on Principles of Distributed Computing, PODC 1999, pp. 23–32 (1999)
12. Maekawa, M.: A $\sqrt{N}$ Algorithm for Mutual Exclusion in Decentralized Systems. ACM Transactions on Computer Systems 3(2), 145–159 (1985)
13. Manabe, Y., Park, J.: A Quorum-Based Extended Group Mutual Exclusion Algorithm Without Unnecessary Blocking. In: Proceedings of the 10th International Conference on Parallel and Distributed Systems, ICPADS 2004, p. 341. IEEE Computer Society, Washington, DC (2004)
14. Pedoe, D.: An Introduction to Projective Geometry. Macmillan, New York (1963)
15. Peleg, D., Wool, A.: Crumbling Walls: A Class of Practical and Efficient Quorum Systems. Distributed Computing 10(2), 87–97 (1997)
16. Ricart, G., Agrawala, A.K.: An Optimal Algorithm for Mutual Exclusion in Computer Networks. Communcations of the ACM 24(1), 9–17 (1981)
17. Wu, K.P., Joung, Y.-J.: Asynchronous Group Mutual Exclusion in Ring Networks. IEE Proceedings on Computer and Digital Techniques 147(1), 1–8 (2000)

A Note on Developing Optimal and Scalable Parallel Two-List Algorithms

Fouad B. Chedid[1,2]

[1] College of Arts and Applied Sciences
Dhofar University, Oman
[2] Department of Computer Science
Notre Dame University - Louaize, Lebanon
fchedid@du.edu.om, fchedid@ndu.edu.lb

Abstract. We show that developing an optimal parallelization of the two-list algorithm is much easier than we once thought. All it takes is to observe that the steps of the search phase of the two-list algorithm are closely related to the steps of a merge procedure for merging two sorted lists, and we already know how to parallelize merge efficiently. Armed with this observation, we present an optimal and scalable parallel two-list algorithm that is easy to understand and analyze, while it achieves the best known range of processor-time tradeoffs for this problem. In particular, our algorithm based on a CREW PRAM model takes time $O(2^{n/2-\alpha})$ using 2^{α} processors, for $0 \le \alpha \le n/2 - 2\log n + 2$.

1 Introduction

The Subset Sum Problem (SSP for short) is the following:
INPUT: A set S of n positive integers and a positive integer t.
OUTPUT: A way to decide whether there is a subset $S' \subseteq S$ such that the sum of the elements in S' is equal to t.

SSP is known to be NP-complete [9]. There is a classical two-list algorithm for SSP [11] where the set S is partitioned into two subsets S_1 and S_2 of size $n/2$ each, and then all subset-sums for S_1 (S_2) are generated in nondecreasing (nonincreasing) order in a list A (B), and finally the lists A and B are searched concurrently for a pair of numbers that sum to t. The two-list algorithm is the following (W.l.o.g., we assume that n is a power of 2):
Algorithm Two-List(S, t)
Let $S = \{a_1, a_2, \ldots, a_n\}$.
Let $S_1 = \{a_1, a_2, \ldots, a_{n/2}\}$ and $S_2 = \{a_{n/2+1}, a_{n/2+2}, \ldots, a_n\}$.
1. Generate all subset-sums for S_1 (S_2) in nondecreasing (nonincreasing) order in a list A (B).
2. Let $N = 2^{n/2}$. Let $i = j = 1$
3. if $(A[i] + B[j] = t)$ then stop. A solution is found.
4. if $(A[i] + B[j] < t)$ then $i = i + 1$, else $j = j + 1$
5. if $(i > N)$ or $(j > N)$ then stop. There is no solution.
6. Goto 3

Y. Xiang et al. (Eds.): ICA3PP 2012, Part II, LNCS 7440, pp. 148–155, 2012.
© Springer-Verlag Berlin Heidelberg 2012

Example:

$S = \{5, 4, 7, 9, 2, 8\}, c = 20$

$S_1 = \{5, 4, 7\}; S_2 = \{9, 2, 8\}$

$A = (0, 4, 5, 7, 9, 11, 12, 16)$

$B = (19, 17, 11, 10, 9, 8, 2, 0)$

Step 1) $A[1] + B[1] = 19 < c \Longrightarrow i = i + 1$

Step 2) $A[2] + B[1] = 23 > c \Longrightarrow j = j + 1$

Step 3) $A[2] + B[2] = 21 > c \Longrightarrow j = j + 1$

Step 4) $A[2] + B[3] = 15 < c \Longrightarrow i = i + 1$

Step 5) $A[3] + B[3] = 16 < c \Longrightarrow i = i + 1$

Step 6) $A[4] + B[3] = 18 < c \Longrightarrow i = i + 1$

Step 7) $A[5] + B[3] = 20 = c \Longrightarrow$ solution $= \{5, 4\} \cup \{9, 2\}$.

A straightforwad algorithm for Step 1 in Algorithm Two-List takes time $O(n \cdot 2^{n/2})$ (simply generate all subset sums for S_1 (S_2) and then sort them in nondecreasing (nonincreasing) order in a list A (B)). There is an algorithm, due to Cosnard et al. [6], that avoids the small extra $\log 2^{n/2}$ factor caused by sorting. This algorithm performs Step 1 above in time $O(2^{n/2})$. The algoritm of Casnard et al. is the following:

Algorithm Cosnard et al.(S_1)

Consider $S_1 = \{a_1, a_2, \ldots, a_{n/2}\}$

1. Initially, $A = \{0, a_1\}$.

2. For $i = 2$ to $n/2$ do

3.   Compute the sum of a_i and each element in A, and then store
       the results in a new list A'.

4.   Merge A and A' and store the results back in A.

5. EndFor

Calculating the run time of this algorithm is straightforward knowing that the time complexity of merging two sorted lists of size p and q is $O(p+q)$. Step 3 in Algorithm Cosnard et al. takes time $O(2^{i-1})$. Step 4 takes time $O(2^{i-1} + 2^{i-1}) = O(2^{i-1})$. So, the run time of this algorithm is $\sum_{i=2}^{n/2}(O(2^{i-1})+O(2^{i-1})) = O(2^{n/2})$.

Finally, Steps 2-6 of Algorithm Two-List take time $O(2^{n/2})$ ($=$ length of lists A and B). So, the run time of Algorithm Two-List is $O(2^{n/2})+O(2^{n/2}) = O(2^{n/2})$.

Though developed in the 1970s, the two-list algorithm continues to be the best known sequential algorithm for SSP. Its run time of $O(2^{n/2})$ has even been suggested by some to be the lower bound on solving SSP sequentially, which if true would imply that P $\neq$ NP.

With the advent of parallelism, much effort has been done in order to reduce the computation time of problems in all research areas. For NP-complete problems, we know that unless P=NP, some exponential factor should appear in parallel solutions, either as the time complexity, the number of processors used, or even as the memory requirements. The two-list algorithm has been substantially explored in the parallel algorithms community. Parallel two-list algorithms appear in [4],[7],[8],[10],[12],[13],[14],[15],[16].

In this paper, we observe that the steps of the search phase of the two-list algorithm are closely related to the steps of a merge procedure for merging two sorted lists. In particular, the steps used for searching the lists A and B for a pair of numbers that sum to t are similar to the steps used for merging A and $t - B$, stopping when we hit equality (when we find a collision in the lists). Linking this observation to the fact that we already know how to parallelize merge efficiently [1] immediately gives a new optimal and scalable parallel two-list algorithm that is easy to understand and analyze, while it achieves the best known range of processor-time trade-offs for this problem [16].

The rest of this paper is organized as follows. Section 2 reviews related work from the literature. Our contribution is included in Section 3. Section 4 is the conclusion.

2   Related Work

Recall that the cost of a parallel algorithm is the product of its run time and the number of processors used. Given a sequential algorithm A for a problem P, a parallelization A' of A is said to be optimal if the cost of A' matches the run time of A. A parallel algorithm A'' for P is said to be cost-optimal if the cost of A'' matches the lower bound on solving P sequentially.

Let n be the size of the problem instance of SSP. One of the early parallel two-list algorithms appears in [12]. In that paper, the author describes an algorithm that takes time $T_p = O(2^{n/2})$ using $P = 2^{n/6}$ processors for a cost of $T_p \times P = O(2^{2n/3})$, which is not optimal. Another important parallelization of the two-list algorithm is the parallel one-list algorithm of Ferreira [7], which takes time $O(n \cdot (2^{n/2})^\epsilon)$ using $(2^{n/2})^{1-\epsilon}$ processors, for $(0 \leq \epsilon \leq 1)$ for a cost of $O(n \cdot 2^{n/2})$, which is optimal to within a multiplicative logarithmic term.

In 1994, Chang et al. [3] claimed a parallelization of the two-list algorithm of cost $O(2^{5n/8})$ using $2^{n/8}$ processors. The time complexities of the generation phase and the search phase of the Chang et al.'s algorithm are reported in [3] to be $O((n/8)^2)$ and $O(2^{n/2})$, respectively. In 1997, Lou and Chang [14] described a novel optimal parallelization of the search phase of the two-list algorithm that runs in time $O(2^{3n/8})$ using $2^{n/8}$ processors. Combining the generation phase of Chang et al.'s algorithm and their own search phase, Lou and Chang claimed an optimal parallelization of the two-list algorithm of cost $(O((n/8)^2) + O(2^{3n/8})) \cdot 2^{n/8} = O(2^{n/2})$. The main idea of the Lou and Chang's algorithm is that after generating the lists A and B, each of these lists gets divided into blocks of size $(e = 2^{3n/8})$ each (there will be $b = 2^{n/8}$ blocks per list). If we denote the blocks of the list A by $A_0, A_1, \ldots, A_{b-1}$, and similarly for the list B, and denote the members of the block A_i by $A_i[0], \ldots, A_i[e - 1]$, and similarly for the block B_j, then the algorithm makes the following clever observation:

Lemma 1. *Any pair of blocks (A_i, B_j) such that the sum of the smallest (largest) elements in A_i and B_j is greater (smaller) than t cannot contain a solution among its members, and therefore can be discarded from the search space.*

For the sake of clarity, we have included below the steps of the algorithm of Lou and Chang as suggested by the work in [14].

Algorithm Lou and Chang
1. Divide each of the lists A and B into blocks of size $(e = 2^{3n/8})$ each (there will be $b = 2^{n/8}$ blocks per list). Denote the blocks of the list A by $A_0, A_1, \ldots, A_{b-1}$, and similarly for the list B. Denote the members of the block A_i by $A_i[0], \ldots, A_i[e-1]$, and similarly for the block B_j.
2. Let $i = j = 0$
3. if $(A_i[0] + B_j[e-1] > c)$ then $j = j + 1$
4. else if $(A_i[e-1] + B_j[0] < c)$ then $i = i + 1$
5. else (A_i, B_j) is a candidate block pair for a solution. Then,
    5.1. append B_j to a list L_i associated with the block A_i
    5.2. Let $k = j + 1$
    5.3. while (A_i, B_k) is a candidate block pair for a solution do
             Append B_k to the list L_i and increment k
6. let $j = k - 1$ and $i = i + 1$
7. if $(i > b - 1)$ or $(j > b - 1)$ then stop.
8. goto 3
9. In parallel, redistribute all candidate block pairs found in lists L_i $(0 \leq i \leq b-1)$ (there are at most $2b$ of them) so that each processor P_i $(0 \leq i \leq b - 1)$ gets assigned at most two pairs.
10. For each processor P_i $(0 \leq i \leq b - 1)$, in parallel, do
    Search the blocks assigned to P_i using the same sequential search routine as in the basic two-list algorithm.

We mention that the above steps are written following closely two results from [14]. In particular, Steps 3-4 above are based on Lemma 1 above. Steps 5-6 are based on the following result:

Lemma 2. *Let L_i be the list of candidate blocks $B_{x_1}, B_{x_2}, \ldots, B_{x_m}$ pertaining to the block A_i (Step 5.1 in the algorithm). Then, the blocks in L_i are adjacent one by one; that is, $x_k = x_{k-1} + 1, \forall k$ $(2 \leq k \leq m)$ and hence $L_i \cap L_{i+1} = \{B_{x_m}\}$ or is empty, $\forall i$ $(0 \leq i \leq b - 1)$.*

The run time of the Lou and Chang's algorithm is dominated by the sequential time spent in executing Steps 1-8 and the parallel time spent in executing Steps 9-10. The worst-case time complexity of Steps 1-8 is $O(b)$ (length of the lists A and B in blocks). The time spent in Steps 9-10 is determined by a third result from [14].

Lemma 3. *There are at most $2b$ pairs of candidate block pairs.*

The run time of Step 9 is $O(1)$. The run time of Step 10 is $O(e)$. Thus, the overall run time of the algorithm is $O(b) + O(e) = O(2^{n/8}) + O(2^{3n/8}) = O(2^{3n/8})$. So, the cost of this parallel algorithm is $O(2^{3n/8}) \cdot 2^{n/8} = O(2^{n/2})$.
    In 2002, Sanches *et al.* [15] proved that the results about the generation phase of Chang *et al.*'s algorithm are incorrect invalidating both Chang *et al.*'s and Lou and Chang's results.

In 2003, Kenli [13] described the first truly optimal parallel two-list algorithm. The paper [13] describes an optimal parallel two-list algorithm based on a EREW model that takes time $O(2^{n/4} \cdot (2^{n/4})^\epsilon)$ using $2^{n/4(1-\epsilon)}$ processors, for $0 \leq \epsilon \leq 1$. Note that the time complexity of this algorithm ranges from $O(2^{n/4})$ to $O(2^{n/2})$, which is exponential. The paper [5] describes an optimal parallel two-list algorithm based on a CREW model that takes time $O(2^{n/2-\alpha})$ using 2^α processors, for $0 \leq \alpha \leq n/4$. Note that the time complexity of this algorithm ranges from $O(2^{n/4})$ to $O(2^{n/2})$. An optimal parallel two-list algorithm with polynomial running time first appears in [16]. The paper [16] describes an algorithm based on a CREW model that takes time $O(2^{n/2-\alpha})$ using 2^α processors, for $0 \leq \alpha \leq n/2 - 2\log n$. As far as we know, this algorithm achieves the best known range of processor-time trade-offs for this problem. In particular, it brings the parallel run time down to $O(n^2)$.

We mention that all three optimal and scalable parallelizations of the two-list algorithm in [13],[16], and [5] are based on an optimal and scalable parallelization of the algorithm of Cosnard et al. [6] for the generation phase (See Section 1) and an optimal and scalable variant of the algorithm of Lou and Chang for the search phase [14].

3   This Work

We show that the steps of the search phase of the two-list algorithm are closely related to the steps of a merge procedure for merging two sorted lists. Let (S, t) be an instance of the subset sum problem, where S is an n-element set. Let A and B be as specified in Section 1. Let B' be a new list such that $B'[i] = t - B[i], \forall i, 1 \leq i \leq 2^{n/2}$. The following algorithm merges A and B' and stores the results in a new list C, stopping when it finds a collision in A and B' :

Algorithm Modified-Merge(A, B', C)
1. Let $N = 2^{n/2}$. Let $i = j = 1$.
2. if $(A[i] = B'[j])$ then stop. A solution is found.
3. if $(A[i] < B'[j])$ then $\{C[k] = A[i], i = i + 1, k = k + 1\}$
4. else $\{C[k] = B'[j], j = j + 1, k = k + 1\}$
5. if $(i > N)$ then
6.   for $p = j$ to N do $\{C[k] = B'[p], k = k + 1\}$
8.   stop. There is no solution.
9. else if $(j > N)$ then
10.   for $q = i$ to N do $\{C[k] = A[q], k = k + 1\}$
12.   stop. There is no solution.
13. goto 2

Clearly, the steps of this algorithm are closely related to the steps of the search phase of the two-list algorithm (See Steps 2-6 of Algorithm Two-List in Section 1). Immediately, we obtain a parallel algorithm for the search phase of the two-list algorithm that is as good as the parallel algorithm of Lou and Chang in [14]. This is true because we already know [1] that on a CREW PRAM with $P = 2^{n/8}$ processors, two sorted lists of size $N = 2^{n/2}$ can be merged in time $T_p = O(N/P + \log N) = O(2^{n/2}/2^{n/8} + \log 2^{n/2}) = O(2^{3n/8})$.

We next describe the main result of this paper. The following algorithm is an optimal and scalable parallel two-list algorithm that achieves the best known range of processor-time tradeoffs for SSP [16]. Assume a number of processors $P = 2^{\alpha}$, for $0 \le \alpha \le n/2 - 1$.

Algorithm Parallel-Two-List (S)
Let $S = \{a_1, a_2, \ldots, a_n\}$.
Let $S_1 = \{a_1, a_2, \ldots, a_{n/2}\}$ and $S_2 = \{a_{n/2+1}, a_{n/2+2}, \ldots, a_n\}$.
1. Parallel-Generation (S_1, A)
2. Parallel-Generation (S_2, B)
3. Parallel-Modified-Merge $(A, t - B, C)$

An algorithm for Step 1 in Parallel-Two-List appears in our paper [5]. In [5], we described an optimal and scalable parallelization of the algorithm of Cosnard et al. (See Section 1) for generating an ordering of all subset sums of a set. The algorithm is the following:

Algorithm Parallel-Generation (S_1, A)
1. Sequentially, generate a nondecreading ordering A of all of the subset-sums of $\{a_1, a_2, \ldots, a_{n/2-\alpha}\}$.
2. For i = 1 to α do {
3.   In parallel, compute the sum of $a_{n/2-\alpha+i}$ and each element in A, and then store the results in a new list A'.
4.   In parallel, merge A and A' and store the results back in A.
5. EndFor

Step 1 in Parallel-Generation takes time $O(2^{n/2-\alpha})$ by the sequential algorithm of Cosnard et al. (See Section 1). Step 3 takes time $O(2^{n/2-\alpha+i-1}/2^{\alpha}) = O(2^{n/2-2\alpha+i-1})$. Step 4 takes time $O(2^{n/2-\alpha+i-1}/2^{\alpha} + n/2 - \alpha + i - 1) = O(2^{n/2-2\alpha+i-1} + n/2 - \alpha + i - 1)$. Hence, the time complexity of Parallel-Generation is

$$O(2^{n/2-\alpha}) + \sum_{i=1}^{\alpha}(O(2^{n/2-2\alpha+i-1}) + O(2^{n/2-2\alpha+i-1} + n/2 - \alpha + i - 1)) =$$

$$O(2^{n/2-\alpha} + \alpha.n/2 - \alpha^2/2 - \alpha/2) = O(2^{n/2-\alpha} + \alpha.n/2) = O(2^{n/2-\alpha} + n^2/4),$$

since $\alpha < n/2$.

This time complexity is $O(2^{n/2-\alpha})$, if $2^{n/2-\alpha} \ge n^2/4$, or equivalently if $0 \le \alpha \le n/2 - 2\log n + 2$.

Step 3 in Parallel-Two-List takes time $O(2^{n/2}/2^{\alpha} + n/2) = O(2^{n/2-\alpha})$, if $2^{n/2-\alpha} \ge n/2$, or equivalently if $0 \le \alpha \le n/2 - \log n + 1$. Combining the time complexities of Steps 1, 2, and 3 in Parallel-Two-List shows that the time complexity of this algorithm is $O(2^{n/2-\alpha})$, for $0 \leq \alpha \leq n/2 - 2\log n + 2$. With these bounds on α, the run time of Parallel-Two-List ranges from $O(2^{n/2})$ down to $O(n^2)$. Its cost is $O(2^{n/2-\alpha}) \cdot 2^{\alpha} = O(2^{n/2})$, which is optimal. These results match the best known range of processor-time tradeoffs for this problem [16].

4   Conclusion

This paper considered optimal parallelizations of the two-list algorithm for the subset-sum problem. We observed that the search phase of the two-list algorithm is closely related to a merge procedure for merging two sorted lists. Using this obseration, we described an optimal and scalable parallel two-list algorithm that is easy to understand and analyze, while it achieves the best known range of processor-time tradeoffs for this problem.

References

1. Akl, S.G.: The Design and Analysis of Parallel Algorithms. Prentice-Hall, Englewood Cliffs (1989)
2. Amirazizi, H.R., Hellman, M.E.: Time Memory Processor trade-offs. IEEE Transactions on Information Theory 34(3), 502–512 (1988)
3. Chang, H.K.-C., Chen, J.J.-R., Shyu, S.-J.: A Parallel Algorithm for the Knapsack Problem Using a Generation and Searching Techniques. Parallel Computing 20(2), 233–243 (1994)
4. Chedid, F.B.: An Optimal Parallelization of the Two-List Algorithm of Cost $O(2^{n/2})$. Parallel Computing 34(1), 63–65 (2008)
5. Chedid, F.B.: A Scalable Parallelization of the Two-List Algorithm of Optimal Cost $O(2^{n/2})$. In: Proceedings of Algorithms and Complexity in Durham, ACiD 2007, King's College, London. Texts in Algorithmics, vol. 9, pp. 35–42 (2007)
6. Cosnard, M., Ferreira, A.G., Herbelin, H.: The Two-List Algorithm for the Knapsack Problem on a FPS T20. Parallel Computing 9(33), 385–388 (1989)
7. Ferreira, A.G.: A Prallel Time/Hardware Tradeoff $T.H = O(2^{n/2})$ for the Knapsack Problem. IEEE Transactions on Computers 40(2), 221–225 (1991)
8. Ferreira, A.G., Robinson, J.M.: Fast and Scalable Parallel Algorithms for Knapsack-Like Problems. Journal of Parallel and Distributed Computing 49, 1–13 (1996)
9. Garey, M.R., Johnson, D.S.: Computers and Intractability: A Guide to the Theory of NP-Completeness. W. H. Freeman and Company, New York (1979)
10. Goldman, A., Trystran, D.: An Efficient Parallel Algorithm for Solving the Knapsack Problem on Hypercubes. Journal of Parallel and Distributed Computing 64(11), 1213–1222 (2004)
11. Horowitz, E., Sahni, S.: Computing Partitions With Applications to the Knapsack Problem. Journal of ACM 21(2), 277–292 (1974)
12. Karnin, E.D.: A Parallel Algorithm for the Knapsack Problem. IEEE Transactions on Computers 33(5), 404–408 (1984)
13. Li, K., Li, Q., Hui, W., Jiang, S.: Optimal Parallel Algorithm for the Knapsack Problem Without Memory Conflicts. Journal of Computer Science and Technology 19(6), 760–768 (2004)

14. Lou, D.-C., Chang, C.-C.: A Parallel Two-List Algorithm for the Knapsack Problem. Parallel Computing 22, 1985–1996 (1997)
15. Sanches, C.A.A., Soma, N.Y., Yanasse, H.H.: Comments on Parallel Algorithms for the Knapsack Problem. Parallel Computing 28, 1501–1505 (2002)
16. Sanches, C.A.A., Soma, N.Y., Yanasse, H.H.: An Optimal and Scalable Parallelization of the Two-List Algorithm for the Subset-Sum Problem. European Journal of Operational Research 176, 870–879 (2007)

Small Business-Oriented Index Construction of Cloud Data

Kai Peng, Hua Zou, Rongheng Lin, and Fangchun Yang

State Key Lab. of Networking and Switching Technology
Beijing University of Posts and Telecommunications
Beijing, China
pkbupt@gmail.com,
{zouhua,rhlin,fcyang}@bupt.edu.cn

Abstract. With the development of cloud computing, data owners (businesses and individuals) are motivated to outsource their local complex database systems to public cloud for flexibility and economic savings. But for the consideration of user's privacy, personal data has to be special treatment locally before outsourcing to the cloud server. Considering the large number of data users and documents in cloud, it is crucial for data owner to construct an index for their data collection, which increases the cost of the data owner. Related works focus on the searches on encrypted database but rarely consider the overhead of the index construction for data owner and the extensions of the index. Although traditional index construction methods of information retrieval have been widely studied, direct application of these methods would not be necessarily suitable for our scenario. Thus, enabling an efficient index construction service is of paramount. In this paper, we define and solve the problem of index construction on small business (SBIC). Among various index methods, we choose inverted index method. An inverted index is an index data structure storing a mapping from content to its locations in a set of documents. The purpose of it is to allow fast full text searches. We firstly propose a basic SBIC scheme using Lucene (an open source project for web search engine), and then significantly improve it to meet efficient keyword extraction requirement and multi-type files demand. Thorough analysis design goals(see section 2.3) of proposed schemes is given, extensive experimental results on the dataset further show proposed scheme indeed introduce low overhead on time and space.

Keywords: Cloud computing, Index construction, Lucene.

1   Introduction

Cloud computing has recently emerged as a new paradigm for hosting and delivering services over the Internet [1]. It economically enables a fundamental paradigm shift on how data services are deployed and delivered. Both individuals and businesses are motivated to outsource their local complex database management system into the cloud, especially when the data produced by them that need to be stored and utilized

Y. Xiang et al. (Eds.): ICA3PP 2012, Part II, LNCS 7440, pp. 156–165, 2012.

is rapidly increasing [5]. To protect data privacy and combat unsolicited accesses in cloud ,in addition, commercial public cloud is "honest but curious"(see section 2.1), data may has to be special treatment locally before outsourcing to the cloud server [2]; this, however, increases the overhead on data owner. Considering the large number of data users and huge amount of documents in cloud, an index can be used for quickly locating the related documents that contain the keywords. Thus, it is crucial for data owner to construct an index before outsourcing. Related works [3-9] focus on improving the retrieval methods for query users (Those are authorized to retrieval the database as their interests by submitting t given keywords) over encrypted data, others' attention centered on the design of access control mechanism [10-12], while those techniques rarely considerate the time and space overhead of index construction for data owner and also the extensions of index. In addition, although traditional index construction methods of information retrieval [14] have been widely developed in web search and large database system, direct application of these methods would not be necessarily suitable for our scenario, as these techniques mainly deployed on large server of big company. We define and solve the problem of efficient index construction on small business (SBIC). For these companies, they don't have enough money to set up cluster server for such data management. Thus, enabling an efficient index construction service for small business is of paramount. Among various index construction methods, we choose inverted index method. An inverted index (also referred to as postings file or inverted file) is an index data structure storing a mapping from content, such as words or numbers, to its locations in a database file, or in a document or a set of documents [15]. It can achieve the balance between time and space. Our contribution can be summarized as follows.

1) We explore the problem of index construction over data owner for small-business, and establish a set of design goals (see section 2.3) for such a system to become a reality.

2) We propose two SBIC schemes following the aforementioned goals.

3) Thorough analysis investigating requirements of our proposed schemes, and experiments on the dataset further show proposed schemes indeed introduce low overhead on time and space.

The reminder of the paper is organized as follows. We first introduce notations, application scenario, and our design goals in Section 2. Section 3 describes SBIC framework and gives our SBIC achieving design goals, followed by Section 4, which evaluates our approach experimentally on dataset. Section 5 shows the related work on both search on encrypted database and IR (Information retrieval), and we conclude and discuss future work in Section 6.

2   Problem Formulation

2.1   Notations

Commercial Public Cloud Server (CS). CS is considered as "honest-but-curious" in our model, which is consistent with the most related works on outsourced data. CS stores the outsourced data without tampering it and honestly executes every search operation and returns documents associated with the given queries, however, it also tries to learn the underlying plaintext of user's data [13].

Data Owner (DO). Small businesses or individuals have a set of documents to be outsourced to CS.

F – The plaintext document collection, denoted as a set of m data documents. It contains many different types of file like TXT, DOC, PDF, etc.

I –The index associated with F.

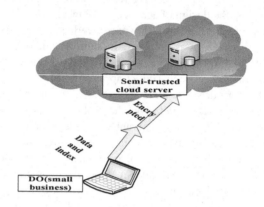

Fig. 1. Architecture of the index construction over cloud data

2.2   Application Scenario

Considering our scenario involving two entities, as illustrated in Fig. 1: *DO* and *CS*. *DO* has a collection of data documents F to be outsourced to CS. To enable the searching capability over the database for effective data utilization, DO, before outsourcing, will first construct an index I from F, and then encrypt both the data F and the index I, outsource both the encrypted document collection and the index I to *CS*. We focus on how to improve the efficiency and extensions of index construction.

2.3   Design Goals

To enable the cost of index construction as low as possible and easy to extend   under the aforementioned model, our system design should achieve requirements as follows.

Time and Space Cost: To make sure the time of index construction within an acceptable range and the storage space is as small as possible.

Relevant Keywords Extraction: To extract the mostly relevant keywords from the big data collection for each file, the performance of the algorithm must keep stable even for dealing with big data.

Extensions of the Index (e.g. Support multi-type files): The algorithm can be extended to support multi-type files including TXT Type in the cloud data and also performs quite stable .In addition, the query users will benefit from these extensions.

3   Framework

3.1   SBIC _I: Basic Scheme

(1). The Idea of the Algorithm and Main Class

As TXT files are basic form of data in information retrieval, SBIC_I should well support the index construction of them. Our algorithm is based on Lucene. It   traverses all the files in source folder and calls the embedded analyzer in Lucene, and then stores the index files into target file folder. The knowledge of Lucene can be found on [16].

Main Class and Function

Document: A document is the base process unit in Lucene. The document contains the *title, time, author and content,* which maps to the specific file in general.

IndexWriter : It can be used to construct the inverted index files in Lucene.

StandardAnalyzer: Embedded analyzers in Lucene. Choose different analyzers according to different languages.

(2). In the Setup Phase

The program initiates the scheme by calling IndexConstruct (*dataDir, indexDir*).The details are **given in Algorithml1 (SBIC_I: Basic Scheme).**

Upon receiving the indexDir and dataDir, the IndexConstruct( ) calls IndexWriter and IndexDir. First constructs initialized files of index, and then calls IndexDir (*writer, dataDir),* which traverses all the files in dataDir. After that, updates the index files via IndexFiles ( ) in given file folder until finishing the last one.

(3). Discussion

The above scheme well satisfies the inverted index construction of big data consisting of TXT. However, the embedded word segmentation algorithm in Lucene counts the term of all words, and then construct index for all of them. Actually, as the big data in the cloud, there is no need to do so. For one thing, we can save a lot of space for data owner in our scheme. For another, relevant keywords can achieve efficient retrieval for query users.

3.2   3.2 SBIC_II Scheme

(1). Keyword Extraction Algorithm

The TF*IDF weight is a numerical statistic which reflects how important a word is to a document in a collection or corpus [17]. It is widely used as a weighting factor in several areas such as information retrieval and data mining. TF (term frequency) is simply the number of times a given term or keyword appears within a file (to measure the importance of the term in a special file) [3]. IDF (inverse document frequency) is mainly used for preventing the impact to the keywords by common words.

The basic definition is as follows:

$$idf(t, F) = \log \frac{|F|}{|\{d \in F : t \in d\}|}$$

Algorithm 1.   SBIC_I: Basic Scheme
```
1:  procedure Main ()
2:  indexnumber<-IndexConstruct (dataDir,indexDir);
3:  end procedure

4:  procedure IndexConstruct (dataDir,indexDir);
5:  IndexWriter (indexDir,standardAnalyzer)
6:  IndexDir (writer,dataDir);
7:  return indexnumber;
8:  end procedure

9:  procedure IndexDir (writer,dir)
10: IndexDir (writer,f); // Recursive
11: IndexFiles ();
12: end procedure

13: procedure IndexFiles ()
14: document.add (); // Get content of document
15: writer.addDocument (doc);
16: end procedure
```

|F|: The total number of documents in the collection. |F| is the length of file F; it is usually normalized to prevent a bias towards longer documents.

|{d}|: number of documents where the term t appears (i.e, $tf(t, d) \neq 0$). Actually, it is common to modify the formula to $1+|d \in F : t \in d|$ for avoiding a division-by-zero caused by the term is not in the corpus[17].

(2). The Implementation of the Algorithm
Traversal all the files in given path, and compile statistics of keyword (frequency) term in the dataset and calculate the length of the file, and then make them normalized, finally call the TF*IDF to calculate the final scores of keywords.

(3). In the Setup Phase
   1), The data owner traverse all the files in the path by using readDirs and then normal the term of keywords in the lib by calling NormalTF ( ).

Ouput Parameter: *normalTF*.

2).Upon receiving the parameters from Part I).The user calls CalculateIDF (*normalTF,   fileList*) to calculate the final score for all of the keywords.

3).The owner chooses the mostly relevant keywords from the ranked list, and then construct   an index by using SBIC_I system.

Algorithm 2. (SBIC_II system)

```
1: procedure main ()
2: normal <- NormalTF (dir);
3: End procedure

4: procedure NormalTF (dir)
5: fileList=readDirs (dir);
6: CalculateTF (fileList);
7: return normalTF;
8: end procedure

9: procedure CalculateIDF (normalTF,fileList)
10: IDF=log (|F|/1+|Ft|)
11: end procedure
```

---

(4). Discussion and Analysis

Discussion: In information retrieval, there are a large number of unstructured documents like TXT, DOC, PDF, and etc. System II can only support keyword extraction of TXT type, which limits the application of multi-type. Therefore, we need to modify our scheme to support them. Through the analysis of the previous algorithm, we find that (see Algorithm2) can be modified to achieve the desired goals. As we traverse the files, we add a judgmental process. We choose different parsers according to the extension of file. The main idea is to get the text content by calling the specific parser, and then do TF*IDF. Taking DOC for example, we choose POI (We can also use textmining). The details are given in **Algorithm3 (Improved SBIC_II scheme).**

Analysis: System I achieves the inverted index construction of big data consisting of TXT, which provides a basis method for the data owner over cloud computing. Considering the storage overhead of index, we introduce keyword extraction algorithm before index construction in System II .In order to support other unstructured documents in the cloud, we improve system II by introducing file parsers. Improved system II achieves all the established design goals (see section 2.3).

Algorithm 3. (Improved SBIC_II scheme)

```
1:  procedure main ()
2:  normal <- NormalTF ("path");
3:  end procedure

4:  procedure NormalTF ()
5:   fileList = readDirs (dir);
 //The main modifications are as follows
6:   if (.doc) then
7:   do WordParser
8:   end if
9:   if (.xsl) then
10: do ExcelParser
11: end if
12: else if (.pdf) then
13: do PdfParser
14: end if
15: else
16:    (here add other parsers)
17: end
18: CalculateTF (fileList);
19: return normalTF;
20: end procedure

21: procedure CalculateIDF (normalTF,fileList)
22: IDF=log (|F|)/1+|Ft|)
23: end procedure
```

---

4   Performance Analysis

In this section, we demonstrate a thorough experimental evaluation of the proposed technique on a dataset: BIT NLPIR Dataset (for TXT Test) [18] and then we convert the TXT files into DOC format for DOC Test. The whole experiment system is implemented by Java language on a windows Server. The performance of our technique is evaluated regarding the requirements of two proposed SBIC schemes, as well as the balance between time and space.

Time Analysis

1)、 *Time of Index construction for TXT dataset.* Tab.1 shows the file information before and after index construction. A number of factors such as number of files, memory space and hard disk space should be taken into consideration. Here, we mainly discuss the time cost. The average time of index construction is 0.4ms. Thus, we can conclude that the inverted index is quite a time saving method.

2) Time of keyword extraction. Time of TF*IDF (both TXT and DOC) is absolutely linear. The doc files in the dataset are all converted from the txt files. From fig 2, we can conclude that the different time cost for TXT and DOC only caused by the file format.

Space Analysis: From Tab.1, we can conclude that the final index files account for percentage of eight ratios of the source files. That is, the inverted index is space saving. Furthermore, relevant keyword extraction algorithm makes the storage much more economical.

Conclusion: Our TF*IDF algorithm supports multi-type files and it keeps stable even as the size get larger. After extracting the mostly relevant keywords and construct the space saving inverted index by using Lucene. Our proposed schemes enjoy the constant overhead between time and space which makes it can be widely used in the cloud paradigm, especially for those small businesses.

Table 1. Before and after index construction

	Soure files	Index files
Num	8704	13
Mem	784KB	2.82MB
Space	34MB	2.86MB
Time	0 ms	3544ms

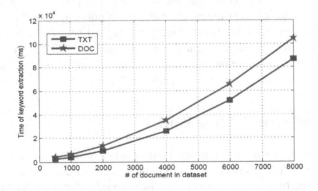

Fig. 2. 8000 files are divided into six groups for TXT and DOC test.500, 1000, 2000, 4000, 6000, and 8000

5   Related Work

Search on Encrypted Database. Recently, the importance of encrypted data search has received attention in information retrieval community [3-9].Many of them focus on the search of data for query users (Those are authorized to search the database as their interests by submitting *t* given keywords) over encrypted data .This of course greatly meets the query users to retrieval the encrypted data directly in the cloud. [3-5] provide single keyword ranked search, fuzzy keyword search, and multi-keyword search over outsourced data. Yang et.al.'s [9] mainly solve the multi-user search problem for the outsourced cloud data. [10-12] mainly focus on efficient access control mechanism caused by increasing query users in cloud. While these technique rarely consider the time and space overhead of index construction for data owner, and do not propose a common index construction which can be easy modified to meet the increasing retrieval needs. Thus, enabling an efficient and easily extended index construction service is of paramount.

IR (Information retrieval). Traditional index construction methods in IR have been well studied. Among those works, most of them focus on enhancement of retrieval requirements in web search engine or large database system, these techniques mainly ignore the hardware costs. The bitmap index is quite a fast retrieval method which has been widely used in oracle database. However, it usually occupies large storage space. Taking TREC database for example, a bit-map index requires 40GB, almost 20 times larger than the collection itself [14]. A signature file is another common technique applied to document retrieval. In certain circumstances, it can save a lot of space, however, this method will performance low efficiency in data search especially when facing negated terms [14].In short, all these existing schemes do not performance very well when considering both the cost and extensions of index, and thus they are not suitable for our scenario (see section 2.2).Note that, the inverted index is suitable for ours. It can achieve the balance between time and space. Although the literature [3] proposes ranked keyword search scheme using inverted index, their algorithm only supports TXT Type (RFC dataset), in addition, they focus on solving the ranked search for the query users without consideration of the overhead for data owner. In our SBIC_II scheme, multi-type files keyword extraction algorithm not only reduces storage space for data owner, but also improves the retrieval efficiency for query users.

6   Conclusion and Future Work

In this paper, we define and solve the problem of efficient index construction on small business, and establish a variety of design requirements for data owner. Among various index construction methods, we choose the inverted index. In order to achieve the efficient establishment of the index, and in order to improve the retrieval needs in the future. We firstly propose a basic SBIC system using Lucene, and then significantly improve it to meet efficiency keyword extraction and support multi-type files. Thorough analysis requirements and time and space of proposed schemes are given, and experiments on the dataset show our schemes introduce low overhead on both time and space. As our future work, we will explore supporting other efficient vector space index construction method, and also try to improve the efficiency of encryption for data owner.

Acknowledgement. This work is supported by the National 863 High-tech Project of China under Grant No. 2011AA01A102.

References

1. Zhang, Q., Cheng, L., Boutaba, R.: Cloud computing: state-of-the-art and research challenges. Proc. Journal of Internet Services and Applications 1(1), 7–18 (2010)
2. Kamara, S., Lauter, K.: Cryptographic Cloud Storage. In: Sion, R., Curtmola, R., Dietrich, S., Kiayias, A., Miret, J.M., Sako, K., Sebé, F. (eds.) FC 2010 Workshops. LNCS, vol. 6054, pp. 136–149. Springer, Heidelberg (2010)
3. Wang, C., Cao, N., Li, J., Ren, K., Lou, W.: Secure ranked keyword search over encrypted cloud data. In: Proc. ICDCS 2010, pp. 253–262 (2010)
4. Li, J., Wang, Q., Wang, C., Cao, N., Ren, K., Lou, W.: Fuzzy keyword search over encrypted data in cloud computing. In: Proc. INFOCOM 2010 Mini-Conference, San Diego, pp. 1–5 (March 2010)
5. Cao, N., Wang, C., Li, M., Ren, K., Lou, W.: Privacy-Preserving Multi-Keyword Ranked Search over Encrypted Cloud Data. In: Proc. INFOCOM 2011, Shanghai, pp. 829–837 (April 2011)
6. Chuah, M., Hu, W.: Privacy-Aware Bedtree Based Solution for Fuzzy Multi-Keyword Search over Encrypted Data. In: Proc. ICDCSW 2011, pp. 273–281 (2011)
7. Wang, C., Ren, K., Yu, S., Urs, K.M.R.: Achieving Usable and Privacy-Assured Similarity Search over Outsourced Cloud Data. In: Proc. INFOCOM 2012, Orlando (March 2012)
8. Cao, N., Yang, Z., Wang, C., Ren, K., Lou, W.: Privacy-Preserving Query over Encrypted Graph-Structured Data in Cloud Computing. In: Proc. ICDCS 2011, pp. 393–402 (2011)
9. Yang, Y., Lu, H., Weng, J.: Multi-User Private Keyword Search for Cloud Computing. In: Proc. CLOUDCOM 2011, Athens, pp. 264–271 (2011) ISBN:146730090X
10. Goyal, V., Pandey, O., Sahai, A., Waters, B.: Attribute-Based Encryption for Fine-Gained Access Control of Encrypted Data. In: Proc. ACM CCS 2006, pp. 89–98 (2006)
11. Di Vimercati, S.D.C., Foresti, S., Jajodia, S., Paraboschi, S., Samarati, P.: Over-Encryption: Management of Access Control Evolution on Outsourced Data. In: Proc. VLDB Endowment 2007, pp. 123–134 (2007)
12. Yu, S., Wang, C., Ren, K., Lou, W.: Achieving Secure, Scalable, and Fine-Grained Data Access Control in Cloud Computing. In: Proc. INFOCOM 2010, pp. 1–9 (2010)
13. Chai, Q., Gong, G.: Verifiable Symmetric Searchable Encryption for Semi-Honest-but-Curious Cloud Servers
14. Witten, I.H., Moffat, A., Bell, T.C.: Managing gigabytes: Compressing and indexing documents and images. Morgan Kaufmann Publishing, San Francisco (1999)
15. Inverted Index, http://en.wikipedia.org/wiki/Inverted_index
16. Cutting, D.: Lucene, http://lucene.apache.org/
17. TF*IDF, http://en.wikipedia.org/wiki/Tf*idf
18. Zhang, H.: NLPIR dataset, http://www.datatang.com/datares/go.aspx?dataid=605109

High-Performance Matrix Multiply on a Massively Multithreaded Fiteng1000 Processor

Jie Liu, Lihua Chi, Chunye Gong, Han Xu, Jie Jiang, Yihui Yan, and Qingfeng Hu

Section 605, College of Computer Science, National University of Defense Technology,
Changsha, China, 410073
liujie@nudt.edu.cn

Abstract. Matrix multiplication is an essential building block of many linear algebra operations and applications. This paper presents parallel algorithms with shared A or B matrix in the memory for the special massively multithreaded Fiteng1000 processor. We discuss the implementations of parallel matrix multiplication algorithms on the multi-core processor with many threads. To gain better performance, it is important to choose the 2D thread spatial topography, the memory layer for the placement and the sizes of the matrices. Parallel codes using C and assembly language under OpenMP parallel programming environment are designed. Performance results on Fiteng1000 processor show that the algorithms have well good parallel performance and achieve near-peak performance.

Keywords: matrix multiplication, OpenMP, parallel algorithm.

1   Introduction

The limitations known as power, memory, and instruction-level parallelism (ILP) walls led to the stagnation in single-core single-thread performance, and a switch to multiple separate processing cores on a chip. This has led to changes in computer architecture, including emerging massively multi-core and many-core processors. Multi-threading has become more acceptable, with dual threads present in many main-line microprocessors, and some chips such as Fiteng1000 (FT1000) processor [1] support even more. The Fiteng1000 processor with massively multithreaded nature is based on the employment of 8 cores per chip in combination with simultaneous 64 threads multithreading capabilities. So the entire programming paradigms must shift to take advantage of the performance of the massively multithreaded processor.

General matrix-matrix multiplication (Gemm) is an essential building block of many linear algebra operations and applications [2, 3]. Since the hardware environments change frequently, the process of development of new approaches for Gemm does not stop, and the most effective solutions are implemented using machine dependent techniques.

On conventional serial and multi-core architectures with little threads, the high-performance implementation of Gemm is well understood. Gunnels [4, 5, 6] gave a

Y. Xiang et al. (Eds.): ICA3PP 2012, Part II, LNCS 7440, pp. 166–176, 2012.

formal linear algebra methods environment (FLAME) based on a family of high-performance matrix multiplications on those architectures. Kazushige Goto developed his version of BLAS library named GotoBLAS [7, 8, 9] which was handcrafted for many various hardware architectures. Jeff [10] extended the algorithm for matrix multiplication by Goto to the spatially distributed processor and described the optimizations of the innermost kernel. Ernie Chan [11] proposed an algorithm by arranging the data structures and making the matrix blocks become the fundamental units of data, resulting in algorithms-by-blocks as opposed to the more traditional blocked algorithms for SMP and multi-core architectures. Bryan Maker [12] showed that the performance of 2D partitioning was better that 1D partitioning and gave low-level optimization avoiding redundant copying of B sub-matrices on multithreaded SMP and multi-core architectures.

However, the high-performance implementation of Gemm on conventional serial and multi-core architectures with little threads is not fit to a massively multithreaded processor, just like Fiteng1000 processor with simultaneous 64 threads. In this paper, we discuss parallel algorithms for the special massively multithreaded processors. We present parallel algorithms with shared A or B matrix in the memory avoiding the redundant packing data for the special massively multithreaded Fiteng1000 processors. We discuss the implementations of parallel matrix multiplication algorithms on the multi-core processor with many threads. We choose the 2D thread spatial topography, the memory layer for the placement and the sizes of the matrices. Parallel codes using C and assembly language under OpenMP parallel programming environment are designed. Performance results on Fiteng1000 processors show that the algorithms have good parallel performance and achieve near-peak performance.

Section 2 discusses the basic conventional Gemm algorithms of general high performance matrix multiply. Section 3 discusses extentions to the conventional algorithm for the massively multithreaded processor. Section 4 evaluates the performance. Section 5 summarizes and describes future work.

2   The Architecture of Fiteng1000 Processor

Fiteng1000 processor, which was introduced in Nov. 2010 by NUDT and used as partly processors of TianHe-1A supercomputer, allows multiple Chip-level Multi-Threading (CMT) processors to be used within a single system. Fiteng1000 processor contains eight physical processor cores . The eight cores are connected via a high bandwidth crossbar to eight memory banks of shared 4MB L2 cache. Each core can execute up to eight threads simultaneously. One core provides two integer execution units (EXU), one floating point and graphics unit (FPU) and a specialised stream processing unit (SPU) for cryptographic acceleration. The floating-point and memory pipelines are shared by all eight threads. The eight threads are hard-partitioned into two groups of four, and the four threads within a group share a single integer pipeline. While all eight threads run simultaneously, at any given time at most two threads will be active in the physical core, and those two threads will be issuing either a pair of integer pipeline operations, an integer operation and a floating-point operation, an integer operation and a memory operation, or a floating-point operation and a memory operation. The L2 cache banks are connected to two memory controllers (MCU). Table 1 summarizes the main features of Fiteng1000 processor.

Table 1. Fiteng1000 processor

Hz	L1I cache(core)	L1D cache(core)	L2 Cache	cores	threads
800MHz	16KB	8KB	4MB	8	64

Algorithm 1: Sequential matrix multiplication

for $i \leftarrow 0$ to $M-1$ do
  for $j \leftarrow 0$ to $N-1$ do
   for $k \leftarrow 0$ to $K-1$ do
    $C[i][j] \leftarrow C[i][j] + A[i][k]*B[k][j]$
   endfor
  endfor
endfor

Fig. 1. Sequential matrix multiplication algorithm

Algorithm 2: Blocked matrix multiplication

for $ii \leftarrow 0$ to $M-1$ step b_m do
 for $jj \leftarrow 0$ to $N-1$ step b_n do
  for $kk \leftarrow 0$ to $K-1$ step b_k do
   for $i \leftarrow ii$ to $ii+P$ do
    for $j \leftarrow jj$ to $jj+Q$ do
     for k $\leftarrow kk$ to $kk+R$ do
      $C[i][j] \leftarrow C[i][j]+A[i][k]*B[k][j]$
     end for
    end for
   end for
  end for
 end for
end for

Fig. 2. Blocked matrix multiplication algorithm

3   Conventional Gemm Algorithm

Consider the prototypical computation $C := AB + C$, where C, A, and B are $M \times N$, $M \times K$, and $K \times N$ matrices, respectively. The sequential matrix multiplication algorithm is given in figure 1. Computation for each element of C needs one column of A and one row of B. The ratio of arithmetic operations to memory accesses is only $O(K)/O(K)$. For large M, N and K, the performance of sequential matrix multiplication algorithm given in figure 1 is poor. The blocked method is the effective way to improve the performance of matrix multiplication algorithm. Assume for simplicity that $M = b_m \times m$, $N = b_n \times n$ and $K = b_k \times k$, where b_m, b_n, b_k, m, n and k are all integers. The blocked matrix multiplication algorithm, given in figure 2, improves the localization of reference and takes advantage of the $O(MNK)/O(MN+MK+NK)$ ratio of arithmetic operations to memory accesses. Blocked algorithm creates three more inner loops, which calculate a product of a submatrix $\tilde{A}_{il}(i=0, ..., m-1, l=0, ..., k-1)$ of A and a submatrix $\tilde{B}_{lj}(l=0, ..., k-1, j=0, ..., n-1)$ of B and updates a submatrix $\tilde{C}_{ij}(i=0, ..., m-1, j=0, ..., n-1)$ of C with the partial result.

Algorithm 3: Streamed B and C matrix multiplication

for $j \leftarrow 0$ to $n-1$ do
  for $l \leftarrow 0$ to $k-1$ do
  Pack $\tilde{B}_{lj}$ into $\bar{B}$
  for $i \leftarrow 0$ to $m-1$ do
    Pack $\tilde{A}_{il}$ into $\bar{A}$
    Call gemm_kernel(b_m, b_n, b_k, $\bar{A}$, $\bar{B}$, $\tilde{C}_{ij}$, LDC)
  end for
  end for
end for

Fig. 3. Streamed B and C matrix multiplication algorithm

Algorithm 4: Streamed A and C matrix multiplication

for $i \leftarrow 0$ to $m-1$ do
  for $l \leftarrow 0$ to $k-1$ do
  Pack $\tilde{A}_{il}$ into $\bar{A}$
  for $j \leftarrow 0$ to $n-1$ do
    Pack $\tilde{B}_{lj}$ into $\bar{B}$
    Call gemm_kernel(b_m, b_n, b_k, $\bar{A}$, $\bar{B}$, $\tilde{C}_{ij}$, LDC)
  end for
  end for
end for

Fig. 4. Streamed A and C matrix multiplication algorithm

The high-performance inner kernel named gemm_kernel() for submatrix multiplication $\tilde{C} = \tilde{A}\tilde{B} + \tilde{C}$ is exploited by vendor and library researchers, such as Intel's MKL, IBM's ESSL, ATLAS and GotoBLAS. In order to achieve near-optimal performance, the subroutine gemm_kernel() is using optimization techniques such as unrolling, data prefetching and instruction reordering.

Based on the subroutine gemm_kernel(), choosing the reasonable blocked size of b_m, b_n and b_k, the overall performance of Gemm is driven by that of each individual general panel-panel multiplication. The algorithm requires two data packing routines. One is packing $\tilde{B}_{lj}$ into a contiguous buffer. The other is packing $\tilde{A}_{il}$ into a contiguous buffer. When b_n is large, b_m and b_k is relative small, the streamed A algorithm is given in figure 3. This algorithm is the Goto's streaming matrix multiply algorithm. On the current conventional architectures, the size of $\tilde{A}_{il}$ is chosen to fill about half of the L2 cache. The cost of packing B is large and should be amortized over as many blocks of A as possible. The key is to orchestrate the computation so that $\tilde{A}_{il}$ stays in the L2 cache and B and C are streamed from memory. Similarly, when b_m is large, b_n and b_k is relative small, the streamed B algorithm is given in figure 4. This algorithm is different from the Goto's streaming matrix multiply algorithm. On the current conventional architectures, the size of $\tilde{B}_{lj}$ is chosen to fill about half of the L2 cache. The cost of packing A is large and should be amortized over as many blocks of B as possible. The key is to orchestrate the computation so that $\tilde{B}_{lj}$ stays in the L2 cache and A and C are streamed from memory.

Algorithm 5: Parallel algorithm with streamed A and C

Local r, c, $\bar{A}$ and $\bar{B}$
for all $P(r, c)$ where $0 \leq r < p_r$ and $0 \leq c < p_c$ do
  for $i \leftarrow r \times m_r$ to $r \times m_r + m_r$ do
    for $l \leftarrow 0$ to $k\text{-}1$ do
      Pack $\tilde{A}_{il}$ into $\bar{A}$
      for $j \leftarrow c \times n_c$ to $c \times n_c + n_c$ do
        Pack $\tilde{B}_{lj}$ into $\bar{B}$
        Call gemm_kernel(b_m, b_n, b_k, $\bar{A}$, $\bar{B}$, $\tilde{C}_{ij}$, LDC)
      end for
    end for
  end for
endfor

Fig. 5. Parallel matrix multiplication algorithm with streamed A and C

4 Parallel algorithms for a Massively Multithreaded Architecture

Many studies have been focused on parallel algorithms of matrix multiplication for distributed memory and SMP/multicore architectures. The most distributed memory matrix multiplication algorithms are discussed in [15]. And parallel algorithms for SMP-like architectures are given in [12] and [16]. Similar to the algorithm in [12], we extend it to exploit the parallelism for more concurrent threads.

Algorithm 6: Parallel algorithm avoiding the redundant packing of $\tilde{A}_{il}$

Global $\bar{A}$
Local r, c and $\bar{B}$
for all $P(r, c)$ where $0 \leq r < p_r$ and $0 \leq c < p_c$ do
  for $i \leftarrow r \times m_r$ to $r \times m_r + m_r$ do
    for $l \leftarrow 0$ to k-1 do
      One thread of the rth row packs $\tilde{A}_{il}$ into $\bar{A}$
      for $j \leftarrow c \times n_c$ to $c \times n_c + n_c$ do
        Pack $\tilde{B}_{lj}$ into $\bar{B}$
        Call gemm_kernel(b_m, b_n, b_k, $\bar{A}$, $\bar{B}$, $\tilde{C}_{ij}$, LDC)
      end for
    end for
  end for
endfor

Fig. 6. Parallel matrix multiplication algorithm avoiding the redundant packing of $\tilde{A}_{il}$

Algorithm 7: Parallel algorithm avoiding the redundant packing of $\tilde{B}_{lj}$

Global $\bar{B}$
Local r, c and $\bar{A}$
for all $P(r, c)$ where $0 \leq r < p_r$ and $0 \leq c < p_c$ do
  for $j \leftarrow c \times n_c$ to $c \times n_c + n_c$ do
    for $l \leftarrow 0$ to k-1 do
      One thread of the cth column packs $\tilde{B}_{lj}$ into $\bar{B}$
      for $i \leftarrow r \times m_r$ to $r \times m_r + m_r$ do
        Pack $\tilde{A}_{il}$ into $\bar{A}$
        Call gemm_kernel(b_m, b_n, b_k, $\bar{A}$, $\bar{B}$, $\tilde{C}_{ij}$, LDC)
      end for
    end for
  end for
endfor

Fig. 7. Parallel matrix multiplication algorithm avoiding the redundant packing of $\tilde{B}_{lj}$

Work for matrix multiplication is assigned to threads using a two-dimensional partitioning of data. To achieve a 2D work partitioning, P threads logically form a $p_r \times p_c$ grid, with $P = p_r \times p_c$. Assume that $P(r, c)$ $(0 \leq r < p_r, 0 \leq c < p_c)$ is the thread in the

rth row and cth column. And assume for simplicity that $m = p_r \times m_r$ and $n = p_c \times n_c$, where m_r and n_r are both integers. Parallel matrix multiplication algorithm with streamed A and C is illustrated in figure 5. In the algorithm 5, submatrix $\tilde{A}_{il}$ and $\tilde{B}_{lj}$ are both redundant packing to contiguous buffers in memory or L2 cache. The packing of $\tilde{A}_{il}$ is a memory-to-memory copy for every threads on the same row. For the size of $\tilde{A}_{il}$ is large, the redundant packing which need reading from and writing to memory results to competition for the limited bandwidth to memory. The algorithm avoiding the redundant packing of $\tilde{A}_{il}$ is given in figure 6. Creating redundant copies of $\tilde{B}_{lj}$ is unavoidable, and the submatrix has to be loaded into and ends up in the L2 cache. Similarly to the algorithm 6, parallel matrix multiplication algorithm avoiding the redundant packing of $\tilde{B}_{lj}$ is given in figure 7.

5   Implementation on a Massively Multithreaded Fiteng1000 Processor

The low level kernel of a matrix multiply algorithm is highly dependent on the structure of the real processor. The Fiteng1000 processor is targeted on server workloads with high throughput requirements via low-frequency core design and massive chip multithreading capabilities. The most important characteristic of Fiteng1000 processor is that the L2 cache is shared and the number of threads is large. The performance of matrix multiplication is greatly dependent on the placement of data and the implementation of practical algorithms.

5.1   Choosing the Memory Layer and Data Movement

To gain better performance, it is important to choose the memory layer for the placement of the matrices. The Gemm in the algorithm 6 is decomposed into multiple calls to GEPB ($\bar{A}$ panel, $\bar{B}$ block, $\tilde{C}_{ij}$ panel). The Gemm in the algorithm 7 is decomposed into multiple calls to GEBP ($\bar{A}$ block, $\bar{B}$ panel, $\tilde{C}_{ij}$ panel). For the analysis of algorithm 6 and 7 is similar, we mainly discuss the data placement of algorithm 7.

Assume that the initial data of matrix A, B and C is kept in the memory of Fiteng1000 processor. The same rows data of matrix A are reused for every threads in the rth row. It is typically worthwhile to copy the part of matrix A into a contiguous work arrray $\bar{A}$ by one thread in the rth row. In figure 8 the data placement and movement are proposed for one row of all two-dimensional threads. The arrows show the directions of data movement.

Each thread packs $\tilde{B}_{lj}$ from the memory into $\bar{B}$. $\bar{B}$ is a congruous buffer in the L2 cache, and it remains so until no longer needed. After packed arrray $\bar{A}$ by one thread in the rth row, each thread takes part data from a contiguous work arrray $\bar{A}$ to L1 cache or register. Each thread takes part data of C to L1 cache or register, and

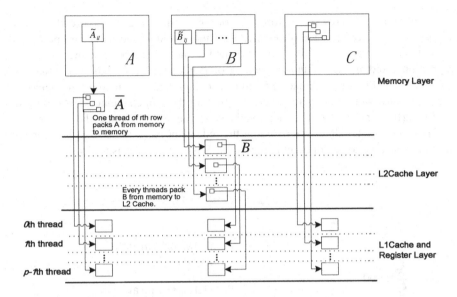

Fig. 8. Data placement and movement for threads in the rth row

deposits result data from L1 cache or register to memory. The key of performance is orchestrate the computation so that $\bar{B}$ stays in the L2 cache and $\bar{A}$ and C are streamed from memory to L1 cache or register.

5.2   Parameters Chosen

The implementation of GEPB kernel routine is the key to get high performance of matrix multiplication. Now concentrate on GEPB kernel routine, and assume that $\tilde{C}_{ij} = \overline{A}\overline{B} + \tilde{C}_{ij}$ is to be computed.

As explained in Goto's high level algorithm[7], the size of $\bar{B}$ is chosen to fill about half of the L2 cache or the memory addressable by the TLB on current conventional architectures. Different from the most conventional processors, the L2 cache of Fiteng1000 processor is shared by eight cores or 64 threads. We chose the size of $\bar{B}$ for each thread to fill about 1/128 of the L2 cache.

Each thread will take a sub-matrix $\tilde{A}$ from $\bar{A}$, a sub-matrix $\tilde{B}$ from $\bar{B}$ and a sub-matrix $\tilde{C}$ from $\tilde{C}_{ij}$. $\tilde{B}$ stays in the L2 cache, and $\tilde{A}$ and $\tilde{C}$ are streamed from memory. $\tilde{A}$ is stored in the L1 caches. We limit each slice of $\tilde{A}$ to no more than half of the L1 cache capacity. A number of elements of $\tilde{C}$ at a time are kept in registers and update. We use half of the available registers storing $\tilde{C}$. The remaining registers are used to prefetch elements of $\tilde{A}$ and $\tilde{B}$.

6   Experiments

Experiments were performed on a Fiteng1000 processor with 64 threads. We used OpenMP as the threading mechanism within the GCC. We implement algorithm 5, 6 and 7, and optimize the code for the better performance.

In Figure 9 we show the performance of algorithm 5, 6 and 7 where all matrices are square. The performance of parallel algorithm avoiding the redundant packing of A is about 4% higher than that with streamed A and C. The performance of parallel algorithm avoiding the redundant packing of B is about 1.8% higher than that with streamed A and C. Every thread of 64 threads copies data from memory to memory at the same time, which results to the competition for the limited memory data I/O width of Fiteng1000 processor. Packing overhead is roughly 6% once the size reaches 1024x1024. Parallel algorithm avoiding the redundant pack, the size of packing data is cut down about to one of eight in algorithm 5 using 8x8 threads topology.

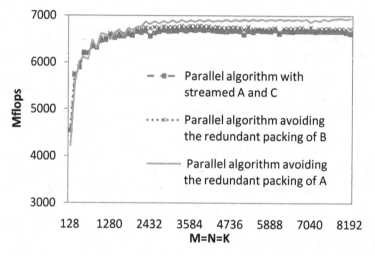

Fig. 9. The performance of algorithm 5, 6 and 7 where all matrices are square

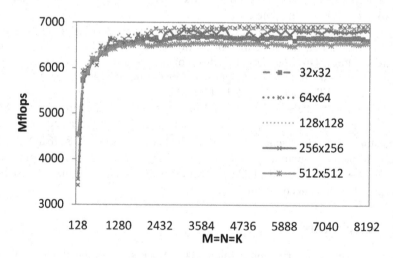

Fig. 10. The effect of different $\bar{B}$ buffer dimensions

The L2 cache of Fiteng1000 processor is shared by 64 threads, so the size of $\bar{B}$ affects the performance of parallel algorithm. In figure 10, we show the performance of algorithm 7 for the different dimensions of the $\bar{B}$. In Goto's algorithm, the best choice for the size of the $\bar{B}$ buffer is keeping its size as half of the L2 cache, and the dimensions of $\bar{B}$ are 512x512. For the Fiteng1000 processor, if each thread used half of the L2 cache, the performance is bad because the L2 cache is shared by 64 threads and L2 cache conflicts are heavy. Figure 11 shows that the best performance is gained by the 32x32 dimension of $\bar{B}$.

7   Conclusion

We examine the adaptation of high-performance parallel matrix multiply algorithms to a special massively multithreaded processor named Fiteng1000. We present parallel algorithms with shared A or B matrix in the memory avoiding the redundant packing data. To gain better performance, we choose the 2D thread spatial topology, the multi-memory layer for the data placement and the varied sizes of the buffer matrices. Parallel codes using C and assembly language under OpenMP parallel programming environment are designed. Performance results on Fiteng1000 processors show that performance of parallel algorithm avoiding the redundant packing of A is about 4% higher than that with streamed A and C, and achieves near-peak performance.

Acknowledgments. This research work is supported by the National Natural Science Foundation of China under grant No.60970033, also by the National High Technology Research and Development Program of China under grant No.2012AA01A301. We would like to thank the anonymous reviewers for their helpful comments.

References

1. http://www.nscc-tj.gov.cn/resources/resource_1.asp
2. Anderson, E., Bai, Z., Bischof, C., Demmel, J., Dongarra, J., Croz, J.D., Greenbaum, A., Hammarling, S., McKenney, A., Ostrouchov, S., Sorensen, D.: LAPACK Users' Guide-Release 2.0. SIAM (1994)
3. Dongarra, J.J., Du Croz, J., Hammarling, S., Duff, I.: A set of level 3 basic linear algebra subprograms. ACM Trans. Math. Soft. 16(1), 1–17 (1990)
4. Gunnels, J.A., Gustavson, F.G., Henry, G.M., van de Geijn, R.A.: A Family of High-Performance Matrix Multiplication Algorithms. In: Dongarra, J., Madsen, K., Waśniewski, J. (eds.) PARA 2004. LNCS, vol. 3732, pp. 256–265. Springer, Heidelberg (2006)
5. Gunnels, J.A., Gustavson, F.G., Henry, G.M., van de Geijn, R.A.: FLAME: Formal linear algebra methods environment. ACM Trans. Math. 4, 422–455 (2001)
6. Gunnels, J.A., Henry, G.M., van de Geijn, R.A.: A Family of High-Performance Matrix Multiplication Algorithms. In: Alexandrov, V.N., Dongarra, J., Juliano, B.A., Renner, R.S., Tan, C.J.K. (eds.) ICCS 2001. LNCS, vol. 2073, pp. 51–60. Springer, Heidelberg (2001)

7. Goto, K., van de Geijn, R.: High-performance implementation of the level-3 BLAS. FLAME Working Note #20, Tech. rep. TR-2006-23, Department of Computer Sciences, The University of Texas at Austin (2006)
8. Goto, K., van de Geijn, R.A.: On reducing TLB misses in matrix multiplication. Tech. rep. CS-TR-02-55, Department of Computer Sciences, University of Texas at Austin (2002)
9. Goto, K., van de Geijn, R.: Anatomy of high-performance matrix multiplication. ACM Trans. Math. Soft. 34(3) (2008)
10. Jeff, D., Behnam, R., Stephen, W.K., van de Robert, G., Goto, K., Doug, B.: PPoPP 2008, Salt Lake City, Utah, USA, Februrary 20-23, pp. 63–72 (2008)
11. Ernie, C., Enrique, S.Q., Gregorio, Q., Robert van de, G.: SuperMatrix out-of-order scheduling of matrix operations for SMP and Multi-Core Architectures. In: SPAA 2007, San Diego, Califonia, USA, June 9-11, pp. 116–125 (2007)
12. Marker, B., Van Zee, F.G., Goto, K., Quintana-Ortí, G., van de Geijn, R.A.: Toward Scalable Matrix Multiply on Multithreaded Architectures. In: Kermarrec, A.-M., Bougé, L., Priol, T. (eds.) Euro-Par 2007. LNCS, vol. 4641, pp. 748–757. Springer, Heidelberg (2007)

BIDE-Based Parallel Mining of Frequent Closed Sequences with MapReduce

Dongjin Yu[1], Wei Wu[2], Suhang Zheng[1], and Zhixiang Zhu[1]

[1] School of Computer, Hangzhou Dianzi University, Hangzhou, China
yudj@hdu.edu.cn
[2] Zhejiang Provincial Key Laboratory of Network Technology and Information Security,
Hangzhou, China
ww@topcheer.cn

Abstract. Parallel processing is essential to mining frequent closed sequences from massive volume of data in a timely manner. On the other hand, MapReduce is an ideal software framework to support distributed computing on large data sets on clusters of computers. In this paper, we develop a parallel implementation of BIDE algorithm on MapReduce, called BIDE-MR. It iteratively assigns the tasks of closure checking and pruning to different nodes in cluster. After one round of *map-combine-partition-reduce*, the closed frequent sequences with round-specific length and the candidates for the next round of computation are generated. Since the candidates and their pseudo project databases are independent with each other, BIDE-MR achieves high speed-ups. We implement BIDE-MR on an Apache Hadoop cluster and use BIDE-MR to mine the vehicles which frequently appear together from massive records collected at different monitoring sites. The results show that BIDE-MR attains good parallelization.

Keywords: frequent closed sequences, parallel algorithms, BIDE, MapReduce.

1   Introduction

Sequential pattern mining is trying to find the relationships between occurrences of sequential events, or in other words, to find if there exist any frequently occurring patterns related to time or other sequences. Since many business transactions, telecommunications records and weather data are time sequence data, discovery of sequential patterns is an essential data mining task with broad applications, such as targeted marketing, customer retention and weather forecasting. Among several variations of sequential patterns, closed sequential pattern is the most useful one since it retains all the information of the complete pattern set but is often much more compact than it. Some well-known algorithms, such as BIDE[1-2], CloSpan[3] and CMP-Miner[4] have been proposed for mining closed sequential patterns. BIDE adopts a closure checking scheme, called BI-Directional Extension, which mines closed sequential patterns without candidate maintenance. CloSpan follows a candidate *maintenance-and-test* paradigm to prune the search space and check if a newly found candidate sequential pattern is likely to be closed. CMP-Miner mines closed patterns in a time-series database where each record in the database contains multiple time-series sequences.

Y. Xiang et al. (Eds.): ICA3PP 2012, Part II, LNCS 7440, pp. 177–186, 2012.

With advances in data collection and storage technologies, large data sources have become ubiquitous. Today, organizations routinely collect terabytes of data on a daily basis with the intent of gleaning non-trivial insights on their business processes. To benefit from these advances, it is imperative that sequence mining techniques scale to such proportions. Such scaling can be achieved through the design of new and faster algorithms and/or through the employment of parallelism. However, achieving such scaling is not straightforward and only a handful of research efforts in the data mining communities have attempted to address these scales.

Fortunately, the past few years have witnessed the emergence of several platforms for the implementation and deployment of large-scale analytics. MapReduce, which has been popularized by Google, is a scalable and fault-tolerant data processing model that enables to process a massive volume of data in parallel with many low-end computing nodes [5]. The MapReduce model consists of two primitive functions: Map and Reduce. During the Map step, the master node takes the input, partitions it up into smaller sub-problems, and distributes them to worker nodes. The worker node processes the smaller problem, and passes the answer back to its master node. During the Reduce step afterwards, the master node collects the answers to all the sub-problems and combines them in some way to form the output. Users can define the Map() and Reduce() functions however they want the MapReduce framework works.

This paper presents the parallel implementation of BIDE on MapReduce framework, called BIDE-MR. It iteratively distributes the tasks of closure checking and pruning to different nodes in cluster. After one round of *map-combine-partition-reduce*, the closed frequent sequences with round-specific length and the candidates to be checked for the next round of computation are generated. Since the candidates and their pseudo project databases are independent with each other, BIDE-MR achieves high speed-ups. To the best of our knowledge, previous work on parallel closed sequential pattern mining has mainly focused on multi-core computer architectures [6-7] or MPI [8]. There is no parallel algorithm that targets on MapReduce framework.

The rest of the paper is organized as follows. In Section 2, we discuss the related works. The problem is defined in Section 3 and the traditional serial BIDE algorithm is given in Section 4. In Section 5, we describe the parallel implementation of BIDE on MapReduce in detail. The results from the real case are then presented in Section 6. Finally, the last section concludes the paper.

2   Related Works

Sequential pattern mining, since its introduction in [9], has become an essential data mining task, with broad applications, including market and customer analysis, web log analysis and pattern discovery in protein sequences. Some efficient sequential pattern mining algorithms have been proposed in the literature such as CloSpan [3], BIDE [2] and SeqStream [10]. Many studies present convincing arguments that for mining frequent patterns, one should not mine all frequent patterns but the closed ones because the latter leads to not only more compact yet complete result set but also better efficiency [8-9, 11-12]. In the dynamic sequence database environment, sequences (or items) are often added to and deleted from databases and thus the mining of closed frequent itemsets over streaming data become more difficult. For such online mining of closed frequent itemsets, one of the most important issues is about how to maintain the set of closed frequent itemsets. In [13], Chang et. al. presented a compact structure CSTree to keep closed sequential patterns, while in [14], Li, Ho and Lee proposed a one-pass algorithm, NewMoment, to maintain the set of closed frequent itemsets in data streams with a transaction-sensitive sliding window. Episode mining used to discover the events occurring often in the vicinity of each other is another well-studied field in sequential pattern discovery. Such approaches include mining closed episodes with simultaneous events [15], with minimal and non-overlapping occurrences [16], etc.

Parallel frequent pattern discovery algorithms exploit parallel and distributed computing resources to relieve the sequential bottlenecks of serial frequent pattern mining algorithms. Although there have been numerous studies on sequential-pattern mining, the study on parallel sequential-pattern mining is still limited and is largely confined to mining the complete set of sequential patterns such as pSPADE[17]. Many partition based approaches in distributed databases are mainly employed for preserving individual confidentiality, but not for the efficient mining [18-20]. Guralnik and Karypis presented in [21] some parallel sequential-pattern mining approaches toward a distributed-memory system for mining the complete set of sequential-patterns, via the tree-projection-based sequential algorithm. However, to the best of our knowledge, there are only a few parallel algorithms that target closed sequential-pattern mining. In [8], Cong, Han and Padua developed an algorithm, called Par-CSP, to conduct parallel mining of closed sequential patterns on a distributed memory system. Par-CSP partitions the work among the processors by exploiting the divide-and-conquer property so that the overhead of inter-processor communication is minimized. Moreover, it applies dynamic scheduling and selective sampling to avoid processor idling and load imbalance. In [22], Luo and Chung proposed a parallel algorithm, named PMSPX, which mines close frequent sequences by using multiple samples to exclude infrequent candidates. In PMSPX, the asynchronous local closed frequent sequence mining on each processing node followed by synchronous global mining approach minimizes the synchronization and communication among the processing nodes.

3   Problem Definition

A **sequence** S is an ordered list of events, denoted as $< e_1, e_2, ..., e_m >$, or simply $e_1 e_2 ... e_m$, where e_i is an event, or an item, i.e., $e_i \in I = \{i_1, i_2, ..., i_n\}$, for $1 \ll i \ll m$. The number of events, or the instances of items, in a sequence S is called the length of the sequence S, and a sequence with a length l is also called a l-sequence.

A sequence $S_a = a_1 a_2 ... a_n$ is contained in another sequence $S_b = b_1 b_2 ... b_m$, or in other words, S_a is the **sub-sequence** of S_b or S_b is the **super-sequence** of S_a, if there exist integers $1 \ll i_1 < i_2 < \cdots < i_n \ll m$ such that $a_1 = b_{i_1}, a_2 = b_{i_2}, ..., a_n = b_{i_n}$.

An input **sequence database** SDB is a set of tuples (sid, S), where sid is a sequence identifier, and S an input sequence.

The **support** of a sequence S_a in a sequence database SDB is the number of tuples of S_a that SDB contains, denoted as $|S_a|$.

Given a support threshold min_sup, a sequence S_a is a **frequent sequence** on SDB if $|S_a| \gg min\_sup$. If sequence S_a is frequent and there exists no super-sequence of S_a with the same or bigger support, S_a is called as a **frequent closed sequence**.

Given an input sequence S_a which contains a prefix sequence $e_1 e_2 \dots e_i$, the remaining part of S_a after the first instance of prefix is called the **projected sequence of prefix sequence** $e_1 e_2 \dots e_i$ in S_a. Given an input sequence database SDB, the complete set of projected sequences of prefix $e_1 e_2 \dots e_i$ in SDB called the **projected database** of prefix $e_1 e_2 \dots e_i$ in SDB. Instead of physically constructing the projected database, **pseudo projected databases** only keep a set of pointers, one for each projected sequence, pointing at the starting position in the corresponding projected sequence.

The problem can be then defined as following. Given an input sequence database SDB and a support threshold min_sup, find in SDB all frequent closed sequences with support equal to or bigger than min_sup.

4   BIDE: BI-directional Extension Based Frequent Closed Sequence Mining

According to the definition of a frequent closed sequence, if an n–sequence, $S = e_1 e_2 \dots e_n$, is non-closed, there must exist at least one event e', which can be used to extend sequences S to get a new sequence S' with the same support. The sequence S can be extended in two ways:

1) $S' = e_1 e_2 \dots e_n e'$ and $|S| = |S'|$, where e' is a **forward-extension event (or item)** and S' a **forward-extension sequence** of S.

2) $S' = e' e_1 e_2 \dots e_n$ or $\exists i (1 \leq i < n), S' = e_1 e_2 \dots e_i e' e_{i+1} \dots e_n$, and $|S| = |S'|$, where e' is a **backward-extension event (or item)** and S' a **backward-extension sequence** of S.

The BIDE algorithm is illustrated as follows. The detail can be found in [2].

1) scan the sequence database SDB once to find the frequent 1-sequences, treat each frequent 1-sequence as a prefix S_p while all prefixes form the prefix set P.

2) if there exists no S_p in prefix set P, terminate the procedure.

3) for each prefix S_p in prefix set P with depth-first order, build projected database and compute its backward-extension items if S_p cannot be pruned, otherwise delete S_p in prefix set P and then go to 2).

4) scan the pseudo projected database of prefix S_p to find its locally frequent items, or the forward-extension items.

5) if there is no backward-extension item nor forward-extension item, output S_p as a frequent closed sequence.

6) grow prefix set P by appending S_p with its locally frequent items if exists any, and go to 2).

BIDE adopts a strict depth-first search order and can output the frequent closed patterns in an online fashion. It avoids the curse of the candidate maintenance-and-test paradigm and does not need to maintain the set of historic closed patterns. In addition, it prunes the search space more deeply and checks the pattern closure in a more efficient way in contrast to some other closed pattern mining algorithms like CloSpan algorithm.

5   The BIDE-MR Algorithm

To make sequential pattern mining practical for large datasets, the mining process must be efficient, scalable, and have a short response time. Since the projected datasets of the frequent k-sequences are independent in BIDE, its parallel implementation is convenient and thus could lead to the great improvement of its performance. The following presents a BIDE-based algorithm, called BIDE-MR, which conducts the parallel mining of closed sequential patterns on Apache Hadoop. The Apache Hadoop software library is a framework that allows for the distributed processing of large data sets across clusters of computers using a simple programming model [23]. As the free and open source implementation of MapReduce, Hadoop MapReduce allows for distributed processing of large data sets on compute clusters. It exploits a master/slave architecture, implemented by Apache Hadoop Distributed File System, or HDFS. An HDFS cluster consists of a single NameNode, a master server that manages the file system namespace and regulates access to files by clients. In addition, there are also a number of DataNodes in HDFS, usually one per node in the cluster, which manage storage attached to the nodes that they run on.

BIDE-MR distributes the tasks with respect to each node on the same level in the sequence tree, such as backward-extension, forward-extension and pruning, to one DataNode in HDFS, while constructing and traversing the sequence tree. If extension events exist, the newly extended prefix sequences as the children of the current node are then assigned to another new DataNode in HDFS to fulfill further extension and pruning. In this way, BIDE-MR identifies the closed sequences with certain length in just one loop, or one job in Hadoop MapReduce's word.

BIDE-MR exploits Hadoop MapReduce as the software framework for distributed processing of large data sets on compute clusters. The mappers identify the candidate k-sequences and calculate their local counts from the split of data in the local DataNode. The candidates are then partitioned and to be reduced on different DataNodes in parallel. Those have supports equal to or bigger than min_sup are separated on different Datanodes again and checked if they could be pruned or closed via bi-directional extension. In this way, the closed frequent k-sequences are finally obtained. The above loop could be repeated to obtain the closed frequent $k + 1$-sequences.

The following shows BIDE-MR in detail.

BIDE-MR(SDB, len, min_sup)
Input
    SDB: sequence database
    len: the longest length of the closed frequent sequence
    min_sup: minimum support threshold
Output
    CFS: set of frequent closed sequences found
1: split SDB into n blocks, each SDB_i assigned to one DataNode;
2: execute in parallel on each DataNode:
2:   $bout_{1,i}$ = frequent 1-sequences(SDB_i, min_sup)
3: $bout_1 = bout_{1,1} \cup bout_{1,2} \cup ... \cup bout_{1,n}$
4: $k = 1$;
5: split $bout_k$ into m blocks, each $bout_{k,j}$ assigned to one DataNode

```
6:  execute in parallel on each DataNode:
7:      bout_{k+1,j} = PAR_BIDE(bout_{k,j}, k, min _sup)
8:  bout_{k+1} = bout_{k+1,1} ∪ bout_{k+1,2} ∪ ...∪ bout_{k+1,m}
9:  k = k + 1;
10: if k ≤ len, go to 5
11: output the closed frequent sequences: CFS_1 ∪ CFS_2 ∪ ...∪ CFS_{len}
```

PAR_BIDE(FS, k, min _sup)

Input

   FS: candidate frequent sequences

   k: length of the frequent sequence

   min _sup: minimum support threshold

Output

   CFS_k: closed frequent k-sequences

   $bout_{k+1}$: extended candidate frequent $(k + 1)$-sequences

```
12: for (each sequence s in FS) do {
13:   PPD^s = pseudo projected database (FS)
14:   if (!prunable(s, PPD^s)) {
15:     if (!backward-extensible(s, PPD^s)) {
16:       if (!forward-extensible(s, PPD^s)) {
17:         CFS_k = CFS_k ∪ {s}
18:       }
19:       else bout_{k+1} = bout_{k+1} ∪ {s + extensible items}
20:     }
21:   }
22: }
12: return bout_{k+1}
```

Figure 1 shows the running process of BIDE-MR.

6   Performance Evaluation

6.1   Test Environment and Dataset

The experiment was performed on a cluster of 4 computers, each with E7500 2.93GHZ CPU and 2G memory, and Ubuntu 10.04 and Apache Hadoop 0.20.2 installed. Among these 4 computers, one runs both the NameNode and DataNode software, while other three run only the instance of DataNode.

Because the synthetic datasets have far different characteristics from the real-world ones, in our experiments we only used some real datasets to do the tests. We chose the vehicle passing-through records collected at different monitoring sites and ran BIDE-MR on these data to mine the Vehicles Frequently Appearing Together, or VFATs, which are sometimes regarded as one of the valuable hints when solving a criminal case. The test datasets contained 2.5 million records that were collected at 183 monitoring sites during 3 months.

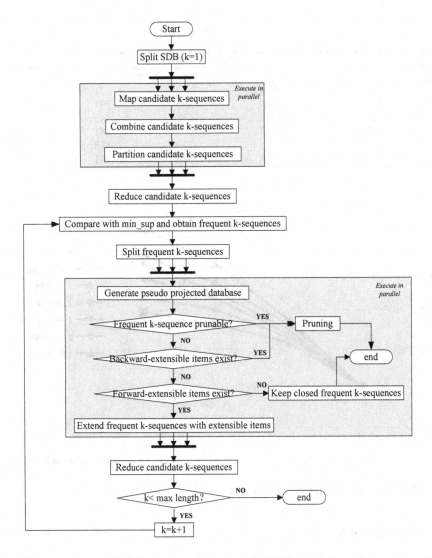

Fig. 1. Running process of BIDE-MR algorithm

6.2 Experimental Results

Table 1 gives the runtime of BIDE-MR in seconds on different sizes of test data. The result shows that BIDE-MR runs faster with more participant DataNodes. In other words, BIDE-MR is quite scalable especially with larger amount of test data. Figure 2 presents the speed-ups of BIDE-MR with different numbers of DataNodes and sizes of test data.

Table 1. Result of experiments

Number of records	Run time (in seconds)			
	Single data node	2 data nodes	3 data nodes	4 data nodes
100,000	129	82	71	65
500,000	584	356	291	270
1,000,000	735	438	342	305
1,500,000	1077	623	481	416
2,000,000	1398	773	598	516
2,500,000	1928	1036	741	632

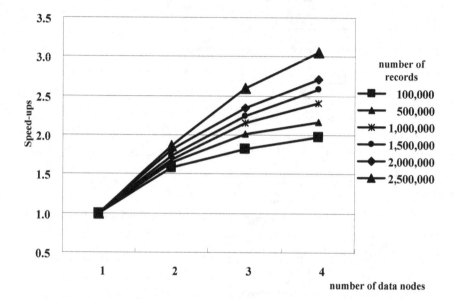

Fig. 2. Speed-ups with respect to the numbers of data nodes and sizes of test data

7   Conclusions

In this paper, we propose a parallel closed sequential pattern mining algorithm BIDE-MR. It takes full advantage of MapReduce paradigm on the Apache Hadoop cluster. Our experimental results on real data show that BIDE-MR attains good parallelization efficiencies. To the best of our knowledge, it is the first MapReduce-based solution for the closed pattern mining problem. In the future, we will conduct the more extensive experiments with larger scales to demonstrate its scalability on the Apache Hadoop cluster consisting of thousands of machines.

Acknowledgments. The work is supported by Natural Science Foundation of Zhejiang (No.LY12F02003), the open project of Zhejiang Provincial Key Laboratory of Network Technology and Information Security. The authors would like to thank anonymous reviewers who gave valuable suggestion to improve the quality of the paper.

References

1. Wang, J., Han, J., Li, C.: Frequent Closed Sequence Mining without Candidate Maintenance. IEEE Transactions on Knowledge and Data Engineering 19(8), 1042–1056 (2007)
2. Wang, J., Han, J.: BIDE: Efficient mining of frequent closed sequences. In: 20th International Conference on Data Engineering, pp. 79–90. IEEE Computer Society (2004)
3. Yan, X., Han, J., Afshar, R.: CloSpan: Mining Closed Sequential Patterns in Large Databases. In: SDM 2003, San Francisco, CA, pp. 166–177 (2003)
4. Lee Anthony, J.T., Wu, H.-W., Lee, T.-Y., Liu, Y.-H., Chen, K.-T.: Mining closed patterns in multi-sequence time-series databases. Data and Knowledge Engineering 68(10), 1071–1090 (2009)
5. Dean, J., et al.: MapReduce: Simplified data processing on large clusters. Communications of the ACM 51(1), 107–113 (2008)
6. Lucchese, C., Orlando, S., Perego, R.: Parallel Mining of Frequent Closed Patterns: Harnessing Modern Computer Architectures. In: 7th IEEE International Conference on Data Mining, pp. 242–251 (2007)
7. Benjamin, N., Alexandre, T., Jean-Francois, M., Takeaki, U.: Discovering Closed Frequent Itemsets on Multicore: Parallelizing Computations and Optimizing Memory Accesses. In: 2010 International Conference on High Performance Computing and Simulation, pp. 521–528 (2010)
8. Shengnan, C., Jiawei, H., David, P.: Parallel Mining of Closed Sequential patterns. In: 11th ACM SIGKDD International Conference on Knowledge Discovery in Data Mining, pp. 562–567 (2005)
9. Agrawal, R., Srikant, R.: Mining sequential patterns. In: 11th IEEE International Conference on Data Engineering, pp. 3–14 (1995)
10. Chang, L., Wang, T., Yang, D., Luan, H.: SeqStream: Mining closed sequential patterns over stream sliding windows. In: 8th IEEE International Conference on Data Mining, pp. 83–92 (2008)
11. Lin, M.Y.: Mining closed sequential patterns with time constraints. Journal of Information Science and Engineering 24(1), 33–46 (2008)
12. Bolin, D., David, L., Jiawei, H., Siau-Cheng, K.: Efficient mining of closed repetitive gapped subsequences from a sequence database. In: 25th IEEE International Conference on Data Engineering, pp. 1024–1035 (2009)
13. Chang, L., Wang, T., Yang, D., Luan, H., Tang, S.: Efficient algorithms for incremental maintenance of closed sequential patterns in large databases. Data and Knowledge Engineering 68(1), 68–106 (2009)
14. Li, H.-F., Ho, C.-C., Lee, S.-Y.: Incremental updates of closed frequent itemsets over continuous data streams. Expert Systems with Applications 36(2, pt. 1), 2451–2458 (2009)
15. Nikolaj, T., Boris, C.: Mining closed episodes with simultaneous events. In: 17th ACM SIGKDD International Conference on Knowledge Discovery and Data Mining, pp. 1172–1180 (2011)
16. Zhu, H., Wang, P., He, X., Li, Y., Wang, W., Shi, B.: Efficient episode mining with minimal and non-overlapping occurrences. In: 10th IEEE International Conference on Data Mining, pp. 1211–1216 (2010)
17. Zaki, M.J.: Parallel sequence mining on shared-memory machines. Journal of Parallel and Distributed Computing 61(3), 401–426 (2001)
18. Rozenberg, B., Gudes, E.: Association rules mining in vertically partitioned databases. Data and Knowledge Engineering 59(1), 378–396 (2006)

19. Kapoor, V., Poncelet, P., Trouss, F., et al.: Privacy preserving sequential pattern mining in distributed database. In: 15th ACM Conference on Information and Knowledge Management, CIKM 2006, pp. 758–767 (2006)
20. Nguyen, S.N., Orlowska, M.E.: A partition-based approach for sequential patterns in large sequence databases. Knowledge-Based Systems 21(2), 110–122 (2007)
21. Guralnik, V., Karypis, G.: Parallel tree-projection-based sequence mining algorithms. Parallel Computing 30(4), 443–472 (2004)
22. Luo, C., Chung Soon, M.: Parallel mining of maximal sequential patterns using multiple samples. Journal of Supercomputing 59(2), 852–881 (2012)
23. The Apache Software Foundation, http://hadoop.apache.org

Efficient Task Scheduling for Hard Real-Time Tasks in Asymmetric Multicore Processors

Sung Il Kim, Jong-Kook Kim[*], Hyoung Uk Ha, Tae Ho Kim, and Kyu Hyun Choi

School of Electrical Engineering, Korea University, Anam Dong, Seoul, Korea
jongkook@korea.ac.kr

Abstract. In the future it is very likely that asymmetric multi-core processors (AMP) will be used because of their proposed power efficiency and higher performance. In order to use the device intelligently and efficiently, it is essential to exploit the heterogeneity of AMPs. To fully exploit AMP systems, intelligent scheduling of tasks or intelligent resource management becomes one of the critical issues. In this paper, an AMP system is emulated, SPEC CPU2006 benchmark applications are executed as tasks, and heuristic methods for task scheduling are designed. Tasks are independent, non-preemptive, and have deadline (hard real-time) constraints. They arrive aperiodically and task migration is enabled. The performance metric is the total number of tasks completed by their deadline. The heuristic methods that are designed are compared with classic methods and the naïve Linux scheduler. Experimental results show that our task scheduling method completed 2.8 times more tasks than the naïve Linux scheduler for the proposed AMP environment.

Keywords: asymmetric, heterogeneous, multicore, multiprocessor, task scheduling, real-time, algorithms.

1 Introduction

The architecture of the processor had been changed from single-core integration to multi-core integration on a die by making multiple simple cores instead of one complex core which allowed less power consumption and significant throughput improvement in comparison to the single-core processor. Thus, a lot of research and studies were focused on the symmetric (or homogeneous) multi-core processors, where each core has the same architecture and same clock cycle speed. However, some recent research studies asymmetric (or heterogeneous) multi-core processor (AMP) systems and more and more research efforts will be focused on AMP systems because different applications have different affinity towards different architecture cores. Some research results show that AMPs can deliver both low power consumption and high performance while exploiting massive parallelism with specialized processing units [1][2][3]. However, AMP inherently has many issues that the current OS is not yet designed to handle. Especially, it is difficult to exploit the

---

[*] Corresponding author.

Y. Xiang et al. (Eds.): ICA3PP 2012, Part II, LNCS 7440, pp. 187–196, 2012.

heterogeneity/affinity of resources and tasks. It becomes more complex to exploit the heterogeneity of the resources when other constraints are introduced (e.g., deadline and/or power). To efficiently utilize such AMP systems, it is important to solve the task scheduling problem. An efficient and intelligent task scheduler enables the system to increase throughput, reduce makespan, while minimizing the power consumption under given constraints. The problem of task scheduling is proven to be in general a NP-complete problem [4]. Therefore, heuristic approaches must be designed to intelligently utilize the resources of an AMP system.

A simple way to emulate an AMP system is by using dynamic voltage and clock frequency scaling (DVFS) [5] technique to manipulate the homogeneous multi-core processor system ([6][7][8][9]). The DVFS scheme reduces the power consumption because the power consumption of the processor is proportional to the clock frequency and to the square of the supply voltage [10] while delaying the completion of tasks or applications. In our research, the DVFS scheme supported is used to introduce four fast cores and four slow cores in a single system as a type of an AMP system. The tasks in this environment are independent, non-preemptive, and have deadline (hard real-time) constraints. They arrive aperiodically and task migration is enabled. The goal of this research is to schedule intelligently in order to complete as many tasks as possible by their deadline.

The heuristic methods that are designed for this environment are dynamic methods in the sense that they consider information about the change in the system. Our methods are compared to some of the classic methods in the literature and also to the naive Linux scheduler. Results show that our best method completes 2.8 times more tasks than the original Linux scheduler.

To the best of our knowledge, this is the first AMP research that uses the applications of the SPEC CPU2006 benchmark suite as tasks, introduces hard deadlines to those tasks, and assumes a system where tasks are requested aperiodically. The result and its analysis will inspire how to design algorithms in a hard real-time AMP environment where the tasks arrive dynamically.

The next section describes related research. In Section 3, the AMP system used for this research is introduced. The task scheduling methods that are designed for the AMP system are depicted in Section 4. In Section 5, the simulation setup and environment is presented. Section 6 analyzes the results and the last section summarizes the paper.

2   Related Works

There have been quite a few studies that deal with task scheduling for an example of the AMP system. For non-real-time systems research, most of AMP scheduling methods utilize the characteristics of tasks and assign tasks to appropriate cores to exploit the task features. The research by Kumar et al. [3], designed, simulated, and evaluated an AMP system which consisted of a combination of Alpha processors. The proposed scheduling algorithm was based on the online sampling of relative IPC. It monitors relative IPC during sampling phase, assigns tasks using that information, and executes tasks during steady phase. However, load imbalance burden high IPC core with focused workloads. Shelepov et al. [6] designed an algorithm which exploits memory re-use distance for task scheduling. Memory re-use distance is gathered by offline profiling. This algorithm is a static approach, therefore, the runtime environment and application status cannot be utilized. Koufaty et al. proposed bias scheduling [12] that exploits the boundedness of threads. For high computational thread, it is beneficial that the thread should be assigned to the sophisticated core, whereas, thread which has many stalls cannot exploit high computational performance of the sophisticated core because of the latency for the off-chip memory request or the lack of core resources.

For real-time systems, Y. Yu and V. K. Prasanna [15] proposed energy efficient resource allocation algorithm which is based on integer linear programming with no guarantees that feasibility of a derived solution [15]. J. M. Calandrino et al. [16] focused on providing larger throughput for the non-real-time tasks when periodic real-time tasks arrive in the system allowing higher priority to the non-real-time tasks. In [17], approximation algorithm was proposed for a DVS system and a non-DVS processing element in a single environment.

Compared with previous research our research focuses on scheduling aperiodic hard real-time tasks onto an actual AMP system that consists of four fast and four slow cores. Also, real benchmark applications are run as tasks.

3   The Asymmetric Multicore Processor System

3.1   System Model

The system model is shown in Figure 1. The *task generator* generates independent tasks aperiodically by randomly picking from the task set (i.e., SPEC CPU2006). When a task arrives, the *task scheduler* identifies the task and dynamically gathers information from the AMP system to schedule using a designated algorithm and assign the task to an appropriate core. If a certain core is idle, the *queue manager* executes the task in the front of the wait queue of that core. For passive guarantee of task completion, whether the task can complete before its deadline will be tested just before its execution. It is assumed that only one task is executed on a core at any given time because when multiple tasks are run simultaneously cannot guarantee the execution time of the tasks. After finishing task execution and when the core becomes idle, the system generates an event signal to the *task scheduler* and the *queue manager*. This will allow the *task scheduler* to allocate a task to the wait queue of the system and/or the *queue manager* to execute a task in the wait queue. A task can be determined as completed, failed, or dropped, where the task is completed if the task finishes within its deadline, failed if the executed task does not meet its deadline, dropped if the task is not executed.

3.2   Energy Model

The power consumption (P) equation of the processor is $P = CV_s^2 f$, where C is capacitance, V_s is supply voltage, and f is clock frequency. Assuming that $f \propto V_s$ for

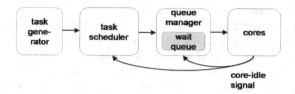

Fig. 1. The block diagram of the system model

simplification, then $P \propto V^3$, which is the same equation in [8]. The energy consumption of the task is equal to the execution time multiplied by the power consumption of the core. In this paper, because fast cores support 1.5 times higher clock frequency than that of slow cores, the task on fast cores consumes around 2.25 times $(=1.52^2)$ higher energy.

4   Task Scheduling Methods

4.1   Overview

The notations used to describe the scheduling methods are listed in Table 1. The machine available time, MAT_j, is time when a core becomes idle. Expected completion time is the expected time to finish a given task. ($CT_{i,j} = MAT_j + wait_j + ETC_{i,j}$)

Table 1. The notations

t_i	task i
C_j	core j
$t_{i,j}$	task i on core j
MAT_j	machine (core) available time of C_j
$ETC_{i,j}$	expected execution time to complete for $t_{i,j}$
$ATC_{i,j}$	actual execution time to complete for $t_{i,j}$
$wait_j$	total sum of expected execution time in wait queue of C_j
$CT_{i,j}$	expected completion time of $t_{i,j}$
d_i	deadline of t_i

4.2   Baseline Algorithms

For comparison purposes classic algorithms are chosen from [13] and modified for the system environment modeled in this paper and the original Linux scheduler is used for the baseline. The **Linux scheduler** basically assigns tasks onto cores and the tasks are not pinned to a specific core. Linux kernel 2.6.34 is used in our experiment, allowing up to eight tasks to execute simultaneously. The Linux scheduler was given the advantage of having eight fast cores. The **Random** algorithm assigns a task to a randomly selected core. Each core has equal probability to be selected. The **Opportunistic Load Balancing (OLB)** assigns a task to the core j which has the minimum wait time (= wait$_j$ + MAT$_j$). The **Minimum Completion Time (MCT)** assigns a task to the core which has minimum expected completion time (= wait time + ETC$_{i,j}$). The **Opportunistic Minimum Execution Time (OMET)** is designed where the system has one wait queue and the tasks in the queue are sorted by execution time in increasing order. The tasks are then sent one by one only when there is an idle machine. The **Two-phase Greedy** calculates the minimum CT of the tasks from the set S of non-executed tasks then chooses the minimum out of them and allocates the chosen task onto the minimum CT core. Then repeats the procedure until all tasks in the set S is allocated to the wait queues of the cores.

4.3   Avalanche

The Avalanche heuristic is based on the idea to restrict task's execution on certain cores. In this environment, tasks that have longer execution times are restricted to run on faster cores, increase the chance of it being completed. The tasks are divided into 4 classes according to their expected execution time as shown in Table 2. Cores 0~3 are slow cores and cores 4~7 are fast ones. A given task is assigned by the MCT method using the class specification. This approach may cause slow cores to be idle because only a few fast tasks may be introduced to the system. This will lead to significant low utilization of the slow cores, while fast cores may be full of tasks. Therefore, when a core becomes idle, task migration from fast core to slow core occurs if the executing task only a small amount of time left to complete (shown in Table 3). The remaining execution time should be small enough to not hinder upcoming short tasks and complete by its deadline on the idle core. The values described in Table 3 are determined by preliminary experiments.

Table 2. Class of the task

Class	ETC$_{i,slow}$	Core Range
class 1	less than 20	core 0~7
class 2	less than 110	core 1~7
class 3	less than 250	core 5~7
class 4	above 250	core 6, 7

Table 3. The condition of task migration

Target core	Migrate task from	Execution time
core 0	core 1~4	less than 5
core 1~4	core 1~7	less than 40

4.4   Reserve Core MCT (RC MCT)

Intuitively, the long execution time of an executing task or long wait time in the queue will increase the probability of dropping a newly arrived task. The intuition behind the RC MCT method is to use core reservation to try and stop dropping many short tasks that may be followed by some number of long tasks. This is attempted by allowing the long execution tasks to occupy a number of reserved fast core(s), while short tasks can be executed on cores that are not reserved. If a newly arrived task cannot meet the deadline on any other core than the reserved core by using the MCT method, then the task is assigned to the reserved core. If this assignment cannot complete the task by its deadline, the longest task in the wait queue of the reserved core will be dropped to make space for the new task.

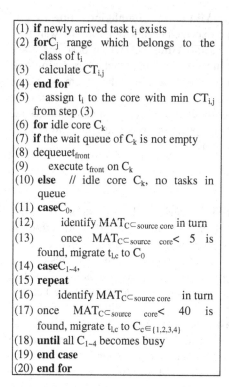

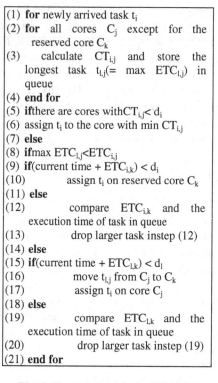

Fig. 2. The pseudo code for Avalanche

Fig. 3. The pseudo code for RC MCT

5   Experimental Setup

The machine used in this experiment is a symmetric multi-processor that supports the DVFS feature. The system consists of Supermicro X8DTi mainboard with dual package of Intel Xeon E5620, 16 GB of DDR3 PC3-10600 memory. The Intel Xeon E5620 is a quad core processor that has a 12MB Shared L3 cache and the clock cycle speed that ranges from 1.6 Ghz to 2.4 Ghz. The clock frequency of a processor is scaled with EIST to 1.6 Ghz and the other processor to 2.4 Ghz. Therefore, four cores run at 1.6 Ghz (slow cores) while the other four cores run at 2.4 Ghz (fast cores). The operating system is Linux Fedora13 64bit with kernel 2.6.34. All 29 applications (with training input sizes) in the SPECCPU2006 are used as independent tasks of which execution time varies from 1.62 seconds to 292 seconds. The actual execution time of tasks when run alone on a fast and a slow core is measured ten times each and is averaged to be used as the expected execution time of the tasks on the fast cores and slow cores respectively. The deadline of a task is equal to two times longer than its execution time on the slow core plus the arrival time of the task to ensure that the task has a chance of being completed.

The task arrival time is modeled by a Poisson distribution with a mean inter-task arrival time of six seconds. This resulted in a task-abundant environment, where not all tasks can complete within their deadline. For the results, ten trials are conducted for each heuristic and averaged, and the whole system is run for 7200 seconds. An average of 995.35 tasks is introduced to the system during two hours. Tasks that have deadline exceeding the simulation time are not considered.

6   Results

Figure 4 shows the overall average performance (completed tasks, failed tasks, and dropped tasks) of the algorithms. For the upper bound, we used the method proposed in [13] Section 4.7. The Avalanche algorithm performed the best in terms of the task completion percentage. The performance of Linux scheduler shows task completion rate of 25.05%, which is even worse than the random algorithm, despite the fact that Linux scheduler was given the advantage of having eight fast cores. The OLB was the worst performing method, but when the Linux scheduler was run on the four fast and four slow core setting, the Linux was worse than OLB. For the Linux, tasks are not assigned to a specific core (not pinned) and sometimes the task float among the cores. This causes significant migration overhead. The Linux schedules the tasks FCFS (first-come first-served) method regardless of the status of the system or the tasks.

RC MCT performs better than all other methods except for the two phase greedy, OMET, and Avalanche. However, RC MCT is one of the methods that use the least amount of power (shown in Figure 6). When compared to MCT, which it enhances, RC MCT completed around 10% more tasks and uses about 10% less power. The RC MCT reserves one fast core for long tasks, thus reducing the burden of executing long tasks on other cores. In the experiment, the reserved core always suffers from task congestion.

Avalanche handles the task congestion problem by categorizing tasks into classes. Long tasks are assigned to the fast cores to exploit the high computational ability. It reduces the total execution time of tasks, restricts long tasks to execute on slow cores, and allows short tasks to be executed with less task congestion. Avalanche shows the shortest execution time per a completed task (Figure 5), it means that it handles short tasks properly and not blocked by long tasks. In some cases, the slow cores suffer from task starvation because short tasks complete and leave the core faster than long tasks. If there is no task that belongs to the appropriate task class, the core will be idle state making low utilization of slow cores. The Avalanche method attempts to migrate longer tasks to the idle cores to cover the low utilization of the slow cores while also allowing other long tasks to execute on the fast cores. Avalanche is one of the methods that allows a lot of tasks to fail (at approximately 1.7%). This is a high percentage as each of the wait queues determines whether the task that will execute next can complete by its deadline using the estimated time to complete information and drop it if the core cannot complete it. So, there can only be a very small number of tasks being failed if there is only a small error between the estimated time to complete information and the actual time to complete information. Therefore, the failed tasks for Avalanche is mainly from the task migrations as the migration cost (delay) was not included in the estimation of whether a task that is migrated can complete.

The two phase greedy method also performs pretty well as it always considers the whole system of cores while it attempts to reassign all tasks in all of the wait queues whenever there is a change in the system. However it uses a lot of power as it only considers time and not power when allocating tasks onto the cores.

7   Summary

In the future, the multi-core computer system or mobile devices will be driven by asymmetric (or heterogeneous) multi-core processors (AMPs) because of power efficiency, high performance, and affinity to different applications/tasks. An intelligent task scheduler will be essential for this system to exploit heterogeneities and other information to boost the performance of the AMP system in terms of time and power. The goal of this research was to complete as many tasks as possible by their deadline while using an AMP system. In this paper, modified previous methods and also proposed algorithms to support intelligent task-core assignments on a real system with four fast and four slow cores using the SPEC CPU2006 benchmark applications as independent tasks. Due to the deadline constraint, task-oversubscription, and unknown arrival time, it is difficult for a task scheduling method to perform optimally. Therefore, a method that is carefully designed is needed to intelligently complete as many tasks as possible. One of our algorithms, Avalanche, achieved 70.74% task completion percentage with one of the lowest power consumption, which is close to the upper bound considering that eight fast core were used for the upper bound calculation where the upper bound completed 90.39% of the tasks.

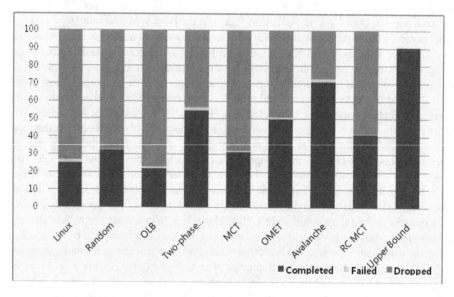

Fig. 4. Percentage of completed, failed, and dropped tasks

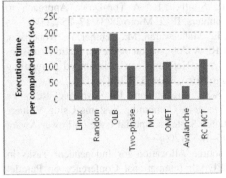
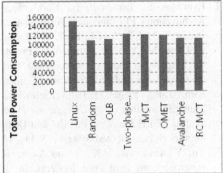

Fig. 5. Execution time per completed task   **Fig. 6.** Total power consumption

Acknowledgement. This research is supported in part by the National Research Foundation of Korea grant no. 2009-0076378.

References

1. Kumar, R., Tullsen, D.M., Jouppi, N.P., Ranganathan, P.: Heterogeneous Chip Multiprocessors. IEEE Trans. on Computer 38(11), 32–38 (2005)
2. Hill, M.D., Marty, M.R.: Amdahl's law in the multicore era. IEEE Trans. on Computer 41(7), 33–38 (2008)
3. Kumar, R., Tullsen, D.M., Ranganathan, P., Jouppi, N.P., Farkas, K.I.: Single-ISA Heterogeneous Multi-Core Architectures for Multithreaded Workload Performance. In: Proc. of the Annual International Symposium on Computer Architecture (2004)
4. Garey, M.R., Johnson, D.S.: Computers and Intractability: A Guide to the Theory of NP-Completeness, pp. 238–239. W.H. Freeman and Co. (1979)
5. Burd, T.D., Brodersen, R.W.: Energy efficient CMOS Microprocessor Design. In: Proc. of the Hawaii International Conference on System Sciences, vol. 1, pp. 288–297 (1995)
6. Shelepov, D., Fedorova, A., Blagodurov, S., Saez Alcaide, J.C., Perez, N., Kumar, V., Jeffery, S., Huang, Z.F.: HASS: A Scheduler for Heterogeneous Multicore Systems. Operating Systems Review 43(2), 66–75 (2009)
7. Saez, J.C., Prieto, M., Fedorova, A., Blagodourov, S.: A Comprehensive Scheduler for Asymmetric Multicore Systems. In: Proc. of ACM European Conference on Computer Systems (2010)
8. Winter, J.A., Albonesi, D.H., Shoemaker, C.A.: Scalable Thread Scheduling and Global Power Management for Heterogeneous Many-Core Architectures. In: Proc. of the 9th International Conference on Parallel Architectures and Compilation Techniques (2010)
9. Lakshminarayana, N.B., Lee, J., Kim, H.: Age Based Scheduling for Asymmetric Multiprocessors. In: Proc. of the Conference on High Performance Computing Networking, Storage and Analysis (2009)
10. Weiser, M., Welch, B., Demers, A., Shenker, S.: Scheduling for Reduced CPU Energy. In: Proc. Usenix Symp. Operating Systems Design and Implementation, pp. 13–23 (1994)
11. Koufaty, D., Reddy, D., Hahn, S.: Bias Scheduling in Heterogeneous Multi-core Architectures. In: Proc. of the ACM European Conference on Computer Systems (2010)

12. Eyerman, S., Eeckhout, L., Karkhanis, T., Smith, J.E.: A Top-Down Approach to Architecting CPI Component Performance Counters. IEEE Micro 28(3), 17–25 (2008)
13. Braun, T.D., Siegel, H.J., Beck, N., Boloni, L., Maheswaran, M., Reuther, A., Robertson, J., Theys, M., Yao, B., Hensgen, D., Freund, R.: A Comparison of Eleven Static Heuristics for Mapping a Class of Independent Tasks onto Heterogeneous Distributed Computing Systems. J. Parallel and Distributed Computing 61(6), 810–837 (2001)
14. Kim, J.-K., Siegel, H.J., Maciejewski, A.A., Eigenmann, R.: Dynamic Resource Management in Energy Constrained Heterogeneous Computing Systems Using Voltage Scaling. IEEE Trans. on Parallel and Distributed Systems, Special Issue on Power-Aware Parallel and Distributed Systems 19(11), 1445–1457 (2008)
15. Yu, Y., Prasanna, V.K.: Power-Aware Resource Allocation for Independent Tasks in Heterogeneous Real-Time Systems. In: IEEE 9th International Conference on Parallel Distributed Systems, pp. 341–348 (2002)
16. Calandrino, J.M., Baumberger, D., Li, T., Hahn, S., Anderson, J.H.: Soft Real-time Scheduling on Performance Asymmetric Multicore Platforms. In: Proc. of the 13th IEEE Real-Time and Embedded Technology and Applications Symposium (2007)
17. Hung, C.-M., Chen, J.-J., Kuo, T.-W.: Energy-Efficient Real-Time Task Scheduling for a DVS System with a Non-DVS Processing Element. In: Proc. of the IEEE Real-Time Systems Symposium (2006)

An Implementation of Parallel 2-D FFT Using Intel AVX Instructions on Multi-core Processors

Daisuke Takahashi

Faculty of Engineering, Information and Systems, University of Tsukuba
1-1-1 Tennodai, Tsukuba, Ibaraki 305-8573, Japan
daisuke@cs.tsukuba.ac.jp

Abstract. In this paper, we propose an implementation of a parallel two-dimensional fast Fourier transform (FFT) using Intel Advanced Vector Extensions (AVX) instructions on multi-core processors. The combination of vectorization and a block two-dimensional FFT algorithm is shown to effectively improve performance. We vectorized FFT kernels using the AVX instructions. Performance results of two-dimensional FFTs on multi-core processors are reported. We successfully achieved a performance of over 61 GFlops on an Intel Xeon E5-2670 (2.6 GHz, two CPUs, 16 cores) and over 24 GFlops on an Intel Core i7-3930K (3.2 GHz, one CPU, six cores) for a $2^{12} \times 2^{12}$-point FFT.

1   Introduction

The fast Fourier transform (FFT) [1] is an algorithm widely used today in science and engineering. Today, a number of processors have short vector SIMD instructions, e.g., Intel's SSE/SSE2/SSE3/SSSE3/SSE4/AVX, AMD's 3DNow!, and Motorola's AltiVec. These instructions provide substantial speedup for digital signal processing applications. Efficient FFT implementations with short vector SIMD instructions have also been investigated thoroughly [2,3,4].

Many FFT algorithms work well when the data sets fit into the cache. However, when the problem size exceeds the cache size, the performance of these FFT algorithms decreases dramatically. The key issue in the design of large FFTs is minimizing the number of cache misses. Thus, both vectorization and high cache utilization are particularly important with respect to high performance on processors that have short vector SIMD instructions. A block two-dimensional FFT algorithm [5] improves performance by utilizing the cache memory effectively.

In this paper, an implementation of a parallel two-dimensional FFT using Intel Advanced Vector Extensions (AVX) instructions on multi-core processors is presented.

We implemented the parallel block two-dimensional FFT algorithm on multi-core processors, and the obtained performance results are reported herein.

Section 2 describes a vectorization of FFT kernels. Section 3 describes a block two-dimensional FFT algorithm used for problems that exceed the cache size. Section 4 describes the in-cache FFT algorithm used for problems that fit into a data cache and parallelization. Section 5 gives performance results. In section 6, we provide some concluding remarks.

Y. Xiang et al. (Eds.): ICA3PP 2012, Part II, LNCS 7440, pp. 197–205, 2012.
© Springer-Verlag Berlin Heidelberg 2012

```
            SUBROUTINE FFT(A,B,W,M,L)
            COMPLEX*16 A(M,L,*),B(M,2,*),W(*)
            COMPLEX*16 C0,C1
            DO J=1,L
      !DIR$ VECTOR ALIGNED
               DO I=1,M
                 C0=A(I,J,1)
                 C1=A(I,J,2)
                 B(I,1,J)=C0+C1
                 B(I,2,J)=W(J)*(C0-C1)
               END DO
            END DO
            RETURN
            END
```

Fig. 1. An example of a vectorizable radix-2 FFT kernel

2   Vectorization of FFT Kernels

Intel AVX [6] is a new 256 bit extension to the SSE/SSE2/SSE3/SSSE3/SSE4 instruction sets. AVX supports 256-bit wide SIMD registers (YMM0–YMM15) in 64-bit mode.

The most direct way to use the AVX instructions is to insert the assembly language instructions inline into source code. However, this can be time-consuming and tedious, and assembly language inline programming is not supported on all compilers. Instead, Intel provides easy implementation through the use of API extension sets referred to as intrinsics [7]. The latest version of the FFTW library (version 3.3.1) [1] uses the AVX intrinsics to access SIMD hardware.

The Intel C/C++ and Fortran compilers also support automatic vectorization of floating-point loops using AVX instructions.

In this paper, this automatic vectorization was used. An example of a vectorizable radix-2 FFT kernel is shown in Fig. 1. The directive "!DIR$ VECTOR ALIGNED" in Fig. 1 instructs the compiler to use aligned data movement instructions for all array references when vectorizing.

Here, the arrays A and B are the input array and the output array, respectively. The twiddle factors [8] are stored in the array W. The problem size n corresponds to M×L×2.

In the radix-2 FFT kernel, the innermost loop lengths are varied from 1 to $n/2$ for n-point FFTs during $\log_2 n$ stages. For the first stage of the FFT kernel in Fig. 1, the innermost loop length is 1. In this case, the double-nested loop can be collapsed into a single-nested loop to expand innermost loop length, as shown in Fig. 2.

---

[1] http://www.fftw.org/

```
        SUBROUTINE FFT1ST(A,B,W,L)
        COMPLEX*16 A(L,*),B(2,*),W(*)
        COMPLEX*16 CO,C1
!DIR$ VECTOR ALIGNED
        DO J=1,L
          CO=A(J,1)
          C1=A(J,2)
          B(1,J)=CO+C1
          B(2,J)=W(J)*(CO-C1)
        END DO
        RETURN
        END
```

Fig. 2. First stage of a vectorizable radix-2 FFT kernel

3 A Block Two-Dimensional FFT Algorithm

The two-dimensional discrete Fourier transform (DFT) is given by

$$y(k_1, k_2) = \sum_{j_1=0}^{n_1-1} \sum_{j_2=0}^{n_2-1} x(j_1, j_2)\omega_{n_2}^{j_2 k_2}\omega_{n_1}^{j_1 k_1},$$

where $\omega_{n_r} = e^{-2\pi i/n_r}$ $(1 \leq r \leq 2)$ and $i = \sqrt{-1}$.

The two-dimensional FFT based on the multicolumn FFT algorithm [9] is as follows:

Step 1: Transpose
$$x_1(j_2, j_1) = x(j_1, j_2).$$

Step 2: n_1 individual n_2-point multicolumn FFTs
$$x_2(k_2, j_1) = \sum_{j_2=0}^{n_2-1} x_1(j_2, j_1)\omega_{n_2}^{j_2 k_2}.$$

Step 3: Transpose
$$x_3(j_1, k_2) = x_2(k_2, j_1).$$

Step 4: n_2 individual n_1-point multicolumn FFTs
$$y(k_1, k_2) = \sum_{j_1=0}^{n_1-1} x_3(j_1, k_2)\omega_{n_1}^{j_1 k_1}.$$

The distinctive features of the two-dimensional FFT can be summarized as follows:

- Two multicolumn FFTs are performed in Steps 2 and 4. Each column FFT is small enough to fit into the data cache.

– The two-dimensional FFT has two transpose steps, which typically are the chief bottlenecks in cache-based processors.

We combine the multicolumn FFTs and transpositions in order to reduce the number of cache misses, and we modify the conventional two-dimensional FFT algorithm to reuse the data in the cache memory. In the following, n_b is the block size. Each processor is assumed to have a multi-level cache memory. A block two-dimensional FFT algorithm [5] can be written as follows.

Step 1: Consider the data in main memory as an $n_1 \times n_2$ complex matrix. Fetch and transpose the data n_b rows at a time into an $n_2 \times n_b$ matrix. The $n_2 \times n_b$ array fits into the L2 cache.

Step 2: For each group of n_b columns, perform n_b individual n_2-point multicolumn FFTs on the $n_2 \times n_b$ array in the L2 cache. Each column FFT also fits into the L1 data cache.

Step 3: Transpose each of the resulting $n_2 \times n_b$ matrices, and return the resulting n_b rows to the same locations in the main memory from which they were fetched.

Step 4: Perform n_2 individual n_1-point multicolumn FFTs on the $n_1 \times n_2$ array.

4   In-Cache FFT Algorithm and Parallelization

We use the radix-2, 4, and 8 Stockham autosort FFT algorithm [10] for in-cache FFTs.

Although the Stockham autosort FFT algorithm requires a scratch array the same size as the input array, the algorithm does not include digit-reverse permutation. Table 1 shows the real inner-loop operations for radix-2, 4, and 8 double-precision complex FFT kernels.

In view of the Byte/Flop ratio, the radix-8 FFT is preferable to the radix-2 and 4 FFTs. Although higher radix FFTs require more floating-point registers to hold intermediate results, the Sandy Bridge processor has 16 YMM 256-bit registers.

A power-of-two point FFT (except for 2-point FFT) can be performed by a combination of radix-8 and radix-4 steps containing at most two radix-4 steps. That is, the power-of-two FFTs can be performed as a length $n = 2^p = 4^q 8^r$ ($p \geq 2$, $0 \leq q \leq 2$, $r \geq 0$).

Fig. 3 gives the Fortran program for the block two-dimensional FFT algorithm. Here, the arrays A and WORK are the input/output array and the work array, respectively. The parameters NB and NP are the blocking parameter and padding parameter, respectively.

We parallelized the block two-dimensional FFT by using OpenMP. The outermost loop of each FFT step shown in Fig. 3 is distributed across the cores.

```
        COMPLEX*16 A(N1,N2),WORK(N2+NP,NB)
! Step 1 (Transpose)
!$OMP PARALLEL DO
      DO II=1,N1,NB
        DO JJ=1,N2,NB
          DO I=II,MIN(II+NB-1,N1)
            DO J=JJ,MIN(JJ+NB-1,N2)
              WORK(J,I-II+1)=A(I,J)
            END DO
          END DO
        END DO
! Step 2 (N1 individual N2-point multicolumn FFTs)
        DO I=II,MIN(II+NB-1,N1)
          CALL IN_CACHE_FFT(WORK(1,I-II+1),N2)
        END DO
! Step 3 (Transpose)
        DO J=1,N2
          DO I=II,MIN(II+NB-1,N1)
            A(I,J)=WORK(J,I-II+1)
          END DO
        END DO
      END DO
! Step 4 (N2 individual N1-point multicolumn FFTs)
!$OMP PARALLEL DO
      DO J=1,N2
        CALL IN_CACHE_FFT(A(1,J),N1)
      END DO
```

Fig. 3. A block two-dimensional FFT algorithm

5   Performance Results

To evaluate the implemented parallel two-dimensional FFT, referred to as FFTE (version 5.0)[2], we compared its performance against that of the FFT library of FFTW (version 3.3.1) [2] and the Intel Math Kernel Library (MKL, version 10.3 update 9) [11]. The FFTW and the MKL support AVX instructions.

The elapsed times obtained from 10 executions of complex forward FFTs were averaged, where the input and output were in normal order. The FFTs were performed on double-precision complex data, and the table for twiddle factors was prepared in advance. In the FFTW, the "patient" planner was used.

The specifications for the two platforms used are shown in Table 2. Hyper-Threading (HT) [12] was disabled on both platforms.

The compilers used were the Intel C Compiler (icc, version 12.1) and the Intel Fortran Compiler (ifort, version 12.1). For the FFTE, the compiler options used were specified as "ifort -O3 -xAVX -openmp". The compiler option "-O3" specifies to optimize for maximum speed and enable more aggressive

---

[2] http://www.ffte.jp/

Table 1. Real inner-loop operations for radix-2, 4, and 8 double-precision complex FFT kernels based on the Stockham FFT

	Radix-2	Radix-4	Radix-8
Loads	4	8	16
Stores	4	8	16
Multiplications	4	12	32
Additions	6	22	66
Byte/Flop ratio	6.400	3.765	2.612

Table 2. Specification of machines

Platform	Intel Xeon E5-2670	Intel Core i7-3930K
Number of CPUs	2	1
Number of cores	16	6
CPU Type	Intel Xeon E5-2670 Sandy Bridge-EP 2.6 GHz	Intel Core i7-3930K Sandy Bridge-E 3.2 GHz
L1 Cache (per core)	I-Cache: 32 KB D-Cache: 32 KB	I-Cache: 32 KB D-Cache: 32 KB
L2 Cache (per core)	256 KB	256 KB
L3 Cache (shared)	20 MB	12 MB
Main Memory	DDR3-1600 SDRAM 128 GB	DDR3-1600 SDRAM 16 GB
OS	Linux 2.6.32-131.0.15.el6.x86_64	Linux 2.6.32-220.7.1.el6.x86_64

optimizations, and "-xAVX" specifies to generate the AVX instructions. The compiler option "-openmp" specifies to enable the compiler to generate multi-threaded code based on the OpenMP directives. For the FFTW and the MKL, the compiler options used were specified as "icc -O3 -xAVX -openmp". All programs were run in 64-bit mode.

5.1   Performance Results on Intel Xeon E5-2670

Tables 3, 4, and 5 compare the FFTE, the FFTW, and the MKL in terms of their run times and GFlops. The first column gives the problem size, and the remaining ten columns show the average elapsed times in seconds and the average execution performance in GFlops. The GFlops values are each based on $5n \log_2 n$ for a transform of size $n = 2^m$.

The FFTE is faster than the FFTW on two CPUs, 16 cores. On the other hand, the FFTE is slower than the MKL on one CPU, whereas for $n_1 \times n_2 = 2^8 \times 2^8$, $n_1 \times n_2 = 2^9 \times 2^{10}$, and $n_1 \times n_2 = 2^{10} \times 2^{10}$, the FFTE is faster than the MKL on two CPUs, 16 cores.

5.2   Performance Results on Intel Core i7-3930K

Tables 6, 7 and 8 compare the FFTE, the FFTW, and the MKL in terms of their run times and GFlops. The first column gives the problem size, and the

Table 3. Performance of FFTE 5.0 on Intel Xeon E5-2670

$n_1 \times n_2$	1 CPU, 1 core		1 CPU, 2 cores		1 CPU, 4 cores		1 CPU, 8 cores		2 CPUs, 16 cores	
	Time	GFlops	Time	GFlops	Time	GFlops	Time	GFlops	Time	GFlops
$2^8 \times 2^8$	0.00064	8.154	0.00034	15.298	0.00019	27.402	0.00012	45.223	0.00012	42.173
$2^8 \times 2^9$	0.00134	8.332	0.00070	15.845	0.00037	29.998	0.00021	52.752	0.00021	51.877
$2^9 \times 2^9$	0.00274	8.596	0.00142	16.604	0.00073	32.243	0.00039	60.860	0.00037	63.931
$2^9 \times 2^{10}$	0.00619	8.044	0.00319	15.624	0.00164	30.339	0.00084	59.300	0.00067	74.540
$2^{10} \times 2^{10}$	0.01373	7.635	0.00690	15.200	0.00350	29.949	0.00182	57.661	0.00128	81.854
$2^{10} \times 2^{11}$	0.04155	5.300	0.02094	10.513	0.01124	19.587	0.00711	30.985	0.00390	56.405
$2^{11} \times 2^{11}$	0.09021	5.115	0.04567	10.102	0.02425	19.025	0.01430	32.275	0.00798	57.852
$2^{11} \times 2^{12}$	0.18788	5.135	0.09537	10.115	0.05047	19.116	0.02950	32.703	0.01649	58.518
$2^{12} \times 2^{12}$	0.38818	5.186	0.19699	10.220	0.10191	19.756	0.05853	34.394	0.03274	61.491

Table 4. Performance of FFTW 3.3.1 on Intel Xeon E5-2670

$n_1 \times n_2$	1 CPU, 1 core		1 CPU, 2 cores		1 CPU, 4 cores		1 CPU, 8 cores		2 CPUs, 16 cores	
	Time	GFlops	Time	GFlops	Time	GFlops	Time	GFlops	Time	GFlops
$2^8 \times 2^8$	0.00062	8.450	0.00035	14.969	0.00023	23.019	0.00011	46.516	0.00016	33.221
$2^8 \times 2^9$	0.00129	8.673	0.00069	16.120	0.00044	25.527	0.00024	46.313	0.00025	44.280
$2^9 \times 2^9$	0.00261	9.042	0.00147	16.048	0.00085	27.816	0.00048	48.775	0.00056	41.811
$2^9 \times 2^{10}$	0.00540	9.219	0.00290	17.186	0.00155	32.136	0.00089	55.716	0.00128	38.986
$2^{10} \times 2^{10}$	0.01122	9.345	0.00587	17.864	0.00317	33.094	0.00192	54.713	0.00182	57.606
$2^{10} \times 2^{11}$	0.03203	6.874	0.01744	12.627	0.00940	23.426	0.00619	35.555	0.00521	42.230
$2^{11} \times 2^{11}$	0.08235	5.603	0.04416	10.447	0.02303	20.033	0.01480	31.182	0.01206	38.242
$2^{11} \times 2^{12}$	0.17078	5.649	0.08669	11.128	0.04704	20.507	0.02708	35.620	0.03313	29.122
$2^{12} \times 2^{12}$	0.35976	5.596	0.24015	8.384	0.12514	16.088	0.06877	29.274	0.05892	34.169

Table 5. Performance of Intel MKL 10.3 on Intel Xeon E5-2670

$n_1 \times n_2$	1 CPU, 1 core		1 CPU, 2 cores		1 CPU, 4 cores		1 CPU, 8 cores		2 CPUs, 16 cores	
	Time	GFlops	Time	GFlops	Time	GFlops	Time	GFlops	Time	GFlops
$2^8 \times 2^8$	0.00052	10.146	0.00028	19.015	0.00015	34.201	0.00010	54.893	0.00013	39.376
$2^8 \times 2^9$	0.00106	10.546	0.00055	20.356	0.00029	38.355	0.00017	65.615	0.00021	52.833
$2^9 \times 2^9$	0.00227	10.410	0.00117	20.097	0.00061	38.642	0.00032	72.996	0.00036	65.255
$2^9 \times 2^{10}$	0.00515	9.677	0.00263	18.958	0.00133	37.413	0.00068	73.055	0.00069	72.256
$2^{10} \times 2^{10}$	0.01119	9.374	0.00565	18.546	0.00296	35.481	0.00154	68.047	0.00151	69.695
$2^{10} \times 2^{11}$	0.03300	6.672	0.01695	12.995	0.00921	23.922	0.00600	36.707	0.00365	60.326
$2^{11} \times 2^{11}$	0.07170	6.434	0.03704	12.457	0.02065	22.343	0.01371	33.660	0.00752	61.392
$2^{11} \times 2^{12}$	0.14771	6.531	0.07523	12.824	0.04253	22.683	0.02838	33.994	0.01510	63.878
$2^{12} \times 2^{12}$	0.30907	6.514	0.15863	12.692	0.08800	22.879	0.05935	33.922	0.03133	64.257

remaining eight columns show the average elapsed times in seconds and the average execution performance in GFlops.

The FFTE is faster than the MKL for the cases of $n_1 \times n_2 = 2^{10} \times 2^{10}$ and $n_1 \times n_2 \geq 2^{11} \times 2^{11}$ on one CPU, six cores. On the other hand, for $n_1 \times n_2 \leq 2^9 \times 2^{10}$ the FFTE is slower than the MKL on one CPU, six cores. For the Intel Core

Table 6. Performance of FFTE 5.0 on Intel Core i7-3930K

$n_1 \times n_2$	1 CPU, 1 core		1 CPU, 2 cores		1 CPU, 4 cores		1 CPU, 6 cores	
	Time	GFlops	Time	GFlops	Time	GFlops	Time	GFlops
$2^8 \times 2^8$	0.00060	8.705	0.00032	16.325	0.00018	29.284	0.00014	37.841
$2^8 \times 2^9$	0.00126	8.829	0.00066	16.977	0.00035	32.144	0.00026	42.592
$2^9 \times 2^9$	0.00260	9.061	0.00132	17.831	0.00068	34.588	0.00050	46.998
$2^9 \times 2^{10}$	0.00582	8.555	0.00301	16.571	0.00154	32.290	0.00116	42.998
$2^{10} \times 2^{10}$	0.01705	6.151	0.00862	12.167	0.00473	22.173	0.00369	28.432
$2^{10} \times 2^{11}$	0.04073	5.406	0.02077	10.604	0.01154	19.089	0.00903	24.393
$2^{11} \times 2^{11}$	0.08835	5.222	0.04497	10.261	0.02439	18.920	0.01848	24.972
$2^{11} \times 2^{12}$	0.18770	5.140	0.09527	10.126	0.05063	19.052	0.03827	25.205
$2^{12} \times 2^{12}$	0.43003	4.682	0.21556	9.340	0.11219	17.946	0.08071	24.943

Table 7. Performance of FFTW 3.3.1 on Intel Core i7-3930K

$n_1 \times n_2$	1 CPU, 1 core		1 CPU, 2 cores		1 CPU, 4 cores		1 CPU, 6 cores	
	Time	GFlops	Time	GFlops	Time	GFlops	Time	GFlops
$2^8 \times 2^8$	0.00058	9.031	0.00033	15.704	0.00019	28.326	0.00014	36.319
$2^8 \times 2^9$	0.00122	9.143	0.00067	16.563	0.00045	25.046	0.00032	34.716
$2^9 \times 2^9$	0.00246	9.580	0.00138	17.130	0.00076	31.228	0.00055	42.669
$2^9 \times 2^{10}$	0.00520	9.574	0.00279	17.860	0.00153	32.562	0.00120	41.530
$2^{10} \times 2^{10}$	0.01390	7.544	0.00800	13.107	0.00427	24.588	0.00353	29.671
$2^{10} \times 2^{11}$	0.03194	6.894	0.01721	12.793	0.00987	22.307	0.00811	27.170
$2^{11} \times 2^{11}$	0.07219	6.392	0.03669	12.577	0.02142	21.537	0.01820	25.350
$2^{11} \times 2^{12}$	0.15193	6.350	0.07825	12.329	0.04298	22.443	0.03287	29.348
$2^{12} \times 2^{12}$	0.33713	5.972	0.17134	11.750	0.09340	21.556	0.09964	20.205

Table 8. Performance of Intel MKL 10.3 on Intel Core i7-3930K

$n_1 \times n_2$	1 CPU, 1 core		1 CPU, 2 cores		1 CPU, 4 cores		1 CPU, 6 cores	
	Time	GFlops	Time	GFlops	Time	GFlops	Time	GFlops
$2^8 \times 2^8$	0.00048	10.968	0.00026	20.370	0.00014	36.624	0.00014	38.507
$2^8 \times 2^9$	0.00099	11.301	0.00052	21.549	0.00027	41.006	0.00024	46.777
$2^9 \times 2^9$	0.00211	11.178	0.00110	21.475	0.00057	41.675	0.00047	50.537
$2^9 \times 2^{10}$	0.00478	10.414	0.00245	20.324	0.00126	39.698	0.00098	50.615
$2^{10} \times 2^{10}$	0.01415	7.409	0.00763	13.752	0.00423	24.802	0.00382	27.484
$2^{10} \times 2^{11}$	0.03192	6.900	0.01670	13.187	0.01008	21.846	0.00901	24.442
$2^{11} \times 2^{11}$	0.06911	6.676	0.03616	12.759	0.02158	21.378	0.01910	24.154
$2^{11} \times 2^{12}$	0.15036	6.416	0.07851	12.287	0.04510	21.388	0.04101	23.522
$2^{12} \times 2^{12}$	0.31902	6.311	0.16559	12.158	0.09414	21.386	0.08392	23.990

i7-3930K processor, up to $2^9 \times 2^{10}$-point FFTs fit into the 12 MB L3 cache. Moreover, the MKL works well when the data sets fit into the cache. These are two reasons why for $n_1 \times n_2 \leq 2^9 \times 2^{10}$, the FFTE is slower than the MKL on one CPU, six cores.

6   Conclusion

In this paper, we proposed the implementation of the parallel two-dimensional FFT using Intel AVX instructions on multi-core processors.

We vectorized FFT kernels using the AVX instructions, and parallelized the block two-dimensional FFT by using OpenMP. The performance of the implemented parallel two-dimensional FFT remains at a high level even for a larger problem size, owing to cache blocking.

We succeeded in obtaining a performance of over 61 GFlops on an Intel Xeon E5-2670 (2.6 GHz, two CPUs, 16 cores) and over 24 GFlops on an Intel Core i7-3930K (3.2 GHz, one CPU, six cores) for a $2^{12} \times 2^{12}$-point FFT.

These performance results demonstrate that the implemented FFT utilizes cache memory effectively and exploits the AVX instructions.

Acknowledgments. This work was supported by a Grant-in-Aid for Scientific Research on Innovative Areas (No. 22104003) of The Ministry of Education, Culture, Sports, Science and Technology, Japan.

References

1. Cooley, J.W., Tukey, J.W.: An algorithm for the machine calculation of complex Fourier series. Math. Comput. 19, 297–301 (1965)
2. Frigo, M., Johnson, S.G.: The design and implementation of FFTW3. Proc. IEEE 93, 216–231 (2005)
3. Püschel, M., Moura, J.M.F., Johnson, J., Padua, D., Veloso, M., Singer, B.W., Xiong, J., Franchetti, F., Gacic, A., Voronenko, Y., Chen, K., Johnson, R.W., Rizzolo, N.: SPIRAL: Code generation for DSP transforms. Proc. IEEE 93, 232–275 (2005)
4. McFarlin, D.S., Arbatov, V., Franchetti, F., Püschel, M.: Automatic SIMD vectorization of fast Fourier transforms for the Larrabee and AVX instruction sets. In: Proc. 25th International Conference on Supercomputing, ICS 2011, pp. 265–274 (2011)
5. Takahashi, D.: Implementation and evaluation of parallel FFT using SIMD instructions on multi-core processors. In: Proc. 2007 International Workshop on Innovative Architecture for Future Generation High-Performance Processors and Systems, IWIA 2007, pp. 53–59 (2007)
6. Intel Corporation: Intel 64 and IA-32 Architectures Software Developer's Manual, Volume 1: Basic Architecture (2012)
7. Intel Corporation: Intel C++ Compiler XE 12.1 User and Reference Guides (2011)
8. Brigham, E.O.: The Fast Fourier Transform and its Applications. Prentice-Hall, Englewood Cliffs (1988)
9. Van Loan, C.: Computational Frameworks for the Fast Fourier Transform. SIAM Press, Philadelphia (1992)
10. Swarztrauber, P.N.: FFT algorithms for vector computers. Parallel Computing 1, 45–63 (1984)
11. Intel Corporation: Intel Math Kernel Library Reference Manual (2012)
12. Marr, D.T., Binns, F., Hill, D.L., Hinton, G., Koufaty, D.A., Miller, J.A., Upton, M.: Hyper-threading technology architecture and microarchitecture. Intel Technology Journal 6, 1–11 (2002)

A Semantic Impact in Decentralized Resource Discovery Mechanism for Grid Computing Environments

Abdul Khalique Shaikh[1], Saadat M. Alhashmi[1], and Rajendran Parthiban[2]

[1] School of IT, Monash University, Sunway Campus, Bandar Sunway, Malaysia
{shaikh,alhashmi}@monash.edu
[2] School of Engineering, Monash University, Sunway Campus, Bandar Sunway, Malaysia
rajendran.parthiban@monash.edu

Abstract. The requirement of semantic technology has been augmented day by day in IT related applications due to various features including interoperability. Effective development and organization of semantic knowledge are essential for maximum throughput in any application. We extend and develop two sub-domain computer resource ontologies and utilize them in a resource discovery process of a Grid computing environment to reduce the job rejection rate. Grid computing aggregates distributed computing resources to execute computationally complex jobs. The selection of resources in a Grid system involves finding and locating resources based on users' requirements. Identifying an appropriate resource selection mechanism for Grid jobs is a major concern because overall performance of a Grid depends on it and it also helps to schedule and allocate resources. We compute semantic similarity threshold values and employ both extended ontolgies in a decentralized resource discovery model of Grid Computing. The simulation is carried out using GridSim and PlanetSim to evaluate the effectiveness of a semantic resource discovery model. The results show improved success probability for complex jobs and reduce communication overheads compared to the non semantic resource discovery model.

Keywords: Grid Computing, Semantic, Ontology, Resource Discovery.

1 Introduction

Due to the various features of semantic technology [1], its usage has been dramatically increased over the years in IT applications. A number of researchers are also trying to get full benefits of semantic technology in resource management of Grid Computing environment. A resource discovery process which is a prominent function of resource management can be enhanced by using semantic features. The main purpose of a Grid system is to aggregate physical and logical computing resources for executing computationally complex applications such as large scale structural testing, sensor analysis, weather forecasting and drug design [2]. These types of complex applications need huge amounts of computing resources. Prior to submitting jobs to a Grid system, appropriate resources are selected to execute these jobs. Resources in a

Y. Xiang et al. (Eds.): ICA3PP 2012, Part II, LNCS 7440, pp. 206–216, 2012.

Grid system are highly distributed and are dynamic in nature. Moreover, these resources are under the control of different virtual organizations with their own rules and policies [3]. Ian Foster states in [4] that unlike global identification of resources in P2P systems, it is very difficult to define global naming scheme for attribute based resource identification in Grid computing environment. So it is highly probable that the same resources might be published with different names and it could be possible to miss some relevant resources in syntax-based technique. Hence, the resource discovery process in a Grid system is very challenging. Due to the usage of fixed schema between users requirement and providers availability in Grid environments, the job rejection ratio is very high. Moreover, lack of coordination between users and providers in a highly heterogeneous Grid environment often results in user jobs failing in finding relevant resources [5].To overcome the above limitations, the usage of semantic technology can be considered to reduce the job rejection ratio, because semantic matching helps to remove the tight coordination between resource providers and users. The overall effectiveness of the system depends on the level of coordination and cooperation among users, providers, resources and services [6]. In order to enhance job success probability and reduce communication overheads, there is a need for better coordination between users and providers that could be improved by adding semantic features.

To add the features of semantic in a resource discovery function of Grid computing resource management, we extend two exiting ontologies i.e. *Processor* and *Operating System* from [7] and compute semantic similarity threshold values with the help of formula defined in [22].

To minimize the job rejection and communication heads, we employ these two ontologies in a decentralized resource discovery process. A decentralized resource discovery process is more successful in large number of nodes as it provides better scalability and fault tolerance compared to a centralized resource discovery process.

Our main contributions include extension in existing grid computing resource ontologies and present sub-domain ontology structure for a Grid Computing environment. Also, we develop a semantic decentralized model to evaluate how semantic can be useful in a Grid Computing environment. On the basis of our simulation results, we believe that integration of sub-domain ontology into a Grid resource discovery model can be beneficial in increasing job success probability and reducing communication cost.

The remaining sections of the papers are organized as follows:

Section 2 reviews existing semantic resource discovery systems. Section 3 explains the process of ontologies deployment. Section 4 presents experiments and Section 5 shows results. Finally, Section 6 concludes the paper with possible future work.

2   Related Work

Currently, most of the real existing grid systems including CONDOR[8], Globus[9] gLite[10] encompass a syntax-based matching resource discovery mechanism that gives limited and fixed results. However, following related work discusses semantic resource discovery models in a Grid Computing environment.

Somasundaram et al. [11] has proposed semantic Grid architecture to describe and searching resources where authors introduce a knowledge layer at top of resource broker. Authors show some comparisons of semantic and non-semantic results on very low scale where domain based ontology is being used that shows some relationship between CPU and RAM concepts. However, both concepts are irrelevant each other in terms of function. In this scenario, if users demand very low semantic threshold value, it might be possible to offer RAM instead of CPU for a job. So it is not realistic approach to use domain specific ontology in a Grid resource discovery process.

Vidal et al. proposed a semantic approach based on ontolgies to manage resources in a Grid system. Authors develop the grid resources and applications ontologies including *Processor* and *Operating system* resources. However, existing concepts are not enough to cover all relevant terms. Hence, we extend these two ontologies by adding more concepts which are acquired from top 500 high performance computing website [12] and prominent hardware & software companies.

Juan Li [13] propose an efficient discovery framework which organizes a grid system by implementing ontology domain knowledge and semantic link network. According to author, experimental results confirm the effectiveness of the design in efficiency and robustness. The drawback includes artificial data is used in non Grid simulator environment.

A P2P semantic-based system, Atlas is proposed in [14] for distributed storage and retrieval of Resource Description Framework (RDF). This is built on top of the Distribution Hash Table (DHT) bamboo and supports pull and push query scenario. It is currently being used to realize the metadata service of Semantic Open Grid Service Architecture (S-OGSA) in a fully distributed and scalable way. Authors of [14] claim that resource discovery services for semantic grid can be made scalable, fault tolerant, robust and adaptive. However, the query evaluation and experimental results with realistic grid computing semantic data are missing. Moreover, the current version of Atlas [15] evaluates the system with distributed digital library application that supports storing, updating and queering RDFs data on top of DHT. A novel semantic supported agent-based decentralized Grid resource discovery mechanism has been proposed in [16]. This heuristic algorithm has been developed to find out neighbor resources and introduces the concepts of semantic similarity of domain ontology using a decentralized approach. The experimental results show that the success probability of resource discovery increases with the decrease in semantic similarity threshold. The level of the job complexity is inversely proportional to success probability. Authors in [16] claim that the algorithm has a flexibility to efficiently and dynamically discover resources. However, their experiment results show that the job success probability is very low under average job complexity and average semantic threshold values. Also, no realistic semantic concepts are used in their research work. Different from above approaches, we present sub-domain specific ontologies for grid resources and deploy in a decentralized resource discovery process of Grid computing.

3   Semantic Impact

In this section, we explain the impact of semantic technology in resource discovery mechanism of a Grid system. It also presents the features of our semantic framework used for resource ontology discovery in a Grid system. Grid resources belong to different virtual organizations with their own rules and policies, so it is possible for same resources to be published with different terminology. A semantic approach can be useful to identify the relationship between those resources [17]. It is stated that in paper [11], ontologies can improve the quality of information and facilitate to increase the efficiency of resource management in a Grid system. Moreover, ontology defines resource descriptions and builds a semantic bridge between the resource descriptions and users' demands [18]. In addition to this, ontology can help in expanding the search by representing the equivalence of related concepts of ontologies in terms of some standards semantics.

Protégé ontology editor and framework [19] is being widely used among semantic research community to design and extend ontologies of various fields. We use the same framework to extend the ontologies of *Processor* resource and *Operating System* resource. Ontology for both resources can be seen in fig. 1 and fig. 2. After developing both ontologies, we compute semantic similarity threshold values among concepts of ontologies. Semantic similarity is defined as the relationship between ontology concepts. The similarity of concepts represents the degree of commonality between these concepts. No standard procedure is available to measure the semantic similarity. However, a survey paper [20] compares and contrasts the various models to measure the semantic similarity distance between ontology concepts. In paper [20], authors state that the selection of measurement process is very complicated for certain applications as human similarity judgment process is varied person to person based on context and experience. For our application, we select the semantic measurement formula based on network model because of the following reasons:

- Network model measures similarity based on the notion of the distance short path algorithm
- The mathematical model based on graph theory so we can easily find out the relationship of the objects
- Its element representation is applicable to both object and concepts
- Its knowledge representation is structured way which is important for similarity measurement in terms of making explicit relationship between concepts
- It supports both notion of similarity i.e. semantic distance as dissimilarity and commonalities versus differences.

Network model based semantic measurement formula has been proposed in Andreasen et al. [21] and also used in a decentralized semantic resource discovery model [16]. Authors derive conceptual similarity using the notion of "similarity graph". In this, ontology is represented as a graph with concepts as nodes and relationships connecting these concepts as edges.

4   Calculation of Semantic Threshold Values

In this section, we present the method to compute semantic similarity threshold values between concepts of developed ontologies. We use semantic similarity formula which is published in Andreasen et al. [21]. Authors in [21] introduce following equation and use a function, sim (x,y) to measure the degree of similarity, which is proportional to the common concepts x and y share. We utilize this method to calculate semantic similarity values between concepts of resource ontologies. The semantic similarity distance between concepts of resources is also known as a semantic threshold value and could be derived from (1).

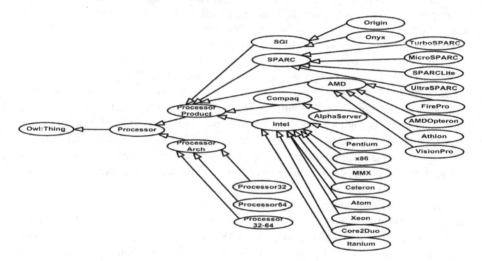

Fig. 1. Ontology for Resource *Processor*

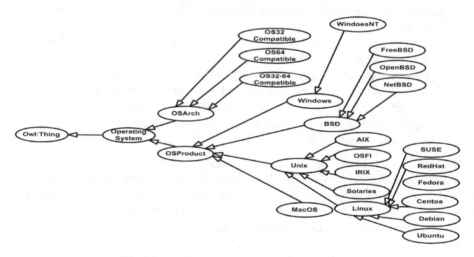

Fig. 2. Ontology for Resource *Operating System*

$$Sim(x,y) = \rho \frac{|\alpha(x) \cap \alpha(y)|}{|\alpha(x)|} + (1-\rho)\frac{|\alpha(x) \cap \alpha(y)|}{|\alpha(y)|} \qquad (1)$$

In (1), rho is a factor that determines the degree of influence of generalization of ontology concepts. The value of rho lies between 0 and 1. If value of rho is 1, that means perfect generalization, with each and every concept defined properly and 0 means very poor generalization. We set the different rho value such as 0.25, (0.5),(0.75) and (1.00). However, results showed in this paper by using rho value 0.75. In following formula, $\alpha(x)$ is the set of nodes reachable from x and $\alpha(x) \cap \alpha(y)$ the reachable nodes shared by x and y. Sim(x,y) = 0 means x and y are completely dissimilar and Sim(x,y) = 1 means full similarity. Table 1 shows the semantic threshold values of *operating system* ontology with rho value 0.75. For example, above method can be used to calculate semantic threshold values between *AIX* concept and *BSD* concept in operating system ontology.

$$Sim(AIX, BSD) = \rho \frac{|\alpha(AIX) \cap \alpha(BSD)|}{|\alpha(AIX)|} + (1-\rho)\frac{|\alpha(AIX) \cap \alpha(BSD)|}{|\alpha(BSD)|}$$

$$Sim(AIX, BSD) = .75\,\frac{2}{4} + (1-.75)\frac{2}{3}$$

$$Sim(AIX, BSD) = .54$$

Table 1. Semantic threshold values for *Operating System* ontology

	Operating System	OSArch	OSProduct	OS32Compatible	OS64Compatible	OS32-62Compatible	Windows	BSD	Unix	MacOS	Windows NT	FreeBSD	OpenBSD	NetBSD	AIX	OSFI	IRIX	Solaries	Linux	SUSE	RedHat	Fedora	Centos	Debiian	Ubuntu
Operating System	1.00	0.88	0.88	0.83	0.83	0.83	0.83	0.83	0.83	0.81	0.81	0.81	0.81	0.81	0.81	0.81	0.81	0.81	0.81	0.80	0.80	0.80	0.80	0.80	0.80
OSArch	0.63	1.00	0.50	0.92	0.92	0.92	0.46	0.46	0.46	0.44	0.44	0.44	0.44	0.44	0.44	0.44	0.44	0.44	0.44	0.43	0.43	0.43	0.43	0.43	0.43
OSProduct	0.63	0.50	1.00	0.46	0.46	0.46	0.92	0.92	0.92	0.88	0.88	0.88	0.88	0.88	0.88	0.88	0.88	0.88	0.88	0.85	0.85	0.85	0.85	0.85	0.85
OS32Compatible	0.50	0.75	0.38	1.00	0.67	0.67	0.33	0.33	0.33	0.31	0.31	0.31	0.31	0.31	0.31	0.31	0.31	0.31	0.31	0.30	0.30	0.30	0.30	0.30	0.50
OS62Compatible	0.50	0.75	0.38	0.67	1.00	0.67	0.33	0.33	0.33	0.31	0.31	0.31	0.31	0.31	0.31	0.31	0.31	0.31	0.31	0.30	0.30	0.30	0.30	0.30	0.30
OS32-64Compatible	0.50	0.75	0.38	0.67	0.67	1.00	0.33	0.33	0.33	0.31	0.31	0.31	0.31	0.31	0.31	0.31	0.31	0.31	0.31	0.30	0.30	0.30	0.30	0.30	0.30
Windows	0.50	0.38	0.75	0.33	0.33	0.33	1.00	0.67	0.67	0.63	0.94	0.63	0.63	0.63	0.63	0.63	0.63	0.63	0.63	0.60	0.60	0.60	0.60	0.60	0.60
BSD	0.50	0.38	0.75	0.33	0.33	0.33	0.67	1.00	0.67	0.63	0.94	0.94	0.94	0.94	0.94	0.94	0.94	0.94	0.94	0.90	0.90	0.90	0.90	0.90	0.90
Unix	0.50	0.38	0.75	0.33	0.33	0.33	0.67	0.67	1.00	0.63	0.63	0.94	0.94	0.94	0.94	0.94	0.94	0.94	0.94	0.90	0.90	0.90	0.90	0.90	0.90
MacOS	0.50	0.38	0.75	0.33	0.33	0.33	0.67	0.67	0.67	1.00	0.63	0.63	0.63	0.63	0.63	0.63	0.63	0.63	0.63	0.60	0.60	0.60	0.60	0.60	0.60
Windows NT	0.44	0.31	0.63	0.27	0.27	0.27	0.81	0.54	0.54	0.54	1.00	0.50	0.50	0.50	0.50	0.50	0.50	0.50	0.50	0.48	0.48	0.48	0.48	0.48	0.48
FreeBSD	0.44	0.31	0.63	0.27	0.27	0.27	0.54	0.81	0.54	0.54	0.50	1.00	0.75	0.75	0.50	0.50	0.50	0.50	0.50	0.48	0.48	0.48	0.48	0.48	0.48
OpenBSD	0.44	0.31	0.63	0.27	0.27	0.27	0.54	0.81	0.54	0.54	0.50	0.75	1.00	0.75	0.50	0.50	0.50	0.50	0.50	0.48	0.48	0.48	0.48	0.48	0.48
NetBSD	0.44	0.31	0.63	0.27	0.27	0.27	0.54	0.81	0.54	0.54	0.50	0.75	0.75	1.00	0.50	0.50	0.50	0.50	0.50	0.48	0.48	0.48	0.48	0.48	0.48
AIX	0.44	0.31	0.63	0.27	0.27	0.27	0.54	0.54	0.81	0.54	0.50	0.50	0.50	0.50	1.00	0.75	0.75	0.75	0.75	0.71	0.71	0.71	0.71	0.71	0.71
OSFI	0.44	0.31	0.63	0.27	0.27	0.27	0.54	0.54	0.81	0.54	0.50	0.50	0.50	0.50	0.75	1.00	0.75	0.75	0.75	0.71	0.71	0.71	0.71	0.71	0.71
IRIX	0.44	0.31	0.63	0.27	0.27	0.27	0.54	0.54	0.81	0.54	0.50	0.50	0.50	0.50	0.75	0.75	1.00	0.75	0.75	0.71	0.71	0.71	0.71	0.71	0.71
Solaries	0.44	0.31	0.63	0.27	0.27	0.27	0.54	0.54	0.81	0.54	0.50	0.50	0.50	0.50	0.75	0.75	0.75	1.00	0.75	0.71	0.71	0.71	0.71	0.71	0.71
Linux	0.44	0.31	0.63	0.27	0.27	0.27	0.54	0.54	0.81	0.54	0.50	0.50	0.50	0.50	0.75	0.75	0.75	0.75	1.00	0.71	0.71	0.71	0.71	0.71	0.71
SUSE	0.40	0.28	0.55	0.23	0.23	0.23	0.47	0.47	0.70	0.47	0.43	0.43	0.43	0.43	0.64	0.64	0.64	0.64	0.85	1.00	0.80	0.80	0.80	0.80	0.80
RedHat	0.40	0.28	0.55	0.23	0.23	0.23	0.47	0.47	0.70	0.47	0.43	0.43	0.43	0.43	0.64	0.64	0.64	0.64	0.85	0.80	1.00	0.80	0.80	0.80	0.80
Fedora	0.40	0.28	0.55	0.23	0.23	0.23	0.47	0.47	0.70	0.47	0.43	0.43	0.43	0.43	0.64	0.64	0.64	0.64	0.85	0.80	0.80	1.00	0.80	0.80	0.80
Centos	0.40	0.28	0.55	0.23	0.23	0.23	0.47	0.47	0.70	0.47	0.43	0.43	0.43	0.43	0.64	0.64	0.64	0.64	0.85	0.80	0.80	0.80	1.00	0.80	0.80
Debiian	0.40	0.28	0.55	0.23	0.23	0.23	0.47	0.47	0.70	0.47	0.43	0.43	0.43	0.43	0.64	0.64	0.64	0.64	0.85	0.80	0.80	0.80	0.80	1.00	0.80
Ubuntu	0.40	0.28	0.55	0.23	0.23	0.23	0.47	0.47	0.70	0.47	0.43	0.43	0.43	0.43	0.64	0.64	0.64	0.64	0.85	0.80	0.80	0.80	0.80	0.80	1.00

The computed semantic threshold values for *Operating System* ontology concepts are shown in Table 1.

5   Experimental Setup

To simulate semantic features on a decentralized resource discovery model, we use GridSim and PlanetSim simulators [22], which support discrete event and time based simulations. GridSim provides facilities for the modeling and simulation of resources with different capabilities, configurations and domains [23], whereas PlanetSim facilitates to build a decentralized network and nodes. As semantic API classes are not provided with these simulators, we extended some existing classes and mapped ontology concepts and semantic similarity threshold values in it. In this model, we utilize Chord overlay network [24] and distributed hash service using PlanetSim that presents layered and modular architecture in time efficient manner [22, 25]. With the help of this architecture, resources and users' job requests are routed through to find resources for jobs.

We evaluate the performance of the resource discovery model with semantic and non semantic cases in terms of successful jobs and communication overheads. We ran series of simulations to evaluate and compare the performance of semantic and non-semantic resource discovery models. We use the following parameters for both semantic and non-semantic experiment except semantic threshold values which is only apply for semantic experiment.

> Number of Nodes/Resources = 128
> Jobs query rate =20-200 per/second in steps of 20
> Total Processor Architecture Concepts = 31
> Total Operating System Concepts = 25
> Semantic Threshold= 0.5

The experiment is aimed at enhancing job success probability and reducing communication cost by adding semantic features in a decentralized resource discovery process. We use sub-domain specific ontology for each type of resource separately. In this implementation, we compute semantic similarity threshold values using equation (1).

We observe the successful jobs and number of messages under both semantic and non-semantic decentralized resource discovery models. In our experiment, we utilize resource attributes including *processor* architecture and *operating system* from ontology concepts.

Once a network and nodes are established, providers can publish resources on network and then randomly generated keys are obtained against each resource node. With the help of these generated keys, users are able to find the appropriate resources for their jobs. Each job finds its requirement such as number of CPUs, processor architecture and operating system by comparing with each resource. If the requirements of jobs match with any existing resources, then the jobs are submitted successfully. Otherwise the jobs are rejected. In this way, we measure the relationship between successful jobs and query rates. Since we are not considering semantic matching in the first experiment, users' requests match with resource availability based on exact keywords matching. In the second experiment, we add semantic features and use two sub-domain specific ontologies for *Processor* and *Operating System* resources. We run this experiment under 128 nodes network with various job query rates i.e. 20 to 200 in steps of 20. In order to find appropriate resources for jobs, each job deals with existing resources with semantic data to find a match and then picks those resources. Once this is done, the job is considered submitted. The semantic search mechanism helps to find relevant resources for a job based on semantic similarity threshold 0.5 when exact match is not found. However, the value of semantic threshold can be varied and selected based on users' requirement. By using semantic features job success probability can be enhanced and communication heads can be reduced. We consider time shared allocation policy for selection of grid resources for jobs that use round-robin method to allocate the jobs. The results of both semantic and non-semantic experiments are shown in the next sub-section.

6   Results

This section presents the comparison of results for both semantic and non-semantic cases. Fig.3 shows the relationship between percentage of successful jobs and job query rates for both cases. Based on the same input parameters except semantic threshold values for both semantic and non-semantic cases, the result shows that the percentage of successful jobs is around 20 % higher than non semantic.

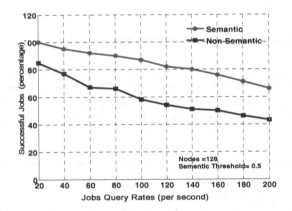

Fig. 3. Successful Jobs vs. Job query rates (per sec)

The reason for this is to the semantic helps in removing tight coupling between users' requirements and available resources. This coupling is stretched to the limit when there is more demand per unit time. In other words, the job success probability increases when we add semantic features in a decentralized resource discovery process of grid computing. It is also observed that the number of resource ontology concepts can have affect on the experimental results.

Fig.4 shows the difference in communication overheads between semantic and non-semantic cases. Under the same criteria, total messages in the semantic case are lower than the non-semantic case. There are two rationales: one is that the semantic matching provides high probability of finding relevant resources which do not need to

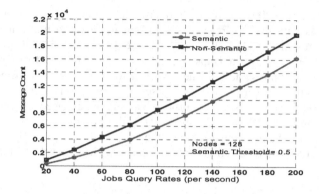

Fig. 4. Message Count vs. Job query rates (per sec)

travel to other nodes in the network. Whenever a job finds semantic relevant resource then, it schedules for a user's request. The second is to that the decentralize Chord protocol that knows only a small amount of routing information about other nodes. With the help of this information, the node helps to find resource quickly and avoids overheads in the system.

7   Conclusion and Future Directions

The paper discusses the benefits of semantic features with sub-domain ontology concepts in a resource discovery process of a Grid computing environment. Two extended ontologies of *Processor* and *Operating system* have been utilized in decentralized resource discovery model. After computing semantic threshold values among all concepts of both ontologies, we have developed and implemented semantic and non semantic resource discovery models. We compared theses models with semantic and non-semantic cases. Our results show that the semantic model outperforms non-semantic resource discovery model in terms of job success probability and communication overheads. As future work, we are planning to consider the possibilities of limitations in semantic features. This could be included to cover the compatibility of resources in our model to avoid job rejection at the time of jobs submission. For instance, some resources are semantically relevant but in terms of function they may not be compatible with users' jobs. Also, in some cases users stipulate some special requirements where exact matching is essential. We also aim to extend Grid Computing resource ontology by including more hyponyms, hypernyms and synonyms to increase possibilities of identifying relevant resources.

References

1. Braines, D., et al.: Semantic Web Techniques to Support Interoperability in Distributed Networked Environments. In: Annual Conference of the International Technology Alliance, ACITA 2008, London, UK (2008)

2. Lacks, D., Kocak, T.: Developing reusable simulation core code for networking: The grid resource discovery example. Journal of Systems and Software 82(1), 89–100 (2009)

3. Caminero, A., et al.: Extending GridSim with an Architecture for Failure Detection. In: 13th International Conference on Parallel and Distributed Systems, ICPADS 2007 (2007)

4. Iamnitchi, A., Foster, I., Nurmi, D.C.: A peer-to-peer approach to resource location in grid environments. International Series in Operations Research and Management Science, pp. 413–430. Springer (2003)

5. Shaikh, A.K., Alhashmi, S.M., Parthiban, R.: A Semantic Decentralized Chord-Based Resource Discovery Model for Grid Computing. In: IEEE 17th International Conference on Parallel and Distributed Systems, ICPADS 2011 (2011)

6. Ranjan, R., Buyya, R.: Decentralized overlay for federation of Enterprise Clouds. In: Handbook of Research on Scalable Computing Technologies, p. 191 (2009)

7. Vidal, A.C.T., et al.: Applying semantics to grid middleware. Concurrency and Computation: Practice and Experience 21(13), 1725–1741 (2009)

8. Frey, J., et al.: Condor-G: A Computation Management Agent for Multi-Institutional Grids. Cluster Computing 5, 237–246 (2002)

9. Schopf, J.M., et al.: Monitoring the Grid with the Globus Toolkit MDS4. Journal of Physics 46, 521–525 (2006)

10. Kretsis, A., Kokkinos, P., Varvarigos, E.: Developing Scheduling Policies in gLite Middleware. In: 9th IEEE/ACM International Symposium on Cluster Computing and the Grid 2009. IEEE Computer Society (2009)

11. Vidal, A.C.T., et al.: Semantics-based grid resource management. In: 5th International Workshop on Middleware for Grid Computing. ACM, Newport Beach (2007)

12. Top500 Super Computer List, http://www.top500.org/ (accessed on December 2011)

13. Juan, L.: Grid resource discovery based on semantically linked virtual organizations. Future Generation Computer Systems 26(3), 361–373 (2010)

14. Kaoudi, Z., et al.: Semantic Grid Resource Discovery in Atlas. In: Knowledge and Data Management in GRIDs, pp. 185–199 (2007)

15. Kaoudi, Z., et al.: Atlas: Storing, updating and querying RDF(S) data on top of DHTs. Web Semantics: Science, Services and Agents on the World Wide Web 8(4), 271–277 (2010)

16. Liangxiu, H., Berry, D.: Semantic-Supported and Agent-Based Decentralized Grid Resource Discovery. Future Generation Computer Systems 24(8), 806–812 (2008)

17. Chen, L., Tao, F.: An Intelligent Recommender System for Web Resource Discovery and Selection. In: Intelligent Decision and Policy Making Support Systems, pp. 113–140 (2008)

18. Ranjan, R., Harwood, A., Buyya, R.: Peer-to-Peer Based Resource Discovery in Global Grids: A Tutorial. IEEE Communications Surveys & Tutorials 10(2) (2008)

19. Stanford Center for Biomedical Informatics Research Group. Ontology Editor & Knowledge base Framework, http://protege.stanford.edu/ (accessed on December 2011)

20. Schwering, A.: Approaches to Semantic Similarity Measurement for Geo-Spatial Data: A Survey. Transactions in GIS 12(1), 5–29 (2008)

21. Andreasen, T., Bulskov, H., Knappe, R.: From ontology over similarity to query evaluation. In: 2nd CologNET-ElsNET Symposium-Questions and Answer: Theoretical and Applied Perspective (2003)

22. García, P., Pairot, C., Mondéjar, R., Pujol, J., Tejedor, H., Rallo, R.: PlanetSim: A New Overlay Network Simulation Framework. In: Gschwind, T., Mascolo, C. (eds.) SEM 2004. LNCS, vol. 3437, pp. 123–136. Springer, Heidelberg (2005)

23. Buyya, R., Murshed, M.: GridSim: a toolkit for the modeling and simulation of distributed resource management and scheduling for Grid computing. Concurrency and Computation: Practice and Experience 14(13-15), 1175–1220 (2002)

24. Stoica, I., et al.: Chord: a scalable peer-to-peer lookup protocol for internet applications. IEEE/ACM Transactions on Networking 11(1), 17–32 (2003)

25. Pujol-Ahulló, J., et al.: An extensible simulation tool for overlay networks and services. In: The 24th ACM Symposium on Applied Computing, New York, USA (2009)

Design of n-Gram Based Dynamic Pre-fetching for DSM

Sitaramaiah Ramisetti[1], Rajeev Wankar[2], and C.R. Rao[2]

[1] CVR College of Engineering Hyderabad India
sitara_r@cvr.ac.in
[2] Department of Computer and Information Sciences University of Hyderabad,
Hyderabad, India
rajeev.wankar@gmail.com, crrcs@uohyd.ernet.in

Abstract. Many earlier reported works have shown that data pre-fetching can be an efficient answer to the well-known memory stalls. If one can reduce these stalls, it leads to performance improvement in terms of overall execution time for a given application. In this paper we propose a new n-gram model for prediction, which is based on dynamic pre-fetcher, in which we compute conditional probabilities of the stride sequences of previous n steps. Here n is an integer which indicates data elements. The strides that are already pre-fetched are preserved so that we can ignore them if the same stride number is referenced by the program due to principle of locality of reference, with the fact that it is available in the memory, hence we need not pre-fetch it. The model also gives the best probable and least probable stride sequences, this information can further be used for dynamic prediction. Experimental results show that the proposed model is far efficient and presents user certain additional input about the behavior of the application. The model flushes once number of miss-predictions exceed pre-determined limit. One can improve the performance of the existing compiler based Software Distributed Shared Memory (SDSM) systems using this model.

Keywords: SDSM, n-gram, pre fetching, Markov Chain.

1   Introduction

Pre-fetching is the process of making the data pre-loaded in to main memory before it is being referenced by the program in execution. For pre-fetching objects/data, we need the prior knowledge of the addresses being referenced. The basic methodologies are hardware pre-fetching and software pre-fetching. For Hardware pre-fetching to take place we require additional hardware at the processor level. Software based pre-fetching is done either by the compiler, wherein the compiler introduces the code that is required for pre-fetching to take place, Jackal DSM [6] is one of the classic examples of DSM that uses it. Another example is loop unrolling where the same addresses are frequently referred hence the compiler will instrument the code required for this; a compiler is able to perform a static analysis of the source code to generate some instruction hints [1]. This form of the optimization is static in nature.

Y. Xiang et al. (Eds.): ICA3PP 2012, Part II, LNCS 7440, pp. 217–224, 2012.

Several approaches ranging from dynamic hardware to static software mechanisms have been studied in the past. A stand alone dynamic software data pre-fetching solution Entirely SOftware and DYnamic data Pre-fetcher (ESODYP) was proposed by Beyler et.al. [2]. ESODYP is based on a memory strides Markov model. It runs in two main phases: a short training phase where a graph coding sequences of occurring memory strides is constructed and an optimizing phase where predicted addresses are pre-fetched. Information in the graph is updated continuously by monitoring accessed strides.

Better runtime optimization (dynamic optimization) is possible only when the application program's behavior is known, or a trace run is performed to identify the addresses that are required for pre-fetching. Hence dynamic analysis and optimizations is an important research area. To obtain dynamic data (address of variables and pointers), we need a model which is able to predict the addresses that are likely to be referenced by the program at run time. This can be achieved by probability estimation of the addresses that are likely to be referenced by the program. We have taken ESODYP as a reference model for both implementation and comparison because the proposed model is based on Markov chain.

Markov chain based model keeps track of the addresses that are pre-fetched. The Markov model stores stride numbers instead of the physical addresses, referencing time will effectively reduced due to the fact that if the referenced stride is in memory we need not pre-fetch it, instead, we can increase reference count of stride (node) to make it more probable for future references. In an operating system analogy the stride typically represents a page of addresses of certain size. Considering memory strides instead of actual addresses can give the predictor a better chance to keep all the information retrievable by the program with the least memory necessary. We propose a new algorithm based on n-gram model for prediction. We also present experimental results for comparison of this model with ESODYP for the set of applications under consideration. In this paper section 2 explains n-Gram model, section 3 presents proposed algorithm, section 4 explains computation of Conditional Probability Transition Matrix (CPTM), section 5 presents results and discussion and finally in section 6 we conclude.

2   n-Gram Model

For any n-gram model the underlying concepts are better explained using words occurrence in a language as an example (usually referred as n-gram language model) [3].

In an n-gram language model, we treat two histories as equivalent if they end in the same n - 1 words, i.e., we assume that for $k \geq n$, $P_r(w_k|w_1^{k-1}) = P_r(w_k|w_{k-n+1}^{k-1})$, Where P_r represents probability of word $w's$ occurrence. For a vocabulary of size V, a 1-gram model has $(V-1)$ independent parameters, one for each word minus one for the constraint that all of the probabilities add up to 1. A 2-gram model has $V(V-1)$ independent parameters of the form $P_r(w_2|w_1)$ and $(V-1)$ of the form $P_r(w)$ for a total of $V^2 - 1$ independent parameters. In general, an n-gram model has $V^n - 1$ independent parameters: $V^{n-1} - 1$ (V - 1) of the form $Pr(w_1|w_1^{n-1})$, which we call the order-n parameters, plus the V^{n-1} parameters of an (n - 1) gram model.

We estimate the parameters of an n-gram model by examining a sample of text t_1^T which we call the training text, in a process called training. If $C(w)$ is the number of times that the string w occurs in the string t_1^T, then for a 1-gram language model the maximum likelihood estimate for the parameter Pr (w) is $C(w)/T$.

To estimate the parameters of an n-gram model, we estimate the parameters of the (n - 1)-gram model that it contains and then choose the order-n parameters so as to maximize $P_r(t_n^T|t_1^{n-1})$. Thus, the order-n parameters are

$$P_r(w_n|w_1^{n-1}) = \frac{C(w_1^{n-1}w_n)}{\sum_w C(w_1^{n-1}w)} \tag{1}$$

In the literature n-gram model is typically applied to the language model, we have given the same for readers to understand concept. Our technique makes use of the stride numbers for pre-fetching in place of words used in the language model.

3   Proposed Algorithm

We observe the following problems with the above representation of the given application using the n-gram model.

1. For some strings where occurrences are sparse in nature that leads to (denominator of equation 1 being zero), we should not perform computations for these nodes.
2. The n in n-gram model is predefined where as in the present language model, n cannot be predefined.

Keeping the above two issues, an algorithm is proposed by considering sparse matrix representation with an incremental n.

```
Algorithm: Dynamic Pre-fetching
Input:   Stride Numbers:
Output: Linked lists of each gram (with stride sequence),
count and pointer to next node
Begin
Repeat
{
pNew = Create i^th  gram node  with i-1 list size per each
node;
Add pNew node to the list;
If pNew->list is already existing in one of the nodes
then
        Update pNew->count
Compute the conditional probability;
Increment i;
}
Until conditional probability of each gram is 1;
end;
```

The input for nodes is sequence of strides numbers that are referenced by the application which are to be eventually pre-fetched for fulfilling the seamless execution of the applications. We have considered the random stride sequence of 1, 2, 16, 2, 32, 2, 16, 2, 32, 4, 9, 25, 36, 9, 4 as a reference stride sequence for building n-gram model. A typical matrix representation of 1-gram model and 2-gram model for the above sequence is given in fig. 1.

1-gram	1	2	4	9	16	25	32	36
1	0	1	0	0	0	0	0	0
2	0	0	0	0	2	0	2	0
4	0	0	0	1	0	0	0	0
9	0	0	1	0	0	1	0	0
16	0	2	0	0	0	0	0	0
25	0	0	0	0	0	0	0	1
32	0	1	1	0	0	0	0	0
36	0	1	1	0	0	0	0	0

2-gram	1	2	4	9	16	25	32	36
1	0	1	0	0	0	0	0	0
2	0	0	0	0	5	0	5	0
4	0	0	0	1	0	0	0	0
9	0	0	5	0	0	5	0	0
16	0	1	0	0	0	0	0	0
25	0	0	0	0	0	0	0	1
32	0	0	0	0	0	0	0	5
36	0	0	0	0	0	0	0	1
	1	2	4	9	16	25	32	36
1,4	0	0	0	0	0	1	0	0
1,9	0	0	0	0	0	0	0	0
1,16	0	0	0	0	0	0	0	0
1,25	0	0	0	0	0	0	0	0
1,32	0	0	0	0	0	0	0	0
1,36	0	0	0	0	0	0	0	0

	1	2	4	9	16	25	32	36
36,1	0	0	0	0	0	0	0	0
36,2	0	0	0	0	0	0	0	0
36,4	0	0	0	0	0	0	0	0
36,9	0	0	2	0	0	0	0	0
36,16	0	0	0	0	0	0	0	0
36,25	0	0	0	0	0	0	0	0
36,32	0	0	0	0	0	0	0	0
36,36	0	0	0	0	0	0	0	0

Fig. 1. 1-gram and 2-gram representation for the above stride sequence

In the given $n \times n$ matrix above referenced stride sequence 1, 2, 16, 2, 32, 2, 16, the item $(1, 2) = 1$ indicate that the sequence 1 followed by 2 occurs only once (count $= 1$) in the above given sequence. Similarly item $(2, 16) = 2$ represents 2, 16 sequence occurs twice in the above stride sequence. Similarly for 2-gram the node $(36, 9, 4) = 2$ indicate that node sequence of 36 followed by 9 as 2-gram followed by 4 is occurring twice in the given sequence. An application program (transportation problem) when executed on a system and its memory contains 32 blocks of 512 bytes (stride size 512), the sequence indicated represents memory address reference that program is accessing is *base address + strideno * stridesize*. First, strides 1 is accessed then stride 2 and then stride 16 so on.

Similar tables can be generated and stored for observing for 3-gram, 4-gram... n-gram. From the above tables we can observe that the tables to be represented in the memory require multi dimensional array representation and thus occupy large memory. Especially when the application program requires large memory or frequent data references then stride sequence will be long and the table sizes for given n-grams increases exponentially.

As part of n-gram implementation, we need to compute conditional probability for each and every entry in the table. This leads to exceptions like divide by zero when denominator for CPTM becomes zero. Hence the node representation which is proposed in our implementation will be ideal choice and will be optimal. Hence the proposed algorithm uses the linked list data structures for implementation for the n-gram.

Observing the sparse nature of the above stride occurrences following node structure is proposed:

Dynamic Stride List	Conditional Probability	PointerToNextNode
A0, A1 ,A2 , ..., An-1 Previous stride List	probability of An being the next stride	link

4   Computation and Importance of Conditional Probability Transition Matrix (CPTM)

For a given gram (1-gram...n-gram) the number of stride references are stored in a linked list. The frequency of occurrences of strides is represented in the form of a $n \times n$ matrix, where n represents stride number, indicating the sequence in which the strides are referred in the application. We use this matrix to compute Conditional Probability Transition Matrix (CPTM) using following procedure:

These lists are traversed for a given gram which is represented as a CPTM of size $n \times n$, where rows and columns represent the stride numbers and references to strides as a count. The element at (1,1) in 1-gram matrix represents stride-1 followed by stride-1 as a sequence, and how many times this stride sequence is referred by the application program.

We compute the sum of references of the strides for that row of strides and the conditional probability is defined as individual reference divided by the sum of the references for that row. We compute conditional probabilities of the different strides and sequences (based on gram number). As the stride is been accessed by the model, the address is mapped to stride number and the presence of the stride number in the list is checked by using a suitable hashing technique. If the stride is present then its corresponding count is incremented. We also estimate conditional probabilities starting from 1-gram continuing to n-grams by computing conditional probabilities and then summing these conditional probabilities to check for termination. The termination condition for n will be the sum of conditional probabilities for that n will be unity. We also can arrive at the optimal gram for the given series of strides, which can be a configurable parameter.

The model after computing the conditional probability will be able to find out best probable stride for a given sequence. The computed stride can be pre-fetched in advance and the list is updated once the stride is pre-fetched. If the stride is not in the list then it is a clear case of miss, now this new stride is pre-fetched. If the stride is present in the lists, then the corresponding list is updated to indicate that the new stride is in the memory.

The model gets updated incrementally when a new stride arrive. We can also make the model configurable for maximum number of misses, once this pre-defined limit reaches the model may be reset, so that the prediction can start a fresh and the memory data structures can be released and training can start a fresh(flushing).

Our method is efficient in the way that whenever the new address is computed the whole process of computing and updating lists and computing probabilities are done in one single and effective manner. The maximum number of strides to be stored in the memory depends on dynamic memory allocated for storing the list, which is again a configurable parameter for a given application.

5   Results and Discussions

We have considered three example programs for our study. We have taken the following examples for comparison of dynamic pre-fetching to evaluate the performance of two models (ESODYP and proposed) in terms of speed up of execution.

1. **Transport problem:** The program computes the efficient and economical mechanism of moving goods from sources to destinations. We integrated this application (the application program passes control to the model as a function call with the address as input, computation of stride number and maintenance of stride data structures and prediction is done by model) with the ESODYP model for monitoring the execution time, recorded the execution time.

   We have inserted the function call in C language [2] to call models (ESODYP and n-gram) to record the stride reference and hence updating of stride reference and probability of reference for prefetching. We have integrated the same transport application with the n-gram model and recorded the execution time. We have instrumented the necessary changes in the application program to pass control to the n-gram model and checked the execution time for this as well. We chose Linux OS, and we included the system calls Gettimeofday(starttime,0x0) to compute the execution time (with both models used for stride prediction).

   We chose 3 sources and 4 destination and cost of transportation and size of the material in tons is given as input. The execution time for the Transport problem with ESODYP is 52 μsecs. (micro-seconds). Similarly the execution time for the Transport Problem with n-gram model is 38 μsecs. Thus over all speedup of about 1.3682 is observed for this problem.

2. **N-Queens Problem:** The N queen's problem is to find how many ways the number of queens can be placed on a chess board. This is also a computational intensive application with large memory access. We have instrumented the necessary code for both ESODYP and n-gram models. We have considered a maximum of 16 queens to be placed on a chess-board. We have incremented the number of queens starting from 1 to 16 and

recorded the execution time with both ESODYP and n-gram models. The results of the study are given   in Table 1 for comparison.

It is observed that the n-gram model is faster. For 3 queens ESODYP takes about 8 μsec, as compared to 2 μsec for n-gram, which is 4 times faster.

Table 1. Comparing ESODYP and proposed n-gram model

No.of Queens	ESODYP (time in μsecs.)	n-gram (time in μsecs.)
13	35793	34791
14	201689	197641
15	1237099	1215419

It can be observed that the execution time for n-gram is approximately same as with the ESODYP because as the linked list size increases and grams increase, the formation time for the linked list and subsequent search time increases for this application (the same can be observed with any DFS based application).

3. **Satisfiability Problem:** The satisfiability problem is to determine if a formula in propositional calculus, which is an expression that can be constructed using literals *and* and/or *or*, is true for some assignment of truth values to the variables. The problem checks for 30 equations to be compared for the satisfiability condition.

The Execution times for satisfiability problem with ESODYP model was 4:45.89 minutes (4 minutes 45.89 seconds) and with n-gram model was 2:21.23 minutes. This shows a speed up of 2.02.

We can infer from the above three reference applications that the n-gram model performs much better when the memory references are more, and significantly better than the ESODYP for applications involving dynamic pre-fetching. The n-gram model gives better performance for applications that are memory intensive and/or computational bound. We have integrated the applications with the model where memory stride references are required. For all the applications which are memory intensive, the performance is much better. This model can be used for applications such as Distributed Shared Memory implementation where the program and data requires frequent pre-fetching for performance improvement.

6   Conclusion

The approach presented in this paper is faster than ESODYP as later uses forest of graphs to search for referenced stride, whereas n-gram model uses optimized linked lists and effective hashing for referencing. We can see from above three reference applications that the n-gram model performs much better than ESODYP when the application require more memory references and involve dynamic pre-fetching. By extending similar analogy we can conclude that for the DSM, n-gram model will perform better than ESODYP, this is because of the fact that any DSM implementation requires large code and frequent memory references for both data and program code.

References

1. Beyls, K., D'Hollander, E.: Compile-time cache hint generation for epic architectures. In: Proceedings of the 2nd workshop on Explicitly Parallel Instruction Computing Architectures and Compiler Techniques (November 2002)
2. Beyler, J.C., Clauss, P.: ESODYP: An entirely software and dynamic data prefetcher based on a Markov model. In: Proceedings of the 12th Workshop on Compilers for Parallel Computers, A Coruna, Spain, pp. 118–132 (January 2006)
3. Brown, P.F., DeSouza, P.V., Mercer, R.L., Della Pietra, V.J., Lai, J.C.: Class-Based n-gram Models of Natural Language. Journal of Computational Linguistic Archive 18(4) (December 1992)
4. Veldema, R., Bhoedjang, R.A.F., Bal, H.E.: JACKAL, A compiler based Implementation of Java for cluster of workstations. In: Proceedings of SIGPLAN's Principles and Practices of Parallel Computing, PPoPP 2001 (2001)
5. Klemm, M., Beyler, J.C., Lampert, R.T., Philippsen, M., Clauss, P.: Esodyp+: Prefetching in the Jackal Software DSM. In: Kermarrec, A.-M., Bougé, L., Priol, T. (eds.) Euro-Par 2007. LNCS, vol. 4641, pp. 563–573. Springer, Heidelberg (2007)

On Construction of Cloud IaaS for VM Live Migration Using KVM and OpenNebula[*]

Chao-Tung Yang[**], Shao-Feng Wang, Kuan-Lung Huang, and Jung-Chun Liu

Department of Computer Science, Tunghai University, Taichung City 40704, Taiwan
{Ctyang,jcliu}@thu.edu.tw,
{vickwang180,peter760504}@gmail.com

Abstract. The goal of this paper is to build a cloud IaaS environment, which integrates KVM and OpenNebula open sources to provide a cloud virtual environment for users. For the user interface part, this work can reduce the complexity of accessing cloud resources for the user. This paper realizes a web interface that is easy for users to understand, access, and operate with it. The experimental results show the performance of KVM virtual machines with analyses of live migration of virtual machines.

Keywords: Cloud computing, Virtualization, IaaS, KVM, OpenNebula.

1 Introduction

Cloud computing is currently a popular topic, but also all the main axis of development in recent years, the main points of infrastructure as a service (IaaS), Platform as a Service (PaaS), Software as a Service (SaaS), cloud computing is not a new technology; it is a new concept [1, 2]. The early stages of the laboratory started in the creation and development of gird computing cluster and other distributed computing technologies and related issues, for the vigorous development in recent years is also very interested in cloud computing [13, 15].

This paper focuses on the cloud computing infrastructure, particularly virtual machines and physical monitoring components [3, 4, 5, 6, 7, 8, 9]. The goal is to build a system which can provide users with access to apply and use the virtual machine, as well as monitor the physical system. The monitored information includes CPU utilization, disk usage, virtual machine space, and memory usage. This system also uses a mechanism for migration: when a problem occurs, the administrator can shift the user's virtual machine to another physical machine operation, and the user will not feel any abnormalities. Meanwhile, this paper has also carried on the system perfor-mance test using the KVM and OpenNebula [10, 11, 12, 14, 22, 23].

---

[*] This study was supported in part by the National Science Council, Taiwan ROC, under grant numbers NSC 100-2218-E-029-001, NSC 101-2221-E-029-014 and NSC 101-2622-E-029-008-CC3.
[**] Corresponding author.

Y. Xiang et al. (Eds.): ICA3PP 2012, Part II, LNCS 7440, pp. 225–234, 2012.

2   Background Review

2.1   Virtualization

Virtualization is simply the logical separation of requests for some services from the physical resources where the service is actually provided. In practical terms, virtualization allows applications, operating systems, or system services in a logically distinct system environment to run independently of a specific physical computer system. Obviously, all of these must run on a certain computer system at any given time, but virtualization provides a level of logical abstraction that liberates applications, system services, and even the operating system that supports them from being tied to a specific piece of hardware. Virtualization, focusing on logical operating environments, makes applications, services, and instances of an operating system portable across different physical computer systems. Virtualization can execute applications under many operating systems, manage IT more efficiently, and allot computing resources with other computers [2].

Virtualization has hardware imitate much hardware through a Virtual Machine Monitor, and each virtual machine functions as a complete individual unit. A virtual machine is composed of memories, CPUs, unique complete hardware equipment, and so on. It can run any operating system as Guest OS without affecting other virtual machines. In general, most virtualization strategies fall into one of two major categories:

Full virtualization also called native virtualization is similar to emulation. As in emulation, unmodified operating systems and applications run within a virtual machine. Full virtualization differs from emulation because operating systems and applications run on the same architecture as the underlying physical machine. This allows a full-virtualization system to run many instructions directly on raw hardware. The hypervisor in this case monitors access to the underlying hardware and gives each guest operating system the illusion of having its own copy. It no longer has to use software to simulate a different basic architecture (Fig. 1).

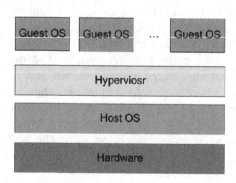

Fig. 1. The architecture of full virtualization

For Para-virtualization, the hypervisor exports a modified version of the underlying physical hardware. The exported virtual machine has the same architecture, which is not necessarily the case in emulation. Instead, targeted modifications make it simpler and faster to support multiple guest operating systems. For example, the guest operating system might be modified to use a special hyper called application binary interface (ABI) instead of using certain architectural features. This means that only small changes are typically necessary in the guest operating systems, but any changes make it difficult to support closed-source operating systems that are only distributed in binary form, such as Microsoft Windows. As in full virtualization, applications are still in run without modifications.

Para-virtualization such as full virtualization uses a hypervisor and virtual machine; the term refers to its virtualized operating systems as well. However, unlike full virtualization, para-virtualization requires changes to the virtualized operating system. This allows the VM to coordinate with the hypervisor and reduces the use of the privileged instructions typically responsible for major performance penalties in full virtualization.

Para-virtualized virtual machines typically outperform fully-virtualized virtual machines. However, it is necessary to modify the para-virtualized virtual machine or operating system to be hypervisor-aware (Fig. 2).

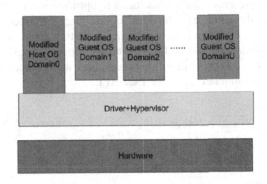

Fig. 2. The architecture of para-virtualization

To evaluate the viability of differences between virtualization and non-virtualization, this paper uses the virtualization software Xen. Xen is a virtual machine monitor (hypervisor) that allows you to use one physical computer to run many virtual computers — for example, a web server application and a test server run on the same physical machine or Linux and Windows run simultaneously. Although a virtualization system is not the only one is available, Xen combines features making it uniquely suited for many important applications. Xen runs on commodity hardware platforms and is open-source as well. Xen is fast and scalable, and provides server-class features such as live migration. Xen provides better efficiency, supports different operating system work simultaneously, and gives each operating system an independent system environment.

2.2   Open Source for Virtualization

KVM is open source software used in the Linux kernel virtualization infrastructure and its full name is: "kernel-based virtual machine". It is supported x86 architecture and hardware for virtualization technology (such as the Intel VT or AMD-V) Linux virtualization solutions. KVM contains a processor which provided the kernel virtualization can be loaded core module kvm.ko (kvm-intel.ko or kvm-amd.ko). It also requires modified QEMU software (qemu-kvm), as the interface of the virtual machine. KVM can operate multiple virtual machines in the same time (ps: It means that multiple virtual machines using the same image) for each virtual machine, configured the hardware environment. In the Linux kernel 2.6.20 above the core contains the the KVM core.

2.3   Virtualization Management

The virtual machine is not only available user interface, but it is the computer with actual loading. Management of virtual machines and management of physical systems are equally important. Virtualization Management includes a set of integrated management tools, can be minimize complexity and simplify the operation. It should centrally manage physical and virtual IT infrastructure, increased server utilization, but also across multiple virtualization platforms to optimize dynamic resources.

OpenNebula is the industry standard open-source product for data center virtualization, offering the most feature-rich, customizable solution to build virtualized enterprise data centers and private cloud infrastructures on Xen, KVM and VMware deployments, and providing cloud consumers with choice of interfaces, from open cloud to de-facto standards, like the EC2 API.

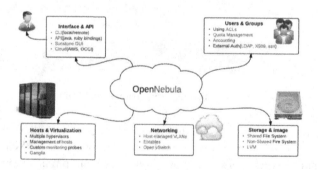

Fig. 3. The architecture of OpenNebula [16]

The OpenStack is the IaaS (Infrastructure as a Service) software so that anyone can create your own cloud computing services. There are three main components [19].

- OpenStack Compute: Provision and manage large networks of virtual machines.
- OpenStack Object Store: Create petabytes of secure, reliable storage using standard hardware.
- OpenStack Glance: Catalog and manage massive libraries of server images.

2.4   Related Work

The most important paper about live migration is [20]. Discussion in this paper is also the implementation of the live migration in Xen. To avoid difficulties of the migration in the process level and residual dependency, instead of the process, the VM with its application regarded as the migration unit. The main goal of live migration is to reduce the time of down time and total migration time. Down time is the he time of shutdown during migration. And total migration time is the VM that can run in the target host without error and source host discarded the old VM. The method of live migration in this paper is "Pre-Copy". It's the same with KVM. Another important paper about live migration is "Post-Copy Live Migration of Virtual Machines" [21]. The method proposed in this paper is "Post-Copy". The purpose of pre-copy method is trying to reduce the down time. But the purpose of post-copy method is trying to reduce the total migration time. Which is good or bad depends on the case. But if we can accept the obvious downtime, we don't need live migration. And it's the reason for most live migration is "Pre-Cpoy" type.

3   System Implementation

3.1   System Overview

In Figure 4 shows the components of the three Cloud Models and point out the emphasis of this paper. This system has the web-based interface to manage virtual machine. And the system shows the CPU utilization, host loading, memory utilization and VMs information etc.

Besides managing individual VMs' life cycles, this study also designs the core to support service deployment. Such services typically include a set of interrelated components (for example, a Web server and database back end) requiring several VMs. Thus, a group of related VMs becomes a first-class entity in OpenNebula. Besides managing the VMs as a unit, the core also handles the context information delivery (such as the Web server's IP address, digital certificates, and software licenses) to the VMs [17].

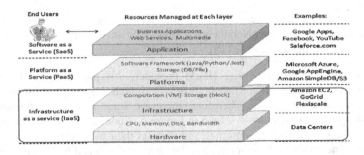

Fig. 4. IaaS

3.2   System Architecture

We use OpenNebula to build the IaaS environment. OpenNebula is a virtual infrastructure engine that enables the dynamic deployment and reallocation of virtual machines in a pool of physical resources. OpenNebula extends the benefits of virtualization platforms from a single physical resource to a pool of resources, decoupling the server, from both the physical infrastructure and the physical location [3]. OpenNebula contains one front end and multiple back ends. OpenNebula orchestrates storage, network, virtualization, monitoring, and security technologies to enable dynamic placement of multi-tier services (groups of interconnected virtual machines) on distributed infrastructures, combining both data center resources and remote cloud resources, according to allocation policies [3](Figure 5).

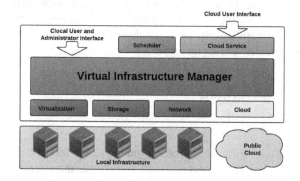

Fig. 5. The Orchestration of OpenNebula [16]

OpenNebula is composed of three main components:

- the OpenNebula Core is a centralized component that manages the life cycle of a VM by performing basic VM operations, and also provides a basic management and monitor interface for the physical hosts
- The Capacity Manager governs the functionality provided by the OpenNebula core. The capacity manager adjusts VM placement based on a set of predefined policies
- Virtualizer Access Drivers. To provide an abstraction for the underlying virtualization layer, OpenNebula uses pluggable drivers that expose the basic functionality of the hypervisor [18].

As an Infrastructure as a Service (IaaS) provider, this paper applies an ideas of virtualizes in the cloud system to economize power, web interface and user friendly to manage the virtual machines. Therefore, there are some distinct on framework of cloud; our system architecture is shown in Figure 6. About user friendly, users simply connect to the site through the Internet, and then set their own needs, you can create a virtual machine, the user does not need to know what happened back may need to set any object, they can be consistent with their own needs of virtual machines. The Screen is shown from Figures 7. And we can make VM to live migrated on line by the web-based interface (Figures 8).

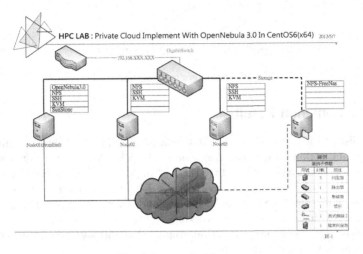

Fig. 6. System Architecture

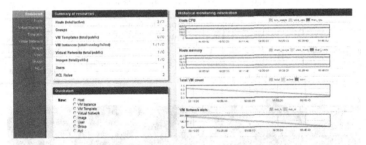

Fig. 7. Initial presentation of OpenNebula

Fig. 8. Live migration of the VM from Node 3 to Node 2

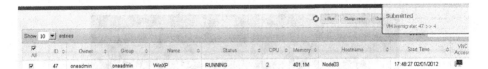

Fig. 9. Submitted

Fig. 10. Live migration was successful

4   Experimental Results

The host list of the test environment is tabulated in Table 1. In the experiment, we tested the ping action during live migration of the VM. At first, the initial status of environment is confirmed (Figure 11). The VM of Node 2 will then be live-migrated to Node 3. We will do the ping action in Node 2 before live migration and keep the ping action until completion of the VM migration (Figure 12). From Figures 13 and 14, we observe that VM continues working during the live migration of VM. The process of ping is successful without interruption but still with some fluctuations of replying time as shown in Figure 15.

Table 1. Environment Specification

Environment Specification						
	CPU	Memory	Disk	Network	OS	Software
Node01	I7-860 2.8GHz	4GB	1TB			OpenNebula Front End Node
Node02	I7-990 3.47GHz	12GB	2TB	1Gb	CentOS6 X64	Open Nebula Node
Node03	I7-3960X 3.3GHz	16GB	6TB			

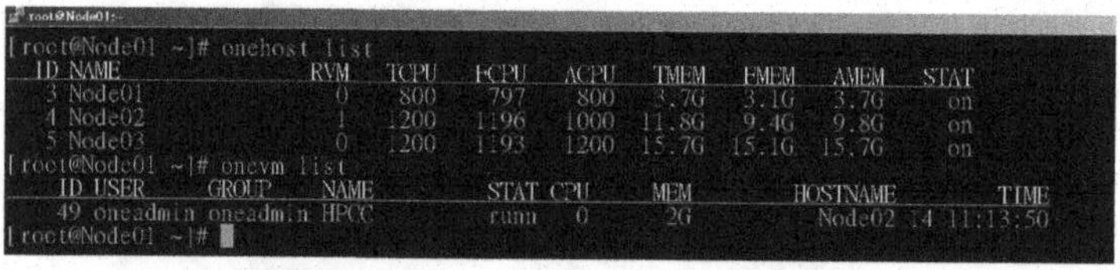

Fig. 11. The initiation of live migration

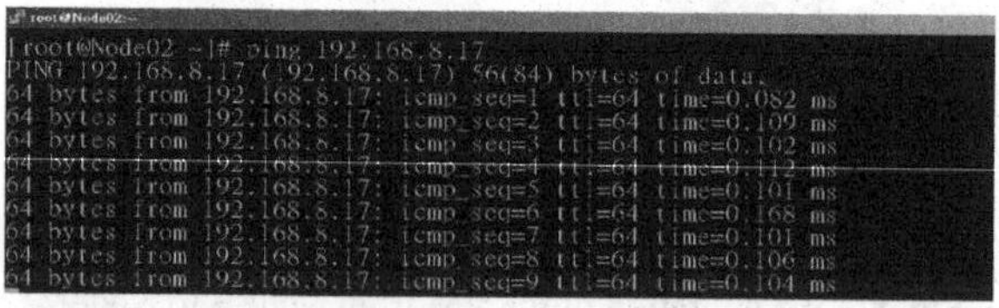

Fig. 12. The ping of live migration

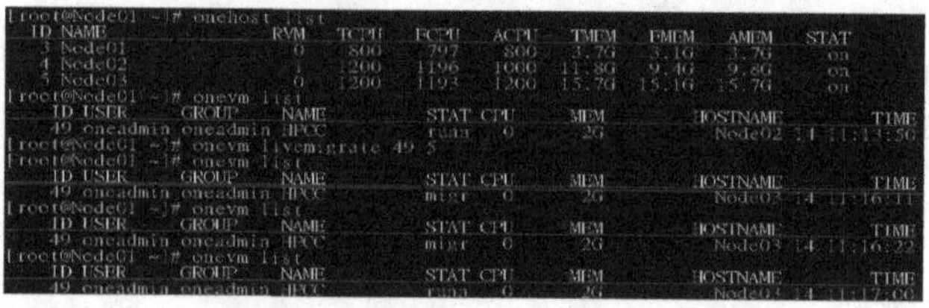

Fig. 13. The end of live migration

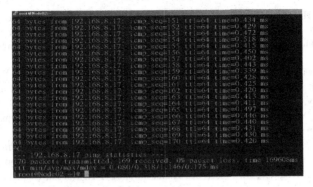

Fig. 14. The ping result after live migration finish

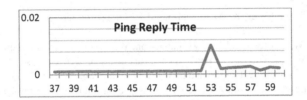

Fig. 15. Collect ping reply time

5   Conclusions

In this paper we implement a cloud with KVM infrastructure and a monitoring web-site, in which users can apply for their use and monitoring of VM states. For a user friendly perspective, from the website main page, it is easy to understand the type to match the user's application and do monitoring with very simple steps. Unlike the previous paper, Xen was adopted as the virtualization technology; here we use KVM as a major virtualization technology. In addition, this paper also tests live migration and implementation efficiency. Although there is still a gap from the best performance, the final results are found very satisfactory.

References

1. Nagarajan, A.B., Mueller, F., Engelmann, C., Scott, S.L.: Proactive fault tolerance for HPC with Xen virtualization. In: Proceedings of the 21st Annual International Conference on Supercomputing, Seattle, Washington, June 17-21, pp. 23–32 (2007)
2. Zhang, B., Wang, X., Lai, R., Yang, L., Wang, Z., Luo, Y., Li, X.: Evaluating and Optimizing I/O Virtualization in Kernel-based Virtual Machine (KVM). In: Ding, C., Shao, Z., Zheng, R. (eds.) NPC 2010. LNCS, vol. 6289, pp. 220–231. Springer, Heidelberg (2010)

3. Tseng, C.-H., Yang, C.-T., Chou, K.-Y., Tsaur, S.-C.: Design and Implementation of a Virtualized Cluster Computing Environment on Xen. Presented at the The second International Conference on High Performance Computing and Applications, HPCA (2009)

4. Oi, H., Nakajima, F.: Performance Analysis of Large Receive Offload in a Xen Virtualized System. In: Proceedings of 2009 International Conference on Computer Engineering and Technology, ICCET 2009, Singapore, vol. 1, pp. 475–480 (January 2009)

5. Milojičić, D., Llorente, I.M., Montero, R.S.: OpenNebula: A Cloud Management Tool. IEEE Internet Computing 15(2), 11–14 (2011)

6. Endo, P.T., Gonçalves, G.E., Kelner, J., Sadok, D.: A Survey on Open-source Cloud Computing Solutions. In: VIII Workshop em Clouds, Grids e Aplicações, pp. 3–16 (2011)

7. Barham, P., Dragovic, B., Fraser, K., Hand, S., Harris, T., Ho, A., Neugebauer, R., Pratt, I., Warfield, A.: Xen and the Art of Virtualization. In: SOSP 2003: Proceedings of the Nineteenth ACM Symposium on Operating Systems Principles, pp. 164–177. ACM Press, New York (2003)

8. Qumranet, White Paper: KVM Kernel-based Virtualization Driver, Qumranet, Tech. Rep. (2006)

9. van Hagen, W.: Professional Xen Virtualization. Wrox Press Ltd., Birmingham (2008)

10. Emeneker, W., Stanzione, D.: HPC Cluster Readiness of Xen and User Mode Linux. In: 2006 IEEE International Conference on Cluster Computing, pp. 1–8 (2006)

11. Zhang, X., Dong, Y.: Optimizing Xen VMM Based on Intel Virtualization Technology. In: 2008 International Conference on Internet Computing in Science and Engineering, ICICSE 2008, pp. 367–374 (2008)

12. Dong, Y., Li, S., Mallick, A., Nakajima, J., Tian, K., Xu, X., Yang, F., Yu, W.: Extending Xen with Intel Virtualization Technology. Journal, ISSN, Core Software Division, Intel Corporation, 1–14 (August 10, 2006)

13. Cloud computing, http://en.wikipedia.org/wiki/Cloud_computing

14. KVM, http://www.linux-kvm.org/page/Main_Page

15. Xen, http://www.xen.org/

16. http://www.opennebula.org

17. Raj, H., Schwan, K.: High Performance and Scalable I/O Virtualization via Self-Virtualized Devices. In: The Proceedings of HPDC 2007, pp. 179–188 (2007)

18. Waldspurger, C.A.: Memory Resource Management in VMware ESX Server. SIGOPS Oper. Rev. 36(SI), 181–194 (2002)

19. http://openstack.org/

20. Clark, C., Fraser, K., Hand, S., Hanseny, J.G., July, E., Limpach, C., Pratt, I., Warfield, A. (eds.): Live Migration of Virtual Machines. University of Cambridge Computer Laboratory y Department of Computer Science 15 JJ Thomson Avenue. UK University of Copenhagen, Denmark (2005)

21. Hines, M.R., Deshpande, U., Gopalan, K.: Post-Copy Live Migration of Virtual Machines, Computer Science, Binghamton University (SUNY)

Performance Evaluation of OpenMP
and CUDA on Multicore Systems[*]

Chao-Tung Yang[1,**], Tzu-Chieh Chang[1], Kuan-Lung Huang[1],
Jung-Chun Liu[1], and Chih-Hung Chang[2]

[1] Department of Computer Science, Tunghai University, Taichung City 40704, Taiwan
ctyang@thu.edu.tw, {s942826,peter760504}@gmail.com
[2] Department of Information Management, Hsiuping University of Science Technology,
Taichung City 41280, Taiwan
chchang@hust.edu.tw

Abstract. Nowadays, not only CPU but also GPU goes along the trend of
multi-core processors. Parallel processing presents not only an opportunity but
also a challenge at the same time. To explicitly parallelize the software by
programmers or compilers is the key for enhancing the performance on
multi-core chip. In this paper, we first introduce some of the automatic parallel
tools based OpenMP, which could save the time to rewrite codes for parallel
processing on multicore system. Then we focus on ROSE and explore it in
depth. And we also implement an interface to reduce its complexity of use and
use some automatic parallelization for CUDA.

Keywords: Auto-Parallel, Parallel Programming, Multicore, OpenMP, CUDA.

1 Introduction

In this paper, we introduce some of the automatic parallel tools for parallel processing
on multicore system. These tools can automatically transform sequential C/C++ codes
to parallel C/C++ codes or to generate parallel programs by using OpenMP directives
or CUDA. Then we focus on ROSE to explore in depth. And we implement an
interface to simplify the complexity of use. And we must to have an experiment on
these tools, to let us know the available of these tools. And when we use them to
enhance the performance, how much benefit we can get actually. Then, we used these
tools to do parallel programming on some benchmarks, and compared the
performance.

We propose a solution not only to simplify the use of hardware acceleration in
conventional general purpose applications, but also to keep the application code portable.
We propose a parallel programming approach using hybrid CUDA, OpenMP and MPI

---

[*] This study was supported in part by the National Science Council, Taiwan ROC, under grant
numbers NSC 100-2218-E-029-001, NSC 101-2221-E-029-014 and NSC 101-2622-E-029-
008-CC3.

[**] Corresponding author.

Y. Xiang et al. (Eds.): ICA3PP 2012, Part II, LNCS 7440, pp. 235–244, 2012.
© Springer-Verlag Berlin Heidelberg 2012

[6] programming, which partitions loop iterations according to the performance weighting of multi-core [4] nodes in a cluster. Because iterations assigned to one MPI process are processed in parallel by OpenMP threads run by the processor cores in the same computational node, the number of loop iterations allocated to one computational node at each scheduling step depends on the number of processor cores in that node.

2   Background

2.1   CUDA

CUDA (Compute Unified Device Architecture) is architecture of parallel computing developed by NVIDIA. The architecture is consisting of three parts, library, runtime, and CUDA driver. Developers can access the virtual instruction set and memory of the parallel computational units which are in CUDA GPUs by using CUDA programming. Through the technology of CUDA, users can calculate by using the GPUs from the GeForce 8 series onwards, including Quadro and the Tesla. CUDA architecture is compatible with OpenCL. Neither in CUDA C-language or in OpenCL, the instructions will be transform into the codes of PTX by the driver, and then calculate by the graphics core. CUDA's parallel programming model maintains a low learning curve for programmers familiar with standard programming languages such as C. And current release is CUDA Toolkit 4.0 that supports various operating systems, including Microsoft Windows, Linux, and Mac OS X.

2.2   OpenCL

OpenCL [12] is a framework of programming on heterogeneous platforms which may consist of CPUs, GPUs, and other processors. OpenCL is developed by Apple Inc. and Khronos Group. OpenCL is consisting of a language and APIs. The language based on C99 is used to write kernels; and the APIs are used to define and control the platforms. OpenCL uses task-based and data-based parallelism to parallel computing. AMD/ATI and Nvidia have adopted OpenCL into graphics card drivers.

2.3   OpenMP

Open Multi-Processing (OpenMP) [14] is an application programming interface (API), a kind of shared memory architecture API which provides a multithreaded capacity. OpenMP supports multi-platform shared memory multiprocessing programming in C, C++ and FORTRAN on much architecture which including UNIX and Microsoft Windows platforms. It consists of a set of compiler directives, library routines, and environment variables that influence run-time behavior. We can parallel a loop easily by invoking subroutine calls from OpenMP thread libraries and inserting the OpenMP compiler directives. In this way, the threads can obtain new tasks, the un-processed loop iterations, directly from local shared memory.

3   Auto-parallel Tools

About the issue of auto-parallel, there are some tools which could accord to our source code to generate the binary file or parallel code automatically.

ROSE is a source-to-source compiler infrastructure of open source which builds source-to-source program transformation and analysis tools for large-scale Fortran, C/C++, and OpenMP applications. There are many functions in ROSE such as static analysis, program optimization, arbitrary program transformation, domain-specific optimizations, complex loop optimizations, performance analysis, and cyber-security.

4   Experimental Results

4.1   CPU (OpenMP Version)

At the first of the experiment, we tried to combine the source-to-source compiler and the source-to-binary compiler. First, generate the OpenMP code through the source-to-source compiler, and then compile the code by using the source-to-binary compiler. In the experiment, we recorded the parameters what we used with each kind of compiler, and also verified that whether the parallelism program execute with multicore. In Figure 1 to Figure 3, "-apo" is the parameter of Open64 compiler which could do auto-parallel to the sequential code. "-mp" is the parameter of Open64 compiler and PGI compiler which could support OpenMP code. "-fast" is the parameter of PGI compiler which could optimize the sequential code. "-parallel" is the parameter of Intel compiler which could do auto-parallel to the sequential code.

"-openmp" is the parameter of Intel compiler which could support OpenMP code. "-Mconcur" is the parameter of PGI compiler which could do auto-parallel to the sequential code. The environment of the system is CPU: Intel(R) Xeon(R) CPU E5520 @ 2.27GHz (8 cores). RAM: 8GB.

In Figure 1, Intel compiler gets the best performance on optimized version even better than some parallel programs. In parallel version, Intel compiler with OpenMP code of ROSE also gets the best performance.

In Figure 1 and Figure 3, it is clearly to show the difference of performance on each kind of compiler. In Figure 5-6, the compilers of GNU, PGI, and Open64 have similar performance, only the compiler of Intel improve the performance obviously form the same code.

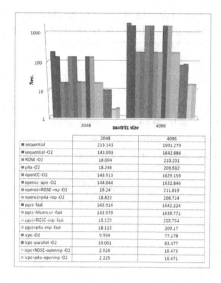

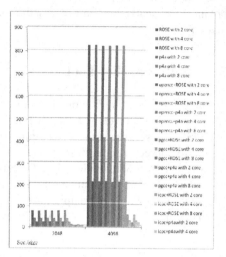

Fig. 1. Matrix Multiplication runs on the CPU with 8 cores

Fig. 2. Matrix Multiplication runs with 2cores to 8 cores

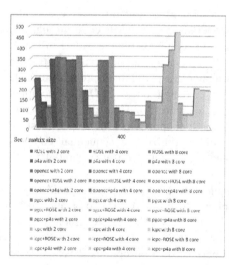

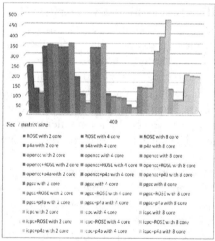

Fig. 3. Solve problem by Jacobi method on the CPU with 8 cores

Fig. 4. Jacobi program runs with 2 cores to 8 cores

4.2   GPU (CUDA Version)

Second, we measure the performance on the GPU, and the experimental environment is CPU: Intel(R) Xeon(R) CPU E5410 @ 2.33GHz (8 cores). RAM: 4GB. GPU: Tesla C1060.

The compilers mentioned earlier, not everyone is support automatically translate to CUDA. PAR4ALL and PGI are the tools that we used in the current environment, and then using these tools to generate CUDA application runs on GPU and comparing with C application runs on CPU. The benchmarks of this part are the same with the benchmarks of 6.1, but the method of parallelize is different.

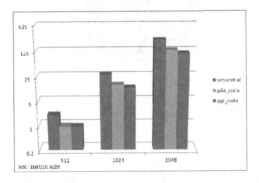

Fig. 5. Matrix Multiplication runs on GPU

Finally, we measure the performance on Arm11MP Core, and the experimental environment as follow: CPU: ARMv6-compatible processors rev 0 (v6l), bogoMIPS: 83.76, 83.55, 83.35, and 83.35, RAM: 128M.

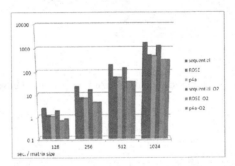

Fig. 6. Matrix Multiplication runs on embedded system

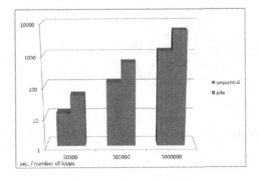

Fig. 7. Nbody runs on embedded system

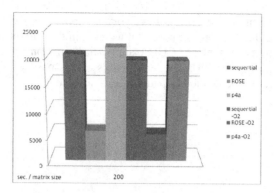

Fig. 8. Solve problem by jacobi method on embedded system

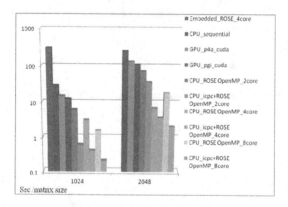

Fig. 9. Matrix Multiplication executes on three kinds of environment

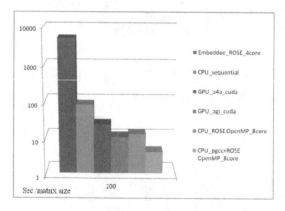

Fig. 10. Jacobi program executes on three kinds of environment

Only ROSE and PAR4ALL are the compilers of source-to-source, so we measured the performance on the platform of Arm11MP core for these tools. In Figure 6 and Figure 7, the performance results are similar as the performance results in 4.1. In Figure 8, PAR4ALL didn't give us a better performance, even worse than sequential. From all of the experiment in 4, we think the tool of PAR4ALL is unstable because it has more problems than others.

Finally, we compared the performance in the three kinds of environment. From Figure 9 and Figure 10, the best performance is the OpenMP code of ROSE compiled by Intel compiler. We think that perhaps automatic parallel technology of CUDA is not mature, so we get the results. In theory, the performance of CUDA should better than OpenMP.

4.3   Part of Hybrid Parallel Programming

We built a hybrid CUDA GPU cluster consisting of one Tesla C1060 and a Tesla S1070, each with Gigabit Ethernet NIC interconnected via a D-LINK DGS-3100-24 Gigabit switch. To verify our approach, illustrate our cluster environment, and describe the terminology for our application, we implemented programs with MPI/OpenMP for execution on our testbed. We then verify the performance of our scheme upon the hybrid CUDA GPU cluster to solve problems in Matrix Multiplication, MD5 and Merge Sorting. From Figure 9 to Figure 11 we take log of 10 at execution time to emphasize the differences.

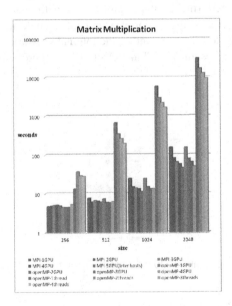

Fig. 11. Matrix multiplication with problem sizes from 256 to 2048

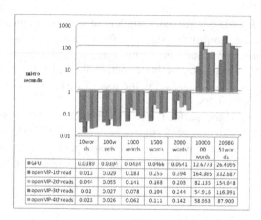

Fig. 12. MD5 hashing on 10 to 2,098,651 words

Figure 9 shows that the performance of GPU on processing the massively parallel execution as the application of Matrix Multiplication form 256 to 2048. In this case, the execution results on MPI and OpenMP upon GPU are close. Comparing to the performance between GPU and CPU with this instance, the performance of GPU obviously exceeds CPU. With the small problem size such as 256 by 256 Matrix Multiplication; the speedup of performance is negligible. The degree of speedup accumulates with the increasing of the problem size. Also, Figure 10 reveals that single GPU presents better performance than single CPU with multiple threads on MD5 hashing computation. Again, the performance of GPU could not be observed in the small problem size due to the constraint on the internal overhead of starting execution. Figure 11 shows that the results of MPI and OpenMP are approximate to each other.

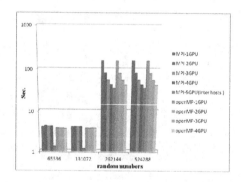

Fig. 13. Sorting numbers 640 times from 65,536 to 524288 floating point

5   Conclusions

We have studied several automatic parallel tools which can translate sequential codes into parallel codes to save the time for rewriting codes for parallel processing on multicore systems. We have verified the availability of these tools, and we have also implemented an interface for ROSE to simplify the complexity of use. From our experiments, we know that these auto-parallel tools almost could help us effortlessly transform non-parallel codes to parallel codes running on multicore systems. From experimental results, we make a table to show what tool is best in each environment in Table 1. The perfect auto-parallelizing compiler is yet to be produced; however, there are some cases where auto-parallelization is perfectly suited.

Table 1. The best tool in each environment

program environment	matrix	Nbody	jacobi
CPU	Intel+ROSE	X	PGI+ROSE
GPU	PGI	PGI	PGI
embedded system	ROSE	X	ROSE

And we propose a parallel programming approach using hybrid CUDA and MPI programming, which partition loop iterations according to the number of C1060 GPU nodes in a GPU cluster which consists of one C1060 and one S1070. During the experiment, loop iterations assigned to one MPI process and processed in parallel by CUDA run by the processor cores in the same computational node. The experiment reveals that the hybrid parallel multicore GPU currently processing with OpenMP and MPI as a powerful approach of composing high performance clusters.

References

1. Yang, C.T., Huang, C.L., Lin, C.F.: Hybrid CUDA, OpenMP, and MPI Parallel Programming on Multicore GPU Clusters. Computer Physics Communications 182(1), 266–269 (2010)
2. Yang, C.T., Huang, C.L., Lin, C.F., Chang, T.C.: Hybrid Parallel Programming on GPU Clusters. In: International Symposium on Parallel and Distributed Processing with Applications, ISPA 2010, pp. 142–147 (September 2010)
3. Goddeke, D., Strzodka, R., Mohd-Yusof, J., McCormick, P., Buijssen, S., Grajewski, M., Tureka, S.: Exploring weak scalability for FEM calculations on a GPU-enhanced cluster. Parallel Computing 33(10-11), 685–699 (2007)
4. Bodin, F., Bihan, S.: Heterogeneous multicore parallel programming for graphics processing units. Scientific Programming 17, 325–336 (2009)
5. Dolbeau, R., Bihan, S., Bodin, F.: HMPP: A hybrid multi-core parallel programming environment. In: The Proceedings of the Workshop on General Purpose Processing on Graphics Processing Units, GPGPU 2007, Boston, Massachussets, USA, October 4 (2007)
6. Alonso, P., Cortina, R., Martinez-Zaldivar, F.J., Ranilla, J.: Neville elimination on multi- and many-core systems: OpenMP, MPI and CUDA. J. Supercomputing, doi:10.1007/s11227-009-0360-z (SpringerLink Online Date: November 18, 2009) (in press)
7. Che, S., Boyer, M., Meng, J., Tarjan, D., Sheaffer, J.W., Skadron, K.: A performance study of general-purpose applications on graphics processors using CUDA. Journal of Parallel and Distributed Computing 68(10), 1370–1380 (2008)

8. Liao, C., Quinlan, D.J., Panas, T., de Supinski, B.R.: A ROSE-Based OpenMP 3.0 Research Compiler Supporting Multiple Runtime Libraries. In: Sato, M., Hanawa, T., Müller, M.S., Chapman, B.M., de Supinski, B.R. (eds.) IWOMP 2010. LNCS, vol. 6132, pp. 15–28. Springer, Heidelberg (2010)
9. Liao, C., Quinlan, D.J., Willcock, J.J., Panas, T.: Semantic-Aware Automatic Parallelization of Modern Applications Using High-Level Abstractions. International Journal of Parallel Programming 38(5-6), 361–378 (2010)
10. Carribault, P., Pérache, M., Jourdren, H.: Enabling Low-Overhead Hybrid MPI/OpenMP Parallelism with MPC. In: Sato, M., Hanawa, T., Müller, M.S., Chapman, B.M., de Supinski, B.R. (eds.) IWOMP 2010. LNCS, vol. 6132, pp. 1–14. Springer, Heidelberg (2010)
11. Close To Metal wiki, http://en.wikipedia.org/wiki/Close_to_Metal
12. CUDA, http://en.wikipedia.org/wiki/CUDA
13. MPI, http://www.mcs.anl.gov/research/projects/mpi/
14. Open MP Specification, http://openmp.org/wp/about-openmp/
15. POSIX Threads Programming, https://computing.llnl.gov/tutorials/pthreads/
16. Intel® Threading Building Blocks, http://www.threadingbuildingblocks.org/
17. Intel, http://software.intel.com/en-us/articles/intel-parallel-studio-xe/
18. The Potland Group, http://www.pgroup.com/index.htm
19. PAR4ALL, http://www.par4all.org/
20. MPICH, A Portable Implementation of MPI, http://www.mcs.anl.gov/research/projects/mpi/mpich1/index.htm
21. The CUDA Compiler Driver NVCC, http://moss.csc.ncsu.edu/~mueller/cluster/nvidia/2.0/nvcc_2.0.pdf
22. Specification Tesla S1070 GPU Computing System, http://www.nvidia.com/docs/IO/43395/SP-04154-001_v02.pdf
23. Arm11MP Core, http://www.arm.com/products/processors/classic/arm11/arm11-mpcore.php
24. NVIDIA CUDA Programming Guide, http://developer.download.nvidia.com/compute/cuda/2_3/toolkit/docs/NVIDIA_CUDA_Programming_Guide_2.3.pdf

Complexity of the Resource Allocation/Matching Problem with Weight Based Ceilings

Charles Karemera and John Ngubiri*

Makerere University,
College of Computing and Information Sciences,
Department of Computer Science
karemecha@yahoo.fr, ngubiri@cit.mak.ac.ug

Abstract. Assigning elements of one set to elements of another set is a common occurrence. This has to be done so that certain objectives are met. In some situations, matching between two different sets is done according to preferences of either one set or both. At the same time, in many cases, a ceiling beyond which the allocations can no longer be made exist. Oftentimes, such a ceiling is made on numbers not on weights (for homogeneous tasks/actors, numbers and weights are synonymous). In this paper, we consider allocations where the tasks and actors are not necessarily homogeneous and the allocation ceilings are based on weights rather than numbers. We develop the algorithm using the Gale and Shapely algorithm for the stable marriage problem as the novel set up. We show that the problem can be solved in polynomial time with worst case being quadratic and best case being linear. We also make sensitivity studies on selected parameters.

Keywords: Dynamic Resource Allocation, Matching, Stable Marriage.

1 Introduction

Task allocation can be looked at as a variant of a general two sided matching problem. The basic idea of such a game is that there are two sets of actor - task entities which are to be matched. Gale and Shapley [6] formulated a typical matching problem in terms of a stable marriage. A man (boy) is matched to a woman (girl) such that the two get the best satisfaction possible given the available choices and the preference lists. Such a matching goes beyond looking for an acceptable pairing. A stable marriage is in such a way that alternative options will lead to more dissatisfaction within the couple. This problem formulation can be extended to solve many allocation problems in real life. Indeed, many researchers [1][4][7][9][10] have made studies that applied many variants of the original Gale and Shapley [6] approach.

---

* Corresponding author.

Y. Xiang et al. (Eds.): ICA3PP 2012, Part II, LNCS 7440, pp. 245–254, 2012.

Solutions to the task allocation problem can be grouped in two main categories: Centralized and Decentralized approaches. Centralized approach relies on a well-informed central decision point to produce task allocation and is widely used in industrial engineering like scheduling parallel machines in a factory [5]. Shen [13] noted that heuristic algorithms are the majority applied to solve task allocation problem in centralized approach. In decentralized approaches, decisions are made by multiple decision makers, based on the local knowledge and interactions. Decision makers happen to be system members. In either approach, many constraints must be respected [10].

In this paper, we study the complexity of the resource allocation/matching problem where the ceilings are based on weight rather than numbers. We do this by improving the original Gale and Shapley [6] algorithm and cater for the dynamic resource allocation problem. We show that the overall complexity of the problem is quadratic with linear best case performance. The rest of the paper is organized as follows. In Section 2, we discuss and formulate the dynamic resource allocation problem. In Section 3, we formulate improve the original Gale and Shapely [6] stable marriage matching algorithm to cater for the dynamic resource allocation problem. We then study the complexity of the improved algorithm in Section 4 and make discussions and recommend future research in Section 5.

2   The Dynamic Resource Allocation (DRA) Problem

Most work (like [2][4][8]) on resource allocation considers homogeneous tasks and actors. Actors and tasks are matched up to when the ceiling is met. These ceilings are mostly in terms of numbers. Many real life problems are made up of heterogeneous tasks and actors with varying capacities. In the heterogeneous tasks, each task require different amount of resources from the actors. The concept of the actor being to a certain level of utilization is therefore looked at in terms of the total resources required from it rather than the number of tasks its handling. Algorithms solving homogeneous tasks instances can be applied to the heterogeneous task allocation set up with minor corrections. However, their complexity and performance sensitivity to the heterogeneity parameters are unknown.

2.1   Mathematical Formulation of DRA

We can formalize the dynamic resource allocation problem as follow: A problem consists of a set of m actors A=$\{a_1, a_2, ..., a_m\}$, and a set of n tasks T=$\{t_1, t_2, ..., t_n\}$, tasks are in disjoint classes $\{TC_1, TC_2, ..., TC_\tau\}$.

Given

- The size vector $z = z_1, z_2, ..., z_n$ where z_i = resources required by t_i
- The capacity matrix C:=$(c_{i,j})_{m \times n}$ where $(c)_{i,j}$= capacity of a_i to perform t_j
- The ceiling matrix $\hat{C} = (\hat{c}_{i,j})_{m \times \tau}$ where $\hat{c}_{i,j}$ = maximum total resource a_i can devote to TC_j tasks.

Find

An allocation matrix A=$(a_{i,j})_{m\times n}$ ($a_{i,j}$ is 1(0) if a_i is (not) allocated to t_j) satisfying the following constraints:

1. The task atomicity condition:
    $|\underline{a}_j| = 1 \; \forall j = 1, 2, ..., n$ where $\underline{a}_j$ is the vector obtained by extracting the jth column from A
2. The task satisfeability condition:
    $l_{i,j} \geq z_j \; \forall \; l_{i,j} \neq 0$ where L:= $(l_{i,j})_{m\times n}$ such that $l_{i,j} = c_{i,j} \times a_{i,j}$
3. Task class ceiling condition
    $t_{i,k} \leq \hat{c}_{i,k}$ where T:=$(t_{i,k})_{m\times \tau}$ such that $t_{i,k} = \sum_{j=1}^{j=n} l_{i,j}^{k}$ and $L^k := (l_{i,j}^{k})_{m\times n}$
    such that $l_{i,j}^{k} = l_{i,j}$ is 1(0) if $t_j \in (\notin)TC_k$

3   DRA and SMP

We now discuss the stable marriage problem as a novel starting point to the dynamic resource allocation problem.

3.1   The Stable Marriage Problem

The Stable Marriage Problem (SMP) seeks to find a good/stable matching between men and women given the preference lists of each. In the preference lists, each person expresses his/her preference over members of the opposite sex. The result (pairings) must be stable, which means that there is no man-woman pair with an incentive to elope. Note that, the algorithm used to solve SMP has the running time O (n^2). Informally, it can be expressed as a sequence of steps with the men proposing to the women (and possibly vice versa).

Generally, Stable Marriage instance consists of two finite equal-sized sets of men and women. Each man $m_i (1 \leq i \leq n)$ranks women in strict order forming his preference list. In the same way, each woman $w_j (1 \leq j \leq n)$ ranks men in strict order forming her preference list. Everybody, ideally, wants to get married to someone at the top of his or her list, but mutual attraction is not symmetric and frustration and compromises are unavoidable.

The SMP can have different instances such as Incomplete Preference Lists, Preference Lists with Ties, Incomplete Preference Lists with Ties, etc. By using Hospital Residents Algorithm, we make changes so that it so as to solve the problem of allocating tasks dynamically with the incomplete preference choices.

3.2   Hospitals Residents Set Up

The HR is a well-known extension of the classical SMP [6]. It is a many to one (polygamous) extension of SMP. It considers the preferences of residents and preferences of hospitals. But in this case, the preference lists of residents may be incomplete.

As definition of blocking pairs, we may apply that of SM instance by regarding a hospital as single if the number of assigned residents is less that its quota of residents. Alternatively, we can reduce the HR into SM by replacing each hospital with a quota q by its q copies. Any stable matching assigns the same number of residents to all hospitals. Furthermore, if a hospital obtains residents fewer than its quota in one stable matching, then the hospital gets the same set of residents in any stable matching.

3.3   Hospitals Residents Algorithm

Algorithm 1. Hospitals Residents Algorithm

Require: Initialize M:= $\emptyset$;
  while $\exists$ resident r_i unassigned with a non-empty list **do**
    h_j := first hospital on r_i' s list
    r_i applies to h_j
  end while
  M := M $\cup(r_i$, h_j)
  if h_j is over-subscribed) **then**
    r_k := worst resident in $M(h_j)$ w.r.t h_j's list
    M := M $\setminus (r_k$, h_j)
  end if
  if (h_j is full) **then**
    r_k := worst resident in M (h_j) according to h_j's list;
    for (each successor r_l of r_k on h_j's list) **do**
      delete the pair (r_l, h_j)
    end for
  end if

It has been shown that, the worst case complexity of HR is O $(n \times m')$ which is linear time using extended Gale and Shapley algorithm.

3.4   The Improved HR Algorithm for DRA

In order to address DRA, the following changes on HR has been made:

1. In MHRA set up, actors are considered as Residents and Tasks are looked at as Hospitals.
2. In Hospitals Residents Problem, matching is based on preferences lists of two sides. Whereas in MHRA, an assignment is based only on one side (actors)
3. It is known that in Hospitals Residents problem, the assignment is based on preferences. But, in MHRA, the assignment is based mostly on ceiling-weight of actors.
4. In Hospitals Residents set up again, a resident r_i is supposed to work in one hospital h_j and each hospital h_h is allowed to be assigned 0 up to C_i residents depending on its (hospital) capacity C_i. In MHRA this is different,

because every actors a_i is allowed to work on different tasks depending on his/her capacity. Also, in MHRA every task is atomic.

5. Finally , in Hospitals Residents Problems blocking pairs are allowed but in MHRA are not.

3.5   Assumptions

We modify the one-to-many version of SMP/Algorithm to address DRA and the modified algorithm will try to allocate tasks by considering the following assumptions:

1. The tasks- preference according to the capacity of actor i.e. a range of tasks he/she is confident to handle by order of priorities or not;
2. One task must be done by only one actor ;
3. The ceiling of every actor ;
4. The algorithm should allocate less or equal weight capacity to the actors, but it should not go beyond his/her ceiling limitation ;
5. It will loop until all tasks are being allocated even if some actors are not given any tasks

If there are some tasks which are not assigned or do not have qualified actors to tackle them, they will remain unallocated. We emphasize that, this algorithm is biased because it is actor optimal. But, on the other hand it is good because it guarantees the system top manager that the actors is capable to do what he/she is qualified for.

3.6   Capacity Matrix

Here, the task allocator will fill the Capacity matrix C according to the following rules:

1. Consider the order in how the actors have come to submit their preferences;
2. Rearrange actors as follows:
    – According to their quotas, meaning that the actor who has the highest quota will be actor a_1, and so on.
    – In case some actors have the same quotas, he will follow how they have come, (he will check again manner 1. above)

The above Capacity Matrix C shows the list of all actors and quota q_a which indicates the number of tasks an actor a can work handle according to his/her capacity. We remind the readers that, as every actor has his/her own capacity represented in terms of quota q, it is clear that the table above has gaps as all actors have different capacities.

In order to have a full table, we introduce the ghost tasks after checking the highest quota and the lowest one. Then, we fill all gaps by ghost tasks noted as zeros until we get the full table. These ghost tasks will not affect the capacity of actors because of their zeros weight.

Table 1. Actors, their required tasks and their quotas

A_i	Tasks						
a_1	$t_{1,1}$	$t_{1,2}$	$t_{1,3}$	. $t_{1,i}$	. $t_{1,n}$	: q_{a_1}
a_2	$t_{2,1}$	$t_{2,2}$	$t_{2,3}$	. $t_{2,i}$	. $t_{2,n}$	: q_{a_2}
a_3	$t_{3,1}$	$t_{3,2}$	$t_{3,3}$	. $t_{3,i}$	. $t_{3,n}$	: q_{a_3}
.	.	.	.	. .	. .	.
.	.	.	.	. .	. .	.
.	.	.	.	. .	. .	.
a_m	$t_{m,1}$	$t_{m,2}$	$t_{m,3}$	. $t_{m,i}$	. $t_{m,n}$	: q_{a_m}

4   Complexity

For the Complexity, we look at and analyze two different cases. In the first case, tasks have different priorities and in the second case, the tasks have the same priorities.

4.1   Case One: Tasks Have the Same Priorities

In this version, when tasks have been submitted in other of preferences the MHRA will allocate them with respect to their ranks, meaning that after giving all actors their first rank it will continue to their second task and so on. MHR Algorithm will work as follow:

Before it starts, it is imperative to look at some instruction so that it will produce an optimum result. First of all the task-allocator will distributes tasks in the following manner

When tasks have preferences, it means before MHRA goes to actor a, it has to first satisfy actor $a-1$. That's why at phase φ_1,the actor a_1 is given his/her first choice automatically. But actor a_2 can get his first or second choice. Actor a_3 can get his/her first or second even third choice and so on.

In phase φ_1 as every task to be allocated, has to be compared with only allocated tasks there are $0+1+2+...+m-1$ steps of comparisons which is $O(m^2)$ running time algorithm.

At second phase as always comparison is done on allocated tasks, the last task $t_{m,2}$ will make $(m-1)$ steps of phase φ_1 and $(m-1)$ of phase φ_2.The same process until phase φ_π where the number of steps will be $\pi(m-1)$. So the total running time of our MHRA is total steps done from phase φ_1 up to phase φ_π which is $O(m^2)$.

4.2   Case Two: Tasks Have Different Priorities

Sometimes, tasks may have different priorities; the MHRA will first allocate the first ranked tasks to the actors. By doing this, if MHRA finds similar tasks, it will assign zero to the current actor because that task has been already assigned before. In second phase(i.e. allocating $t_{1,2}$ to a_1)it will first compare $t_{1,2}$ with

Algorithm 2. MHRA with Same Priorities

Require: Assign each Actor to be free
Require: Assign each task to be free
  INPUT: Actors $a_1, a_2, ..., a_m$ and their tasks
  OUTPUT: Every actor and his/her working tasks
  Set $a_1 \leftarrow t_{1,1}$
  Set next$\leftarrow t_{2,1}$
  Set next+1$\leftarrow t_{3,1}$
  Set $t_{j,i}$ the ith task for j^{th} actor
  continue until $a_m \leftarrow t_{m,1}$
  $a_1 \leftarrow t_{1,1}$
  $\Theta_t := t_{1,1}$
  $j = 2, i = 1$
  while $j <= m(lastactor)$ **do**
    if $t_{j,i} \in \Theta_t$ **then**
      $i++$
    else
      $a(j) \leftarrow t_{j,i}$
      $\Theta_t := +t_{j,i}$
    end if
    $j++$
  end while

---

assigned tasks noted as Θ_t at first phase. If $t_{1,2} \notin \Theta_t$, then $t_{1,2}$ is assigned to a_1. In case of similarities, it will go to the next actor a_2 to compare his/her task with Θ_t until a_m. This process continues until it finds free tasks. The same procedure is applied for all phases.

We look at the worst case and best case complexity of the algorithm.

1. Worst Case

   In the worst case, tasks can have similar preferences somehow. In this case, MHRA will allocate all actors their first tasks after doing a comparison of current task to already allocated ones, this is done in first phase φ_1. Though, it will make $0+1+2+3+...+m-1 = \frac{m(m-1)}{2}$ counting steps of comparisons which is O (m^2) of running time, where m represents the number of first preferred tasks for all actors.

   At second phase, as $1, 2$ will not be compared with $t_{1,1}$ because we are certain that they are different. The maximum number of steps the algorithm will take to make all comparisons at phase φ_2 is $(m-1) + (m-1)$ steps. Therefore, the running time algorithm is O (m) at second phase. The same procedure is done for all phases.

   Furthermore, as phases go higher, more steps are executed. At phase φ_π, which is the last phase for all actors , task $t_{1,n}$ will not be compared with its all preceding tasks. This is the same for task $t_{m,n}$. Consequently, on task $t_{m,n}$, the algorithm will make $\pi(m-1)$ steps where π shows the πth phase. The running time algorithm of MHRA at phase φ_π will be O(m). Apart from phase φ_1, it is clear that, the rest phases the MHRA has a running time of O(m), that is why

Algorithm 3. MHRA with different priorities

Require: Assign each Actor to be free
Require: Assign each task to be free
    INPUT: Actors $a_1, a_2, ..., a_m$ and their tasks
    OUTPUT: Every actor and his/her working tasks
    Set $a_1 := t_{1,1}, t_{1,2}, ..., t_{1,i}, ..., t_{1,m}$
    Set $a_m := t_{m,1}, t_{m,2}, ..., t_{m,i}, ..., t_{m,n}$
    Set $t_{j,i}$ as the ith task for j^{th} actor
    increment tasks$= t_{j+1,1}$
    $a_1 \leftarrow t_{1,1}$
    $\Theta_t := t_{1,1}$
    Set $t_{j,i}$ as the ith task for j^{th} actor
    $j = 2$
    $i = 1$
    while $i <= n$ **do**
      while $j <= m$ **do**
        if $t_{j,i} \notin \Theta_t$ **then**
          i++
        else
          $a(j) := t_{j,i}$
          $\Theta_t := +t_{j,i}$
        end if
        $j++$
      end while
      $i++$
    end while

---

the total running time in worst case is $[[(0 + 1 + 2 + ... + m - 1)] + [(m - 1) + (m - 1)] + ... + [\pi(m - 1)]]$ which gives $O(m^2)$.

2. Best Case

For the best case scenario, all tasks are totally different and every actor is given all chosen tasks ie according to his/her quota q_j. Therefore, the running time algorithm is $\sum_{j=1}^{m} q_j$ which gives the running time of $O(m)$ where m represents tasks.

4.3 Sensitivity of MHRA

Generally, when a preference list is used or when tasks have the same priorities for a particular actor, the MHRA does not give the same results except under certain instances. This is due to the fact that when preferences are considered tasks of first rows have more chance to be allocated to their respective actors unlike tasks in the last rows. On the other hand, if tasks have the same priorities, because MHRA allocates tasks by columns, the tasks of first columns are likely to be allocated before the lasts ones. In this case, we limit ourselves to the following instances:

- When the same priorities are considered and the highest quota is greater than the number of actors $q_a > m$, or the highest quotas is equal to the number of actors $q_a = m$ and when the highest quota is less than the number of actors $q_a < m$;
- If preferences are respected and the highest quota is greater than the number of actors $q_a > m$

If Tasks Have the Same Priorities and Tasks with Highest Quotas Are on the Top

1. **If $q_a > m$:** In this case, at phase φ_1 the running time algorithm is $O(m^2)$. In addition, it guarantees a hope to a_1 to be given at least second task after $t_{1,i} = a_i$. But it does not guarantee for the remaining actors. At phase φ_π, the running time of algorithm will be $O(m)$ and therefore, MHRA has a running time of $O(m^2)$.
2. **If $q_a = m$:** At first phase, the running time is $O(m^2)$. This case does not guarantee a_1 to have his/her second allocation even for some others because $lim_{q \to 0} \frac{q_{a_1} - 1}{m-1} = 0$. At final phase φ_π, the comparison steps will be $\pi(m-1)$ which is $O(m)$.
3. **If $q_a < m$:** This case shows that all actors do not have a guarantee to be given second tasks as $lim_{m \to \infty} \frac{q_a}{m} = 0$. Their running time algorithm is $O(m^2)$ as well.

If tasks Have Different Priorities When the priorities of tasks are used, the first phase in the worst case gives a running time algorithm of $O(m^2)$, and $O(m)$ in final phase φ_π. This gives the total running time algorithm of $O(m^2)$ whatever the quotas strategies. In this scenario, we are not interested in the relationship between quotas and the number of actors as in 5.3.1 because the MHRA here deals mainly with columns rather than rows. But at Best case always the MHRA will have a running time of $O(m)$.

5   Conclusion and Future Work

In this paper, we have studied the dynamic resource allocation problem. We have studied its complexity and complexity sensitivity to selected parameters. We have used the Gale and Shapely algorithm as a starting point and generated an algorithm that can address the dynamic resource allocation problem. We then studied the complexity of selected variants of it. We have shown that the problem can be solved in polynomial time (linear and quadratic).

Future research can incorporate costs of associated task/actor assignments as well as fairness and robustness studies. Likewise, cases of divisible tasks (non atomic) as well as collaborating actors (where actors can make groups that work on tasks) can form extension to this work.

References

1. Campbell, A., Wu, A.S.: Learning and Exploiting Knowledge in Multi-Agent Task Allocation Problems. In: Proceedings of the 2007 GECCO Conference Companion on Genetic and Evolutionary Computation, pp. 2637–2642 (2007)
2. Roth, A.E., Sotomayor, M.A.O.: Two-sided matching: a study in game-theoretic modeling and analysis. Econometric Society Monographs, vol. 18. Cambridge University Press, Cambridge (1990)
3. Mills-Tettey, G.A., Stentz, A., Dias, M.B.: The Dynamic Hungarian Algorithm for the Assignment Problem with Changing Costs. Technical Report 7-2007, Robotics Institute-Carnegie Mellon University (July 2007)
4. Gerkey, B.: A formal analysis and taxonomy of task allocation in multirobot systems. Intl. J. of Robotics Research 23(9), 939–954 (2004)
5. Zhou, C.: Using Genetic Algorithms and Heuristics for Job Shop Scheduling with Sequence-Dependent Setup Times. Annals of Operations Research 107(1-4), 65–81 (2001)
6. Gale, D., Shapley, L.S.: College admissions and the stability of marriage. American Mathematical Monthly 69, 9–15 (1962)
7. Gale, D., Sotomayor, M.: Some remarks on the stable matching problem. Discrete Applied Mathematics 11(3), 223–232 (1985)
8. Manlove, D., Irving, R.W., Iwama, K., Miyaziki, S., Morita, Y.: Hard variants of stable marriage. Theoretical Computer Science 276(1-2), 261–279 (2002)
9. de Weerdt, M., van der Krogt, R.: Inefficiencies in Task Allocation for Multiagent Planning with Bilateral Deals. In: Proceedings of the 25th Workshop of the UK Planning and Scheduling Special Interest Group, PlanSIG, pp. 33–38 (2007)
10. McVitie, D.G., Wilson, L.B.: The Stable Marriage Problem. Communications of the ACM 144, 486–492 (2006)
11. Irving, R.: Stable marriage and indifference. Discrete Applied Mathematics 48, 261–272 (1994)
12. Irving, R.W., Manlove, D.F., Scott, S.: The Hospitals/Residents Problem with Ties. In: Halldórsson, M.M. (ed.) SWAT 2000. LNCS, vol. 1851, pp. 259–271. Springer, Heidelberg (2000)
13. Shen, W.: Distributed manufacturing scheduling using intelligent agents. IEEE Intelligent Systems Magazine 17(1), 88–94 (2002)

Wireless Sensor Network Internal Attacker Identification with Multiple Evidence by Dempster-Shafer Theory

Muhammad Ahmed[1], Xu Huang[1], Dharmendra Sharma[1], and Li Shutao[2]

[1] Faculty of Information Sciences and Engineering,
University of Canberra, Australia
[2] College of Electrical and Information Engineering,
Huana University, Changsha, P.R. China
{muhammad.ahmed,xu.huang,dharmendra.sharma}@canberra.edu.au

Abstract. Wireless sensor Network (WSN) is known to be vulnerable to variety of attacks due to the construction of nodes and distributed network infrastructure. In order to ensure its functionality especially in malicious environments, security mechanisms are essential. Malicious or insider attacker has gained prominence and poses the most challenging attacks to WSN. Many works has been done to secure WSN from internal attacker but most of it relay on either training data set or predefined threshold. Without a fixed security infrastructure WSN need to find the internal attacker. Normally, internal attacker node behavioral pattern is different from the other neighbor good nodes in the system, but neighbor node can be attacked as well. In this paper, we use Dempster-Shafer theory (DST) of combined multiple evidence to identify the malicious or internal attacker in WSN. This theory reflects with the uncertain event or uncertainty as well as uncertainty of the observation. Moreover, it gives a numerical procedure for fusing together multiple pieces of evidence from unreliable neighbor with higher degree of conflict reliability.

Keywords: Wireless Sensor Networks, Internal Attacker, Security, Dempster-shafer theory.

1   Introduction

The recent advances in micro-electro-mechanical system technology, wireless communication and digital electronics lead us to wireless sensor networks. It is an emerging technology for collecting data with distributed autonomous sensors for natural or built environment to work in real time. The technology became popular because it radically improves the cost and quality of data gathering to enhance the understanding of the application environment. It consists of processing capability (one or more microcontrollers, CPUs or DSP chips), may contain multiple types of memory (program, data and flash memories), embedded with RF transceiver (usually with a single omni- directional antenna), have a power source (e.g., batteries and solar cells), and accommodate various sensors and actuators [1]. The nodes communicate wirelessly and often self-organize after being deployed. Base station called sink in

Y. Xiang et al. (Eds.): ICA3PP 2012, Part II, LNCS 7440, pp. 255–263, 2012.

which all data is transmitted in an autonomous way has high capacity of storage and analysis power. The architecture may include the topology organization of sink node and global view of the whole network. The application of WSN includes battlefield surveillance, border monitoring, habitat monitoring, intelligent agriculture, home automation, etc. According to the applications the deployment strategy is decided. When the environment is unknown or hostile such as remote harsh fields, disaster are as toxic environment the deployment usually done by scatter by a possible way.

In this information age the world is interconnected via various communications. Security provisioning is a critical requirement for any communication network. Security in the wireless sensor network is challenging and important task because of its characteristics that include, open nature of wireless medium, unattended operation, limited energy, memory, computing power, communication bandwidth, and communication range. Considering those characteristics many algorithms have developed for the secure functionality of WSN. Most of the work has focused on the pair wise key establishment, authentication access control and defense against attack. Most importantly those works mainly focused on the traditional cryptographic information, data authentication in order to build the relationship between the sensors. However, the unreliable communications through wireless channel made the communication technique vulnerable by allowing the sensor nodes to compromise and release the security information to the adversary [2]. The compromised entity of the network acts as a legitimate node. So it is easy for the adversary to perform the insider attacks. When insider attack occurs for a node, this node will behave abnormally such as tampering the massage from other member, dropping the data or broadcast excessive data.

So far, not much attention has been given to save the network from the insider attacker that caused by the abnormally behaved node. In this paper, we have proposed Dempster–Shafer theory (DST) based internal attacker identification mechanism with neighbor nodes parameters observation as DST has the feature of dealing with uncertainty. In our proposed method the system does not need to have any prior knowledge of the pre-classified training data of the nodes.

The paper is organised as follows: section 2 is comprised of the overview of the related work followed by the system architecture and network model in section 3. The detail of the dempester-shafer theory for internal attacker identification process is described in section 4. The evaluation in WSN and mathematical calculation is given in section 5 followed by conclusion in section 6.

2   Related Work

To identify internal attacker in wireless sensors networks several work has been done in the past but DST based method was not given significant attention.

For detection of abnormal behavior of the nodes or internal attacker Staddon et al [3] proposed to trace the failed nodes in sensor networks at the base station assuming that all the sensor measurement will be directed along the sinker based on the routing tree. In this work the sinker has the global view of the network topology and can identify the failed nodes through route update message and it is directional.

Watchdog like technique was proposed by Marti [4], this technique can detect the packet dropping attack by letting nodes listen to the next hope nodes broadcasting transmission. In this multiple watchdog work collaboratively in decision making and reputation system is necessary to provide the quality rating of the participants.

Zhang et al [5] proposed a scheme which is the first work on intrusion detection in wireless ad hoc networks. A new architecture is investigated for collaborative statistical anomaly detection which provides protection from attack on ad hoc routing.

These developments somehow solve the mathematical problems with certain constrain but does not take the internal attacker identification in consideration with the uncertainty of observation by neighbor nodes.

3   System Architecture and Network Model

Our temperature measurement WSN system is based on a single sinker with randomly distributed static node. We assume the neighbor node with one hop will observe the data of the suspected internal attacker. In order to observe, the physical parameter (Temperature) and transmission behavior (packet drop rate) is considered as independent events. The observation of the events becomes the pieces of evidences. In the decision making process with Dempster-Shafer Theory we will combine the independent pieces of evidences.

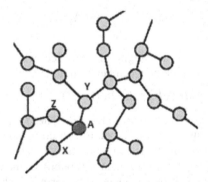

Fig. 1. Three neighbor observing the attacker with one hop

In the Fig 1, neighbor nodes X, Y and Z will observe the suspected internal attacker node A for its temperature (T) and packet drop rate (PDR).

4   Methodology

4.1   Dempster-Shafer Theory

In DST, probability is replaced by an uncertainty interval bounded by belief and plausibility. Belief is the lower bound of the interval and represents supporting evidence. Plausibility is the upper bound of the interval and represents the non-refuting evidence [6]. In this reasoning system, all possible mutually exclusive hypothesis (or events) of the same kind are enumerated in the frame of discernment also known as universal discloser θ. A basic belief assignment (BBA) or mass function is a function m: $2^{\theta} \to [0, 1]$, and it satisfies two following conditions

$$m(\phi) = 0 \tag{1}$$

$$\sum_{A \subseteq \theta} m(A_j) = 1 \tag{2}$$

In which ϕ is the empty set and a BBA that satisfy the condition $m(\phi) = 0$. The basic probability number can be translated as $m(A)$ because the portion of total belief assigned to hypothesis A, which reflects the evidences strength of support. The assignment of belief function maps each hypothesis B to a value $bel(B)$ between 0 and 1. This defined as

$$bel(B) = \sum_{j:A_j \subseteq A} m(A_j) \tag{3}$$

The upper bound of the confidence interval is the plausibility function, which accounts for all the observations that do not rule out the given proposition. It maps each hypothesis B to a value $pls(B)$ between 0 and 1, can be defined as follows.

$$pls(B) = \sum_{j:A_j \cap B \neq \phi} m(A_j) \tag{4}$$

The plausibility function is a weight of evidence which is non-refuting to B. equation (5) shows the relation between belief and plausibility.

$$pls(B) = 1 - bel(\sim B) \tag{5}$$

The hypothesis not B is representing by $\sim B$. The functions basic probability numbers, belief and plausibility are in one-to-one correspondence and by knowing one of them, the other two functions could be derived.

Assuming $m_1(A)$ and $m_2(A)$ are two basic probability number by two independent items of evidence means two independent neighbor node which act as observers in the same frame of discernment. The observations (the pieces of evidence) can be combined using Dempster's rule of combination (known as orthogonal sum) as in equation (6).

$$m(B) = (m_1 \oplus m_2)(B) = \frac{\sum_{i,j:A_i \cap A_j = B} m_1(A_i) m_2(A_j)}{1 - \sum_{i,j:A_i \cap A_j = \phi} m_1(A_i) m_2(A_j)} \tag{6}$$

where $\oplus$ represents the Dempster's combination operator that combines two basic probability assignments or basic belief assignments (BBA) into the third [7]. To normalize the equation we consider L is a normalization constant defined by the equation (7), More than two belief function can be combined with pairwise in any order.

$$L = \frac{1}{K} \tag{7}$$

Where ,

$$K = 1 - \sum_{i,j:A_i \cap A_j = \phi} m_1(A_i) m_2(A_j)$$

The combination rule assigns the belief according to the degree of conflict between the evidences and assigns the remaining belief to the environment and not to common hypothesis. It makes possible to combine with most of their belief assigned to the disjoint hypothesis without the side effect of a counterintuitive behavior. Belief resembles the certainty factors or evidences [8]. The conflict between two belief functions bel_1 and bel_2, denoted by the $Con(bel_1, bel_2)$ is given by the logarithm of normalization constant [9] shown in equation (8)

$$Con(bel_1, bel_2) = \log(L) \tag{8}$$

If there is no conflict between the bel_1 and bel_2 than $Con(bel_1, bel_2) = 0$ and if there is nothing in common between two evidences $Con(bel_1, bel_2) = \infty$. [10] The DST automatically incorporates the uncertainty coming from the conflicting evidences. Following the reference [10] we can come up with a dempester-shafer combination, which can be given as in equation (9)

$$m(B) = (m_1 \oplus m_2)(B) = \frac{L \sum_{i,j:A_i \cap A_j = B} m_1(A_i) m_2(A_j)}{1 + \log(L)} \tag{9}$$

4.2   DST Framework in WSN

DST application in our system works by considering the independent event as temperature T and PDR as described in section 3. Our case the universal discloser or the set of local element can be observed by the one hop neighbor is $\theta = \{T, PDR\}$. Hence the power set becomes

$$2^\theta = \{\phi, \{T\}, \{PDR\}, \{unknown\}\}$$

Where,

$$\{unknown\} = \{T\} \cup \{PDR\}$$

With the T and PDR the basic probability assignments for the nodes X, Y and Z are as follows,

$$m_T(X) = 0.3 \; ; \; m_T(Y) = 0.4 \; ; \; m_T(Z) = 0.2 \; ; \; m_T(U) = 0.1$$
$$m_{PDR}(X) = 0.4 \; ; \; m_{PDR}(Y) = 0.4 \; ; \; m_{PDR}(Z) = 0.2$$

From the above we have,

$$K = \{1 - (0.12 + 0.04 + 0.16 + 0.04 + 0.04 + 0.02)\} = 0.58 \; ;$$

Hence,

$$L = 1.72 \text{ and } \log(L) = 0.23 \; ;$$

Implementing the DST as in equation (12) we can find the individual nodes observation about the suspected node A, based on the independent pieces of information or evidence.

$$m_{T,PDR}(X) = m_T(X) \oplus m_{PDR}(X) = 0.22$$
$$m_{T,PDR}(Y) = m_T(Y) \oplus m_{PDR}(Y) = 0.27$$
$$m_{T,PDR}(Z) = m_T(Z) \oplus m_{PDR}(Z) = 0.08$$

From the above calculation we can see that the node A is compromised with the probability of 0.22, 0.27 and 0.08 by the observation of node X, Y and Z respectively.

The combination between the evidences with high conflicting factor can lead to the inconsistent outcome by the dempster-shafer theory. The conflicting value more than 0.5 indicates more conflict than arguments. In your case the conflicting factor $Con\,(bel_1, bel_2) = \log(L) = 0.23$.

4.3   Framework Execution

In order to find the internal attacker in our case we can execute framework in the section 4.2 with the algorithm shown below. The temperature threshold ∂_T and ∂_{PDR} is the threshold for the Packet drop rate which is set based on the training data.

Algorithm 1
I. Get the view of the neighbor node view

Input: m_T, m_{PDR}, ∂_T, ∂_{PDR}

   m_T[ ]\\ BPA assignment

   m_{PDR}[ ]\\ BPA assignment

II. Execute the equation (12)

   $m_{T,PDR}$[ ]\\

      If $\log(L) < 0.5$

   Output result accepted
      printf "the node is an internal attacker"
   else
      Go to step I

end

5   Results

In this paper we have come up with case studies and applied in our system model and algorithm. We have assigned basic probability for the 2 events observed by the sensors. The calculation is done based on our model of WSN which tabulated in the table 1.

Table 1.

		Sensors View	DST combination	Conflict
Case Study1	X	T=0.3 PDR= 0.4	0.22	
	Y	T=0.4 PDR= 0.4	0.27	0.23
	Z	T=0.2 PDR=0.2	0.08	
Case Study 2	X	T=0.4 PDR= 0.2	0.17	
	Y	T=0.2 PDR= 0.4	0.22	0.25
	Z	T=0.2 PDR=0.4	0.22	
Case Study 3	X	T=0.35 PDR= 0.25	0.16	
	Y	T=0.25 PDR= 0.45	0.18	0.20
	Z	T=0.4 PDR=0.2	0.16	

From the three case studies we can find the internal attacker percentage based on the DST combination result. Fig 2 shows DST combination for each sensor. In which we can see the graphical representation of the three cases. The BBA assignment was different in three different cases but the combination decision is almost same about the sensor node A that it is an internal attacker. Most of the combination probability is between 0.16 to 0.22 on the other hand lowest and highest probability that the A is an internal attacker is 0.08 and 0.27, considering the result we can tell that node a in an internal attacker.

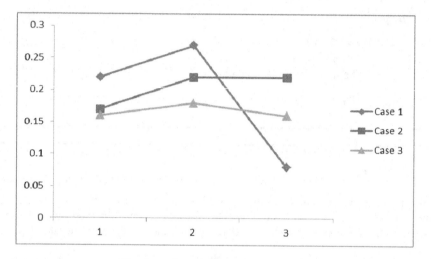

Fig. 2. DST combination of each sensor

6   Conclusion

In this paper an internal attacker identification framework in wireless sensor network is proposed with Dempster-Shafer theory of evidence combination method. The mathematical calculation shows that the result depends on the neighbor nodes observation of the event. Moreover, the conflict increases with the number of sources. In future, we would like to create a database for the nodes normal behavior and simulate in the hardware platform.

References

1. Huang, X., Ahmed, M., Sharma, D.: Timing Control for Protecting from Internal Attacks in Wireless Sensor Networks. In: IEEE ICOIN 2012, Bali, Indonesia (February 2012)
2. Ahmed, M., Hunag, X., Sharma, D.: A Novel Framework for Abnormal Behaviour Identification and Detection for Wireless Sensor Networks. In: ICIS 2012, Kuala Lumpur, Malaysia (2012)
3. Staddon, J., Balfanz, D., Durfee, G.: Efficient tracing of failed nodes in sensor networks. In: WSNA 2002, Atlanta, USA, pp. 122–130 (2002)

4. Marti, S., Giuli, T.J., Lai, K., Baker, M.: Mitigating Routing Misbehavior in Mobile Ad Hoc Networks. In: ACM MOBICOM 2000, Boston, USA, pp. 255–265 (August 2000)
5. Zhang, Y., Lee, W.: Intrusion Detection in Wireless Ad-hoc Networks. In: ACM MOBICOM 2000, Boston, USA, pp. 275–283 (August 2000)
6. Sentz, K.: Combination of Evidence in Dempester-Shafer Theory. System Science and Engineering Department, Binghamton University, SAND 2002-0835 (April 2002)
7. Koks, D., Challa, S.: An Introduction to Bayesian and Dempster-Shafer Data Fusion. Published by DSTO Systems Sciences Laboratory, Australia (November 2005)
8. Tabassian, M., Ghaderi, R., Ebrahimpour, R.: Combination of multiple diverse classifiers using belief functions for handling data with imperfect labels. Expert Systems with Applications 39 (2011)
9. Khalaja, F., Khalajb, M., Khalaj, A.H.: Bounded Error for Robust Fault Detection under Uncertainty, Part 1: Proposed Model Using Dempster-Shafer Theory. Journal of Basic and Applied Scientific Research 2(2), 1233–1240 (2012)
10. Campos, F., Cavalcante, S.: An Extended Approach for Dempster-Shafer Theory. In: Information Reuse and Integration, IRI 2003. IEEE (2003)

A Novel Feature Selection Scheme
for Energy Efficient Wireless Sensor Networks

Moh'd Alwadi and Girija Chetty

Faculty of Information Sciences and Engineering, The University of Canberra
u3019769@uni.canberra.edu.au, girija.chetty@canberra.edu.au

Abstract. Energy efficiency is a key issue in wireless sensor networks where the energy sources and battery capacity are very limited. In this paper we propose a novel pattern recognition based formulation for minimizing the energy consumption in wireless sensor networks. The proposed scheme involves an algorithm to rank and select the sensors from the most significant to the least, and followed by a naïve Bayes classification. Assuming that each feature represents a sensor in the wireless sensor network, various data sets with multiple features are considered to show that feature ranking and selection could play a key role for the energy management. We have examined Isolet, forest fires and ionosphere datasets from the UCI repository to emulate the wireless sensor network scenario. From our simulation results, we show that it is possible to achieve two important objectives using the proposed scheme: (1) Increase the lifetime of the wireless sensor network, by using optimal number of sensors, and (2) Manage sensor failures with optimal number of sensors without compromising the accuracy.

Keywords: wireless sensor networks, feature ranking, feature selection, data sets, accuracy, life time extension factor, WEKA machine learning framework.

1   Introduction

The field of wireless sensor networks (WSN) has become a focus of intensive research in recent years and various theoretical and practical questions have been addressed. WSNs can be used to monitor environmental or physical conditions such as temperature, wind and humidity [1]. Energy management in WSN is a key issue caused by a limited battery capacity and large number of sensors distributed along wide area. In sensor networks, there is no power support with constant power rate. The life time of a sensor is very restricted based on very limited power source. Therefore keeping the energy consumption in the lowest level is always a key issue. Though some approaches have been developed to address this issue, they have met with limited success, in terms of dynamically managing the energy requirements without compromising the accuracy in the event of sensor failures. In this paper we propose a novel pattern recognition based formulation of energy efficient WSNs during sensor failures without compromising the accuracy requirements. In this scheme, we model sensors with the features extracted from the data sets

Y. Xiang et al. (Eds.): ICA3PP 2012, Part II, LNCS 7440, pp. 264–273, 2012.

corresponding to different WSN application scenarios, including acoustic data (Isolet), forest fire data, and ionosphere data set. In our formulation, minimizing the number of sensors for energy efficient management becomes equivalent to minimizing the number of features [2]. For minimizing, we use a feature ranking approach, where the features are ranked according to their significance of use in the wireless sensor network. That means we first rank the sensors from the most significant to the least significant, and then select optimal number of sensors to meet a specified accuracy.

For validating the proposed scheme, we used different publicly available datasets corresponding to wireless sensor networks in UCI Machine Learning repository [3]. We have studied Isolet, forest fires and ionosphere datasets. Each data set consists of different number of sensors (features).

2 Background

Various approaches have been proposed to maximize energy efficiency and management in wireless sensor networks. Nakamura and Loureiro [4] proposed a scheme with four main contributions - an information fusion frame work for WSNs, a novel algorithm that applies information fusion to detect when a routing tree to be rebuilt, a novel routing strategy, based on role assignment which maximizes the gains of an information-fusion application and a critical survey about information fusion in WSNs. Bashyal and Venayagamoorthy [5] proposed a collaborative routing algorithm for WSN longevity, and this approach was based on four different possible node distribution in uniform or non-uniform distribution. Initial network with all surviving nodes, uneven distribution of surviving sensor nodes, an uniform distribution scheme of surviving sensor nodes and an optimal distribution for the last four surviving nodes for area coverage. Richter [6] introduced a scheme with five common steps for general pattern recognition process: signal recording, pre-processing, feature extraction, feature reduction and classification. Narasimhan and Cox [7] proposed a Handoff algorithm for wireless systems where it is necessary to switch or handoff the communication link from one base station to another for two main reasons: to maintain the signal quality and minimize interference caused to other radio links. Song and Allison [8] developed algorithms to break the frequency hopping spread spectrum patterns. In frequency hopping spread spectrum the transmitter broadcasts on one frequency for small amount of time then switches to another frequency using a known switching algorithm called a hopping or hopping pattern. Walchi and Braun [9] proposed an office monitoring system which is able to distinguish abnormal office access from normal access due to severe battery restrictions on the system. Therefore, office access pattern need to be classified. The node-level decision unit of self-learning anomaly detection mechanism for office monitoring with wireless sensor nodes is presented. Yu and He [10] developed the algorithm of resource reservation based on neural networks which is easy to implement and adaptable for different situations. It offers accurate classification about the user's random movement in small size cells and improved resource efficiency when resources are limited in wireless systems. Dziengel, Wittenburg and Schiller [11] presented ongoing work on distributed event detection system for WSNs. In contrast to other approaches, their system is self-contained for example it operates without a central component for co-ordination or processing, and makes active use of the redundantly placed sensor nodes in the network to improve detection accuracy. The experimental results in this paper show that distributed event detection yields higher accuracy than local detection on a single node. Wittenburg et al. [12] presented a system for distributed even detection in WSNs that allows number of sensor nodes to collaborate in order to identify which application- specific even has occurred.

3   Simulation Tools

In the current paper, MATLAB [13] and WEKA [14] have been used to develop the algorithm to rank and classify the sensors. The algorithm ranks the sensors based on the significance of use, from the most significant to the least. The following script is used on MATLAB to rank sensors in a descending order:

```
1       %feature selection
2 -     clear
3 -     M = csvread('covtype.csv');
4 -     [r,c] = size(M);
5 -     X = M(:, 1:c-1);
6 -     Y=M(:,c);
7 -     Sf =IndFeat(X,Y);
8 -     [SfSorted,indx] = sort(Sf,'descend');
9
10 -    figure
11 -    subplot(211), stem(Sf);
12 -    subplot(212), stem(SfSorted);
13 -     grid on
14 -     zoom on
15 -    csvwrite('selFeatures.csv',indx);
```

Fig. 1. Algorithm for feature selection [15]

4   Experiments

For the simulation work, we have studied three different data sets. We can summaries the data sets we used for this work from the UCI repository in the following table.

Table 1. Data sets

Data set	#of instances	#of Attributes	Missing Values?	Associated tasks
ISOLET	7797	617	No	Classification
Forest fires	517	13	N/A	Regression
Ionosphere	351	34	No	Classification

The purpose of ISOLET dataset is to predict which letter or name was spoken. From the table above ISOLET is a large data set with 7797 instances and 617 attributes (features). It is divided into isolet 1+2+3+4 and isolet5. In this paper we used isolet5 part with only 1559 instances and 617 features because of limitations of memory size in the simulation.

Forest fires is a difficult regression task, the aim is to predict the burned area of forest fires. Several of attributes in forest fires data set may be correlates, thus it makes sense to apply some sort of feature selection [16]. In our experiments, the features have been minimized into 5 features as the attributes such as date, time and month are not selected as features.

Ionosphere data set that contains radar data was collected by system in Goose Bay, Labrador. The targets were free electrons in the Ionosphere. "Good" radar returns are those showing evidence of some type structure in the Ionosphere. "Bad" returns are those that do not let their signals pass through the Ionosphere [14]. In experiment 3 we used all 34 attributes in addition to the class   "good" and "bad" has been replaced with "1" and "0" to be able to classify the data set, as our script and WEKA are not compatible in classifying characters.

The main aim of our experiments to show that to what level the number of features selected may affect the accuracy and the life time extension factor (life time of the sensor network before the sensor becomes unavailable). In the following experiments, we will show the accuracy and the life time of a sensor network based on the number of feature used in all sensor networks for ISOLET, forest fires and Ionosphere.

4.1   Experiment 1

The first experiment is on ISOLET dataset. The actual size of data we used consists of 1559 instances with 617 features to remove the data redundancy, whereas the original size of the dataset is 7797 instances and 617 features. After applying our Isolet5 dataset to our feature ranking algorithm, the most significant features are as shown in the following table:

Table 2. Selected features on Isolet5

	1	2	3	4	5	6	7	8	9	10
1	455	453	454	456	457	458	459	460	461	462
2	69	6	101	38	37	70	39	5	262	261
3	7	102	40	71	72	103	43	104	8	44
4	76	73	42	2	41	133	74	75	230	9
5	106	11	110	108	109	78	77	263	105	45
:	107	10	12	293	3	46	264	134	229	135
:	34	111	66	290	98	226	79	47	137	140
:	227	258	294	231	139	136	225	165	332	166
:	138	265	130	112	80	486	259	142	48	232
10	233	141	295	13	81	545	266	167	481	113
:	..	..	...	...	...	...	....	...	...	...
:	....	...	...	...	...	...	...	...	...	...
20	236	467	157	177	329	485	94	147	270	239

The above features have been imported to WEKA and classification experiments performed on most significant 10 features, 20, 30, 40, 50, 100 and 200 features. We used the classify option on WEKA [5], and selected the NaiveBayes classification algorithm. We performed several tests to show the accuracy for each selection and the results as the following:

Table 3. Experiment 1 accuracy

Features	Accuracy	Life time extension factor
10	9.62%	617/10= 61.7
20	11.80%	617/20 = 30.85
30	13.79%	20.56
40	14.62%	15.42
50	16.10%	12.34
100	23.92%	6.17
200	41.05%	3.08

$$Life\ time\ Extension\ factor = \frac{Total\ number\ of\ features}{Number\ of\ features\ used}$$

From the table above it seems to be clear that the accuracy is increased based on the number of features selected. However, this will be at the cost of the life time extension factor. Life time extension factor is increased if the number of features used is less, and redundant features are eliminated. So an appropriate feature ranking and selection algorithm can determine most influential sensors or most significant

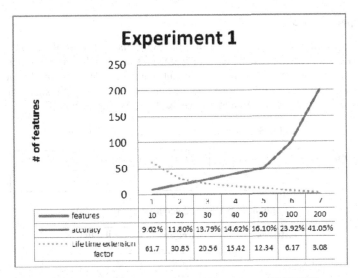

Fig. 2. Accuracy and life time extension factor. (ISOLET5)

features, and allow redundant features to be eliminated. We propose a measure the "life time extension factor" as the total number of sensors in network or the features divided by the number of sensors or features used as per the ranking algorithm [2]. In our experiments the life time extension factor shown in table 3.

From Figure 2 above, it can be seen that the life time extension factor increases with lesser sensors at the cost of accuracy. And the accuracy of a network could be increased at the cost of decreased life time extension factor. In the event of a sensor failure or unavailability, it is possible to maintain the accuracy by increasing the number of features used. To emulate the sensor failure, we assign a probability. We are assuming that our sensor Si is not available with probability p= 0 , 0.01 , 0.05 , 0.10 , 0.50 [2]. In this experiment, we have multiplied our Isolet5 data set with all probability values above. We have selected 10 features and applied feature classification on WEKA and the results as the following table.

Table 4. Experiment 1 accuracy with Probability

Features	Accuracy Without P	Accuracy P= 0.01	Accuracy P=0.05	Accuracy P=0.10	Accuracy P=0.5
10	9.62%	9.55%	9.42%	9.56%	9.56%

We can see from the table above that the system is quite stable with respect to occasional sensor faults. In case of using 20, 30, 40, 50, 100 and 200 features with probability the accuracy will still quite stable. In experiment 2 , 3 and 4 we are not going to repeat the probability multiplication in all datasets because of lack of space and memory size on WEKA.

4.2   Experiment 2

The second experiment based on forest fires dataset. This data set is of size 517 * 13 (517 samples with 13 features). Features have been reduced to 5 because 8 other attributes such as date, time and month were not relevant features. After applying feature ranking algorithm, the following table shows features in the order of their significance, most significant to the least significant feature; we used a naïve Bayes classifier.

Table 5. Selected features on forest fires data set

Feature 1	Feature 2	Feature 3	Feature 4	Feature 5
3	4	5	1	2

Table 6. Experiment 2 accuracy (Forest fires)

Features	Accuracy	Life time extension factor
1 (3)	10.77%	5/1= 5
2 (3,4)	11.04%	5/2 = 2.5
3 (3,4,5)	13.37%	5/3= 1.6
4 (3,4,5,1)	13.56%	5/4= 1.25
5 (3,4,5,1,2)	13.75%	5/5= 1

The relationship between accuracy and lifetime extension factor for the forest fires data set is similar to experiment 1. That is increasing the number of features increases the accuracy at the cost of life time extension factor. Further, in the event of sensor failure or unavailability, it is possible to maintain the specified accuracy by including more sensors for classifying the area affected by fire. However, for a healthy sensor network, using more features or sensors is costing more resources and reduces the life time of the sensor network. It would be energy efficient if lesser number of sensors with more significance can be used.

The accuracy vs. life time extension factor for selected features is as shown below:

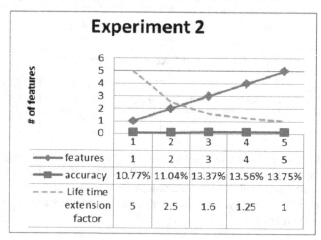

Fig. 3. Accuracy and life time extension factor. (Forest fires)

4.3   Experiment 3

This experiment was based on Ionosphere data set. We used all 34 attributes in addition to the class "good" and "bad" have been replaced with "1" and "0" to be able to classify the data set, as our script and WEKA are not compatible in classifying characters in the data. After applying ionosphere data set into our feature ranking algorithm the most significance to the least significant features are as shown in Table 7 below:

Table 7. Experiment 3 selected features & ranked on Ionosphere dataset

	1	2	3	4	5	6	7	8	9	10
1	2	3	5	7	1	9	31	33	29	21
2	15	23	8	13	25	14	11	12	16	6
3	19	10	18	22	27	4	17	34	28	32
4	20	24	30	26						

Table 8. Experiment 3 Accuracy

Features	Accuracy	Life time extension factor
10	38.74%	34/10 = 3.4
20	35.89%	34/20 = 1.7
30	35.89%	34/30 = 1.1
34	35.89%	34/34 = 1

The accuracy and lifetime extension factor achieved for this dataset is as shown in Table 8 and Figure 4 below:

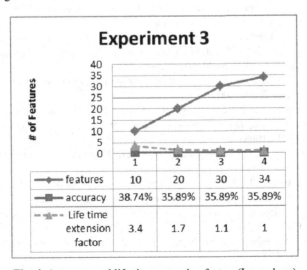

Fig. 4. Accuracy and life time extension factor. (Ionosphere)

We can notice that the accuracy of Ionosphere data set is larger than the accuracy of forest fires in experiment 2 because the number of features used is larger than the number of features in experiment 2. The accuracy when using more than 10 features is getting constant this may affected by the class type of 0 and 1 in the dataset. However, we can conclude that using more features is costing more resources and less life time of the sensor network.

5   Conclusions and Further Plans

Energy sources are very limited in wireless sensor networks. In this paper we propose a feature selection and ranking approach to manage energy in wireless sensor network. Using lesser sensors that are most significant can increase the life time of the network. Further, the proposed feature ranking and selection scheme allows graceful management of sensor network in the event of sensor failures, by increasing the number of sensors to meet the specified accuracy requirements. The proposed scheme was validated by extensive experimental evaluation for different datasets corresponding to wireless sensor networks used in different application scenarios. As future plan, we are going to investigate more data sets to achieve higher accuracy.

References

1. Ping, S.: Delay measurement time synchronization for wireless sensor networks. Intel Research Berkeley Lab (2003)
2. Csirik, J., Bertholet, P., Bunke, H.: Pattern recognition in wireless sensor networks in presence of sensor failures (2011)
3. Frank, A., Asuncion, A.: UCI Machine Learning Repository, p. 213. University of California, School of Information and Computer Science, Irvine, CA (2010), http://archive.ics.uci.edu/ml
4. Nakamura, E.F., Loureiro, A.A.F.: Information fusion in wireless sensor networks. In: Proceedings of the 2008 ACM SIGMOD International Conference on Management of Data 2008, pp. 1365–1372. ACM, Vancouver (2008)
5. Bashyal, S., Venayagamoorthy, G.K.: Collaborative routing algorithm for wireless sensor network longevity. IEEE (2007)
6. Richter, R.: Distributed Pattern Recognition in Wireless Sensor Networks
7. Narasimhan, R., Cox, D.C.: A handoff algorithm for wireless systems using pattern recognition. IEEE (1998)
8. Song, M., Allison, T.: Frequency Hopping Pattern Recognition Algorithms for Wireless Sensor Networks
9. Wälchli, M., Braun, T.: Efficient signal processing and anomaly detection in wireless sensor networks. Applications of Evolutionary Computing, 81–86 (2009)
10. Yu, W., He, C.: Resource reservation in wireless networks based on pattern recognition. IEEE (2001)
11. Dziengel, N., Wittenburg, G., Schiller, J.: Towards distributed event detection in wireless sensor networks (2008)

12. Wittenburg, G., et al.: A system for distributed event detection in wireless sensor networks. ACM (2010)
13. MATLAB (January 20, 2012), http://www.mathworks.com.au/
14. Hall, M., et al.: The WEKA data mining software: an update. ACM SIGKDD Explorations Newsletter 11(1), 10–18 (2009)
15. (February 15, 2012), http://dwinnell.com/IndFeat.m
16. Cortez, P., Morais, A.J.R.: A data mining approach to predict forest fires using meteorological data (2007)

A Comprehensive Survey of the Feature Extraction Methods in the EEG Research

Mohammad A. Rahman, Wanli Ma, Dat Tran, and John Campbell

Faculty of Information Sciences & Engineering, University of Canberra, Australia
{Mohammad.Rahman,Wanli.Ma,Dat.Tran,
John.Campbell}@canberra.edu.au

Abstract. This survey paper categories, compares, and summaries from published technical and review articles in feature extraction methods in Electroence-phalography research and defines the feature, feature extraction, formalizes the relevance of the Electroencephalography data analysis in the health applications. Compared to all related reviews on feature extraction, this survey covers much more technical articles to the best of our knowledge, which describes most of the feature extraction methods used in the Electroencephalography related research domains.

Keywords: Electroencephalography, feature, feature extraction, classification, algorithm, brain computer interface (BCI), machine learning, and data mining.

1 Introduction

A feature is anything that can be determine as being either present or absent in the item [57] and feature extraction is a more general form of this idea; it tries to find new data rows that can be used in combination to reconstruct rows of the original dataset and rather than belonging to one cluster, each row is created from a combination of the features [57]. Feature extraction can be used as a preprocessor for applications including visualization, classification, detection, and verification [24] and extracting informative and discriminative features from EEG signals is often of crucial importance for representing and classifying patterns of brain activations [58].

Electroencephalography (EEG), a non-invasive tool to measure the electrical activity of the brain [2] is the most studied potential non-invasive interface for BCI implementation, among the brain activities monitoring techniques, mainly due to its low cost, ease of use, non-invasive nature, and comparatively easily recording brain signals. A brain computer interface (BCI) aims at translating brain signals into commands and it will be useful for people with severe motor impairments in order to restore communication and movement, on the other hand it could be a new interface for healthy people, e.g., in gaming applications[7]. EEG features extraction plays an important role in conjunction with methods that evaluate this feature in different scenarios such as detection or classification of EEG signals.

The primary objective of this paper is to define existing challenges in this domain for the different types of large data sets and streams. It categorizes, compares, and

Y. Xiang et al. (Eds.): ICA3PP 2012, Part II, LNCS 7440, pp. 274–283, 2012.
© Springer-Verlag Berlin Heidelberg 2012

summarizes relevant data mining-based fraud detection methods and techniques in published academic and industrial research. This paper is organized as follows. Section 2 introduces EEG and relationship between EEG and feature extraction methods. Section 3 shows different feature extraction methods used in the EEG signal processing. Finally, in Section 4 the principal conclusions with the further work are presented.

2   EEG - Electroencephalography

Electroencephalography (EEG) records electrical voltage fluctuations along the scalp of a person. It has a wide application in clinic practice, for example, in epilepsy diagnosis, patient coma monitoring, and brain damage assessment etc. EEG has also found a new application in brain-computer interface due to its non-invasive nature and ubiquitous accessibility. Researchers use the EEG signals collected to instruct computers to perform takes without the need of the traditional input device, such as computer keyboards and mice. Researchers also try to use EEG signals to measure the levels of activities of human brains [10, 61]. The measurements help the researchers to understand not only the activities of but also the health states of human brains, which may further help the health practitioners to improve their training methods, such as meditation and medical Qigong [19], on patients to improve their mental health.

The brain's electrical charge is maintained by billions of neurons. Using the volume conduction process the wave of the ions pumped by the membrane transport proteins can be measured. The difference of the two electrodes voltage over the time while the wave of the ions reaches the electrodes on the scalp generates the EEG. The EEGs are becoming increasingly important measurements of brain activities and they have great potentials for the diagnosis and treatment of mental and brain diseases and abnormalities. The study of the brain electrical activity, through the EEG records, is one of the most important tools for the diagnosis of neurological diseases [24, 5] such as epilepsy, brain tumor and development abnormalities [54].

A standard medical EEG device may have 19 or more electrodes. The device we use is developed by Emotiv [6] for human-computer interface purpose. It is called EPOC neuroheadset and has only 14 electrodes. The device is basically a headset with 14 electrodes attached. When taking EEG signals, the headset is worn by a subject. The electrodes then record the voltage fluctuations on the 14 locations where the electrodes contact the scalp and send them to a close-by computer via wireless transmission. In home environments without the supervision of a physician and absence of electromagnetic shielding, the raw EEG data, especially the most important alpha rhythm, which can be used to detect the mental illness and depression, is polluted by background noise such as Ocular Artifacts (OA), DC adrift and so on[48]. Last decade witnessed the development of cheap EEG devices, for example, EPOC from [20, 42] and increasing interest in EEG based human-computer interfaces.

The EEG is extremely difficult compared other biomedical signals [51] for an untrained observer to understand, partially as a consequence of the spatial mapping of functions onto different regions of the brain and electrode placement. Besides, data processing can be determination of reduced features set including only data needed for quantification, as in evoked response recordings, or feature extraction and subsequent pattern recognition, as in automated spike detection during monitoring for epileptic seizure activity [53].

3   Feature Extraction Methods

The EEG is based on electric signal and features extraction is used is to filter the signal to use in applications. Due to this feature of the EEG signals we categories the feature extraction into three groups such as signal based feature extraction, selection based feature extraction and feature extraction methods for the applications. In these sections we will discuss these three groups of feature extraction methods for EEG research.

3.1   Signal Based Feature Extraction Methods

A technique was proposed by [4] which performs Wavelet Packet Decomposition (WPD) of the EEG segments to obtain the wavelet coefficients at different levels and using Principal Component Analysis (PCA) determined the eigenvalues of these coefficients. A small set of highly significant features from the EEG segments have been extracted and uses them in simple classifiers to accurately classify them into normal, interictal or ictal classes by developing a CAD technique which is capable of classifying EEG segments with clinically acceptable accuracy using less number of features that can be extracted with less computational cost and can be used as an automated, simple, objective, fast, and cost-effective efficient secondary diagnostic tool that provides additional confidence to the clinician's initial diagnosis of the class of the EEG segment[4].

A new decomposing algorithm Haung–Hilbert transform method which is the combination of empirical mode decomposition (EMD) algorithm [31] and Hilbert transform [21] was proposed by [6] to analyze the EEG data to extract features, without any assumptions about the signal such as Fourier and Wavelet transforms. A versatile signal processing and analysis framework for Electroencephalogram (EEG) proposed to decompose into the frequency sub-bands using DWT and a set of statistical features was extracted from the sub-bands to represent the distribution of wavelet coefficients [55]. Principal components analysis (PCA), independent components analysis (ICA) and linear discriminant analysis (LDA) is used to reduce the dimension of data. A support vector machine (SVM) used to classify the EEG dataset using these features were used as an input to show the discrete outputs: epileptic seizure or not.

Three different schemes used by [18] to extract features from the EEG signal such as Relative spectral band energy, Harmonic parameters and Itakura distance. A feature extraction method for motor imagery single trial EEG classification was presented by [32] which used nonnegative matrix factorization (NMF) to select discriminative features in the time-frequency representation of EEG. The discrete wavelet transform (DWT) was proposed by [49] to process signal and signal segments to extract feature as an alternative to the commonly used discrete Fourier transform (DFT). Using a competitive neural network as one of methods of cluster analysis and processing, feature vectors belonging to separate signal segments are classified.

A new method of dimensionality reduction for time series data mining was proposed by [38]. This new method chooses the best coefficients for a set of time series is presented instead of using only the best coefficients and a criterion function is evaluated using all values of a coefficients position to determine a good set of coefficients. For many real life data sets much more energy can be preserved, which is advantageous for data mining tasks.

A technique was developed by [60] which remove irrelevant signal and subsequently extract key features from spatial patterns of EEG signal to perform classification using an optimal temporal filter, specifically, the proposed method transforms the original EEG signal into a spatial pattern and applies the RBF feature selection method to generate robust feature.

An individualized method for selecting Electroencephalogram (EEG) features and electrode proposed by [16] which applies an intelligent genetic search process to EEG signals simultaneously collected from multiple intracranial electrode contacts and multiple quantitative features derived from these signals and is trained on a series of baseline and preseizure records and then validated on other, previously unseen data using split sample validation techniques [16]. A continuous wavelet applied by [29] to analysis to the EEG signals to extract more precise information for the stages and a modified wavelet transform method is proposed and an extraction method of time series of peak frequency based on time-frequency analysis is introduced.

3.2 Selection Based Feature Extraction Methods

A novel fuzzy rule-based system used for detecting epileptic seizures in the IEEG recordings by [2]. This system has three stages such as processing band pass filtering, artifact detection and segmentation, extract feature and make decision based on the rule.

In the feature extraction stages a set of relevant features such as entropy, dominant frequency; average amplitude and coefficient of variation of amplitude were extracted from IEEG segments [2]. An autoregressive (AR) modeling approach used to and the dominant frequency for each IEEG segment, first the spectral frequency band was determined by an autoregressive (AR) modeling approach and used the parametric spectral estimation method because it reduces spectral losses and gives better frequency resolution in the case of short duration data records[30,22] and also Akaike's information criterion [31] to determine an appropriate AR model order for a good approximation of the shape of the power spectrum of seizure and non-seizure segments The Burg method [8], which is considered as an appropriate method for estimating high resolution power spectrum for short data sequences.

A methodology for the automatic detection of normal, pre-ictal, and ictal conditions proposed by [3] from recorded collected EEG signals to extract four entropy features. Seven different classifiers used these features as input to classify the EEG dataset. A solution proposed by [57] modeling the outputs of each electrode as a stochastic process by assuming that the stochastic process (representing the output of an electrode) is stationary and Markov and use conditional entropy feature to capture temporal dependences within an electrode and using mutual information-based features, capture dependences between pairs of electrodes. Classifying the EEG data from n-back tasks used to determine the usefulness of these features and also demonstrated its advantage over simple entropy and MI features that do not incorporate temporal information [57].

The adaptive common spatial patterns (ACSP) [51] which is an adaptive feature extractor is used to extract the most discriminative features related to the current brain states by the method of multi-class common spatial patterns (CSP) through the weighed update of signal covariance's and tested this adaptive feature extractor using the Pseudo-online simulations of EEG signal classification with a support vector machine (SVM) classifier for multi-class mental imagery tasks show the effectiveness of the proposed adaptive feature extractor. The last EEG segment used to update the feature extractor when the ACSP feature extractor is followed by a classification task in BCI applications, and then use the updated feature extractor to extract the features of the current segment [51]. Based on the extracted features, the classifier trained on the previous training sessions could give the estimated label of the current segment and this process runs iteratively as new EEG segments are continually recorded and sent for classification [51].

3.3   Feature Extraction Methods for Applications

The alpha extraction proposed [47] to extract the feature from the EEG dataset which used to design home care in OPTIMI which used to monitor levels of individual mental disorders and collect feedback during treatment using EEG signals. Four methods [47] used to extract the feature such as Decompose raw data, Construct the input mixed matrix and using FastICA, Independent Components (ICs) selection and Obtain the alpha wave using WPT.

A solution which extracted features from the distribution of the epileptic EEG signals, and used as inputs to a feed-forward back propagation neural network which is proposed by [52] and suggested [50] that an epileptic signal has components in both time and frequency, but the conventional time and frequency representations present only one aspect. A signal is localized in both time and frequency domains by means of computation of a time-frequency distribution. The pseudo Wigner-Ville and the smoothed-pseudo Wigner-Ville distribution [1, 56] used this technique.

An analysis of a new methodology for feature extraction in a BCI presented by [13] which is based on identifying the extent of ultrametricity from EEG time-series which was inspired by the idea that there are natural, not necessarily unique, tree or hierarchy structures defined by the ultrametric topology of EEG time-series to determine if coefficients which reflect the extent of ultrametricity can be used as distinct features of different EEG time series, recorded whilst subjects imagine left/right hand movements (motor imagery (MI)).

The familiar AR feature extraction technique traditionally applied in brain-computer interfacing extended by [10] to the ARX case where an evoked or event-related potential is employed as the exogenous input. The ARX model characterizes the signal into its constituent parts of noise (ongoing EEG) and signal (the ensemble average evoked or event-related potential) [11] and the coefficients of the model constitute the feature vector for subsequent classification.

The MIFX extraction algorithm using two-dimensional MI estimate was proposed by [43] to extract feature efficiently by creating a new feature such that the MI between the new feature and the target class is maximized and the redundancy is minimized. The proposed mutual information based feature extraction (MIFX) algorithm performed well in several experiments on different subjects and can improve the classification accuracy of the EEG patterns based on their test result and the results also show that the classification accuracy obtained by MIFX is higher than that achieved by full feature set as claimed by [43].

The coupling measures proposed by [58] which is an appropriate method for feature extraction in BCIs by comparing the performance of coupling features with that of the autoregressive (AR) feature. Moreover [58] suggested the combination of coupling and AR feature can effectively improve the classification accuracy due to their complementarities and used amplitude and phase coupling measures, quantified by a nonlinear regressive coefficient and phase locking value respectively to extract the features and determined these two measures based on three different coupling methods which is determined by neurophysiological a priori knowledge, and applied to a small number of electrodes of interest, leading to six feature vectors for classification. A novel feature extraction procedure (FEP) presented by [12] for extracting features from the electroencephalogram (EEG).

The combined wavelet transforms with basic detection theory used by [49] to develop a new unsupervised method for robustly detecting and localizing spikes in noisy neural recordings which does not require the construction of templates, or the supervised setting of thresholds, it is based on a Bayesian detector where the noise is modeled to be Gaussian in nature. A simulation was presented by [49] on actual EEG recordings under different recording conditions and also demonstrate that falsely detected spikes corresponding to their method resemble actual spikes more than the false positives of other techniques such as amplitude threshold.

A trainable feature extraction algorithm FuRIA proposed by[34] which stands for Fuzzy Region of Interest Activity for BCI which relies on linear and distributed inverse solutions which can learn and use subject-specific features for mental state classification. FuRIA aims at automatically identifying what are, for a given subject, the relevant Regions of Interest (ROI) and their associated frequency bands for the discrimination of mental states. The activity in these ROI and associated frequency bands can be used as features for any classifier.

4 Conclusion

Signal processing (i.e., feature extraction and translation) is a fundamental requirement for operation of brain–computer interfaces (BCIs), which take signals produced by the brain, and translates them into useful output commands with no intervention of muscles [39]. This survey has explored almost all published feature extraction studies and defines the adversary, performance metrics, and the methods and techniques used in feature extraction. After identifying the limitations in methods and techniques of feature extraction, this paper shows that this field can benefit from other related fields specially Single-trial analysis by [14].

References

1. Tzallas, A.T., Tsipouras, M.G., Fotiadis, D.I.: Automatic seizure detection based on time-frequency analysis and articial neural networks. Intell. Neuroscience 7(3), 1–13 (2007)
2. Aarabi, A., Fazel-Rezai, R., Aghakhani, Y.: A fuzzy rule-based system for epileptic seizure detection in intracranial EEG (2009)
3. Acharya, U., Filippo, S., Sree, V., Chattopadhyay, S., Ng, K., Suri, J.: Automated diagnosis of epileptic EEG using entropies (2011)
4. Acharya, U., Sree, S., Alvin, A., Suri, J.: Use of principal component analysis for automatic classification of epileptic EEG activities in wavelet framework (2012)
5. Adeli, H., Zhou, Z., Dadmehr, N.: Analysis of EEG Records in an Epileptic Patient Using Wavelet Transform. Methods 123(I), 69–87 (2003)
6. Cerutti, S., Chiarenza, G., Liberati, D., Mascellani, P., Pavesi, G.: A parametric method of identification of single-trial event-related potentials in the brain. IEEE Trans. Biomed. Eng. 35(9), 701–711 (1988)
7. Coyle, D., Prasad, G., Mcginnity, T.: Extracting Features for a Brain-Computer Interface by Self-Organising Fuzzy Neural Network-based Time Series Prediction. In: Proceedings of the 26th Annual International Conference of the IEEE EMBS San Francisco, CA, USA (2004)
8. Coyle, D., Mcginnity, T., Prasad, G.: Identifying Local Ultrametricity of EEG Time Series for Feature Extraction in a Brain-Computer Interface. In: Proceedings of the 29th Annual International Conference of the IEEE EMBS (2007)
9. Dornhege, G., Blankertz, B., Curio, G., Müller, K.: Combining features for BCI. In: Becker, S., Thrun, S., Obermayer, K. (eds.) Advances in Neural Inf. Proc. Systems (NIPS 2002), vol. 15, pp. 1115–1122 (2003)
10. Dressler, O., Schneider, G., Stockmanns, G., Kochs, E.: Awareness and the EEG power spectrum: analysis of frequencies. British Journal of Anaesthesia 93(6), 806–809 (2004)
11. D'Alessandro, M., Esteller, R., Vachtsevanos, G., Hinson, A., Echauz, J., Litt, B.: Epileptic Seizure Prediction Using Hybrid Feature Selection Over Multiple Intracranial EEG Electrode Contacts: A Report of Four Patients. IEEE Transactions on Biomedical Engineering 50(5) (2003)
12. Exarchos, T., Tzallas, A., Fotiadis, D., Konitsiotis, S., Giannopoulos, S.: A Data Mining based Approach for the EEG Transient Event Detection and Classification. In: Proceedings of the 18th IEEE Symposium on Computer-Based Medical Systems, CBMS 2005 (2005)

13. Estrada, E., Nazeran, H., Nava, P., Behbehani, K., Burk, J., Lucas, E.: EEG Feature Extraction For Classification Of Sleep Stages. In: Proceedings of the 26th Annual International Conference of the IEEE EMBS San Francisco, CA, USA, September 1-5 (2004)

14. Emotiv, BCI (March 17, 2012), http://www.emotiv.com (retrieved)

15. Freeman, W.J.: A neurobiological interpretation of semiotics: meaning, representation, and information. Information Sciences 124, 93–102 (2000)

16. Feldman, M.: Theoretical analysis and comparison of the Hilbert transform decomposition methods. Mech. Syst. Signal Process. 22(3), 509–519 (2008)

17. Gath, I., Feuerstein, C., Pham, D.T., Rondouin, G.: On the tracking of rapid dynamic changes in seizure EEG. IEEE Trans. Biomed. Eng. 39(9), 952–958 (1992)

18. Hild II, K., Erdogmus, D., Torkkola, K., Jose, C.: Feature Extraction Using Information-Theoretic Learning. IEEE Transactions on Pattern Analysis and Machine Intelligence 28(9) (September 2006)

19. Hazarika, N., Chen, Z., Tsoi, A.C., Sergejew, A.: Classification of EEG Signals Using the Wavelet Transform. Signal Process 59(I), 61–72 (1997)

20. Haselsteiner, E., Pfurtscheller, G.: Using time-dependant neural networks for eeg classication. IEEE Transactions on Rehabilitation Engineering 8, 457–463 (2000)

21. Hazarika, N., Chen, J., Tsoi, A., Sergejew, A.: Classification of EEG signals using the wavelet transform. Signal Process. 59(1), 61–72 (1997)

22. http://www.emotiv.com/store/hardware/epoc-bci/epoc-neuroheadset/ (cited on June 23, 2011)

23. Inoue, K., Tsujihata, T., Kumamaru, K., Matsuoka, S.: Feature Extraction of Human Sleep EEG Based on a Peak Frequency Analysis (2005)

24. Kim, D., Oh, H.S.: EMD: A package for empirical mode decomposition and hilbert spectrum. R J. 1(1), 40–46 (2009)

25. Kay, S.: Modern spectral estimation: theory and application. Prentice Hall, New Jersey (1988)

26. Lee, H., Cichocki, A., Choi, S.: Kernel nonnegative matrix factorization for spectral EEG feature extraction (2009)

27. Lee, H., Cichocki, A., Choi, S.: Nonnegative Matrix Factorization for Motor Imagery EEG Classification (2006)

28. Lotte, F., Lecuyer, A., Arnaldi, B.: FuRIA: An Inverse Solution based Feature Extraction Algorithm using Fuzzy Set Theory for Brain-Computer Interfaces. IEEE Transactions on Signal Processing X(X) (2009)

29. Lemm, S., Schafer, C., Curio, G.: Probabilistic modeling of sensorimotor mu rhythms for classication of imaginary hand movements. IEEE Transactions on Biomedical Engeneering 51(6), 1077–1080 (2004)

30. Lotte, F.: The use of Fuzzy Inference Systems for classification in EEG-based Brain Computer Interfaces. In: Proceedings of the Third International Brain-Computer Interface Workshop and Training Course, pp. 12–13 (2006)

31. Lotte, F., Lécuyer, A., Lamarche, F., Arnaldi, B.: Studying the use of fuzzy inference systems for motor imagery classification. IEEE Transactions on Neural System and Rehabilitation Engineering 15(2), 322–324 (2007)

32. Lotte, F., Congedo, M., Lecuyer, A., Lamarche, F., Arnaldi, B.: A Review of Classication Algorithms for EEG-based Brain-Computer Interfaces (2007)

33. Morchen, F.: Time series feature extraction for data mining using DWT and DFT (2003)

34. McFarland, D., Anderson, C., Müller, K., Schlögl, A., Krusienski, D.: BCI Meeting 2005—Workshop on BCI Signal Processing: Feature Extraction and Translation. IEEE Transactions on Neural Systems and Rehabilitation Engineering 14(2) (June 2006)
35. NeuroSky (March 17, 2012), http://www.neurosky.com/ (retrieved)
36. Butow, B., Mullan, P., Clarke, B., Beale, S., Pavlakis, P., Kothe, N., Lam, E., Rosenthal, D.: Impact of medical Qigong on quality of life, fatigue, mood and inflammation in cancer patients: a randomized controlled trial. Annals of Oncology 21(3), 608–614 (2010)
37. Obermeier, B., Guger, C., Neuper, C., Pfurtscheller, G.: Hidden markov models for online classication of single trial EEG. Pattern Recognition Letters, 1299–1309 (2001)
38. Oveisi, F., Erfanian, A.: A Tree-Structure Mutual Information-Based Feature Extraction and Its Application to EEG-Based Brain-Computer Interfacing. In: Proceedings of the 29th Annual International Conference of the IEEE EMBS, August 23-26 (2007)
39. Pfurtscheller, G., Neuper, C., Flotzinger, D., Pregenzer, M.: EEG-based discrimination between imagination of right and left hand movement. Electroencephalography and Clinical Neurophysiology 103, 642–651 (1997)
40. Pfurtscheller, G., Neuper, C.: Motor Imagery and Direct Brain-Computer Communication. Proceedings of the IEEE 89(7), 1123–1134 (2001)
41. Penny, W., Roberts, S.: EEG-based communication via dynamic neural network models. In: Proceedings of International Joint Conference on Neural Networks (1999)
42. Peng, H., Hu, B., Qi, Y., Zhao, Q., Ratcliffe, M.: An Improved EEG Denoising Approach in Electroencephalogram (EEG) for Home Care. In: 2011 5th International Conference on Pervasive Computing Technologies for Healthcare (PervasiveHealth) and Workshops (2011)
43. Prochazka, A., Kukal, J., Vysata, O.: Wavelet Transform Use for Feature Extraction and EEG Signal Segments Classification. In: 3rd International Symposium on Communications, Control and Signal Processing, ISCCSP 2008 (2008)
44. Ramachandran, N., Chellappa, A.K.: Feature Extraction from EEG using Wavelets: Spike Detection Algorithm. In: International Symposium on Modern Computing (JVA 2006), pp. 120–124 (2006)
45. Rivero, D., Fernandez-Blanco, E., Dorado, J., Pazos, A.: A New Signal Classification Technique by Means of Genetic Algorithms and kNN. IEEE (2011)
46. Sun, S., Zhang, C.: Adaptive feature extraction for EEG signal classification. In: International Federation for Medical and Biological Engineering (2006)
47. Smart, O., Maus, D., Marsh, E., Dlugos, D., Litt, B., Meador, K.: Mapping and mining interictal pathological gamma (30–100 Hz) oscillations with clinical intracranial EEG in patients with epilepsy (2012)
48. Subasi, A., Gursoy, M.: EEG signal classification using PCA, ICA, LDA and support vector machines (2010)
49. Ly, S., Li, Y.: Analysis and classification of EEG signals using a hybrid clustering technique. In: The 2010 IEEEIICME International Conference on Complex Medical Engineering (2010)
50. Segaran, T.: Programming Collective Intelligence Building Smart Web 2.0 Applications, p. 226 (August 2007)
51. Tzallas, A.T., Tsipouras, M.G., Fotiadis, D.I.: Epileptic Seizure Detection in EEGs Using Time-Frequency Analysis. IEEE Transactions on Information Technology in Biomedicine 13(5), 703–710 (2009)
52. Wu, L., Neskovic, P.: Feature extraction for EEG classification: representing electrode outputs as a Markov stochastic process. In: European Symposium on Artificial Neural Networks, pp. 567–572 (2007)

53. Wei, Q., Wang, Y., Gao, X., Gao, S.: Amplitude and phase coupling measures for feature extraction in an EEG-based brain–computer interface. IOP Publishing Ltd. (2007)
54. Wu, L., Neskovic, P.: Feature extraction for EEG classification:representing electrode outputs as a Markov stochastic process (2007)
55. Xu, W., Guan, C., Siong, C., Ranganatha, S., Thulasidas, M., Wu, J.: High Accuracy Classification of EEG Signal. IEEE (2004)
56. Lin, Y.-P., Wang, C.-H., Jung, T.-P., Wu, T.-L., Jeng, S.-K., Duann, J.-R., Chen, J.-H.: EEG-Based Emotion Recognition in Music Listening. IEEE Transactions on Biomedical Engineering 57(7) (2010)
57. Wu, L., Neskovic, P.: Feature extraction for EEG classification: representing electrode outputs as a Markov stochastic process. In: European Symposium on Artificial Neural Networks, pp. 567–572 (2007)
58. Wei, Q., Wang, Y., Gao, X., Gao, S.: Amplitude and phase coupling measures for feature extraction in an EEG-based brain–computer interface. IOP Publishing Ltd. (2007)
59. Wu, L., Neskovic, P.: Feature extraction for EEG classification:representing electrode outputs as a Markov stochastic process (2007)
60. Xu, W., Guan, C., Siong, C., Ranganatha, S., Thulasidas, M., Wu, J.: High Accuracy Classification of EEG Signal. IEEE (2004)
61. Lin, Y.-P., Wang, C.-H., Jung, T.-P., Wu, T.-L., Jeng, S.-K., Duann, J.-R., Chen, J.-H.: EEG-Based Emotion Recognition in Music Listening. IEEE Transactions on Biomedical Engineering 57(7) (2010)

Development of a Smart e-Health Portal
for Chronic Disease Management

Maryam Haddad and Girija Chetty

Faculty of Information Sciences and Engineering
University of Canberra, Australia
Maryam.haddad@canberra.edu.au

Abstract. In developed countries, chronic disease now accounts for more than 75% of health care expenditure and nearly an equivalent percentage of disease related deaths. In response to these changes in disease demographics and the economic imperatives caused by an aging population, service delivery models are shifting their focus from episodic care to continuity of care, from institutional care to community and home-based care, from disease treatment to disease prevention, and from an individual approach to a multidisciplinary team based approach. In this paper, we present the work in progress for a novel smart eHealth portal platform that supports patient empowerment and inclusiveness, due to integration of monitoring and decision support tools, the multimedia and Web 2.0 social networking components, and with design based on multi-layer security and scalability.

Keywords: e-Health Portal, Chronic Disease, Decision support.

1 Introduction

Health information technology has great potential to promote efficiency in patient care and increase patient provider communication, and patient engagement in their treatment [1]. Technology has been changing health care for more than a century, and with each new technological advancement—be it telephone, e-mail, the Internet, electronic health records (EHRs), personal health records (PHRs), or social media—there has been both celebration and apprehension [2, 3]. Practitioners see the advantages of efficiency and accessibility but often feel concerned by how each tool may overwhelm them as patients seek care or gain access to misinformation. Privacy is also a consideration [2]. As a result of these concerns, health care has been among the slowest to embrace advances in communication and information technology [4].

Yet technology holds the potential to improve both individual and organizational health outcomes [5, 6]. Moreover, increasing the patients' knowledge about their current risk factors, while facilitating collaboration with them to achieve their health goals, can improve clinical outcomes [7]. Portability, timeliness, efficiency [8], scalability [9, 10], and few barriers based on geography or mobility [11] could also be mentioned as advantages of e-health technology. E-health programs can be tailored [12], can deliver support as needed [45] and prevent relapse [13-17], increase access

Y. Xiang et al. (Eds.): ICA3PP 2012, Part II, LNCS 7440, pp. 284–291, 2012.
© Springer-Verlag Berlin Heidelberg 2012

to healthcare professionals, and may lower healthcare costs [18, 19]. With the introduction of the patient-centered medical home (PCMH) [20], opportunities exist for behavioral scientists to work with healthcare practices to design electronic technologies to achieve practice and patient goals [45].

The main focus of this study is on management of chronic diseases, particularly diabetes. Chronic illnesses account for 70% of deaths and for the expenditure of over 75% of direct health care costs [21], and direct costs are now estimated at over $1.5 trillion [22]. Chronic diseases are those that can only be controlled and not, at present, cured. They include diabetes, asthma, arthritis, heart failure, chronic obstructive pulmonary disease, dementia and a range of disabling neurological conditions [23]. Indirect costs of chronic diseases, in the form of lost productivity and non-reimbursed personal costs, add several more hundreds of billions of dollars each year.

Most diabetes management happens outside of clinics [24] yet patients look to healthcare providers for counseling and support. Unfortunately, due to limitations in staffing and reimbursement, counseling patients on diet, exercise, and other important self-management behaviors is not accomplished as part of routine primary care [25, 26]. Research shows that in-person interventions can improve behavioral and biologic outcomes [27-30], but questions remain about whether their relatively high cost might be reduced using technology without limiting their effectiveness. Well designed, patient-centered [20, 31-33] e-health technologies could enhance access to diabetes self-management programs and promote dissemination [34].

2   Motivation

The tools for active team based management in monitoring of chronic diseases is needed for next generation health care system, which can be achieved by tele-health technologies such as portals and web based systems. These tools and technologies can enhance collaborative patient care, involving health authorities and professionals, from national to International, from the doctor, to the specialists, to the hospital manager, nurses, radiology and data processing specialists, social security administrators and - of course - the patients, as well as individuals and community. Examples of different systems for collaborative health care systems include health information networks, electronic health records, radiological information systems, telemedicine services, personal wearable and portable communicable systems including those for medical implants, health portals, and many other ICT-based tools assisting disease prevention, diagnosis, treatment, health monitoring and lifestyle management for chronic diseases.

2.1   e-Health Data Integration

In Australia, NEHTA (National E-Health Transition Authority) was established by the Australian states governments to build up electronically and securely exchanging health information between healthcare providers. The project is expected to complete by the end of 2012 [35]. The outcome of the proposed research work might fit as a component in the Australian National E-health System. The research will utilize patient's histories, health information, radiological imaging data, and databases from the national EHRs (Electronic Health Records) for investigating next generation smart portals for chronic disease management. The research is expected to deliver some models and tools that integrate EHRs, HIS (Hospital Information systems) and RIS (radiological information systems), that can provide decision support to physicians and empower the patients in managing the chronic health conditions as follows:

- Providing diagnosing support: The aim is to design intelligent support tools that combines multiple information sources – the EHRs, the HIS data and RIS data for a better decision support for chronic disease management. (Better Evidence based diagnosis).
- Providing Patient Empowerment: The aim is to design communication , networking and social media tools to involve patient in the decision making loop, as chronic health conditions require close involvement of patient in better management of diseases

3   Current e-Health Systems

There are many e-health portals that have been developed using ICTs [36], but they are not designed for seamless collaboration for team based management needed for chronic health conditions. Further, they are not intelligent enough and they don't provide services in terms of analysis and decision support for pharmacological intervention. They also lack imaging support for managing radiological results, and web 2.0 features for patient empowerment. As an example of current e-health portals In Australia Insight Health could be mentioned which basically just lets users to subscribe to the newsletters, or give them health advice on the phone. Other similar health care websites just provide primitive information to the users and they have no tools for collaboration with other patients and support groups (e.g. Everydayhealth, Webmd, etc).

To address the objectives of this project, a smart based portal solution is proposed. Smart based solution allows the vision of virtual health care ecosystem to be realized. The proposed smart based portal can provide value to a variety of stakeholders such as:

- Support for Chronic disease management that allows patients to become part of a medical community, share concerns, resources, and participate in online moderated audio/video chats.
- Support for participation in Clinical trials, allowing patients and their families to search for, and enroll online, in clinical trials for new drugs and treatment plans. This is an excellent example of a Web application which serves both the consumer market and the pharmaceutical company market.
- Support for Teleradiology, where both referring and specialty physicians alike can access reports and images and videos without needing specialized and expensive picture archiving and communication systems (PACS).

- Support for Physician portals, connecting providers, patients, pharmacies, and payers. Patients schedule or request appointments online, access patient-provider messaging in a secure portal environment, and can search online "credentialed" health knowledge bases. For providers, staff can verify patient eligibility online, conduct insurance authorizations online, or send prescriptions to the pharmacy.
- Support for Automatic monitoring and decision support, with visual representation of vital health parameters measured with home based blood pressure, glucose monitors and fall detectors for elderly people. The visual representation of health parameters in terms of graphs, alerts and alarms can facilitate quicker consultations and referrals.

Inclusion of all of these features and capabilities in eHealth portals can represent dramatic improvements in physician workflow and can result in improved patient satisfaction.

4   Smart eHealth Portal Platform

To the best of our knowledge there is no vendor platform which allows implementation of this mentioned virtual ecosystem for eHealth. The proposed smart portal framework empowers patients to have an active role in managing their chronic conditions, and be easily connected to information and people for a better self-care. The preliminary work done so far involved:

- Development of automated decision support and diagnostic component for a diabetic case study using publicly available diabetes dataset
- Implementation of the decision support component in C# which would be then integrated in the smart web portal along with other collaboration, messaging, communication and multilayer access control components.

A brief description of the work in progress so far is described here:

4.1   Introducing Diabetes Case Study Using publicly Available Datasets

For the preliminary work towards development of decision support tools, we examined several established learning and classifier algorithms such as Decision Table, Random Subspace, Naïve Bayes, Logistic, and SMO for their forecasting/prediction of early onset of non-insulin dependent diabetes mellitus (DM) within a five-year period. These algorithms are capable of using a training data set to discover patterns in data. The data used in this preliminary study is from publicly available database available at UCI machine learning repository (http://archive.ics.uci.edu/ml/) from the Pima Indian population near Phoenix, Arizona. The development of decision support component involved using each of the learning algorithms and using a 10-fold cross validation with training and test sets from the database. The trained using 576 cases and each of the learning/classifiers were used to forecast whether another 192 test cases would develop diabetes within five years. Forcing the classifiers to conclude on all test cases produced an accuracy or (sensitivity and specificity) of 73.05 % for Decision Table, 74.74% for RandomSubspace, 75.78% for NaiveBayes, 76.82% for Logistic, 76.82% for SPegasos and 77.08% for SMO classifiers.

4.2   Case Study Population

The population for this study from the database was the Pima Indian population near Phoenix, Arizona. That population has been under continuous study since 1965 by the National Institute of Diabetes and Digestive and Kidney Diseases because of its high incidence rate of diabetes [37-39]. Each community resident over 5 years of age was asked to undergo a standardized examination every two years, which included an oral glucose tolerance test. Diabetes was diagnosed according to World Health Organization Criteria [21]; that is, if the 2 hour post-load plasma glucose was at least 200 mg/dl (11.1 mmol/l) at any survey examination or if the Indian Health Service Hospital serving the community found a glucose concentration of at least 200 mg/dl during the course of routine medical care [7]. In addition to being a familiar database to the investigators, this data set provided a well validated data resource in which to explore prediction of the date of onset of diabetes in a longitudinal manner.

4.3   Initial Results

The results show that sensitivity and specificity of 73.05 % for DecisionTable, 74.74% for RandomSubspace, 75.78% for NaiveBayes, 76.82% for Logistic, 76.82% for SPegasos and 77.08% for SMO classifiers (Table 1). According to (Table 2) the specificity results by using NaiveBayes classifier on single features have been calculated. The prototype decision support software with physical access (built using Visual Studio) is shown in Fig. 1 and Fig. 2.

Table 1. Classifier Vs. Accuracy

Classifier	Accuracy
DecisionTable	73.05%
RandomSubSpace	74.74%
NaiveBayes	75.78%
Logistic	76.82%
SPegasos	76.82%
SMO	77.08%

Table 2. NaiveBayes Classifier on Standalone Features

Feature	Accuracy
Age (years)	64.19%
Diastolic blood pressure (mm Hg)	64.45%
Triceps skin fold thickness (mm)	64.58%
Diabetes pedigree function	65.36%
2-Hour serum insulin (mu U/ml)	65.63%
Body mass index (weight in kg/(height in m)^2)	66.15%
Number of times pregnant	67.19%
Plasma glucose concentration a 2 hours in an oral glucose tolerance test	74.61%

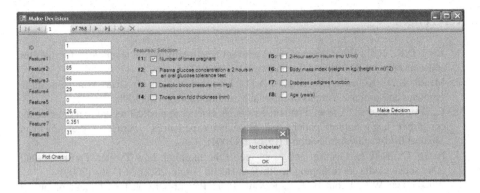

Fig. 1. Prototype Decision Support Software with Visualisation_1

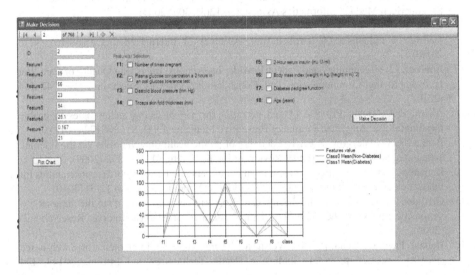

Fig. 2. Prototype Decision Support Software with Visualisation_2

5 Conclusion

In this paper, we propose a novel smart eHealth Portal for chronic disease management and report the work-in-progress for diabetic case study. The proposed smart eHealth Portal for diabetes management enhances the patient inclusiveness, by including decision support tools useful for creating alerts for prompt medical consultation. Further, with a publicly available diabetes datasets, we showed how the visualization can be included in the portal solution. Further work involves creating collaboration tools based on Web2.0 features, and multilevel access control components for physician, administrator and patient access, and integrations difference sources of health data in the portal platform

References

1. King, D.K., et al.: What patients want: relevant health information technology for diabetes self-management. Health and Technology, 1–11 (2012)
2. Mandl, K.D., Kohane, I.S., Brandt, A.M.: Electronic patient-physician communication: problems and promise. Annals of Internal Medicine 129(6), 495 (1998)
3. Earnest, M.A., et al.: Use of a patient-accessible electronic medical record in a practice for congestive heart failure: patient and physician experiences. Journal of the American Medical Informatics Association 11(5), 410 (2004)
4. Hawn, C.: Take two aspirin and tweet me in the morning: how Twitter, Facebook, and other social media are reshaping health care. Health Affairs 28(2), 361–368 (2009)
5. Winkelman, W.J., Leonard, K.J., Rossos, P.G.: Patient-perceived usefulness of online electronic medical records: employing grounded theory in the development of information and communication technologies for use by patients living with chronic illness. Journal of the American Medical Informatics Association 12(3), 306 (2005)
6. Grant, R.W., et al.: Practice-linked online personal health records for type 2 diabetes mellitus: a randomized controlled trial. Archives of Internal Medicine 168(16), 1776 (2008)
7. Boucher, J.L.: Technology and Patient-Provider Interactions: Improving Quality of Care, But Is It Improving Communication and Collaboration? Diabetes Spectrum 23(3), 142–144 (2010)
8. Ahern, D.K., et al.: Promise of and potential for patient-facing technologies to enable meaningful use. American Journal of Preventive Medicine 40(5), S162–S172 (2011)
9. Bennett, G.G., Glasgow, R.E.: The delivery of public health interventions via the Internet: actualizing their potential. Annual Review of Public Health 30, 273–292 (2009)
10. Bonander, J., Gates, S.: Public health in an era of personal health records: opportunities for innovation and new partnerships. Journal of Medical Internet Research 12(3) (2010)
11. Griffiths, F., et al.: Why are health care interventions delivered over the internet? A systematic review of the published literature. Journal of Medical Internet Research 8(2) (2006)
12. Hannah Faye, C., Thad, P., I.L., Welsh, R.: Neural responses to elements of a web-based smoking cessation program. Studies in Health Technology and Informatics 144, 174 (2009)
13. Oenema, A., et al.: Efficacy and use of an internet-delivered computer-tailored lifestyle intervention, targeting saturated fat intake, physical activity and smoking cessation: a randomized controlled trial. Annals of Behavioral Medicine 35(2), 125–135 (2008)
14. Vandelanotte, C., De Bourdeaudhuij, I., Brug, J.: Two-year follow-up of sequential and simultaneous interactive computer-tailored interventions for increasing physical activity and decreasing fat intake. Annals of Behavioral Medicine 33(2), 213–219 (2007)
15. Prochaska, J.O., et al.: Stage-based expert systems to guide a population of primary care patients to quit smoking, eat healthier, prevent skin cancer, and receive regular mammograms. Preventive Medicine 41(2), 406–416 (2005)
16. Glasgow, R.E., et al.: Outcomes of minimal and moderate support versions of an internet-based diabetes self-management support program. Journal of General Internal Medicine 25(12), 1315–1322 (2010)
17. Glasgow, R.E., et al.: Reach and effectiveness of DVD and in-person diabetes self-management education. Chronic Illness 5(4), 243–249 (2009)
18. Strecher, V.: Internet methods for delivering behavioral and health-related interventions (eHealth). Annu. Rev. Clin. Psychol. 3, 53–76 (2007)

19. Piette, J.D., et al.: Impact of automated calls with nurse follow-up on diabetes treatment outcomes in a department of Veterans Affairs health care system. Diabetes Care 24(2), 202–208 (2001)

20. Finkelstein, J., et al.: Patient-Centered Medical Home Cyberinfrastructure: Current and Future Landscape. American Journal of Preventive Medicine 40(5), S225–S233 (2011)

21. Catwell, L., Sheikh, A.: Evaluating eHealth interventions: the need for continuous systemic evaluation. PLoS Medicine 6(8), e1000126 (2009)

22. Car, J., et al.: The impact of eHealth on the quality and safety of healthcare. A Systemic Overview and Synthesis of the Literature. Imperial College London and The University of Edinburgh, London (2008)

23. Koufi, V., Malamateniou, F., Vassilacopoulos, G.: A Highly-Interactive and User-Friendly PHR Application for the Provision of Homecare Services. Smart Healthcare Applications and Services: Developments and Practices, 197 (2010)

24. Wagner, J.: Behavioral interventions to promote diabetes self management. Diabetes Spectrum 24, 61–62 (2011)

25. Jansink, R., et al.: Primary care nurses struggle with lifestyle counseling in diabetes care: a qualitative analysis. BMC Family Practice 11(1), 41 (2010)

26. Kolasa, K.M., Rickett, K.: Barriers to Providing Nutrition Counseling Cited by Physicians. Nutrition in Clinical Practice 25(5), 502–509 (2010)

27. Silberman, A., et al.: The effectiveness and efficacy of an intensive cardiac rehabilitation program in 24 sites. American Journal of Health Promotion 24(4), 260–266 (2010)

28. Lorig, K.R., et al.: A national dissemination of an evidence-based self-management program: a process evaluation study. Patient Education and Counseling 59(1), 69–79 (2005)

29. Toobert, D.J., et al.: Outcomes from a Multiple Risk Factor Diabetes Self-Management Trial for Latinas:Â!' Viva Bien! Annals of Behavioral Medicine 41(3), 310–323 (2011)

30. Toobert, D.J., et al.: Biologic and quality-of-life outcomes from the Mediterranean lifestyle program. Diabetes Care 26(8), 2288–2293 (2003)

31. Piette, J.D.: Interactive behavior change technology to support diabetes self-management. Diabetes Care 30(10), 2425–2432 (2007)

32. Reid, R.J., et al.: Patient-centered medical home demonstration: a prospective, quasi-experimental, before and after evaluation. Am. J. Manag. Care 15(9), e71–e87 (2009)

33. Seidman, J., Eytan, T.A.: Helping Patients Plug In: Lessons in the Adoption of Online Consumer Tools. California HealthCare Foundation (2008)

34. Schillinger, D., et al.: Effects of self-management support on structure, process, and outcomes among vulnerable patients with diabetes. Diabetes Care 32(4), 559–566 (2009)

35. Mangasarian, O.L., Wolberg, W.H.: Cancer diagnosis via linear programming. University of Wisconsin-Madison, Computer Sciences Department (1990)

36. Hlungulu, B., Thinyane, M.: Building an e-health component for a multipurpose communication centre for a marginalized community using FOSS (2010)

37. Bennett, P.H., Burch, T.A., Miller, M.: Diabetes mellitus in American (Pima) indians. The Lancet 298(7716), 125–128 (1971)

38. Knowler, W.C., et al.: Diabetes incidence and prevalence in Pima Indians: a 19-fold greater incidence than in Rochester, Minnesota. American Journal of Epidemiology 108(6), 497–505 (1978)

39. Knowler, W.C., et al.: Diabetes incidence in Pima Indians: contributions of obesity and parental diabetes. American Journal of Epidemiology 113(2), 144–156 (1981)

A Novel Approach to Protein Structure Prediction Using PCA Based Extreme Learning Machines and Multiple Kernels

Lavneet Singh, Girija Chetty, and Dharmendra Sharma

Faculty of Information Sciences & Engineering
University of Canberra, Australia
{Lavneet.singh,giriza.chetty,dharmendra.sharma}@canberra.edu.au

Abstract. In the area of bio-informatics, large amount of data is harvested with functional and genetic features of proteins. The structure of protein plays an important role in its biological and genetic functions. In this study, we propose a protein structure prediction scheme based novel learning algorithms – the extreme learning machine and the Support Vector Machine using multiple kernel learning, The experimental validation of the proposed approach on a publicly available protein data set shows a significant improvement in performance of the proposed approach in terms of accuracy of classification of protein folds using multiple kernels where multiple heterogeneous feature space data are available. The proposed method provides the higher recognition ratio as compared to other methods reported in previous studies.

Keywords: Support Vector Machines (SVM), Extreme Learning Machines (ELM), Protein Folding, Principal Component analysis (PCA), Linear Discriminant Analysis (LDA).

1 Introduction

There is an urgent need of transforming the large harvested human genomic sequences data using effective and efficient computational algorithms to extract the biological knowledge. The structure of protein plays an important role in its biological and genetic functions [1]. Past studies tried to predict protein folding patterns based on an approach involving comparison of between the unknown protein sequences, and the known protein sequences by computing sequence similarities. In contrast, several machine learning methods have been introduced for feature selection and classification to predict protein structures in various folds. Ding and Dubchak [2] proposed the approach based on Support Vector Machines (SVM) and Neural Networks (NN) classifiers. Shen and Chou [3] proposed a model based on nearest neighbor algorithm and it's modified nearest neighbor algorithm called K-local hyperplane (H-KNN) and was implemented by Okun [4]. Nanni [5] also proposed model using Fishers linear classifiers and H-KNN classifiers. Eddy [6] used Hidden Markov Model for protein folding recognition. M Madera and Ch. Lampros [7] and [8] also used the Hidden Markov Models but on reduce state space with small architecture.

Y. Xiang et al. (Eds.): ICA3PP 2012, Part II, LNCS 7440, pp. 292–299, 2012.

The major challenge in above mentioned methods and approaches lies in the complexity of data, which involve a large number of folding classes with only small number of training samples and multiple heterogeneous feature groups, making it harder for pattern discovery in protein folding prediction to reach more than 60%, which is below than normal classification in pattern recognition problems.

To deal with this problem, many studies have been formulated using the fusion and ensemble classifiers for protein fold recognition problems [9][10][11][12][13][14][15][21][22][23].

This ensemble fused classifiers are designed through combining a number of component classifiers on multiple set of features or attributes derived from different combinations of amino acids. For example, OET-KNN (Optimized Evidence-Theoretic K Nearest neighbors) classifier is modeled on each of the nine different feature groups in Shen and Chou [3]. Hence, the performance of ensemble classifiers can increase the classification accuracy of protein folding prediction.

In this paper, we propose a novel extreme learning machine algorithm using multiple kernel learning on preprocessed data using feature selection algorithms - the Principal Component Analysis (PCA) and the Linear Discriminant Analysis (LDA) for multi class protein fold recognition problem, where multiple heterogeneous feature space data are available. The results of our novel algorithm resulted in significant improvement in performance in terms of classification accuracy of protein folds.

2   Extreme Learning Machines

Unlike, traditional popular machine learning algorithms, new Extreme Learning Machine (ELM) [16] [17] [18] is based on single hidden layer feed forward neural networks (SLFNs) with additive neurons which randomly chooses the input weights and hidden neurons biases. Unlike traditional approaches such as Back Propagation (BP) algorithms, ELM doesn't need manual tuning parameters and local minima, providing fast and good classification accuracy rate. ELM doesn't have control parameters as learning epochs etc. and hidden neurons are chosen randomly based on Gaussian Probability Distribution and the output weights are calculated using simple generalized inverse method known as Moore-Penrose generalized pseudo inverse [19].

3   Support Vector Machines

The support vector machine (SVM) is a well-known large margin classifier proposed by Vapnik [13]. The basic concept of the SVM classifier is to find an optimal separating hyper- plane, which separates two classes. The decision function of the binary SVM is

$$f(x) = \sum_{i=1}^{N} \alpha_i y_i K(x_i, x) + b \qquad (1)$$

where b is a constant, $y_i \in \{-1,1\}$, $0 \leq \alpha_i \leq C$, I = 1,2,...............N are non-negative Lagrange multipliers, C is a cost parameter, that controls the trade-off between allowing training errors and forcing rigid margins, x_i are the support vectors and $K(x_i, x)$ is the kernel function.

We use the software LIBSVM library for experiments. LIBSVM is a general library for support vector classification and regression, which is available at http: //www.csie.ntu.edu.tw/~cjlin/libsvm. In this study, we also did comparisons with multiple kernels for better optimization.

3.1   The PCA/ LDA Based Extreme Learning Machines and Support Vector Machines Algorithm

Step 1: Use PCA on training and testing dataset

$$\hat{S} = \frac{1}{N} \sum_{j=1}^{K} \sum_{i=1}^{N_j} (x_{ji} - \hat{\mu})(x_{ji} - \hat{\mu})^T$$

Step2: Use LDA on training and testing dataset

$$\hat{S_W} = \frac{1}{N} \sum_{j=1}^{K} \sum_{i=1}^{N_j} (x_{ji} - \hat{\mu})(x_{ji} - \hat{\mu})^T$$

$$\hat{S_B} = \sum_{j=1}^{K} N_j (\mu_j - \mu)(\mu_j - \mu)^T$$

$$J(T) = \frac{\left| \hat{S}_B \right|}{\left| \hat{S}_W \right|} \quad \textit{Where J(T)=Linear Discriminant Function}$$

Given a training set

$$\hat{S} = \{(x_i, y_i) \in \Re^{m+n}, y_i \in \Re^m\}_{i=1}^{N} \sum \quad \text{, for activation function } g(x) \text{ and the}$$

number of hidden neurons $\hat{N}$;

Step2: For $k = 1,...,\hat{N}$ randomly assign the input weight vector $w_k \in \Re^n$ and bias $b_k \in \Re$.

Step3: Determine the hidden layer output matrix H .

Step4: Calculate H^+ .

Step5: Calculate the output weights matrix $\hat{\beta}$ by $\hat{\beta} = H^+T$.

Step 6: Calculate the decision function of SVM is

$$f(x) = \sum_{i=1}^{N} \alpha_i y_i K(x_i, x) + b)$$

We have used RBF, Sigmoid (Sig) and Linear (Lin) as activation functions in ELM and SVM. In later section, a comparative study has been shown on multi kernels with ELM respect to their learning classification accuracy rate. The parameters C from Eq. (1) and g have certain parametric value. Both values has been experimentally chosen, which was done using a cross-validation procedure on the training dataset. The best recognition ratio was achieved using parameter values gamma = 0.5 and C = 300.

4   Experiments

4.1   Dataset

In our experiments, we have used the features described by Ding and Dubchak [2]. All feature vectors are standardize and normalized to the range of [-1; +1] before applying any classifiers. The proteins in both the training and test sets belong to 27 different protein folds corresponding to four major structural classes: α, β, α/β, α+β. In this study, we compare classification results of protein folds by overall accuracy Q, which is defined as the percentage of correctly recognized proteins to all proteins in the test dataset which can be expressed as Q=c/n where c is the number query proteins whose folds have been correctly recognized and n is the total number of proteins in the test dataset. Table 1 shows extracted parameters from protein sequence with 125 dimensional feature vector for each protein in this dataset.

Table 1. Six Extracted features with their dimensions from Protein Sequence

Protein Features	Dimension
Amino Acids Composition	20
Predicted Secondary Structure	21
Hydrophobicity	21
Van der Waals Volume	21
Polarity	21
Polarizability	21

All the simulations for PCA-ELM and LDA-ELM are carried out in Matlab 10.0 environment running in Pentium dual core, 201 GHZ CPU. Figure 1 demonstrates the principal components (eigen values) of feature vectors of protein sequences.

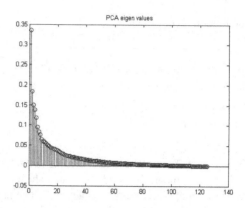

Fig. 1. PCA features of protein sequences

5   Results and Discussion

In this paper, we present a combined generative based classifier and use of feature selection algorithm for protein fold recognition. Table 2 explains the comparison between different methods used in terms of recognition ratio. In comparison with other methods, our proposed PCA and LDA based SVM classifier show higher accuracy rate up to 65.32% and 68.12%. Table 3 presents the recognition ratio of using multiple kernels with proposed PCA and LDA based SVM and PCA and LDA based ELM. It can be seen in Table 3 that in both classifiers, RBF kernels gives the higher accuracy rate comparative to other kernels. In addition, PCA and LDA based ELM classifier from Table 3 shows more promising results in terms of recognition rate upto 82.45% after 50 trials using RBF kernels. As a result, it can be seen that from all classifiers including SVM and proposed SVM, our proposed Extreme Learning Machines shows promising results in terms of higher accuracy rate of protein folds. Table 4 depicts the ELM training time and testing time ranging from 31.2 ms to 67.5 ms as a function of number of hidden neurons (N). This indicates a fast training process unlike training of a gradient descent based BPN which usually gets trapped in multiple local minima's and thus waste time.

Table 2. Comparison among different methods

Method	Recognition Ratio (%)
SVM	63.75
H-KNN	57.4
Bayesian Naives	52.30
Random Forest	53.72
MLP	54.72
LDA-SVM	65.32
PCA-SVM	68.12
LDA-ELM	77.67
PCA-ELM	82.45

Table 3. Comparison among different methods using multiple kernels

Method	Sigmoid Kernels	RBF Kernel	Linear Kernel
LDA-SVM	57.23	65.32	52.11
PCA-SVM	65.78	68.12	51.89
LDA-ELM	72.34	77.67	68.90
PCA-ELM	78.56	82.45	71.35

Table 4. Training and Testing Time computed time spans for PCA/LDA based ELM

Number of Hidden Neurons (N)	ELM Training Time (Sec)	Testing Time (Sec)
20	0.312	0.456
40	0.312	0.545
60	0.675	0.521

6   Conclusions and Future Work

In this study, we compared various classifiers and proposed an improved and more accurate hybrid ensemble classifiers based on Support Vector Machines (SVM and Extreme Learning Machines for protein folding recognition. In contrast to protein folds prediction, it's very hard to classify its various folds with its different amino acids attributes due to the limited training data availability. Our proposed classifier involves dimensionality reduction using PCA and LDA prior to classification This results in significant improvement in recognition accuracy. The combined PCA-SVM and LDA-SVM classifiers results in an accuracy of (65.32%) and (68.12%), as compared to SVM (56.70%) and other above mentioned classifiers. The similar PCA/LDA feature selection for Extreme Learning Machines also results in further improvement in terms of recognition accuracy up to (77.67%) and (82.45%). We also compare our proposed classifiers using multiple kernels approach resulting in promising results. Table 3 reveals that RBF Kernel give the better classification accuracy rate for both ELM and SVM classifiers compared to other kernels. These results seem to be very promising for classification for protein sequences as compared to results reported in the previous work.

Additionally, all our experiments were done on the original protein features developed by Ding and Dubchak [2]. Further work can be done using different feature selection and classification algorithms on other high dimensional protein sequences to reduce the computational power, more accuracy and higher recognition rate. Although, the obtained results are very encouraging, further experiments using different approaches such as SVM with binary decision trees and other ensemble hybrid classifiers will be investigated.

References

1. Chan, H.S., Dill, K.: The protein folding problem. Physics Today, 24–32 (February 1993)
2. Ding, C.H., Dubchak, I.: Multi-class protein folds recognition using support vector machines and neural networks. Bioinformatics 17, 349–358 (2001)
3. Shen, H.B., Chou, K.C.: Ensemble classifiers for protein fold pattern recognition. Bioinformatics 22, 1717–1722 (2006)
4. Okun, O.: Protein fold recognition with k-local hyperplane distance nearest neighbor algorithm. In: Proceedings of the Second European Workshop on Data Mining and Text Mining in Bioinformatics, Pisa, Italy, pp. 51–57 (2004)
5. Nanni, L.: A novel ensemble of classifiers for protein folds recognition. Neurocomputing 69, 2434–2437 (2006)
6. Eddy, S.R.: Hidden Markov models. Current Opinion in Structural Biology 6, 361–365 (1995)
7. Madera, M., Gough, J.: A comparison of profile hidden Markov model procedures for remote homology detection. Nucleic Acids Research 30(19), 4321–4328 (2002)
8. Lampros, C., Papaloukas, C., Exarchos, T.P., Golectsis, Y., Fotiadis, D.I.: Sequence-based protein structure prediction using a reduced state-space hidden Markov model. Computers in Biology and Medicine 37, 1211–1224 (2007)
9. Lampros, C., Papaloukas, C., Exarchos, K., Fotiadis, D.I.: Improving the protein fold recognition accuracy of a reduced state-space hidden Markov model. Computers in Biology and Medicine 39, 907–914 (2009)
10. Shen, H.B., Chou, K.C.: Hum-mPLoc: an ensemble classifier for large-scale human protein subcellular location prediction by incorporating samples with multiple sites. Biochemical and Biophysical Research Communications 355, 1006–1011 (2007)
11. Ghanty, P., Pal, N.R.: Prediction of protein folds: Extraction of new features, dimensionality reduction and fusion of heterogeneous classifiers. IEEE Transactions on Nano-bioscience 8, 100–110 (2009)
12. Guo, X., Gao, X.: A novel hierarchical ensemble classifier for protein folds recognition. Protein Engineering, Design and Selection 21, 659–664 (2008)
13. Kechman, V., Yang, T.: Protein folds recognition with adaptive local hyperplane algorithm. In: Proceedings of IEEE Symposium on Computational Intelligence in Bioinformatics and Computational Biology, Nashville, TN, USA, pp. 75–78 (2009)
14. Chmielnicki, W., Stapor, K.: A hybrid discriminative/generative approach to protein fold recognition. Neurocomuting, 194–198 (2012)
15. Zhang, C.X., Zhang, J.S.: RotBoost: a technique for combining rotation forest and adaboost. Pattern Recognition Letters 29, 1524–1536 (2008)
16. Lin, M.-B., Huang, G.-B., Saratchandran, P., Sudararajan, N.: Fully complex extreme learning machine. Neurocomputing (68), 306–314 (2005)
17. Huang, G.-B., Zhu, Q.-Y., Siew, C.K.: Extreme Learning Machine: Theory and Applications. Neurocomputing (70), 489–501 (2006)
18. Huang, G.-B., Zhu, Q.-Y., Siew, C.K.: Real-Time Learning Capability of Neural Networks. IEEE Transactions on Neural Networks 17(4), 863–878 (2006)
19. Serre, D.: Matrices: Theory and Applications. Springer Verlag, New York Inc. (2002)
20. Vapnik, V.: The Nature of Statistical Learning Theory. Springer, New York (1995)

21. Mishra, A., Singh, L., Chetty, G.: A Novel Image Water Marking Scheme Using Extreme Learning Machine. In: Proceedings of IEEE World Congress on Computational Intelligence (WCCI 2012), Brisbane, Australia (2012)
22. Singh, L., Chetty, G.: Hybrid Approach in Protein Folding Recognition using Support Vector Machines. In: Proceedings of International Conference on Machine Learning and Data Mining (MLDM 2012), Berlin, Germany. LNCS. Springer (2012)
23. Singh, L., Chetty, G.: Review of Classification of Brain Abnormalities in Magnetic Resonance Images Using Pattern Recognition and Machine Learning. In: Proceedings of International Conference of Neuro Computing and Evolving Intelligence, NCEI 2012. LNCS Bioinformatics. Springer, Heidelberg (2012)

A Novel Approach to Guarantee Causal Message Ordering in Pre-planned Wireless Sensor Networks

Chayoung Kim and Jinho Ahn[*]

Dept. of Computer Science, College of Natural Science, Kyonggi University
Suwon, Gyeonggi-do 443-760, Republic of Korea
{kimcha0,jhahn}@kgu.ac.kr

Abstract. Data fusion often depends on the time of occurrence of fused sensor readings, called as temporal ordering, which is defined with respect to a single message, or as causal ordering to guarantee dependency relationships between messages in many-to-many communication patterns. There are some temporal ordering protocols based on physical time synchronization in publish/subscribe (P/S) paradigm of wireless sensor networks, but there exist little research works on development of causal ordering protocols based on logical time in P/S of wireless sensor networks (WSNs). Causal message ordering is more useful for most distributed applications in which a large number of sensor nodes request cooperating to fuse their data in WSNs. Temporal ordering is not sufficient for these distributed applications because it is not defined for dependency relationships between these messages. Also, many-to-many communication patterns attempt to address the problem of providing scalability of data propagation, guaranteeing message delivery order and supporting overlapping multicast groups in WSNs. In this paper, we present a novel approach based on gossiping and firefly synchronization instead of physical time synchronization, guaranteeing the causal message ordering property in P/S of WSNs. In the proposed protocol, every sensor broker disseminates the multicast message including the latest time-stamped information that represents the gossip round in which the message is generated to subscribers for causal message ordering. The latest time-stamped information is represented using colors. Its scalability feature might be highly suitable for the area of the applications requiring only the minimum causal information of message delivery with flexible consistency by cooperating to fuse their data.

Keywords: Sensor network, Group communication, Publish/Subscribe, Scalability, Reliability.

1   Introduction

A wireless sensor network (WSN) consists of a large number of cooperating small-scale nodes capable of wireless communication and sensing [1], [11]. In many applications including geophysical monitoring, habitat monitoring, military systems,

---

[*] Corresponding author.

Y. Xiang et al. (Eds.): ICA3PP 2012, Part II, LNCS 7440, pp. 300–309, 2012.

and business processes, WSNs fulfill complex monitoring tasks [9], [11]. The complex tasks of WSNs are achieved through data fusion, the process of correlating individual sensor readings originating from various nodes into high-level sensing results and often depending on the time of occurrence of fused sensor readings, called as temporal ordering [9], [11]. The temporal ordering [11] is somewhat similar to FIFO property, i.e., the messages will arrive at the receiver in the same order in which the sender sent them. In [11], temporal ordering maintains logical ring structure and provides mechanisms specifying producers to generate sensor events and consumers to want to receive them like in P/S (publish/subscribe) paradigm based on physical time synchronization [6], [10]. So, the protocol [11] is suitable for typical WSN applications like object tracking above mentioned. Recently, there are some protocols for physical time synchronization [6], [10]. But the physical synchronization is a non-trivial problem in sensor networks.

Some protocols, like the protocol in [13], can be applied to many completely decentralized distributed P2P applications such as ubiquitous computing and sensor networks without physical synchronization. In [13], the protocol is based on gossiping and firefly synchronization [12], for the management policy distribution and synchronization over a number of nodes in an application level. Our proposed protocol can be applied to WSN applications like as temporal ordering [11], but it is not physical time synchronization [6], [10]. Our proposed protocol is based on gossiping for completely decentralized distributed applications like in [4] and guarantees causal message ordering, which is somewhat similar to temporal message ordering, based on logical time only.

Our proposed protocol is suitable for distributed applications, in which queries can be much more complex, involving multiple sensors or types of sensors [8]. Causal message ordering is more useful for these distributed applications in which a large number of sensor nodes request cooperating to fuse their data in wireless multiple sensor-typed networks [8], and defined with respect to dependencies between these sensor messages. Temporal ordering [11] is not sufficient for these distributed applications, since it guarantees only FIFO ordering, which is defined with respect to a single message, not to dependencies between these messages.

Therefore we propose a novel approach based on gossiping and firefly synchronization [12] like in as an environment of [13], guaranteeing the causal message ordering in wireless multiple sensor-typed networks [8]. Our proposed protocol is also designed for processing many-to-many communication patterns, leading to make overlapping multicast groups and allowing decoupling between senders and receivers to interact with publishers and subscribers like in producers/consumers mechanisms of temporal ordering [11]. P/S sensors designed as brokers might aggregate the information of the results based on the subscribers' interests, while guaranteeing causal message ordering. The subscribers receive the results aggregated by their brokers by gossip-style dissemination protocols. Recently, gossip protocols seem more appealing in many P/S systems because they are more scalable than traditional reliable broadcast [3] and network-level protocols derived from IP Multicast for the various applications requiring reliable dissemination of events [2]. Gossip protocols have turned out to be adequate for large scale settings by achieving a "high degree of reliability" and strong message delivery ordering guarantees offered by deterministic approaches [2], [4], [5]. Gossip protocols take O(logN) rounds to reach all nodes, where N is the number of nodes. The seminal probabilistic broadcast (pbcast) algorithm of Birman et. al. [2] is originally described as a broadcast presented in the system based on global view and Eugster's algorithm (lpbcast) [4] is implemented for P/S systems as a broadcast based on local view.

In the proposed protocol, because every broker knows about each other, it manages a vector per broker group representing its knowledge for each member of the group, whose element has the number of multicast messages sent to other brokers by this member within this group. In [2], each member has to manage a vector per group and each message should include the whole set of these vectors. On the other hand, in the proposed protocol, every broker disseminates the multicast message including the time-stamped information that represents the gossip round in which the message is generated to subscribers. The time-stamped information is represented using colors. If two messages A and B are generated in different gossip rounds respectively, they can be represented in two different colors. The latest time-stamped information represented in colors of all sensor brokers are also piggybacked on each multicast message and is transmitted to subscribers because the subscribers can verify the observation of causal ordering relation among all messages which sensor brokers have received or sent before this message. That is, the proposed protocol needs a vector, which size is the number of brokers because one color represents only one sensor broker. Therefore, this protocol is appropriate for sensor networks in a pre-planned manner based on firefly synchronization [12] because every sensor broker knows about each other and owns its local clock without global synchronization.

Its features might result in its very low cost communication overhead between brokers and subscribers because of the one-dimensional vector for causal ordering. Its scalability feature might be highly suitable for the area of the applications requiring only the minimum causal information of message delivery with flexible consistency by fusing their data.

2   The Proposed Protocol

2.1   Basic Idea

In this paper, we propose a novel approach based on time-stamped anti-entropy gossiping and firefly synchronization [12] like in an environment of [13], for causal message ordering in wireless multiple sensor-typed networks [8]. Sensor brokers are selected from all of the sensor nodes which are deployed in a pre-planned one. In [11], the protocol provides mechanisms specifying producers to generate sensor events and consumers to want to receive them, like in P/S (publish/subscribe) paradigm. So, our proposed protocol is also designed for processing many-to-many communication patterns, leading to make overlapping multicast groups and allowing decoupling between senders and receivers to interact with publishers and subscribers. P/S sensors designed as brokers might aggregate the information of the results based on the subscribers' interests, while guaranteeing the causally ordered delivery of messages. The subscribers receive the results aggregated by their chosen brokers by gossip-style dissemination protocols. Recently, research on P/S in wireless sensor networks [8] has mainly focused on mobile subscribers and publishers relying on a fixed broker infrastructure to support them. We can see that each sensor broker manages a sensor grid and a moving subscriber marked in red can migrate to another sensor grid in figure 1.

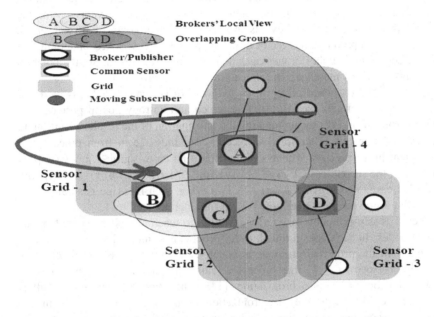

Fig. 1. A Wireless Sensor Network

In the proposed protocol, because every broker knows about each other, it manages a vector per broker group representing its knowledge for each member of the group, whose element has the number of multicast messages sent to other brokers by this member within this group. In [2], each member has to manage a vector per group and each message should include the whole set of these vectors. On the other hand, in the proposed protocol, every broker disseminates the multicast message including the time-stamp information that represents the gossip round in which the message is generated to subscribers. The time-stamped information is represented using colors. If two messages A and B are generated in different gossip rounds respectively, they can be represented in two different colors. The latest time-stamped information represented in colors of all sensor brokers is also piggybacked on each multicast message and is transmitted to subscribers because the subscribers can verify the observation of causal ordering relation among all messages which sensor brokers have received or sent before this message. That is, the proposed protocol needs a vector, whose size is the number of brokers because one color represents only one sensor broker. Therefore, this protocol is appropriate for sensor networks in a pre-planned manner based on firefly synchronization [12] because every sensor broker knows about each other and owns its local clock without global synchronization.

2.2   Algorithm Description

In this section, we describe our proposed protocol through an example of figure 3, which shows how in detail each broker generates a multicast message and aggregates causally ordered delivery information. The proposed protocol manages a vector per group and each message has to include the whole set of all vectors among brokers. A vector [3] piggybacked on each message is dealing with the notation of maintaining the causal relationship that holds among "message send" events with the corresponding "message receive" events. As same as the protocol of Birman et. al. [3], in our proposed protocol, the vector time-stamp (VT) piggybacked on a multicast message m counts the number of messages that causally precedes m. So, the notation $VT_\alpha[i]$ counts multicast messages sent in the group g_α by a process i.

Therefore, in our proposed protocol, the protocol of Birman et. al.[3] is modified for the overlapping groups based on time-stamped anti-entropy gossip protocol and firefly synchronization [12] by aggregating the information of the results according to the subscribers' interests. Therefore, on reception of message m from process $p_i \neq$ process p_j sent in g_α, process p_j delays m until the first case, $\forall g:(g \in g_j): VT_g(m)[i] = VT_g(p_j)[i] + 1$, the second case, $\forall g:(g \in g_j): \wedge \forall k:(pj \in gj \wedge k \neq i): VT_g(m)[k] \leq VT_g(p_j)[k]$, and the third case, $\forall g:(g \in gj): VT_g(m) \leq VT_g(p_j)$. For each message generated by a process j, all group vectors, $\forall g:(g \in g_j): VT_g(p_j)$ are incremented by 1.

In general, gossip protocols take $O(\log_N)$ rounds to reach all nodes, where N is the number of nodes. In each gossip round, every process has initiated a gossip message exactly once. In the proposed protocol, although every process has a local clock, it periodically gossips to $f \geq 1$ other processes (called as fan-out or gossip targets) at random based on firefly synchronization [13]. The synchronization of fireflies flashing can be likened to the synchronization of messages in [12]. So, in our proposed protocol based on this synchronization, each gossip round can be characterized as a unique notation represented using a color. This proposed protocol needs $\log_N + \alpha$ colors because the maximum number of gossip rounds in which all processes receive all messages eventually is $\log_N$ and α may be application specific for buffering. So, if two messages m and m' have been sent at the same gossip round, then they are independent of each other and represented in the same color.

This example of figure 2 shows how in detail each broker participating in $G_1 = \{A, B, C\}$ and $G_2 = \{A, C, D\}$ aggregates the information of causally ordered delivery sent to subscribers. The example of figure 2 sets α to 1. So, the example needs 3 colors because $\log_N$ is 2 and α is 1. In the protocol, although the stale messages might be removed periodically to respect the maximum number of gossip rounds, some processes might be possible to hold the stale messages, which are able to be gossiped about after the maximum number of gossip rounds because each process has its own clock without global synchronization. So, the proposed protocol uses the epoch distinguishing new message from previous message sent by the same process, which is incremented by 1 whenever all colors have been completed exactly once. That is, the color can help subscribers decide what messages are immediately preceding others when the new different colored messages are received. The epoch can make a process to verify which one is preceding when the two same color messages are received.

- Group1 = {A,B,C}, Group2 = {A,C,D}
- If N is 4, MAX Gossip-Round is logN=2.
- We need (logN+1)=3 different colors .

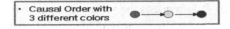

1st	2nd	3rd	4th
● A₁ G1:⟨1,0,0,∗⟩ G2:⟨1,∗,0,0⟩	○ A₁ G1:⟨2,0,0,∗⟩ G2:⟨2,∗,0,0⟩	● B₁ G1:⟨2,1,0,∗⟩ G2:⟨2,∗,0,1⟩	● A₂ G1:⟨3,1,0,∗⟩ G2:⟨3,∗,0,1⟩
	○ D₁ G1:⟨1,0,0,∗⟩ G2:⟨1,∗,0,1⟩		● B₂ G1:⟨3,2,0,∗⟩ G2:⟨3,∗,0,1⟩

Fig. 2. Each gossip round represented in each color

In figure 2, in the first round, broker A generates the first multicast message and makes it tagged with ID "A", the epoch "1" and the current gossip round color "red", denoted "red$_{A1}$". In the second round, brokers A and D generate each message, and make it tagged with ID "A" and "D", the epoch "1" and the current gossip round color "yellow", denoted "yellow$_{A1}$" and "yellow$_{D1}$", respectively. In the third round, B generates the multicast message and makes it tagged with ID "B", the epoch "1" and the current gossip round color "blue", denoted "blue$_{B1}$". And the epoch is incremented by 1 because all colors have been completed exactly once. So, in the fourth round, brokers A and B generate each message, and make it tagged with ID "A" and "B", the epoch "2" and the current gossip round color "red", denoted "red$_{A2}$" and "red$_{B2}$", respectively.

Figure 3 shows how in detail broker groups G_1={A,B,C} and G_2={A,C,D} gossip about the multicast messages including the vector, whose element is the latest gossip round time-stamps represented using colors, which mean when the last time was each broker sent its message to subscribers={S_1,S_2,S_3,S_4}. In the proposed protocol, every broker disseminates the multicast message including the vector because it can verify the observation of causal ordering relation among all messages which sensor brokers have received or sent before this message. In the example of Figure 3, subscriber S_1 subscribes to C in G_1, S_2 and S_3 subscribe to A or B in both G_1 and G_2, and S_4 subscribe to D in G_2. The current colors in the vector are all ⌀ at the beginning. Each broker makes causal ordering of the messages like "red$_{A1}$"   -> "yellow$_{A1}$" = "yellow$_{D1}$" -> "blue$_{B1}$" -> "red$_{A2}$" = "red$_{B2}$". S_1 receives all the messages from broker B. It discards all messages received from broker D without delivering them to the application layer because it does not belong to G_2. On receiving the yellow message from broker A indexed by epoch "1", denoted "yellow$_{A1}$", S_2 requests the red message to broker A indexed by epoch "1", denoted "red$_{A1}$" because it knows that from the piggybacked information of the vector of all the latest gossip round time-stamps represented in colors of all brokers. And on receiving the red message from broker A indexed by epoch "2", denoted "red$_{A2}$", S_2 requests the blue message to broker B indexed by epoch "1", denoted "blue$_{B1}$". S_3 requests all messages to the sending brokers after receiving the red message from broker B indexed by epoch "2", denoted "red$_{B2}$". On receiving the yellow message from broker A indexed by epoch "1", denoted "yellow$_{A1}$", S_2 requests the red message to broker A indexed by epoch "1", denoted "red$_{A1}$". On receiving the red message from broker A indexed by epoch "2", denoted "red$_{A2}$", S_2 requests the yellow message to broker D indexed by epoch "1", denoted "yellow$_{D1}$". And S_4 discards all messages from broker B because it does not belong to G_1.

As figure 3 shows, in this proposed protocol, brokers disseminate the information of the vector , whose element is the latest gossip round time-stamps represented using colors, which mean when the last time was each broker sent its message to subscribers for guaranteeing causally ordered message delivery. The size of the vector is the number of brokers because one color represents only one sensor broker. It is surely the main cause of highly scalable, guaranteeing flexible consistency.

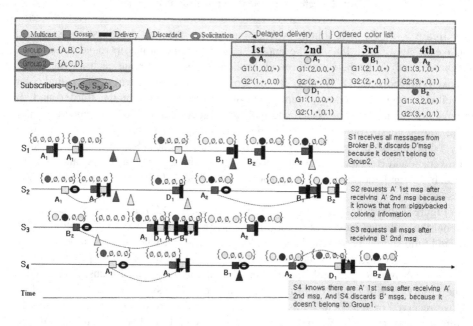

Fig. 3. An example of the vector of the latest gossip rounds from sensor brokers to subscribers

2.3   Proof of the Protocol

Basic idea.
We develop a delivery protocol by which each subscriber S receives messages sent by its broker. Subscriber S delivers them to the application layer only if the messages immediately preceding them have been delivered to S. Otherwise, the messages are not delivered immediately but are buffered until the messages immediately preceding them are delivered. A vector piggybacked on each message, VT_m indicates precisely which multicast messages by broker B_i immediately precede m. A subscriber of m will delay m until VT_m messages have been delivered from B_i. Before multicasting a message m, a broker B_i posts the current gossip round time-stamp on m(in the

proposed protocol, the current gossip round time-stamp is represented using a unique color) and inserts the gossip round time-stamps of the messages immediately preceding m into VT_{Bi}. That is, VT_{Bi} indicates which messages from B_i precede immediately m.

A subscriber S, upon receiving message m including VT_m from B_i, delays its delivery until:

Rule 1:

The gossip round time-stamp of $VT_S[k]$ is as same as that of $VT_m[k]$ for $\forall \in k\{1, 2, ..., n\}$ - i and when k=i, the gossip round time-stamp of $VT_S[k]$ is one-step earlier than that of $VT_m[k]$. This step ensures that subscriber S has received all the messages from B_i that precede m.

1. Causality is never violated (Safety).

Proof:

Consider the actions of a subscriber that receives two messages m_1 and m_2 such that $m_1 \rightarrow m_2$. In this case, m_1 is preceding m_2. So, m_1 and m_2 are generated in the different gossip round by any broker B_i. So, they have different time-stamps each other. By induction on the messages received by subscriber S that m_2 cannot be delivered before m1. Assume that m1 has not been delivered and that subscriber S has received k messages. Since $m_1 \rightarrow m_2$, hence the gossip round time-stamp of VT_{m1} is one-step earlier than that of VT_{m2},

We have the gossip round time-stamp of $VT_{m1}[B_i]$ is one-step earlier than that of $VT_{m2}[B_i]$. -------------------- Relation(1)

Base step:

The first message delivered by S cannot be m_2. Recall that if no messages have been delivered to S, $VT_S[B_i]=0$. However, the gossip round time-stamp of $VT_{m1}[B_i]$ is not one-step earlier than that of $VT_S[B_i]$. (because m_1 is sent by B_i), hence the gossip round time-stamp of $VT_{m2}[i]$ is not one-step earlier than that of $VT_S[B_i]$. By the rule, m_2 cannot be delivered by S.

Inductive step:

Suppose S has received k messages, none of which is a message m such that $m_1 \rightarrow m$. If m1 has not yet been delivered, then

The gossip round time-stamp of $VT_S[B_i]$ is one-step earlier than that of $VT_{m1}[B_i]$. ------------ Relation(2)

From relations (1) and (2) it follows that the gossip round time-stamp of $VT_S[B_i]$ is two-step earlier than that of $VT_{m2}[B_i]$. By application of the rules of the proposed protocol, The *k+1st* message delivered by S cannot be m2.

2. In the absence of failures, every message in overlapping groups is indeed delivered (liveness).

Suppose there exists a multicast message m sent by process Bi that can never be delivered to subscriber S. The rule implies that either

$\exists$ k s.t. the gossip round time-stamp of $VT_S[k]$ is one-step earlier than that of $VT_m[k]$ for k=i, or the gossip round time-stamp of $VT_S[k]$ is earlier than that of $VT_m[k]$, for k≠i.

We consider these cases in turn.

The gossip round time-stamp of $VT_S[k]$ is one-step earlier than that of $VT_m[k]$.

That is, m is not the next message to be delivered to S. Notice that only a finite number of messages can precede m. Since all message are multicast to all processes and channels are lossless and sequenced, it follows that there must be some message m' sent by B_i has not yet delivered, and this is the next message from B_i, i.e., the gossip round time-stamp of $VT_S[k]$ is one-step earlier than that of $VT_m[k]$. If m' is also delayed, it must be under the other case.

$\exists$ k≠i, s.t. The gossip round time-stamp of $VT_S[k]$ is earlier than that of $VT_m[k]$.

There must be some message m'$\rightarrow$m that has either not been received at S, or was received and is delayed. Under the hypothesis that all messages are sent to all processes, m' was already multicast to S. Since the communication system eventually delivers all messages, we may assume that m' has been received by S. The same reasoning that was applied to m can now be applied to m'. The number of messages that must be delivered before m is finite and $\rightarrow$ is acyclic, hence this leads to a contradiction.

3   Conclusions

In this paper, we present a causal order multicast protocol for sensor brokers to aggregate the results in pre-planned wireless sensor networks and to periodically gossip about the results for letting potential consumers subscribe according to their interest topics. In some distributed applications, because queries can be much more complex, involving multiple sensors or types of sensors, various kinds of phenomenon are determined by fusing time-stamped proximity detections at different locations. So, causal ordering protocol from multiple sensors can be applied to such distributed applications, because it is defined with respect to dependency relationships between their messages. Therefore, we propose a novel approach based on time-stamped anti-entropy gossiping and firefly synchronization for causal message ordering among a large number of multicast messages. In the proposed protocol, a sensor broker generates a message m, posts the latest gossip round time-stamp represented using a unique color on the multicast message m. The broker inserts the latest gossip round time-stamps represented using colors, which mean when the last time was each broker sent its message to a one-dimensional vector of length N, where N is the number of brokers in the system. So, each element of the vector represents the multicast message immediately preceding the corresponding message m. The vector is represented using N different colors at most. The multicast message m including the vector time-stamp represented in colors to indicate precisely which multicast messages by a sensor broker immediately precede m is gossiped about from a broker to subscribers. Subscribers deliver the message m to the application layer only if all the messages immediately preceding m have been delivered to subscribers.

Therefore, its features might result in very low cost communication overhead between brokers and subscribers because one-dimensional vector to indicate precisely which multicast messages immediately preceding the corresponding message has been delivered in many-to-many multicast patterns. Therefore, the protocol might be significantly scalable in P/S paradigm in distributed applications in pre-planned wireless sensor networks requiring only the minimum causal information of message delivery with flexible consistency.

References

1. Akyildiz, I., Su, W., Sankarasubramaniam, Y., Cayirci, E.: A survey on Sensor Networks. IEEE Communications Magazine 40, 102–114 (2002)
2. Birman, K., Hayden, M., Ozkasap, O., Xiao, Z., Budiu, M., Minsky, Y.: Bimodal Multicast. ACM Transactions on Computer Systems 17, 41–88 (1999)
3. Birman, K., Schiper, A., Stephenson, P.: Lightweight Causal and Atomic Group Multicast. ACM Transactions on Computer Systems 9, 272–314 (1991)
4. Eugster, P., Guerraoui, R., Handurukande, S., Kouznetsov, P., Kermarrec, A.-M.: Lightweight probabilistic broadcast. ACM Transactions on Computer Systems 21, 341–374 (2003)
5. Freedman, D., Birman, K., Ostrowski, K., Linderman, M., Hillman, R., Frantz, A.: Enabling Tactical Edge Mashups with Live Objects. In: 15th International Command and Control Research and Technology Symposium (ICCRTS 2010), Santa Monica (2010)
6. Hong, Y.-W., Scaglione, A.: A scalable synchronization protocol for large scale sensor networks and its applications. IEEE Journal on Selected Areas in Communications, 1085–1099 (2005)
7. Intanagonwiwat, C., Govindan, R., Estrin, D.: Directed diffusion: A scalable and robust communication paradigm for sensor networks. In: 6th Annual International Conference on Mobile Computing and Networking (MobiCOM 2000), pp. 56–67. ACM, Boston (2000)
8. Pleisch, S., Birman, K.: SENSTRAC: Scalable Querying of SENSor Networks from Mobile Platforms Using TRACking-Style Queries. International Journal of Sensor Networks 3, 266–280 (2008)
9. Pottie, G., Kaiser, W.: Wireless Integrated Network Sensors. Communications of the ACM 43, 51–58 (2000)
10. Römer, K.: Time Synchronization in Ad Hoc Networks. In: ACM Symposium on Mobile Ad Hoc Networking and Computing (MobiHoc 2001), pp. 173–182. ACM, Long Beach (2001)
11. Römer, K.: Temporal Message Ordering in Wireless Sensor Networks. In: IFIP MedHocNet, Mahdia, pp. 131–142 (2003)
12. Tyrrell, A., Auer, G., Bettstetter, C.: Fireflies as Role Models for Synchronization in Ad Hoc Networks. In: International Conference on Bio-Inspired Models of Network, Information, and Computing Systems (BIONETICS), vol. 4. ACM, Cavalese (2006)
13. Wokoma, I., Liabotis, I., Prnjat, O., Sacks, L., Marshall, I.: A Weakly Coupled Adaptive Gossip Protocol for Application Level Active Networks. In: The 3rd International Workshop on Policies for Distributed Systems and Networks, Monterey, pp. 244–247 (2002)

People Identification with RMS-Based Spatial Pattern of EEG Signal

Salahiddin Altahat, Xu Huang, Dat Tran, and Dharmendra Sharma

Faculty of Information Sciences and Engineering
University of Canberra, ACT 2601 Australia
{Salah.Altahat,Xu.Huang,Dat.Tran,Dharmendra.Sharma}@canberra.edu.au
http://www.canberra.edu.au

Abstract. Recently, there are increasing interests in proposing novel people identification methods. In this work we propose to use root mean square
(rms) to create a spatial pattern of the Electroencephalogram (EEG), and
use this pattern in people identification. The proposed method is straight
forward and has low cost of computation comparing to recent published
methods such as auto regression (AR), independent component analysis
(ICA) or wavelet. More importantly, the proposed method gives very
promising results.

Keywords: EEG, person identification, RMS brain signature, brain biometrics.

1 Introduction

Recent years show an increasing attitude to find new methods for people identification. The two main properties for any successful biometric method are high
distinguishing ability and high complexity to imitate. Developing such a method
gives more security and more protection against fraud. There are plenty of methods used to identify people starting from the most famous fingerprint to face
recognition, palm print, voice print, retina, DNA and many more. Recent years
show an increasing interest in using EEG as a people identification method.
Many studies show that EEG signals have unique distinguishing patterns, and
more importantly, it is difficult to change these patterns or to mimic them. The
first try to use EEG signals in people identification was done by Polus *et al.*
[5]. After that many experiments took place in this area, all showing promising
results. These experiments used different pre-processing, feature extraction and
classification methods. Despite the fact that all the previous work in using EEG
as a people identification method shows promising results, there is still room to
improve this method accuracy and stability. In this work we are proposing to
build a concept of **brainprint** assuming that EEG signal alone is able to create
a unique pattern for every human. In this paper we are considering working on
large number of people and using simple feature extraction and classification
methods to provide strong evidence that EEG signals can provide unique pattern for people. Within this work we analyzed 64-electrode EEG samples for 122

Y. Xiang et al. (Eds.): ICA3PP 2012, Part II, LNCS 7440, pp. 310–318, 2012.

people from a public dataset [1], and calculate the equivalent rms value for each electrode signal over 1 second period, thus creating a 64-value inputs for each subject. After that we trained a neural network to classify these people based on their 64-value rms inputs. A very good result has been reached indicating the rms spatial feature extraction method may be used with other methods to enhance the classification.

2   Related Work

Many studies took place for human identification using EEG signal processing. Shedeed in [10] used voting scheme for different feature extraction methods which are Discrete Fourier Transform and Wavelet Packet Decomposition both with different measures, and used neural network backpropagation classifier and reached an accuracy of 100%. However the number of people for identification was only three. Yazdani et al. in [12] work on a partial set of the same dataset we are working on in this work for visual evoked potentials. They used different feature extraction methods which are AR model parameters and the peak of PSD. Then use LDA to reduce features and the KNN classifier. They reached 100% accuracy over 20 subjects when AR model order equals to or greater than 14. However, the proposed feature extraction method is more complex and the number of subjects is less than what we are considering in this work. Riera et al. in [9] select the best five features set among multifeatures preliminary work. The resulted best five features are AR model, Fourier Transform, Mutual Information, Coherence and Cross Correlation. These features were selected on different channel configuration. The size of the sample was 51 people and 36 intruders. They use Fisher's Discriminant Analysis classifier with four different discriminant functions. They reach a performance between 87.5% to 98.1%. The proposed feature extraction methods in their work need high computation, and the sample size considered in this work is approximately doubled. Poulus has many contributions in this field all with small number of subjects. [5][6][7][8] The latest one was Poulus et al. [7] where they reach a classification rate around 99.5%. Palaniappan [3] used a total of 61 channels to record Visual Evoked potential (VEP) EEG signals from 20 subjects. He used the spectral power for the gamma band (30 - 50) Hz as a feature. The reached average accuracy was 99.06% with a 10-fold cross-validation. Also Palaniappan et al. in their work in [4] they update the used methods in [3] and test the used methods against larger sample. The result drops to less than 95% when reaching 40 people sample size.

3   Proposed Method

In this work we are trying to test the EEG uniqueness over a large number of subjects, and also try to use a novel simple method for feature extraction to make EEG identification more applicable. So in this work we will:

1. propose an EEG identification method on a large number of subjects to emphasize EEG uniqueness among people. This will enhance the opportunity to use EEG identification on large scale, or even to use it as a universal human identity.
2. employ relatively low complexity and low computation cost methods in pre-processing and feature extraction, to enhance considering EEG as an online solution for people identification.

To tackle the above issues:

1. we use large public database that contains EEG data for 122 people.
2. we propose rms spatial pattern to create feature vector which is used for the first time in EEG.

3.1 Pre-processing

There are many debates about EEG bandwidth, and what are the lower and higher limits of it [11]. In this work we follow Howard *et al.* [2] where they suggest upper limit to gamma in EEG bandwidth to 60Hz. So, in the preprocessing step, the EEG signals were filtered to get frequencies between 0 and 60 Hz. All frequency components above 60 Hz were disregarded. This filtration is done over all the EEG signals from all the 64 electrodes. Figure 1 shows an example of the effect of the filtration on of the EEG signals.

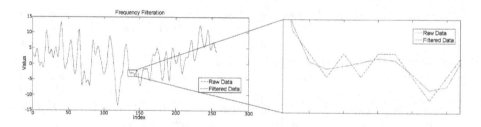

Fig. 1. Frequency Filtration

3.2 Feature Extraction

In the feature extraction step, we only consider one simple feature, which is the rms value for each electrode over one second. The rms value was calculated using Equation 1 over the filtered EEG signal every one second for each electrode. This implies that the EEG from each electrode was divided into one second length segments which is 256 values, and the rms value for all the 256 values was calculated. Finally we got a feature vectors of length 64 rms values, which is the number of electrodes. Figure 2 shows the feature vector collection from EEG using rms values.

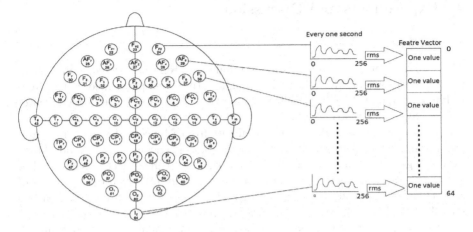

Fig. 2. 64 Channel Feature Vector

The rms value for discrete data is represented by the following formula

$$rms(x) = \sqrt{\frac{1}{n}\sum_{k=1}^{n} x_k^2} \tag{1}$$

The rms value represents active potential of the signal where the power of the signal $p(x)$ is directly proportional to the square of the rms value.

$$p(x) \propto rms^2(x) \tag{2}$$

3.3 Classification

A neural network (NN) classifier was designed to classify the obtained feature vectors. The NN classifier is feedforward error backprobagation network. Also it uses batch mode for weight update after the end of each epoch. The training starts from a random weight sets. The NN engine uses radial basis and the continuous tan sigmoid activation functions. The NN is designed with 64 nodes in the input layer, which is the same number of electrodes. The number of outputs depends on the number of subjects which is 45 for the first experiment and 122 for the second experiment. The network hidden layer size is 200 neurons in the first experiment, and 610 in the second experiment. In the second experiment which was operated on 122 subjects, the NN classifier was trained again with one more hidden layer to increase the performance. We used the MATLAB built in *nntraintool* tool to run the tests. The rms feature vector input was preprocessed by this tool by normalizing the input values between [1, -1].

4   Experiments and Discussion

4.1   Dataset

The used dataset is available through a public data repository for machine learning [1]. This dataset was collected through a study was performed at the Neurodynamics Laboratory of the State University of the New York Health Center at Brooklyn. This study EEG correlates of genetic predisposition to alcoholism. The dataset contains multiple measurements from 64 electrodes placed on subject's scalps which were sampled at 256 Hz (3.9 ms epoch) for 1 second. There were two groups of subjects: alcoholic and control. Each subject was exposed to either a single stimulus (S1) or to two stimuli (S1 and S2) which were pictures of objects chosen from the 1980 Snodgrass and Vanderwart picture set. When two stimuli were shown, they were presented in either a matched condition where S1 was identical to S2 or in a non-matched condition where S1 differed from S2. Zhang *et al.* [13] describes in detail the data collection process. The dataset contains EEG samples for 122 persons, the samples for each person varied from 40 to 120 (so every person has different number of EEG samples). The total number of EEG data files was 11074. Among these files we found 17 files that contain no data. Among the remaining 11057 we found plenty of EEG data files that had all their values or most of them are set to zero. These files were excluded if 32 channels (50%) or more have all their values set to zero. The total number of data files that were considered after this is 11029 files.

4.2   Experiments and Results

The original data contains 77 alcoholic subjects and 45 control subjects. In the first experiment we consider the samples available for all 45 control subjects. The input layer size is 64 inputs which is the number of rms value for each electrodes. The output layer size is 45 outputs which represents the number of subjects (45 control people). Then one hidden layer with a size of 200 neurons was selected. The training stopped when the classifier validation is saturated, and no further improvement achieved. The results were so promising, and the classifier was able to identify 42 of the 45 people correctly, with a mean square error value of 4.3×10^{-3}. We considered the summation of 3 consecutive outputs as the criteria to identify those subjects. Figure 3 shows the mean square error and Figure 4 shows gradient during the training. The training stopped after 747 epochs.

This result encourages considering more subjects in a bigger experiment to include all the dataset for the 122 people. This will test the limits of the rms spatial pattern method and verify its usability in large scale. Also this will verify if this method can be considered with other features as a brain signature or brain print. In the second experiment the input size remains the same which is the 64 rms inputs for the EEG electrodes. The hidden layer size was increased to be 610 neurons arbitrarily, and the output size is 122 which is the number of people.

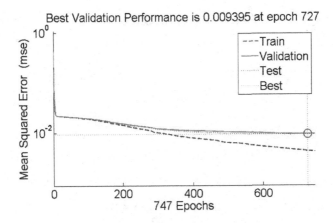

Fig. 3. Mean square error for 45 subjects during the training

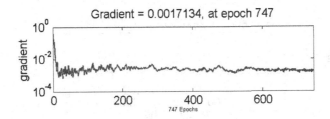

Fig. 4. Gradient for 45 subjects during the training

Although we consider larger sample of people, the results was also promising. The classifier was able to identify 110 people correctly out of 122, with a mean square error value of 0.00262. The other 12 subjects which the classifier was not able to identify, 7 of them were highly confused with other subject in the dataset, and 5 was not identified totally. Figure 5 shows the mean square error and Figure 6 shows the gradient during the training.

To enhance the efficiency of the classifier in the second experiment, we add one more hidden layer, with a size of 400 neurons. The efficiency increases after this enhancement, and the classifier was able to identify 112 people correctly out of 122, but the classifier took longer time to train. The reached mean square error value was 0.00186. The other 10 subjects which the classifier was not able to identify, 6 of them were highly confused with other subject. The other 4 were not identified totally. This last experiment shows that by enhancing the classifier the result might enhance and a better classification rate might be achieved through using the rms spatial pattern only as a feature vector. Figure 7 and Figure 8 separately show the mean square error and the gradient respectively during the training of the second part of this experiment.

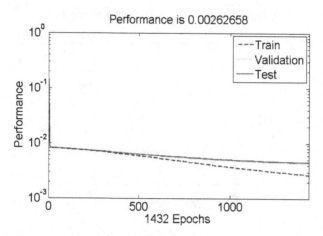

Fig. 5. Mean square error for 122 subjects during the training

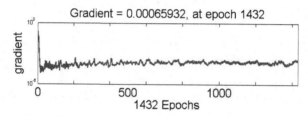

Fig. 6. Gradient for 122 subjects during the training

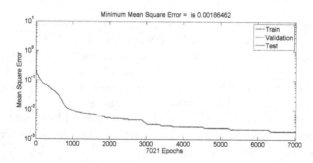

Fig. 7. Mean square error for 122 subjects during the training with enhanced classifier

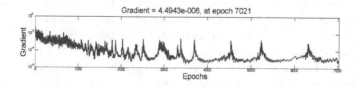

Fig. 8. Gradient for 122 subjects during the training with enhanced classifier

5   Conclusion and Future Work

This work represent a positive clue to consider the rms spatial pattern of the EEG signal as a feature vector for people identification.

For the rms method to be considered as brain property, it needs to be tested to verify its stability and reliability in different situation including:

1. Testing against different brain functions, since this work tests this feature with Visual Evoked Potentials(VEP) signal only.
2. Testing in the case of brain illness and brain injuries, to verify this method stability
3. Testing against brain changes with time and brain aging.

A future work to test this method accuracy against the training dataset size will be conducted.

References

1. Newman, D.J., Asuncion, A.: UCI machine learning repository (2007)
2. Howard, M.W., Rizzuto, D.S., Caplan, J.B., Madsen, J.R., Lisman, J., Aschenbrenner-Scheibe, R., Schulze-Bonhage, A., Kahana, M.J.: Gamma oscillations correlate with working memory load in humans. Cerebral Cortex 13(12), 1369–1374 (2003)
3. Palaniappan, R.: Method of identifying individuals using VEP signals and neural network. IEE Proceedings - Science, Measurement and Technology 151(1), 16–20 (2004)
4. Palaniappan, R., Mandic, D.P.: Eeg based biometric framework for automatic identity verification. J. VLSI Signal Process. Syst. 49(2), 243–250 (2007)
5. Poulos, M., Rangoussi, M., Alexandris, N.: Neural network based person identification using EEG features. In: IEEE International Conference on Acoustics, Speech, and Signal Processing, vol. 2, pp. 1117–1120 (1999)
6. Poulos, M., Rangoussi, M., Alexandris, N., Evangelou, A.: On the use of EEG features towards person identification via neural networks. Med. Inform Internet Med. 26(1), 35–48 (2001)
7. Poulos, M., Rangoussi, M., Alexandris, N., Evangelou, A.: Person identification from the EEG using nonlinear signal classification. Methods Inf. Med. 41(1), 64–75 (2002)
8. Poulos, M., Rangoussi, M., Chrissikopoulos, V., Evangelou, A.: Parametric person identification from the EEG using computational geometry. In: Proceedings of the 6th IEEE International Conference on Electronics, Circuits and Systems, ICECS 1999, vol. 2, pp. 1005–1008 (September 1999)
9. Riera, A., Soria-Frisch, A., Caparrini, M., Grau, C., Ruffini, G.: Unobtrusive biometric system based on electroencephalogram analysis. EURASIP J. Adv. Signal Process 2008 (2008)
10. Shedeed, H.A.: A new method for person identification in a biometric security system based on brain EEG signal processing. In: 2011 World Congress on Information and Communication Technologies (WICT), pp. 1205–1210 (December 2011)

11. Vanhatalo, S., Voipio, J., Kaila, K.: Full-band EEG (FbEEG): an emerging standard in electroencephalography. Clinical Neurophysiology 116(1), 1–8 (2005)
12. Yazdani, A., Roodaki, A., Rezatofighi, S.H., Misaghian, K., Setarehdan, S.K.: Fisher linear discriminant based person identification using visual evoked potentials. In: 9th International Conference on Signal Processing, ICSP 2008, pp. 1677–1680 (October 2008)
13. Zhang, X.L., Begleiter, H., Porjesz, B., Wang, W., Litke, A.: Event related potentials during object recognition tasks. Brain Research Bulletin 38(6), 531–538 (1995)

Gait Based Human Identity Recognition from Multi-view Surveillance Videos

Emdad Hossain and Girija Chetty

Faculty of Information Science and Engineering, University of Canberra
{emdad.hossain,girija.chetty}@canberra.edu.au

Abstract. In this paper we propose a novel multi-view feature fusion of gait biometric information in surveillance videos for large scale human identification. The experimental evaluation on low resolution surveillance video images from a publicly available database showed that the combined LDA-MLP technique turns out to be a powerful method for capturing identity specific information from walking gait patterns. The multi-view fusion at feature level allows complementarity of multiple camera views in surveillance scenarios to be exploited for improvement of identity recognition performance..

Keywords: multi view images, LDA, MLP, identification, feature fusion.

1 Introduction

Human identification from arbitrary views is a very challenging problem, especially when one is walking at a distance. Over the last few years, recognizing identity from gait patterns has become a popular area of research in biometrics and computer vision, and one of the most successful applications of image analysis and understanding. Also, gait recognition is being considered as a next-generation recognition technology, with applicability to many civilian and high security environments such as airports, banks, military bases, car parks, railway stations etc. For these application scenarios, it is not possible to capture the frontal face, and is of low resolution. Hence most of traditional approaches used for face recognition fail; however, several studies have shown that it is possible to identify human from a distance from their gait or the way they walk. Even if frontal face is not visible, it is possible to establish the identity of the person using certain static and dynamic cues such as from face, ear, walking style, hand motion during walking etc. If automatic identification systems can be built based on this concept, it will be a great contribution to surveillance and security area.

However, each of these cues or traits captured from long range low resolution surveillance videos on its own are not powerful enough for ascertaining identity, A combination or fusion of each of them, along with an automatic processing technique can result in satisfactory recognition accuracies. In this paper, we propose usage of full profile silhouettes of persons without frontal faces acquired from multiple views, for capturing complementary or inherent multi-modality available from the gait patterns of the walking human. This also addresses the problems with frontal faces, such as vulnerability to pose, illumination and expression variations. In addition, one of the biggest shortcomings of frontal face is user cooperation - a mandatory

Y. Xiang et al. (Eds.): ICA3PP 2012, Part II, LNCS 7440, pp. 319–328, 2012.

requirement for establishing identity. On other hand, long range biometric information from surveillance videos captures several biometric traits such as side face, ear, body shape, and gait, which are a combination of physiological and behavioral biometrics and this rich complementary information, can be used in development of robust identification approaches. Further, by using certain automatic processing techniques for extracting salient features based on subspace or kernel methods, multivariate statistical techniques and learning classifiers, it is possible to enhance the performance in real world operating scenarios. In this paper we propose use of complementary information available from multiple views, and simple feature extraction technique based on linear discriminant analysis (LDA) along with a learning classifier based on "Multilayer Perceptron" (MLP) for establishing identity. Further, we propose a feature level fusion of multiple views as fusing information at an early stage, is more effective than at later stages (score level fusion or late fusion), because features extracted from different biometrics at feature level can retain inherent multimodality much better at feature level and much more information than those in other fusion stages [2]. The experimental evaluation of the proposed multi-view fusion scheme on a publicly available (CASIA [1]) database shows promising performance for real world video surveillance scenarios. Rest of the paper is organized as follows. The background on the role of gait biometric for establishing identity is described in next section. The details of the proposed multimodal identification scheme is described in Section 3. Section 4 describes the experimental setup and results, and Section 5 concludes the paper with some plans for further research.

2   Background

Current state-of-the-art video surveillance systems, when used for recognizing the identity of the person in the scene, cannot perform very well due to low quality video or inappropriate processing techniques. Though much progress has been made in the past decade on visual based automatic person identification through utilizing different biometrics, including face recognition, iris and fingerprint recognition, each of these techniques work satisfactorily in highly controlled operating environments such as border control or immigration check points, under constrained illumination, pose and facial expression variations. To address the next generation security and surveillance requirements for not just high security environments, but also day-to-day civilian access control applications, we need a robust and invariant biometric trait [3] to identify a person for both controlled and uncontrolled operational environments. In this case, trait selection can play vital role. According to authors in [4], the expectations of next generation identity verification involve addressing issues related to application requirements, user concern and integration. Some of the suggestions made to address these issues were use of non-intrusive biometric traits, role of soft biometrics or dominant primary and non-dominant secondary identifiers and importance of novel automatic processing techniques. To conform to these recommendations; often there is a need to combine multiple physiological and behavioral biometric cues, leading to so called multimodal biometric identification system.

Each of the traits, physiological or behavioral have distinct advantages, for example; the behavioral biometrics can be collected non-obtrusively or even without the knowledge of the user. Behavioral data often does not require any special hardware (other than low cost off the shelf surveillance camera), so, it is very much cost effective. While most behavioral biometrics is not unique enough to provide reliable human identification they have been proved to be sufficiently accurate [5]. Gait, is such a powerful behavioral biometric, but on its own it cannot be considered as a strong biometric to identify a person. But, if we combine some other equally non-intrusive biometric with gait; it is expected to be strong combination for human identification. This could be profile (side) images containing side face or ear biometric traits and used with gait. Here side-face and ear images form the physiological component. Both can be collected unobtrusively without user involvement which is very much important in the public surveillance scenarios. It is possible to capture some or all of these multimodal components, if we use gait image information from multiple camera views, which can capture static and dynamic gait profile of a person from one view, with clear side face and ear from other views. This could be extremely applicable and reliable, as most of security infrastructure in public surveillance scenarios currently use multiple cameras. A multi-modal scheme based on such novel approach using multiple camera views can result in establishing identity from long range video images, which is otherwise difficult because face is not clearly visible in such scenarios. Further, it can also address shortcomings of unimodal biometric systems, which perform person recognition based on a single source of biometric, and are often affected by problems such as noisy sensor data and non-universality. Thus, due to these practical problems, the error rates associated with unimodal biometric systems are quite high and consequently it makes them unacceptable for deployment in security critical applications [6] like public surveillance.

Researchers found that one of the most promising techniques is use of multimodality or combination of biometric traits. Using PCA on combined image of ear and face, researchers in [7, 8] have found that multimodal recognition results in significant improvement over either individual biometrics. But most of these schemes work on highly controlled environment which is not quite the case for real world surveillance scenarios. Recently, few attempts have been expended on combining various biometrics in a bid to improve upon the recognition accuracy of classifiers that are based on a single biometric. Some biometric combinations which have been experimented include face, fingerprint and hand geometry [9]; face, fingerprint and speech [10]; face and iris [11]; face and ear [12]; and face and speech [13]. The multi-view fusion in gait profile however, did not attract much attention from the research community. This could be due to difficulty in processing and shortage of multi-view surveillance data. Next Section presents the proposed multi-view gait fusion scheme.

3   Multiview Gait Fusion Scheme

For experimental evaluation of the proposed multiview gait fusion schems, we used CASIA Gait Database collected by Institute of Automation, Chinese Academy of Sciences [1]. It is a large multi-view gait database, which is created in January 2005. There are more than 300 subjects. We used three (3) different datasets known as

Fig. 1. Sample images

dataset A (36 degree view point) dataset B (90 degree view point) and Dataset C (126 degree view point). All data was captured with normal video camera in 11 different views know as view angles. It takes into account four walking conditions: normal walking, slow walking, fast walking, and normal walking with a bag. All of our data here in this experiment taken from normal walking with free hand. The videos were all captured at night. Figure 1 shows the sample images in different view angles.

For all the experiments, we used 50 subjects from each of the dataset. It means, we used 50 subjects of extracted silhouettes from Dataset A, 50 subjects from B and 50 subjects from C. Each subject consists of 16 images and in total 2400 images for 150 subjects. Figure 2 shows the extracted silhouettes from dataset B and C.

Fig. 2. Extracted silhouettes

For each of the images in these data sets, we extracted the feature vectors in lower dimensional subspaces separately by using PCA (principal component analysis) and Linear Discriminant Analysis (LDA), and used a learning classifier based on well know multi-layer perceptron (MLP) for classifying each person ID. Our multiview fusion experiments involved identity recognition in LDA-MLP subspace for dataset (unimodal) and fusion of multiple views. The details of LDA subspace for extracting discriminating features is described next.

3.1   Linear Discriminant Analysis

The Linear Discriminent Analysis (LDA) similar to principal component analysis (PCA) and factor analysis, looks for linear combinations of variables which can best explain the data. LDA explicitly attempts to model the difference between the classes of data. PCA on the other hand does not take into account any difference in class, and factor analysis builds the feature combinations based on differences rather than similarities. Discriminant analysis is also different from factor analysis in that it is not an interdependence technique: a distinction between independent variables and dependent variables (also called criterion variables) must be made. LDA works when the measurements made on independent variables for each observation are continuous quantities. When dealing with categorical independent variables, the equivalent technique is discriminant correspondence analysis [15]. In our experiment LDA shows very promising as LDA model the difference between class and data

3.2   Multi Layer Perceptron

Multi-Layer perceptron (MLP) is a feedforward neural network with one or more layers between input and output layer. Feedforward means that data flows in one direction from input to output layer (forward). This type of network is trained with the back propagation learning algorithm. MLPs are widely used for pattern classification, recognition, prediction and approximation. Multi-Layer Perceptron can solve problems which are not linearly separable [16]. In our experiments we had 49 input layer, 800 hidden layers (for each data set) and 50 output layers. This is basically based on dimensions, instances and the classes of the dataset. The details of the experiments are described in the next Section.

4   Experimental Results and Discussion

The experiments involved a training phase and a test phase. We used a 10-fold cross-validation for dividing the complete data from into training and test subsets. With 10-fold cross-validation, the original dataset is randomly partitioned into 10 subsets. Of the 10 subsets, a single subset was retained as the validation data for testing the model, and the remaining 9 subsets were used as training data. The cross-validation process is then repeated 10 times (the folds), with each of the 10 subsets used exactly once as the validation data. The 10 results from the folds were then averaged to produce a single estimation. We found that advantage of this method over repeated random sub-sampling is that all observations could be used for training and validation/testing, and each observation could be used for validation exactly once.

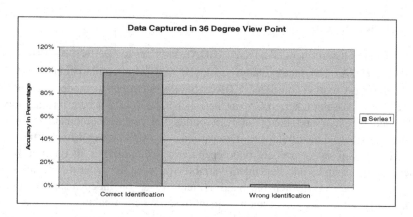

Fig. 3. Rate of Identification in 36 degree view point

In training phase, we built the gait templates for each person using LDA feature vectors for each of the dataset images (Dataset A, B and C) and trained the MLP classifier. In test phase the LDA feature vectors from unseen images in training set were classified with MLP classifier for each of the datasets separately(dataset A, B, C) and by fusion of multiple views. Figure 4 shows the rate of identification in 36 degree view point. The figure 3 shows high level of accuracy with the proposed scheme, for data captured in 36 degree view point. We achieved 98% correct identification by using LDA-MLP approach. And only 2% has been identified with wrong/incorrect identification. On the other hand, the data captured in 90 degree view point resulted in poor results as compare to the data from 36 degree view point. This could be due to difficulty in capturing the identity specific information from 90 degree view point as compared to 36 degrees. Figure 4 shows the results achieved with the data from 90 degree view point.

The result shows, we received 84.5% correct identification for a large data set which has captured in 90 degree view point. And wrong/incorrect identification rate is around 14.5% which is quite large for real world scenario. Figure 5 represents the identification for dataset C (126 degree view point). It can be seen from this figure that it was possible to achieve 88.88% correct identification with the data captured in 123 degree view point. And 11.12% identified were wrongly identified.

After three (3) successful single mode experiments we combined data from all views. We performed feature level fusion of all three extracted set of LDA features, and Figure 6 shows the results of multi-view feature fusion based on gait images from surveillance videos.

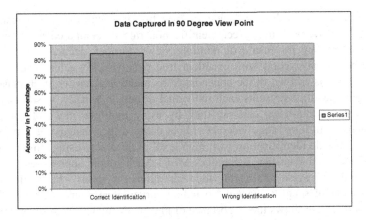

Fig. 4. Rate of Identification in 90 degree view point

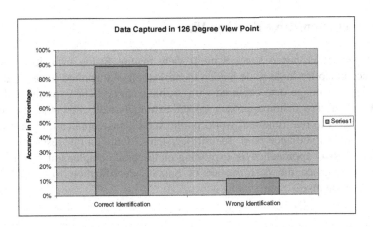

Fig. 5. Rate of Identification in 126 degree view point

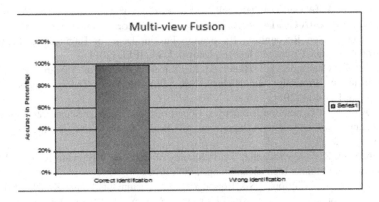

Fig. 6. Result of view point fusion

As can be seen from Figure 8, feature level fusion of multiple views results in a significant improvement in correct identification rate as compared to singe views, with 99 % accuracy for fusion of multiple views. Further, accuracy of each class individually was also good with excellent true positive (TP) rates. The figure for details accuracy is shown in the appendix I. As mentioned earlier, each class in the table in the appendix represents each individual or person. Finally, to summarize our experimental validation we can say that; by using multiple views of surveillance video footage with long range videos (without detailed face images), it is possible to perform large scale identification with high level of accuracy, using simple subspace features (LDA) and classifier techniques(MLP). Such simple approaches can lead to real time and real world intelligent video surveillance systems - the beginning of a new dimension of security systems in public surveillance. Our small experimental efforts reported here shows the importance of multiview images from several cameras and feature level fusion of multiple views as an efficient gait biometric identification.

5   Conclusions and Further Plan

In this paper we proposed a novel multi view feature fusion from low resolution surveillance video for large scale human identification. We applied three (3) different camera views of image data captured with visible cameras. The experimental results shows the multi view fusion approach worked extremely well, indicating the potential of this approach to real time real world public surveillance applications, a truly next generation of surveillance and security systems. Our future research involves investigating novel approaches for exploiting multimodal complementary information available to enhance the performance of human identification for public video surveillance systems.

References

1. Zheng, S.: CASIA Gait Database collected by Institute of Automation, Chinese Academy of Sciences, CASIA Gait Database, http://www.sinobiometrics.com
2. L. Huang, Person Recognition By Feature Fusion, Dept. of Engineering Technology Metropolitan State College of Denver, Denver, USA, IEEE (2011)
3. Bringer, J., Chabanne, H.: Biometric Identification Paradigm Towards Privacy and Confidentiality Protection. In: Nichols, E.R. (ed.) Biometric: Theory, Application and Issues, pp. 123–141 (2011)
4. Jain, A.K.: Next Generation Biometrics, Department of Computer Science & Engineering, Michigan State University, Department of Brain & Cognitive Engineering, Korea University (2009)
5. Yampolskiy, R.V., Govindaraja, V.: Taxonomy of Behavioral Biometrics. In: Behavioral Biometrics for Human Identification, pp. 1–43 (2010)
6. Meraoumia, A., Chitroub, S., Bouridane, A.: Fusion of Finger-Knuckle-Print and Palmprint for an Efficient Multi-biometric System of Person Recognition. IEEE Communications Society Subject Matter Experts for Publication in the IEEE ICC (2011)

7. Berretti, S., Bimbo, A., Pala, P.: 3D face recognaition using isogeodesic stripes. IEEE Transaction on Pattern Analysis and Machine Intelligence 32(12) (2010)

8. Yuan, L., Mu, Z., Xu, Z.: Using Ear Biometrics for Personal Recognition. School of Information Engineering, Univ. of Science and Technology Beijing, Beijing 100083

9. Ross, A., Jain, A.K.: Information fusion in biometrics. Pattern Recognition Letters 24, 2115–2125 (2003)

10. Jain, A.K., Hong, L., Kulkarni, Y.: A multimodal biometric system using fingerprints, face and speech. In: 2nd Int'l Conf. AVBPA, pp. 182–187 (1999)

11. Wang, Y., Tan, T., Jain, A.K.: Combining Face and Iris Biometrics for Identity Verification. In: Kittler, J., Nixon, M.S. (eds.) AVBPA 2003. LNCS, vol. 2688, pp. 805–813. Springer, Heidelberg (2003)

12. Chang, K., et al.: Comparison and Combination of Ear and Face Images in Appearance-Based Biometrics. IEEE Trans. PAMI 25, 1160–1165 (2003)

13. Kittler, J., et al.: On combining classifiers. IEEE Trans. Pattern Anal. Mach. Intell. 20, 226–239 (1998)

14. Smith, L.I.: A tutorial on Principal Components Analysis

15. Linear discriminant analysis, Wikipedia, http://www.wikipedia.org

16. Multi Layer Perceptron, http://www.neoroph.sourceforge.net

17. Platt, J.C.: Sequential Minimal Optimization: A Fast Algorithm for Training Support Vector Machines, Microsoft Research. Technical Report MSR-TR-98-14, (17) (1998)

18. Shlizerman, I.K., Basri, R.: 3D Face Reconstruction from a Single Image Using a Single Reference Face Shape. IEEE Transactions on Pattern Analysis and Machine Intelligence 33(2) (2011)

19. Hossain, E., Chetty, G.: Multimodal Identity Verification Based on Learning Face and Gait Cues. In: Lu, B.-L., Zhang, L., Kwok, J. (eds.) ICONIP 2011, Part III. LNCS, vol. 7064, pp. 1–8. Springer, Heidelberg (2011)

20. Chin, Y.J., Ong, T.S., Teoh, A.B.J., Goh, M.K.O.: Multimodal Biometrics based Bit Extraction Method for Template Security, Faculty of Information Science and Technology, Multimedia University, Malaysia, School of Electrical and Electronic Engineering, Yonsei University, Seoul, Korea, IEEE (2011)

21. Multilayer Perceptron Neural Networks, The Multilayer Perceptron Neural Network Model, http://www.dtreg.com

Appendix I: Detail Accuracy by Class (Person to Person)

=== Detailed Accuracy By Class ===

TP Rate	FP Rate	Precision	Recall	F-Measure	ROC Area	Class
1	0	1	1	1	1	s1
1	0	1	1	1	1	s2
1	0	1	1	1	1	s3
0.875	0.003	0.875	0.875	0.875	0.994	s4
1	0	1	1	1	1	s5
0.875	0.003	0.875	0.875	0.875	0.998	s6
1	0	1	1	1	1	s7
1	0	1	1	1	1	s8
0.938	0	1	0.938	0.968	1	s9
0.938	0.001	0.938	0.938	0.938	1	s10
0.938	0	1	0.938	0.968	1	s11
1	0	1	1	1	1	s12
1	0	1	1	1	1	s13
1	0.001	0.941	1	0.97	1	s14
1	0	1	1	1	1	s15
1	0	1	1	1	1	s16
1	0.001	0.941	1	0.97	1	s17
1	0	1	1	1	1	s18
1	0	1	1	1	1	s19
0.938	0	1	0.938	0.968	1	s20
1	0	1	1	1	1	s21
1	0	1	1	1	1	s22
1	0	1	1	1	1	s23
1	0	1	1	1	1	s24
1	0	1	1	1	1	s25
1	0.001	0.941	1	0.97	1	s26
1	0	1	1	1	1	s27
1	0	1	1	1	1	s28
1	0.001	0.941	1	0.97	1	s29
0.938	0	1	0.938	0.968	1	s30
1	0.003	0.889	1	0.941	1	s31
1	0	1	1	1	1	s32
0.875	0	1	0.875	0.933	1	s33
1	0	1	1	1	1	s34
0.941	0	1	0.941	0.97	0.951	s35
1	0.001	0.938	1	0.968	0.999	s36
1	0	1	1	1	1	s37
0.938	0	1	0.938	0.968	1	s38
0.938	0	1	0.938	0.968	1	s39
1	0	1	1	1	1	s40
1	0	1	1	1	1	s41
1	0	1	1	1	1	s42
1	0	1	1	1	1	s43
1	0	1	1	1	1	s44
1	0	1	1	1	1	s45
0.938	0	1	0.938	0.968	1	s46
1	0	1	1	1	1	s47
0.938	0.004	0.833	0.938	0.882	0.999	s48
1	0.001	0.941	1	0.97	1	s49
1	0	1	1	1	1	s50

Author Index